The rights of the child

A European perspective

Council of Europe Publishing

French edition:

Les droits de l'enfant: une perspective européenne

ISBN 92-871-3005-1

Design: Atelier de création graphique, Council of Europe

Council of Europe Publishing
F-67075 Strasbourg Cedex

ISBN 92-871-3006-X
© Council of Europe, 1996
Printed in Germany

Table of contents

Contents

Introduction

The idea of preparing a collection of Council of Europe legal instruments concerning children came from the Childhood Policies Project of the Council of Europe, a four-year programme (1992-1995) which was in its turn directly inspired by the adoption of the United Nations Convention on the Rights of the Child on 20 November 1989.

The adoption of the International Convention on the Rights of the Child initiated a new debate on the place of children in present-day society. The UN Convention calls for the coherent planning of overall policies for the period of childhood itself, rather than the accumulation of individual measures which affect children without being set in a policy framework.

The Childhood Policies Project sought therefore to reflect at European level policy implications of the United Nations Convention on the Rights of the Child. The UN Convention on the Rights of the Child has set up a holistic, non-hierarchical approach to children's rights, including civil, political, economic, social and cultural rights which are inherent to the human dignity of the child. It is in this context that the upper age-limit for the target group for the Project was set at 18 years.

The Project was based on the following principles:

1.   The importance of the way the child is given the opportunity of expressing his or her views, and of participating in appropriate ways in decision-making processes affecting him or her. The child is to be seen as an active agent, or as a citizen, at the different levels concerning him or her (family, school, community, sport, and so on).

2.   Non-discrimination, particularly in order to ensure equal opportunities for girls and boys.

3.   Considering and taking into account the repercussions on children of the important and accelerating political, social and cultural changes in our societies.

4.   Children should grow up in a family environment which is the natural environment for their full and harmonious development and wellbeing.

5.   Acknowledging that changes in family life mean that there is a need for increasing societal and social responsibility for children, which in turn means an increased need for services such as consultation centres for parents and children, child daycare services, and proper arrangements facilitating the reconciliation of family responsibilities and working life.

6. The needs of children must be taken into account both for them as a population group, and as individuals with specific needs.

7. The close correlation between children and their families decreases as children grow, with a consequent decrease in the overlap between family policies and childhood policies, and an increase in the interaction between childhood policies and social policies in general. This evolution must be considered, appreciated and respected.

8. Because of the present situation of financial crisis in most countries, there is a danger of unduly decreasing the resources and the attention devoted to children. Children in risk situations are particularly vulnerable in a climate of economic restraint for social action programmes, and there are greater numbers of children than ever in such situations, particularly taking into account children in refugee and migrant families, and those from minorities. Measures aimed at preventing unsatisfactory conditions from developing rather than countering the consequences arising from them must be developed.

9. The realities of present day Europe, including the specificities of the countries of Central and Eastern Europe, must be taken into account.

10. Availability of information is a key issue: This should address two levels at least: setting up a network for the exchange of information within the Project and between member states; and raising awareness within the relevant professions and among parents and children about children's rights. The responsibility and the contribution of the media are particularly important.

The following Steering Committees of the Council of Europe took part in the Childhood Policies Project:

Steering Committee on Social Policy (CDPS)
European Social Security Committee (CDSS)
Steering Committee for Employment and Labour (CDEM)
European Committee on Migrations (CDMG)
European Health Committee (CDSP)
Education Committee (CC-ED)
Committee for the Development of Sport (CDDS)
European Steering Committee for Intergovernmental Co-operation in the Youth Field (CDEJ)
European Committee on Legal Cooperation (CDCJ)
European Committee on Crime Problems (CDPC)
Steering Committee on Human Rights (CDDH)
Steering Committee on the Mass Media (CDMM)
Steering Committee for Equality between Women and Men (CDEG)

In order to demonstrate the extraordinary richness of Council of Europe legal instruments concerning children, it was decided to bring them together in one volume, grouped according to broad sectors of interest, with a view to demonstrating to all those involved in children's issues the broad base provided by the Council of Europe for implementing a European Strategy for Children.

European strategy
for children

Recommendation 1286 (1996)[1]
of the Parliamentary Assembly of the Council of Europe
on a European strategy for children

1.   In its Resolution 1011 (1993) on the situation of women and children in the former Yugoslavia, the Assembly urged all the states grouped together in the Council of Europe to subscribe to the principle of "first call for children", to recognise children's rights, their universality and indivisibility and to provide for their essential needs both in Europe and in the rest of the world.

2.   The Assembly decided in Order No. 491 (1993) to develop, in co-operation with Unicef, a strategy for children up to the age of eighteen which at European level could serve as inspiration and guidance for policy-makers and all those who actively support children's causes in their respective activities. It would like to pay particular tribute to Unicef, without whose experience and expertise such a strategy would not have been possible.

3.   The Assembly notes that the rights of the child are still far from being a reality in our own rich and developed continent of Europe and that children are often the first victims of armed conflicts, economic recession, poverty, and in particular budgetary constraints.

4.   Accordingly, it is important for the Assembly that states should be helped to give effect, within their own national situation, to the commitments entered into under the United Nations Convention on the Rights of the Child, to promote a change in the way children, as individuals with rights, are viewed and also to encourage their active and responsible participation within the family and society.

5.   Children are citizens of the society of today and tomorrow. Society has a long-term responsibility to support children and has to acknowledge the rights of the family in the interest of the child. Responding to children's rights, interests and needs must be a political priority. The Assembly is convinced that respect for children's rights and greater equality between children and adults will help preserve the pact between generations and will contribute towards democracy.

6.   The Assembly recommends that the Committee of Ministers urge the member states of the Council of Europe:

     i.   to ratify the United Nations Convention on the Rights of the Child if they have not already done so, to withdraw any reservations made and to

---

1. *Assembly debate* on 24 January 1996 (4th Sitting) (see Doc. 7436, report of the Social, Health and Family Affairs Committee, rapporteur: Mr Cox; and Doc. 7473, opinion of the Committee on Legal Affairs and Human Rights, rapporteur: Mrs Err).
Text adopted by the Assembly on 24 January 1996 (4th Sitting).

implement the convention in the letter and the spirit by reviewing and adapting their legislative and regulatory provisions;

ii. to ratify all the relevant Council of Europe conventions on the rights and protection of the child, in particular the recent European Convention on the Exercise of Children's Rights.

7. The Assembly also recommends that the Committee of Ministers invite the states grouped together in the Council of Europe to make children's rights a political priority by:

i. adopting at national and local level a proactive childhood policy which seeks full implementation of the Convention on the Rights of the Child, which will consider the best interests of the child as a guiding principle of all action and which will anticipate situations instead of trying to deal with emergencies or problems that have already arisen;

ii. making children more visible through the systematic collection of information, in particular reliable, detailed (by age and gender), comparable statistics which will make it possible to identify their needs and the issues which require priority political action;

iii. adopting a comprehensive, consistent and co-ordinated approach to childhood policy, which will encourage multidisciplinary structures to be put in place at all deliberation and decision-making levels, in particular at ministerial level, and foster the creation of national coalitions of all relevant partners;

iv. appointing a commissioner (ombudsman) for children or another structure offering guarantees of independence, and the responsibilities required to improve children's lives, and accessible to the public through such means as local offices;

v. ensuring, especially at policy-making level, that the interests and needs of children are always duly considered and taken into account, for example by introducing practices such as the "child impact statement" which offers a way of determining the probable impact on children of any proposed legislative, regulatory or other measures in whatever field, for example, in the field of legal aid;

vi. investing in children and giving them budgetary priority by allocating adequate and fair resources in relation to spending on the needs of the other sections of the population at all levels (national, regional, local);

vii. guaranteeing the present level of their contributions and subsidies to the various national and international organisations involved in child care.

8. The Committee of Ministers should strongly urge these states:

i. to guarantee, through explicit recognition in their constitutional texts or domestic law, children's civil and political rights, as well as their economic, social and cultural rights, as enshrined in the United Nations Convention on the Rights of the Child;

ii. to guarantee to all children the right to free and high quality education for pre-school, primary and secondary education;

iii. to inform children and also their parents of their rights by widely publicising and disseminating the text of the Convention on the Rights of the Child, by all possible means, including the use of the media and by introducing education on children's rights and responsibilities into the school curriculum from primary level onwards;

iv. to encourage the media, notably visual, to promote children's right to a healthy and balanced development, and in particular in products intended for children, to eliminate violence and to illustrate positive social values;

v. to inform children about the means and remedies available to them in the event of violation of their fundamental rights and, for example, to extend the provision of free help-lines, specialist advocates and child friendly judicial and administrative systems which recognise the claims of individual children for protection against all forms of abuse;

vi. to provide specific training in children's rights for all professionals who come into contact with children, including teachers, the various members of the judicial authorities, social workers, etc.;

vii. to enable the views of children to be heard in all decision-making which affects them, and to enable them to participate actively, responsibly and in a manner appropriate to their capacity, at all levels of society – in the family, in local communities, in schools and other institutions, in judicial hearings and in national government;

viii. to teach children how to act as responsible citizens, to encourage them to take an interest in public affairs and to reconsider the age at which young people can vote;

ix. to promote education for the prevention of racism, political and religious intolerance and violence and for the learning of tolerance and peaceful resolution of conflict;

x. to pay particular attention to the situation and the specific needs of immigrant and refugee children and minority and marginalised children;

xi. to emphasise to parents, families, teachers and all those involved directly or indirectly with children, as they develop into adulthood, that in a civilised society responsibilities and obligations go hand in hand with rights and privileges.

9.   The Assembly also recommends that the Committee of Ministers invite these states to give credibility and consistency to the debate on children's rights by making it a reality outside Europe by:

i.   making a commitment to work towards ensuring that the provisions of the Convention on the Rights of the Child are upheld throughout the world, via all appropriate unilateral or multilateral measures to combat the exploitation of children and to protect them from the effects of armed conflicts;

ii.   promoting international co-operation and in particular by increasing their aid to the developing countries to at least 0,7% of GNP and devoting at least 20% of their aid to basic social services which are indispensable for human development;

iii. adopting a more understanding common attitude to the repayment by these countries of the debt incurred with the international development aid organisations.

10. Finally, the Assembly recommends that the Committee of Ministers:

i. set up, within the Council of Europe, a permanent multidisciplinary intergovernmental structure able to deal with all issues relating to children;

ii. instruct it, as part of its terms of reference, to draw up an annual report on the state of Europe's children, giving a comprehensive account of the situation and an outline of positive achievements and serving as a measure of what else needs to be done to satisfy the requirements of the Convention on the Rights of the Child, and to submit this report to the Parliamentary Assembly; this report will be the subject of an annual discussion within the relevant Parliamentary Assembly committee;

iii. involve other competent international organisations, in particular the United Nations Committee on the Rights of the Child, the European Parliament, Unicef, the various relevant non-governmental organisations, and indeed children themselves in the activities of this structure in the appropriate forms;

iv. transmit the present recommendation to states grouped in the Council of Europe, to the aforementioned organisations and to the Closing Conference of the Multidisciplinary Project on Childhood Policies to be held in Leipzig in spring 1996.

United Nations Convention
on the Rights of the Child

PREAMBLE

The States Parties to the present Convention,

Considering that, in accordance with the principles proclaimed in the Charter of the United Nations, recognition of the inherent dignity and of the equal and inalienable rights of all members of the human family is the foundation of freedom, justice and peace in the world,

Bearing in mind that the peoples of the United Nations have, in the Charter, reaffirmed their faith in fundamental human rights and in the dignity and worth of the human person, and have determined to promote social progress and better standards of life in larger freedom,

Recognizing that the United Nations has, in the Universal Declaration of Human Rights and in the International Covenants on Human Rights, proclaimed and agreed that everyone is entitled to all the rights and freedoms set forth therein, without distinction of any kind, such as race, colour, sex, language, religion, political or other opinion, national or social origin, property, birth or other status,

Recalling that, in the Universal Declaration of Human Rights, the United Nations has proclaimed that childhood is entitled to special care and assistance,

Convinced that the family, as the fundamental group of society and the natural environment for the growth and well-being of all its members and particularly children, should be afforded the necessary protection and assistance so that it can fully assume its responsibilities within the community,

Recognizing that the child, for the full and harmonious development of his or her personality, should grow up in a family environment, in an atmosphere of happiness, love and understanding,

Considering that the child should be fully prepared to live an individual life in society, and brought up in the spirit of the ideals proclaimed in the Charter of the United Nations, and in particular in the spirit of peace, dignity, tolerance, freedom, equality and solidarity,

Bearing in mind that the need to extend particular care to the child has been stated in the Geneva Declaration of the Rights of the Child of 1924 and in the Declaration of the Rights of the Child adopted by the United Nations on 20 November 1959 and recognized in the Universal Declaration of Human Rights, in the International Covenant on Civil and Political Rights (in particular in articles 23 and 24), in the International Covenant on Economic, Social and Cultural Rights (in particular in article 10) and in the statutes and

---

1. Adopted by the General Assembly of the United Nations on 20 November 1989.

relevant instruments of specialized agencies and international organizations concerned with the welfare of children,

Bearing in mind that, as indicated in the Declaration of the Rights of the Child, "the child, by reason of his physical and mental immaturity, needs special safeguards and care, including appropriate legal protection, before as well as after birth",

Recalling the provisions of the Declaration on Social and Legal Principles relating to the Protection and Welfare of Children, with Special Reference to Foster Placement and Adoption Nationally and Internationally; the United Nations Standard Minimum Rules for the Administration of Juvenile Justice ("The Beijing Rules"); and the Declaration on the Protection of Women and Children in Emergency and Armed Conflict,

Recognizing that, in all countries in the world, there are children living in exceptionally difficult conditions, and that such children need special consideration,

Taking due account of the importance of the traditions and cultural values of each people for the protection and harmonious development of the child,

Recognizing the importance of international co-operation for improving the living conditions of children in every country, in particular in the developing countries,

Have agreed as follows:

PART I

Article 1

For the purposes of the present Convention, a child means every human being below the age of 18 years unless, under the law applicable to the child, majority is attained earlier.

Article 2

1.   States Parties shall respect and ensure the rights set forth in the present Convention to each child within their jurisdiction without discrimination of any kind, irrespective of the child's or his or her parent's or legal guardian's race, colour, sex, language, religion, political or other opinion, national, ethnic or social origin, property, disability, birth or other status.

2.   States Parties shall take all appropriate measures to ensure that the child is protected against all forms of discrimination or punishment on the basis of the status, activities, expressed opinions, or beliefs of the child's parents, legal guardians, or family members.

Article 3

1.   In all actions concerning children, whether undertaken by public or private social welfare institutions, courts of law, administrative authorities or

legislative bodies, the best interests of the child shall be a primary consideration.

2.   States Parties undertake to ensure the child such protection and care as is necessary for his or her well-being, taking into account the rights and duties of his or her parents, legal guardians, or other individuals legally responsible for him or her, and, to this end, shall take all appropriate legislative and administrative measures.

3.   States Parties shall ensure that the institutions, services and facilities responsible for the care or protection of children shall conform with the standards established by competent authorities, particularly in the areas of safety, health, in the number and suitability of their staff, as well as competent supervision.

Article 4

States Parties shall undertake all appropriate legislative, administrative, and other measures for the implementation of the rights recognized in the present Convention. With regard to economic, social and cultural rights, States Parties shall undertake such measures to the maximum extent of their available resources and, where needed, within the framework of international cooperation.

Article 5

States Parties shall respect the responsibilities, rights and duties of parents or, where applicable, the members of the extended family or community as provided for by local custom, legal guardians or other persons legally responsible for the child, to provide, in a manner consistent with the evolving capacities of the child, appropriate direction and guidance in the exercise by the child of the rights recognized in the present Convention.

Article 6

1.   States Parties recognize that every child has the inherent right to life.

2.   States Parties shall ensure to the maximum extent possible the survival and development of the child.

Article 7

1.   The child shall be registered immediately after birth and shall have the right from birth to a name, the right to acquire a nationality and, as far as possible, the right to know and be cared for by his or her parents.

2.   States Parties shall ensure the implementation of these rights in accordance with their national law and their obligations under the relevant international instruments in this field, in particular where the child would otherwise be stateless.

Article 8

1.   States Parties undertake to respect the right of the child to preserve his or her identity, including nationality, name and family relations as recognized by law without unlawful interference.

2.   Where a child is illegally deprived of some or all of the elements of his or her identity, States Parties shall provide appropriate assistance and protection, with a view to speedily re-establishing his or her identity.

Article 9

1.   States Parties shall ensure that a child shall not be separated from his or her parents against their will, except when competent authorities subject to judicial review determine, in accordance with applicable law and procedures, that such separation is necessary for the best interests of the child. Such determination may be necessary in a particular case such as one involving abuse or neglect of the child by the parents, or one where the parents are living separately and a decision must be made as to the child's place of residence.

2.   In any proceedings pursuant to paragraph 1 of the present article, all interested parties shall be given an opportunity to participate in the proceedings and make their views known.

3.   States Parties shall respect the right of the child who is separated from one or both parents to maintain personal relations and direct contact with both parents on a regular basis, except if it is contrary to the child's best interests.

4.   Where such separation results from any action initiated by a State Party, such as the detention, imprisonment, exile, deportation or death (including death arising from any cause while the person is in the custody of the State) of one or both parents or of the child, that State Party shall, upon request, provide the parents, the child or, if appropriate, another member of the family with the essential information concerning the whereabouts of the absent member(s) of the family unless the provision of the information would be detrimental to the well-being of the child. States Parties shall further ensure that the submission of such a request shall of itself entail no adverse consequences for the person(s) concerned.

Article 10

1.   In accordance with the obligation of States Parties under Article 9, paragraph 1, applications by a child or his or her parents to enter or leave a State Party for the purpose of family reunification shall be dealt with by States Parties in a positive, humane and expeditious manner. States Parties shall further ensure that the submission of such a request shall entail no adverse consequences for the applicants and for the members of their family.

2.   A child whose parents reside in different States shall have the right to maintain on a regular basis, save in exceptional circumstances, personal relations and direct contacts with both parents. Towards that end and in

accordance with the obligation of States Parties under article 9, paragraph 1, States Parties shall respect the right of the child and his or her parents to leave any country, including their own, and to enter their own country. The right to leave any country shall be subject only to such restrictions as are prescribed by law and which are necessary to protect the national security, public order (*ordre public*), public health or morals or the rights and freedoms of others and are consistent with the other rights recognized in the present Convention.

Article 11

1.   States Parties shall take measures to combat the illicit transfer and non-return of children abroad.

2.   To this end, States Parties shall promote the conclusion of bilateral or multilateral agreements or accession to existing agreements.

Article 12

1.   States Parties shall assure to the child who is capable of forming his or her own views the right to express those views freely in all matters affecting the child, the views of the child being given due weight in accordance with the age and maturity of the child.

2.   For this purpose, the child shall in particular be provided the opportunity to be heard in any judicial and administrative proceedings affecting the child, either directly, or through a representative or an appropriate body, in a manner consistent with the procedural rules of national law.

Article 13

1.   The child shall have the right to freedom of expression; this right shall include freedom to seek, receive and impart information and ideas of all kinds, regardless of frontiers, either orally, in writing or in print, in the form of art, or through any other media of the child's choice.

2.   The exercise of this right may be subject to certain restrictions, but these shall only be such as are provided by law and are necessary:

a)   For respect of the rights or reputations of others; or

b)   For the protection of national security or of public order (ordre public), or of public health or morals.

Article 14

1.   States Parties shall respect the right of the child to freedom of thought, conscience and religion.

2.   States Parties shall respect the rights and duties of the parents and, when applicable, legal guardians, to provide direction to the child in the exercise of his or her right in a manner consistent with the evolving capacities of the child.

3.   Freedom to manifest one's religion or beliefs may be subject only to such limitations as are prescribed by law and are necessary to protect public safety, order, health or morals, or the fundamental rights and freedoms of others.

Article 15

1.   States Parties recognize the rights of the child to freedom of association and to freedom of peaceful assembly.

2.   No restrictions may be placed on the exercise of these rights other than those imposed in conformity with the law and which are necessary in a democratic society in the interests of national security or public safety, public order (*ordre public*), the protection of public health or morals or the protection of the rights and freedoms of others.

Article 16

1.   No child shall be subjected to arbitrary or unlawful interference with his or her privacy, family, home or correspondence, nor to unlawful attacks on his or her honour and reputation.

2.   The child has the right to the protection of the law against such interference or attacks.

Article 17

States Parties recognize the important function performed by the mass media and shall ensure that the child has access to information and material from a diversity of national and international sources, especially those aimed at the promotion of his or her social, spiritual and moral well-being and physical and mental health. To this end, States Parties shall:

a)   Encourage the mass media to disseminate information and material of social and cultural benefit to the child and in accordance with the spirit of Article 29;

b)   Encourage international co-operation in the production, exchange and dissemination of such information and material from a diversity of cultural, national and international sources;

c)   Encourage the production and dissemination of children's books;

d)   Encourage the mass media to have particular regard to the linguistic needs of the child who belongs to a minority group or who is indigenous;

e)   Encourage the development of appropriate guidelines for the protection of the child from information and material injurious to his or her well-being, bearing in mind the provisions of Articles 13 and 18.

Article 18

1.   States Parties shall use their best efforts to ensure recognition of the principle that both parents have common responsibilities for the upbringing and development of the child. Parents or, as the case may be, legal guard-

ians, have the primary responsibility for the upbringing and development of the child. The best interests of the child will be their basic concern.

2.   For the purpose of guaranteeing and promoting the rights set forth in the present Convention, States Parties shall render appropriate assistance to parents and legal guardians in the performance of their child-rearing responsibilities and shall ensure the development of institutions, facilities and services for the care of children.

3.   States Parties shall take all appropriate measures to ensure that children of working parents have the right to benefit from child-care services and facilities for which they are eligible.

Article 19

1.   States Parties shall take all appropriate legislative, administrative, social and educational measures to protect the child from all forms of physical or mental violence, injury or abuse, neglect or negligent treatment, maltreatment or exploitation, including sexual abuse, while in the care of parent(s), legal guardian(s) or any other person who has the care of the child.

2.   Such protective measures should, as appropriate, include effective procedures for the establishment of social programmes to provide necessary support for the child and for those who have the care of the child, as well as for other forms of prevention and for identification, reporting, referral, investigation, treatment and follow-up of instances of child maltreatment described heretofore, and, as appropriate, for judicial involvement.

Article 20

1.   A child temporarily or permanently deprived of his or her family environment, or in whose own best interests cannot be allowed to remain in that environment, shall be entitled to special protection and assistance provided by the State.

2.   States Parties shall in accordance with their national laws ensure alternative care for such a child.

3.   Such care could include, *inter alia*, foster placement, Kafala of Islamic law, adoption, or if necessary placement in suitable institutions for the care of children. When considering solutions, due regard shall be paid to the desirability of continuity in a child's upbringing and to the child's ethnic, religious, cultural and linguistic background.

Article 21

States Parties that recognize and/or permit the system of adoption shall ensure that the best interests of the child shall be the paramount consideration and they shall:

a)   Ensure that the adoption of a child is authorized only by competent authorities who determine, in accordance with applicable law and procedures and on the basis of all pertinent and reliable information, that the adoption is permissible in view of the child's status concerning parents, relatives and legal guardians and that, if required, the persons concerned have given their informed consent to the adoption on the basis of such counselling as may be necessary;

b) Recognize that intercountry adoption may be considered as an alternative means of child's care, if the child cannot be placed in a foster or an adoptive family or cannot in any suitable manner be cared for in the child's country of origin;

c) Ensure that the child concerned by intercountry adoption enjoys safeguards and standards equivalent to those existing in the case of national adoption;

d) Take all appropriate measures to ensure that, in intercountry adoption, the placement does not result in improper financial gain for those involved in it;

e) Promote, where appropriate, the objectives of the present article by concluding bilateral or multilateral arrangements or agreements, and endeavour, within this framework, to ensure that the placement of the child in another country is carried out by competent authorities or organs.

Article 22

1. States Parties shall take appropriate measures to ensure that a child who is seeking refugee status or who is considered a refugee in accordance with applicable international or domestic law and procedures shall, whether unaccompanied or accompanied by his or her parents or by any other person, receive appropriate protection and humanitarian assistance in the enjoyment of applicable rights set forth in the present Convention and in other international human rights or humanitarian instruments to which the said States are Parties.

2. For this purpose, States Parties shall provide, as they consider appropriate, co-operation in any efforts by the United Nations and other competent intergovernmental organizations or non-governmental organizations co-operating with the United Nations to protect and assist such a child and to trace the parents or other members of the family of any refugee child in order to obtain information necessary for reunification with his or her family. In cases where no parents or other members of the family can be found, the child shall be accorded the same protection as any other child permanently or temporarily deprived of his or her family environment for any reason, as set forth in the present Convention.

Article 23

1. States Parties recognize that a mentally or physically disabled child should enjoy a full and decent life, in conditions which ensure dignity, promote self-reliance, and facilitate the child's active participation in the community.

2. States Parties recognize the right of the disabled child to special care and shall encourage and ensure the extension, subject to available resources, to

the eligible child and those responsible for his or her care, of assistance for which application is made and which is appropriate to the child's condition and to the circumstances of the parents or others caring for the child.

3.   Recognizing the special needs of a disabled child, assistance extended in accordance with paragraph 2 of the present article shall be provided free of charge, whenever possible, taking into account the financial resources of the parents or others caring for the child, and shall be designed to ensure that the disabled child has effective access to and receives education, training, health care services, rehabilitation services, preparation for employment and recreation opportunities in a manner conducive to the child's achieving the fullest possible social integration and individual development, including his or her cultural and spiritual development.

4.   States Parties shall promote, in the spirit of international co-operation, the exchange of appropriate information in the field of preventive health care and of medical, psychological and functional treatment of disabled children, including dissemination of and access to information concerning methods of rehabilitation, education and vocational services, with the aim of enabling States Parties to improve their capabilities and skills and to widen their experience in these areas. In this regard, particular account shall be taken of the needs of developing countries.

Article 24

1.   States Parties recognize the right of the child to the enjoyment of the highest attainable standard of health and to facilities for the treatment of illness and rehabilitation of health. States Parties shall strive to ensure that no child is deprived of his or her right of access to such health care services.

2.   States Parties shall pursue full implementation of this right and, in particular, shall take appropriate measures:

a)   To diminish infant and child mortality;

b)   To ensure the provision of necessary medical assistance and health care to all children with emphasis on the development of primary health care;

c)   To combat disease and malnutrition including within the framework of primary health care, through *inter alia* the application of readily available technology and through the provision of adequate nutritious foods and clean drinking water, taking into consideration the dangers and risks of environmental pollution;

d)   To ensure appropriate pre-natal and post-natal health care for mothers;

e)   To ensure that all segments of society, in particular parents and children, are informed, have access to education and are supported in the use of basic knowledge of child health and nutrition, the advantages of breast-feeding, hygiene and environmental sanitation and the prevention of accidents;

f)   To develop preventive health care, guidance for parents and family planning education and services.

3.   States Parties shall take all effective and appropriate measures with a view to abolishing traditional practices prejudicial to the health of children.

4.   States Parties undertake to promote and encourage international co-operation with a view to achieving progressively the full realization of the right recognized in the present article. In this regard, particular account shall be taken of the needs of developing countries.

Article 25

States Parties recognize the right of a child who has been placed by the competent authorities for the purposes of care, protection or treatment of his or her physical or mental health, to a periodic review of the treatment provided to the child and all other circumstances relevant to his or her placement.

Article 26

1.   States Parties shall recognize for every child the right to benefit from social security, including social insurance, and shall take the necessary measures to achieve the full realization of this right in accordance with their national law.

2.   The benefits should, where appropriate, be granted, taking into account the resources and the circumstances of the child and persons having responsibility for the maintenance of the child, as well as any other consideration relevant to an application for benefits made by or on behalf of the child.

Article 27

1.   States Parties recognize the right of every child to a standard of living adequate for the child's physical, mental, spiritual, moral and social development.

2.   The parent(s) or others responsible for the child have the primary responsibility to secure, within their abilities and financial capacities, the conditions of living necessary for the child's development.

3.   States Parties, in accordance with national conditions and within their means, shall take appropriate measures to assist parents and others responsible for the child to implement this right and shall in case of need provide material assistance and support programmes, particularly with regard to nutrition, clothing and housing.

4.   States Parties shall take all appropriate measures to secure the recovery of maintenance for the child from the parents or other persons having financial responsibility for the child, both within the State Party and from abroad. In particular, where the person having financial responsibility for the child lives in a State different from that of the child, States Parties shall promote the accession to international agreements or the conclusion of such agreements, as well as the making of other appropriate arrangements.

Article 28

1. States Parties recognize the right of the child to education, and with a view to achieving this right progressively and on the basis of equal opportunity, they shall, in particular:

a) Make primary education compulsory and available free to all;

b) Encourage the development of different forms of secondary education, including general and vocational education, make them available and accessible to every child, and take appropriate measures such as the introduction of free education and offering financial assistance in case of need;

c) Make higher education accessible to all on the basis of capacity by every appropriate means;

d) Make educational and vocational information and guidance available and accessible to all children;

e) Take measures to encourage regular attendance at schools and the reduction of drop-out rates.

2. States Parties shall take all appropriate measures to ensure that school discipline is administered in a manner consistent with the child's human dignity and in conformity with the present Convention.

3. States Parties shall promote and encourage international co-operation in matters relating to education, in particular with a view to contributing to the elimination of ignorance and illiteracy throughout the world and facilitating access to scientific and technical knowledge and modern teaching methods. In this regard, particular account shall be taken of the needs of developing countries.

Article 29

1. States Parties agree that the education of the child shall be directed to:

a) The development of the child's personality, talents and mental and physical abilities to their fullest potential;

b) The development of respect for human rights and fundamental freedoms, and for the principles enshrined in the Charter of the United Nations;

c) The development of respect for the child's parents, his or her own cultural identity, language and values, for the national values of the country in which the child is living, the country from which he or she may originate, and for civilizations different from his or her own;

d) The preparation of the child for responsible life in a free society, in the spirit of understanding, peace, tolerance, equality of sexes, and friendship among all peoples, ethnic, national and religious groups and persons of indigenous origin;

e) The development of respect for the natural environment.

2. No part of the present article or article 28 shall be construed so as to interfere with the liberty of individuals and bodies to establish and direct

educational institutions, subject always to the observance of the principles set forth in paragraph 1 of the present article and to the requirements that the education given in such institutions shall conform to such minimum standards as may be laid down by the State.

Article 30

In those States in which ethnic, religious or linguistic minorities or persons of indigenous origin exist, a child belonging to such a minority or who is indigenous shall not be denied the right, in community with other members of his or her group, to enjoy his or her own culture, to profess and practise his or her own religion, or to use his or her own language.

Article 31

1. States Parties recognize the right of the child to rest and leisure, to engage in play and recreational activities appropriate to the age of the child and to participate freely in cultural life and the arts.

2. States Parties shall respect and promote the right of the child to participate fully in cultural and artistic life and shall encourage the provision of appropriate and equal opportunities for cultural, artistic, recreational and leisure activity.

Article 32

1. States Parties recognize the right of the child to be protected from economic exploitation and from performing any work that is likely to be hazardous or to interfere with the child's education, or to be harmful to the child's health or physical, mental, spiritual, moral or social development.

2. States Parties shall take legislative, administrative, social and educational measures to ensure the implementation of the present article. To this end, and having regard to the relevant provisions of other international instruments, States Parties shall in particular:

a) Provide for a minimum age or minimum ages for admissions to employment;

b) Provide for appropriate regulation of the hours and conditions of employment;

c) Provide for appropriate penalties or other sanctions to ensure the effective enforcement of the present article.

Article 33

States Parties shall take all appropriate measures, including legislative, administrative, social and educational measures, to protect children from the illicit use of narcotic drugs and psychotropic substances as defined in the relevant international treaties, and to prevent the use of children in the illicit production and trafficking of such substances.

Article 34

States Parties undertake to protect the child from all forms of sexual exploitation and sexual abuse. For these purposes, States Parties shall in particular take all appropriate national, bilateral and multilateral measures to prevent:

a) The inducement or coercion of a child to engage in any unlawful sexual activity;

b) The exploitative use of children in prostitution or other unlawful sexual practices;

c) The exploitative use of children in pornographic performances and materials.

Article 35

States Parties shall take all appropriate national, bilateral and multilateral measures to prevent the abduction of, the sale of or traffic in children for any purpose or in any form.

Article 36

States Parties shall protect the child against all other forms of exploitation prejudicial to any aspects of the child's welfare.

Article 37

States Parties shall ensure that:

a) No child shall be subjected to torture or other cruel, inhuman or degrading treatment or punishment. Neither capital punishment nor life imprisonment without possibility of release shall be imposed for offences committed by persons below 18 years of age;

b) No child shall be deprived of his or her liberty unlawfully or arbitrarily. The arrest, detention or imprisonment of a child shall be in conformity with the law and shall be used only as a measure of last resort and for the shortest appropriate period of time;

c) Every child deprived of liberty shall be treated with humanity and respect for the inherent dignity of the human person, and in a manner which takes into account the needs of persons of his or her age. In particular every child deprived of liberty shall be separated from adults unless it is considered in the child's best interest not to do so and shall have the right to maintain contact with his or her family through correspondence and visits, save in exceptional circumstances;

d) Every child deprived of his or her liberty shall have the right to prompt access to legal and other appropriate assistance, as well as the right to challenge the legality of the deprivation of his or her liberty before a court or other competent, independent and impartial authority, and to a prompt decision on any such action.

Article 38

1.   States Parties undertake to respect and to ensure respect for rules of international humanitarian law applicable to them in armed conflicts which are relevant to the child.

2.   States Parties shall take all feasible measures to ensure that persons who have not attained the age of 15 years do not take a direct part in hostilities.

3.   States Parties shall refrain from recruiting any person who has not attained the age of 15 years into their armed forces. In recruiting among those persons who have attained the age of 15 years but who have not attained the age of 18 years, States Parties shall endeavour to give priority to those who are oldest.

4.   In accordance with their obligations under international humanitarian law to protect the civilian population in armed conflicts, States Parties shall take all feasible measures to ensure protection and care of children who are affected by an armed conflict.

Article 39

States Parties shall take all appropriate measures to promote physical and psychological recovery and social reintegration of a child victim of: any form of neglect, exploitation, or abuse; torture or any other form of cruel, inhuman or degrading treatment or punishment; or armed conflicts. Such recovery and reintegration shall take place in an environment which fosters the health, self-respect and dignity of the child.

Article 40

1.   States Parties recognize the right of every child alleged as, accused of, or recognized as having infringed the penal law to be treated in a manner consistent with the promotion of the child's sense of dignity and worth, which reinforces the child's respect for the human rights and fundamental freedoms of others and which takes into account the child's age and the desirability of promoting the child's reintegration and the child's assuming a constructive role in society.

2.   To this end, and having regard to the relevant provisions of international instruments, States Parties shall, in particular, ensure that:

a)   No child shall be alleged as, be accused of, or recognized as having infringed the penal law by reason of acts or omissions that were not prohibited by national or international law at the time they were committed;

b)   Every child alleged as or accused of having infringed the penal law has at least the following guarantees:

i)   To be presumed innocent until proven guilty according to law;

ii) To be informed promptly and directly of the charges against him or her, and, if appropriate, through his or her parents or legal guardians, and to have legal or other appropriate assistance in the preparation and presentation of his or her defence;

iii) To have the matter determined without delay by a competent, independent and impartial authority or judicial body in a fair hearing according to law, in the presence of legal or other appropriate assistance and, unless it is considered not to be in the best interest of the child, in particular, taking into account his or her age or situation, his or her parents or legal guardians;

iv) Not to be compelled to give testimony or to confess guilt; to examine or have examined adverse witnesses and to obtain the participation and examination of witnesses on his or her behalf under conditions of equality;

v) If considered to have infringed the penal law, to have this decision and any measures imposed in consequence thereof reviewed by a higher competent, independent and impartial authority or judicial body according to law;

vi) To have the free assistance of an interpreter if the child cannot understand or speak the language used;

vii) To have his or her privacy fully respected at all stages of the proceedings.

3.   States Parties shall seek to promote the establishment of laws, procedures, authorities and institutions specifically applicable to children alleged as, accused of, or recognized as having infringed the penal law, and, in particular:

a)   the establishment of a minimum age below which children shall be presumed not to have the capacity to infringe the penal law;

b)   whenever appropriate and desirable, measures for dealing with such children without resorting to judicial proceedings, providing that human rights and legal safeguards are fully respected.

4.   A variety of dispositions, such as care, guidance and supervision orders; counselling; probation; foster care; education and vocational training programmes and other alternatives to institutional care shall be available to ensure that children are dealt with in a manner appropriate to their well-being and proportionate both to their circumstances and the offence.

Article 41

Nothing in the present Convention shall affect any provisions which are more conducive to the realization of the rights of the child and which may be contained in:

a)   The law of a State Party; or

b)   International law in force for that State.

PART II

Article 42

States Parties undertake to make the principles and provisions of the Convention widely known, by appropriate and active means, to adults and children alike.

Article 43

1. For the purpose of examining the progress made by States Parties in achieving the realization of the obligations undertaken in the present Convention, there shall be established a Committee on the Rights of the Child, which shall carry out the functions hereinafter provided.

2. The Committee shall consist of ten experts of high moral standing and recognized competence in the field covered by this Convention. The members of the Committee shall be elected by States Parties from among their nationals and shall serve in their personal capacity, consideration being given to equitable geographical distribution, as well as to the principal legal systems.

3. The members of the Committee shall be elected by secret ballot from a list of persons nominated by States Parties. Each State Party may nominate one person from among its own nationals.

4. The initial election to the Committee shall be held no later than six months after the date of the entry into force of the present Convention and thereafter every second year. At least four months before the date of each election, the Secretary-General of the United Nations shall address a letter to States Parties inviting them to submit their nominations within two months. The Secretary-General shall subsequently prepare a list in alphabetical order of all persons thus nominated, indicating States Parties which have nominated them, and shall submit it to the States Parties to the present Convention.

5. The elections shall be held at meetings of States Parties convened by the Secretary-General at United Nations Headquarters. At those meetings, for which two thirds of States Parties shall constitute a quorum, the persons elected to the Committee shall be those who obtain the largest number of votes and an absolute majority of the votes of the representatives of States Parties present and voting.

6. The members of the Committee shall be elected for a term of four years. They shall be eligible for re-election if renominated. The term of five of the members elected at the first election shall expire at the end of two years; immediately after the first election, the names of these five members shall be chosen by lot by the Chairman of the meeting.

7. If a member of the Committee dies or resigns or declares that for any other cause he or she can no longer perform the duties of the Committee, the State Party which nominated the member shall appoint another expert from among its nationals to serve for the remainder of the term, subject to the approval of the Committee.

8. The Committee shall establish its own rules of procedure.

9. The Committee shall elect its officers for a period of two years.

10. The meetings of the Committee shall normally be held at United Nations Headquarters or at any other convenient place as determined by the Committee. The Committee shall normally meet annually. The duration of the meetings of the Committee shall be determined, and reviewed, if neces-

sary, by a meeting of the States Parties to the present Convention, subject to the approval of the General Assembly.

11. The Secretary-General of the United Nations shall provide the necessary staff and facilities for the effective performance of the functions of the Committee under the present Convention.

12. With the approval of the General Assembly, the members of the Committee established under the present Convention shall receive emoluments from the United Nations resources on such terms and conditions as the Assembly may decide.

Article 44

1. States Parties undertake to submit to the Committee, through the Secretary-General of the United Nations, reports on the measures they have adopted which give effect to the rights recognized herein and on the progress made on the enjoyment of those rights:

a) Within two years of the entry into force of the Convention for the State Party concerned,

b) Thereafter every five years.

2. Reports made under the present article shall indicate factors and difficulties, if any, affecting the degree of fulfilment of the obligations under the present Convention. Reports shall also contain sufficient information to provide the Committee with a comprehensive understanding of the implementation of the Convention in the country concerned.

3. A State Party which has submitted a comprehensive initial report to the Committee need not in its subsequent reports submitted in accordance with paragraph 1(b) of the present article repeat basic information previously provided.

4. The Committee may request from States Parties further information relevant to the implementation of the Convention.

5. The Committee shall submit to the General Assembly, through the Economic and Social Council, every two years, reports on its activities.

6. States Parties shall make their reports widely available to the public in their own countries.

Article 45

In order to foster the effective implementation of the Convention and to encourage international co-operation in the field covered by the Convention:

a) The specialized agencies, the United Nations Children's Fund and other United Nations organs shall be entitled to be represented at the consideration of the implementation of such provisions of the present Convention as fall within the scope of their mandate. The Committee may invite the specialized agencies, the United Nations Children's Fund and other competent bodies as it may consider appropriate to provide expert advice on the implementation of the Convention in areas falling within the scope of their respective mandates. The Committee may invite the specialized agencies, the United Nations Children's Fund and other United Nations organs to submit reports on the implementation of the Convention in areas falling within the scope of their activities;

b) The Committee shall transmit, as it may consider appropriate, to the specialized agencies, the United Nations Children's Fund and other competent bodies, any reports from States Parties that contain a request, or indicate a need, for technical advice or assistance, along with the Committee's observations and suggestions, if any, on these requests or indications;

c) The Committee may recommend to the General Assembly to request the Secretary-General to undertake on its behalf studies on specific issues relating to the rights of the child;

d) The Committee may make suggestions and general recommendations based on information received pursuant to articles 44 and 45 of the present Convention. Such suggestions and general recommendations shall be transmitted to any State Party concerned and reported to the General Assembly, together with comments, if any, from States Parties.

PART III

Article 46

The present Convention shall be open for signature by all States.

Article 47

The present Convention is subject to ratification. Instruments of ratification shall be deposited with the Secretary-General of the United Nations.

Article 48

The present Convention shall remain open for accession by any State. The instruments of accession shall be deposited with the Secretary-General of the United Nations.

Article 49

1. The present Convention shall enter into force on the thirtieth day following the date of deposit with the Secretary-General of the United Nations of the twentieth instrument of ratification or accession.

2. For each State ratifying or acceding to the Convention after the deposit of the twentieth instrument of ratification or accession, the Convention shall enter into force on the thirtieth day after the deposit by such State of its instrument of ratification or accession.

Article 50

1. Any State Party may propose an amendment and file it with the Secretary-General of the United Nations. The Secretary-General shall

thereupon communicate the proposed amendment to States Parties, with a request that they indicate whether they favour a conference of States Parties for the purpose of considering and voting upon the proposals. In the event that, within four months from the date of such communication, at least one third of the States Parties favour such a conference, the Secretary-General shall convene the conference under the auspices of the United Nations. Any amendment adopted by a majority of States Parties present and voting at the conference shall be submitted to the General Assembly for approval.

2.   An amendment adopted in accordance with paragraph 1 of the present article shall enter into force when it has been approved by the General Assembly of the United Nations and accepted by a two-thirds majority of States Parties.

3.   When an amendment enters into force, it shall be binding on those States Parties which have accepted it, other States Parties still being bound by the provisions of the present Convention and any earlier amendments which they have accepted.

Article 51

1.   The Secretary-General of the United Nations shall receive and circulate to all States the text of reservations made by States at the time of ratification or accession.

2.   A reservation incompatible with the object and purpose of the present Convention shall not be permitted.

3.   Reservations may be withdrawn at any time by notification to that effect addressed to the Secretary-General of the United Nations, who shall then inform all States. Such notification shall take effect on the date on which it is received by the Secretary-General.

Article 52

A State Party may denounce the present Convention by written notification to the Secretary-General of the United Nations. Denunciation becomes effective one year after the date of receipt of the notification by the Secretary-General.

Article 53

The Secretary-General of the United Nations is designated as the depositary of the present Convention.

Article 54

The original of the present Convention, of which the Arabic, Chinese, English, French, Russian and Spanish texts are equally authentic, shall be deposited with the Secretary-General of the United Nations.

In witness thereof the undersigned plenipotentiaries, being duly authorized thereto by their respective Governments, have signed the present Convention.

Texts adopted by
the Parliamentary Assembly
and the Committee of Ministers
of the Council of Europe

Social protection,
family policies

Table of contents

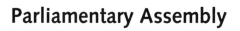

Parliamentary Assembly

Resolution 20[1]
on the social problems of youth

The Consultative Assembly of the Council of Europe,

1. Considers that, as an element in the whole enterprise of the building of Europe, co-ordinating action must be taken to produce a solution for the social problems of youth and childhood and specifically those presented by the professional training of youth, the organisation of international exchanges between young people, the question of stateless children, child welfare, juvenile delinquency and the securing of moral safeguards applicable to children's papers and the cinema;

2. Pays tribute to the work carried out, with these ends in view, and the results already achieved, by the big private organisations; expresses its satisfaction at the endeavours of the European Youth and Childhood Research Bureau to seek concrete solutions for the problems encountered in these different spheres;

3. Instructs the Secretary-General of the Council of Europe to keep in touch with the big official and private organisations, and especially to follow the work of the European Youth and Childhood Research Bureau in the matter of the professional training of youth, and the organisation of international exchanges between young people; instructs the Secretary-General to report to the Committee on Social Questions on the result of these investigations;

4. Calls upon the Governments of the member states of the Council of Europe to support all efforts to bring about co-ordination among the various European bodies concerned with the problems of youth and childhood, and in particular to take all such administrative and financial steps as may be appropriate for the encouragement of wider exchanges among young people.

---

1. See Doc. AS (2) 138, Report. Adopted 21 November 1950 at the conclusion of the debate on the report of the Committee on Social Questions.

Recommendation 29[1]
on the protection of children in the event of war

The Assembly,

Fully aware of the threat to the civilian population, and particularly to children, in time of war;

Believing that all possible steps should be taken for their protection;

Recalling the terms of the Geneva Convention of 12th August, 1949, on the Protection of Civilians in Time of War;

Considering that this Convention has not been ratified by all the member states of the Council of Europe and that the practical measures which it advocated have not yet been taken,

Recommends that the Committee of Ministers invite all member states of the Council of Europe:

i.   To ratify or support the Geneva Convention of 12th August, 1949, on the Protection of Civilians in Time of War;

ii.   To take appropriate measures to provide the protection advocated in that Convention in close collaboration with the national Red Cross Societies, private and public humanitarian bodies, and the International Red Cross Committee;

iii.   To inform the other member states of the practical measures taken, or to be taken, and to exchange information as to the best methods of evacuating and protecting civilians;

iv.   To keep the Assembly informed of the results achieved in this connection.

---

1. This Recommendation was adopted by the Assembly at its Twenty-first Sitting, 26 September 1952 (see Doc. 77, report of the Committee on Social Questions).

Recommendation 561 (1969)[1]
on the protection of minors
against ill-treatment

The Assembly,

1.   Having learned with disquiet that a serious number of children suffer or die each year from what pediatricians call the "beaten child syndrome";

2.   Noting that persons practising cruelty are generally drawn from the social strata which are most under-privileged from an economic and socio-cultural point of view;

3.   Having noted that alcoholism often leads parents to maltreat their own children;

4.   Having learned that the number of maltreated children is often particularly high in families living in unhealthy and over-crowded dwellings;

5.   Considering that in some countries the social services and the competent private organisations are prevented by lack of funds and often by lack of co-ordination from effectively combating cruelty to children;

6.   Noting that the fate of many maltreated children cannot be improved because those best placed to detect cruelty, in particular physicians, are in many cases bound by the obligation to observe professional secrecy or, where they have been relieved of this obligation by legislation governing maltreated children, they are too often reluctant to inform the authority legally responsible;

7.   Noting that severely punitive legal action against the persons practising cruelty cannot improve the lot of maltreated children and rarely changes the attitude of the culprits;

8.   Considering that effective measures against cruelty to children ought essentially to involve preventive action in the social field – together with help and treatment for parents where necessary,

9.   Recommends that the Committee of Ministers invite member governments:

    a.   to take all necessary measures to ensure that the competent ministries and departments are aware of the gravity and extent of the problem of children subject to physical or mental cruelty;

---

1. *Assembly debate* on 30 September 1969 (9th Sitting) (see Doc. 2628, report of the Committee on Social and Health Questions).
Text adopted by the Assembly on 30 September 1969 (9th Sitting).

b. to introduce where it does not already exist, legislation releasing physicians from the obligation of professional secrecy where maltreated children are concerned and requiring them to inform in writing, solely and immediately, the concerned administrative authority of cases detected by them, with a view to improving the fate of these children;

c. to prohibit the administrative authority notified by the physicians from informing the police of a case of cruelty without having itself verified the physical and mental state of the child;

d. to require the administrative authority and the social services to give their attention at the earliest opportunity to cases of maltreatment brought to their notice, by regular supervision of the family in question and by ensuring that the child receives proper care;

e. to provide the social services with the necessary funds and personnel to enable them to take proper care of maltreated children and also to keep a watch on parents liable to commit such cruelty;

f. to request the official services responsible for the care of maltreated children to co-ordinate their action as far as possible with the work undertaken by private organisations;

g. to arrange as soon as possible for compulsory regular medical examination of all children who are not covered by such examinations at school.

Recommendation 675 (1972)[1]
on birth control and family planning
in Council of Europe member states

The Assembly,

1.   Considering that, despite the population explosion of the world as a whole, the population growth of the developed countries does not appear to be such as to require coercive policies;

2.   Considering further that the profound socio-cultural changes that have taken place in West European society over the last fifty years have led to couples claiming the right to decide upon the number and spacing of their children;

3.   Recalling with satisfaction that the Second European Population Conference (1971) considered this right to be a fundamental one;

4.   Deploring that in the member states induced abortion is still frequently used as a means of family planning;

5.   Convinced that the use of contraceptives should be promoted in order to limit the number of abortions and to give couples the possibility of deciding upon the number and spacing of their children,

6.   Recommends that the Committee of Ministers invite member governments of the Council of Europe:

I.   a. to authorise the sale of contraceptives after adequate technical and clinical testing – except for oral contraceptives for which medical prescription is advisable;

b. to create family planning advice bureaux in urban and rural areas, and to encourage the integration of family planning within the general medical and social services;

c. to ensure that young people are provided with suitable sex education, subject to respect for parents' rights and, *inter alia*, to promote premarriage courses;

d. to include teaching on family planning in medical, para-medical and social welfare schools;

e. to support the existence and action of national governmental and non-governmental family planning services as co-ordinating bodies for

---

1. *Assembly debate* on 18 October 1972 (10th Sitting) (see Doc. 3166, report of the Committee on Population and Refugees).
   Text adopted by the Assembly on 18 October 1972 (10th Sitting).

representatives of relevant professional and other organisations, as a discussion forum and channel for information and education;

II. to adopt the following social measures in order to improve the welfare of families with children:

   a. increase in family allowances and perhaps payment of an allowance to mothers remaining at home, especially in the case of families at the lower end of the income scale;

   b. strengthening of mother and child protection services;

   c. improvement of low-cost housing programmes;

   d. establishment of crèches and day-nurseries;

   e. improvement of labour legislation relating to mothers who go out to work;

   f. no penalty should be imposed on any woman regarding her employment and prospects in the event of her becoming pregnant;

   g. encouragement of adoption of children, in particular by implementing the European Convention on Adoption;

   h. legal non-discrimination against unmarried mothers and children born out of wedlock.

Recommendation 751 (1975)[1]
on the position and responsibility of parents in the modern family and their support by society

The Assembly,

1. Observing that the conditions of families are changing towards a more symmetrical internal relationship within which the married partners share the rights and duties more equally;

2. Assured that society has not only a humanitarian duty but also a vital economic and social interest in ensuring that standards in the care of young children are preserved and improved;

3. Observing the need of children for close contact with both mother and father, who therefore carry a joint responsibility as equal partners for the children's upbringing;

4. Recognising that both parents are entitled to the opportunity to participate in the upbringing of children and in paid employment;

5. Recognising as a fundamental principle the right of individual parents to decide for themselves how to fulfil their responsibilities, and the duty of society to provide the means for this choice to be realised, so far as possible without detrimental consequences;

6. Observing that socio-economic changes common to all advanced societies lead to an increasing employment of parents in ways which, in present conditions, may conflict with personal care for their young children;

7. Emphasising that this tension is particularly acute where children are brought up by a single parent, and that the situation of single parents in general is still extremely difficult;

8. Noting that legal and administrative provisions tend to direct parents exclusively into either professional life or work in the home, and thereby restrict their freedom of choice;

9. Considering that upbringing of children must be not purely a matter of physical shelter and care, but should be continually aiming at their long-term emotional, intellectual and social needs;

---

1. *Assembly debate* on 24 January 1975 (21st Sitting) (see Doc. 3531, report of the Committee on Social and Health Questions).
  Text adopted by the Assembly on 24 January 1975 (21st Sitting).

10. Affirming its belief that the complex needs of children in their first years of life – and in particular their need for a stable personal relationship with an adult – are with few exceptions most effectively met through the personal care of a parent;

11. Considering that the interests of parents and children are best served by the entry or re-entry of parents into employment or other work in society outside the home, once the most intense period of family responsibility is ended;

12. Affirming its belief that governments should pursue family policies which promote good relations between all family members and which, regardless of income levels, grant the children a secure growth environment and encourage their emotional, intellectual, cultural and social development;

13. Having regard to Resolution (70) 15 of the Committee of Ministers, on the social protection of unmarried mothers and their children, Resolution AP (74) 2 of the Committee of Ministers (Partial Agreement in the social and public health field), on work by women, particularly in the light of technological progress, including automation, and Recommendation No. 123 (1965) of the International Labour Organisation, concerning the employment of women with family responsibilities,

14. Recommends that the Committee of Ministers:

i. invite member governments to adopt policies in the areas of family law, social legislation, labour and education etc. which promote and safeguard, as far as possible, the equality of men and women, and a genuine partnership between them, in such a way as to enable parents to choose between remaining in the home and taking paid employment, without prejudice in either case to the upbringing of their small children or their own interest in terms of social security and other social benefits;

ii. transmit to member governments the proposals contained in the appendix.

Appendix to Recommendation 751 (1975)

a. To establish a family responsibility allowance, payable to households in which there are children under the age of three or requiring special care and:

i.   not more than one of the two parents is in paid employment, or

ii. there is only one parent.

b. The rate of the allowance specified under *a* shall be fixed at at least 50% of the national minimum wage or of an adequate level to be determined. The allowance shall be fixed at at least twice this amount for category *a*.ii where the beneficiary is not in employment.

c. This allowance is not taxable.

I. Parents at home

A. *Social security*

1.   To credit, without prejudice to other rights acquired or in course of acquisition, the social security contributions, at least in respect of medical and old-age insurance, of any parent wholly occupied in the home for so long as he or she has the full-time care of a young child or children, provided that where there are two parents only one may at any given time benefit from this provision.

2.   To establish an allowance fixed at a reasonable proportion of the national minimum wage or equivalent, payable on account of the certified medical incapacity of any parent normally working full-time in the home with the care of young children.

3.   To reduce, as far as is actuarially and administratively practicable, the qualifying period of contribution for an old-age pension.

4.   To divide equally in case of the cessation of marriage by reason of death, divorce or separation, the old-age pension rights acquired by the two partners of the marriage in the course of its duration.

5.   To eliminate for divorced, separated or widowed persons any provision which would prevent the enjoyment of rights acquired both by dependence and through personal entitlement.

B. *Family property*

1.   To give priority over other claims upon the assets of a divorced or legally separated spouse to the right to maintenance of his or her former spouse when not in employment and having the care of children of the marriage.

2.   To provide that any division of property acquired by a couple in the course of their marriage, and in particular real property, shall take fully into consideration the contribution in terms of effort and responsibility made by both partners even where this has not involved a financial share.

3.   To provide that a husband or wife not formerly the head of the family, who is left with the care of his or her children on the cessation of marriage by reason of death, divorce or separation, shall have the right to the same degree of protection in respect of tenancy or mortgage liabilities as the former spouse enjoyed or would have enjoyed.

C. *Re-entry into employment*

1.   To establish facilities of vocational training appropriate to the needs of mature students of either sex, such facilities to cover the whole range of employment for which training is required.

2.   To encourage women to seek training and employment outside the fields traditionally regarded as women's work and, in appropriate cases, to become teachers and instructors in such fields.

3.   To provide for all parents previously unemployed, within the year following the entry into compulsory schooling of their youngest child, the opportunity to receive a grant of up to one year's duration, sufficient to cover the cost of undergoing vocational training as specified in paragraph C.1 above.

4.   To give priority in the access to facilities of vocational training, and if necessary, in the provision of grants, to single parents.

II. Parents in paid employment

A. *Social security and taxation*

1.   To establish a right to sickness benefit in cash on account of the sickness of a child under the age of 10 living in the care of the beneficiary and payable for 10 days in any year on account of any one child, on the same terms as sickness benefit:

   i.   to any employed parent having the care of such a child whose spouse also is in employment and not receiving such benefit;

   ii.   to any single parent in employment having the care of such a child.

2.   To reorganise systems of direct taxation – for example, by giving the full allowances of an employed person to each spouse where both work – in such a way as to promote equality between working parents of both sexes in the net rewards of their employment.

B. *Organisation of work*

1.   To establish by law the right of either one of the parents to take leave of up to one year from the birth of a child, and thereafter to resume work without loss of status or seniority.

2.   To promote the development of part-time work with full protection for the employee, with priority to be given to parents having the care of young children.

3.   To provide the administrative arrangements which would enable parents with young children to share their employment and family responsibilities, by means which would include the institution of shorter working days.

4.   To promote the development of flexible working arrangements, including personalised working hours, unpaid leave during school holidays etc., which would facilitate the combining of paid employment with the care of children.

C. *Child care facilities*

1.   To increase substantially the number of places available in public and publicly controlled day care facilities for young children, paying equal attention to physical care and to long-term emotional and intellectual needs.

2.   To require any person receiving several children under 10 years of age into day care for payment – whether in a specially established institution or in a private residence – to obtain the permission of the local health and education authority.

3.   To grant permission as specified under paragraph C.2 above only to those ful-filling satisfactory requirements in respect of physical facilities, standards of hygiene, educational capacity and fees charged.

4.   To require persons seeking permission as specified under paragraph C.2 above to undergo a brief initial training at public expense and further periods of continuous training also at public expense, such training to be a condition of the renewal of the permission.

5.   To make every effort to ensure that the requirement to register (C.2 above) and the training and assistance available (C.4 above) are as widely known as possible, and that the formalities should not be carried out in such a way as to deter those con-cerned.

6.   To make the granting of any allowance or credit for the costs of child care by a third person conditional upon the production of evidence that the care provided conforms to the standards laid down.

7.   To create, according to a choice to be made by each government, either grants or tax exemptions which may be claimed where both parents or a single parent are in employment, in respect of a close relative living in the home and undertaking the care of their children.

8.   To give priority for places in public crèches and kindergartens – after those coming from physically or morally harmful home environments – to the children of single parents in paid employment.

Recommendation 1071 (1988)[1]
on child welfare – providing institutional care
for infants and children

The Assembly,

1. Considering that, having regard to that part of the European Social Charter concerning children's environment, all children should have the right to care provisions which complement the care they receive in their own families;

2. Having noted the development of alarming family trends, namely the rise in the number of illegitimate children, single-parent families and divorces;

3. Noting that inadequate provision of institutional child care is partly responsible for the increase in juvenile delinquency, and that the risks of a breakdown in the social relations between parents and children are now very great;

4. Considering that the principles of equal opportunities cannot be respected while excessive disparities in the material conditions of child care persist;

5. Wishing to see recognition given to the enormous efforts made by those professionally involved in the care of young children to encourage development of their full potential;

6. Noting that physical and mental well-being is essential for satisfactory child development;

7. Drawing attention to the cost to society of inadequately providing for the care of young children;

8. Recognising the right of all children to care provisions which complement those made by their own families, the duration of such additional care to be assessed in relation to the specific needs of the children,

9. Recommends that the Committee of Ministers invite the governments of member states:

a. to set up, in the context of European co-operation, a permanent body to:

   i. assess and monitor progress with the decompartmentalisation of services and government departments dealing with child welfare;

---

1. *Text adopted by the Standing Committee*, acting on behalf of the Assembly, on 23 March 1988. See Doc. 5854, report of the Social and Health Affairs Committee.

ii. promote the introduction in every country of a specific policy for child care in and outside the family;

iii. speed up consultations with a view to preparing a charter of children's rights;

b. to make plans to set up administrations (ministries or departments) which could one day propose guidelines for common action on the care of young children, the training of child-care staff and the harmonisation of their status in order to provide conditions that enable families to raise their children properly;

c. to draw up a list of requirements to be met, depending on the number of children born each year, the number of children receiving institutional forms of care complementing family care and the number of different modes of care and requirements within the family-supporting measures existing in Europe;

d. to increase the sums devoted by each government to research on early childhood, and to all public campaigns about children organised by official associations which have undertaken the task to protect children's rights in society;

e. to set up one or more European pilot projects on the care of children under 3, based on management by child-care staff and parents;

f. to urge local, regional and national authorities to reconsider budgetary priorities, in order to lay down guidelines for a policy on the care of young children at their respective levels;

g. to assess local policies regularly;

h. to guarantee all children the right to education regardless of the resources of their families, for example through free education or education allowances;

i. to break down barriers between the various local, regional or national services or administrations responsible for particular aspects of child welfare (health, environment, architecture, care provisions, protection of mothers, etc.);

j. to support financially innovative forms of child care which take account of children's specific physical and psychological needs;

k. to set up an information programme for parents and child-care staff on children's specific needs and the appropriate care conditions for the development of their full potential, the aim of which would be to publicise innovations made by certain families and the type of resources made available to them by local authorities;

l. to hold, at the Council of Europe's initiative, a European conference on children, to be attended by the various specialists involved in child care (parents, teachers, representatives of innovatory bodies and government departments, lawyers, etc.), with a view to defining society's aspirations with regard to child care, children's rights and the financing of children's specific needs.

Recommendation 1074 (1988)[1]
on family policy

The Assembly,

1. Noting the profound changes which have occurred in family structures over recent decades, characterised by greater life expectancy, a sharp drop in the birth-rate, a decrease in the number of marriages and remarriages, an increase in the divorce rate, a proliferation of single-parent families, an increase in other forms of communal life such as cohabitation, and the evolution of the role of women;

2. Observing that other factors, such as alterations in working conditions, the persistence of pockets of structural poverty, the increase in unemployment, illicit drug use, violence and delinquency, and economic migration, have increased tensions within the family;

3. Emphasising none the less that the family has stood up better than other institutions to economic, social and demographic upheavals and, in spite of everything, remains popular for millions of young people;

4. Recognising that the changes which have occurred also have positive aspects such as the replacement of the former marriage-alliance by the marriage-partnership with an improved social, economic and intellectual balance between the partners and, consequently, give hope for the future;

5. Believing that the family is still the place where human relationships are most intense and rich, and the best place for bringing up children and providing care for its elderly, lonely or sick members;

6. Considering that the family with its daily problems and needs is essentially a concrete reality, that it shares in society's economic and cultural life, adapts and evolves with society and that, consequently, any concept of the family as frozen in time would be unrealistic;

7. Convinced, similarly, that the role of the state with regard to family policy is not to give hard and fast replies based on ideology, but to create the circumstances necessary for the establishment of a family unit in which the individual can develop in safety, solidarity and respect for fundamental rights;

8. Recalling that, in this respect, both the European Commission and the European Court of Human Rights have repeatedly held that, under the

---

1. *Assembly debate* on 3 May 1988 (3rd Sitting) (see Doc. 5870, report of the Social and Health Affairs Committee, rapporteur: Mr Pini).
   Text adopted by the Assembly on 3 May 1988 (3rd Sitting).

European Convention on Human Rights, the family life of both "legitimate" and "*de facto*" families has to be respected;

9. Realising that any family policy today must face the new situation resulting from the emancipation of women and its impact on maternity, and must bear in mind two principles: first, the democratisation of the family which implies equality among its members and respect for the rights of each and, secondly, the exercise of free choice by the partners;

10. Believing strongly that the integration of women in economic and professional life and the creation of a climate favourable for child-bearing and bringing up children are not irreconcilable objectives, provided that the value of housework and child-rearing is recognised;

11. Convinced that, to be effective and coherent, specific family policy measures must be co-ordinated and complemented, particularly on the broader scene of social, fiscal and employment policies;

12. Noting that certain sectors of modern life such as social security are in some cases based on an outmoded concept which seems unaware of women's new status, excludes divorce and perpetuates "indirect rights", while tax legislation in many countries continues to discriminate against married couples;

13. Drawing attention in this context to its earlier work, particularly Recommendation 751 (1975) on the position and responsibility of parents in the modern family and their support by society, Recommendation 915 (1981) on the situation of migrant workers in the host countries, Recommendation 1051 (1987) on labour market flexibility in a changing economy, and Recommendation 1071 (1988) on child welfare – Providing institutional care for infants and children;

14. Referring to the position adopted on the role of the family in the report by the Colombo Commission and by the Secretary General of the Council of Europe in his report on social cohesion;

15. Noting the results of the 20th Conference of European Ministers responsible for Family Affairs, held in May 1987, endorsing one of its proposals, for a study on the causes of divorce and its effects on children, but regretting that the conference does not wish to co-operate with the Assembly;

16. Welcoming the fact that the Council of Europe medium-term plan of activities includes several topics on the family, distributed among various sectors such as social, legal and cultural,

17. Recommends that the Committee of Ministers invite the governments of the member states to base their preparation of family policy on the following proposals:

A. *Legislation*

   i. To affirm the pressing need for a general coherent family policy for all families, and to enact laws to ensure its application;

ii. To bring into force national and international legal instruments to consolidate equality between the sexes in the family and the protection of children's rights and, for the latter, particularly by speeding up preparation of the United Nations draft convention;

iii. To pay particular attention to the problems of spouses of different nationalities, such as transmission of nationality, residence permits, divorce and the custody of the children;

iv. To deliberate on questions such as adoption, artificial insemination and surrogate motherhood as they affect family life and particularly the interests of the child and, if appropriate, to prohibit certain practices;

v. To revise criminal and civil legislation concerning violence in the family, and to encourage psychological and other measures of assistance to the victims and perpetrators of violence, without prejudice to the legal procedures concerning the latter;

B. *Working life*

i. To strike a better balance between professional activities and family life, particularly by introducing greater flexibility for working time, part-time work and the age of retirement;

ii. To ensure that "parental leave", which is widely accepted in principle, becomes a reality;

C. *Taxation*

i. To abolish laws and regulations on the aggregation of family incomes, and to accept the principle for separate taxation for spouses;

ii. To introduce a flat-rate child allowance for all children instead of tax reductions;

iii. To introduce tax deduction for costs related to the care of children until they reach school age;

D. *Social security*

i. To recognise the principle of placing a value on housework and education by persons who stay at home for the particular purpose of raising their children;

ii. To examine the possibility of introducing a minimum guaranteed income to assist families in need;

iii. To set up a system of individual rights rather than indirect rights because of the increased risk of family breakup;

iv. To examine the possibility of crediting the periods spent on bringing up children or caring for other dependants (the elderly, the handicapped, etc.) to periods of insurance for the purpose of acquiring old-age and sickness benefits, and for calculating the amounts of such benefits;

v. To ratify the European Convention on Social Security, if they have not already done so, and to ratify the revised European Code of Social Security as soon as it is adopted by the Committee of Ministers, since certain provisions of these instruments have an impact on family welfare;

E. *Housing and urbanisation*

i. To take into account the needs of young families with limited means, and to aim at improving the financing of housing for large families;

ii. To enable children to develop in favourable housing conditions and a favourable environment, through a different approach to urbanisation with the aim of adapting the infrastructure of towns to the needs of people;

iii. To enable generations to live together if they so wish; the return to the family of elderly persons would of course require social infrastructure in order to alleviate the tasks of families for daily needs;

F. *Education*

i. To recognise that the prime responsibility for the upbringing of the child lies with his family; this presupposes a permanent, constructive dialogue between parents and the education authorities;

ii. To guarantee equality of opportunity for children, specifically through special measures for children from economically deprived homes, handicapped children, children of migrant workers, children from ethnic minorities and gifted children;

iii. To set up a system, separate from fostering and adoption, which might be called educational sponsoring, to assist single persons in difficulty to bring up their children, and to facilitate adoption across borders;

iv. To improve care structures for young children, and to adapt them to the needs of families, including particular categories who work at night;

G. *Consumption and information*

To improve opportunities for family associations to express themselves as a group and as users of goods and services, by establishing local, regional and national consultation machinery;

H. *Migration*

To grant migrant workers, by legislation and in administrative procedures, the right to have their families (wives and children) join them in the host country, for example by abolishing visa requirements for spouses and children who are minors.

Resolution 1011 (1993)[1]
on the situation of women and children
in the former Yugoslavia

1.   The Assembly refers in particular to Order No. 486 (1993) on the protection of human rights and the joint declaration of its Social, Health and Family Affairs Committee and Unicef (United Nations Children's Fund), adopted in Geneva on 24 June 1993.

2.   The conflict in the former Yugoslavia is marked by ethnic cleansing and barbarous violence against civilians, in particular women and children. The elementary rules and principles of the laws of war and the protective provisions of humanitarian law have been systematically flouted and violated.

3.   The international community has been powerless to provide an appropriate response, although the United Nations decision to set up an international court expresses its unwavering determination not to leave unpunished the war crimes and crimes against humanity committed during the conflict.

4.   Humanitarian action has shown its limitations; however, in spite of the difficulties encountered, an attempt has been made to offset the international community's shortcomings. Just tribute should be paid to the remarkable work performed by the various humanitarian organisations such as the UNHCR (Office of the United Nations High Commissioner for Refugees), Unicef, ICRC (International Committee of the Red Cross) and the NGOs (non-governmental organisations), and also to their staff, those women and men who devote themselves to helping others, often at the risk of their own lives.

5.   The current lack of subsidies means that this action may have to be discontinued, despite the increase in and diversification of the demand for humanitarian relief. Steps must be taken to continue to ensure the survival of civilian populations and also to treat the trauma caused by war, to reconstruct the vital infrastructure which has been destroyed and to give the population, especially the children, prospects of a future comprising something other than violence, hatred and revenge.

6.   In the last ten years, 90% of victims of armed conflict have been civilians; over one and a half million children have been killed, four million suffer from disabilities resulting from war, and a reported five million live in refugee camps. Moreover, in the conflict of the former Yugoslavia it is once again the

---

1. *Assembly debate* on 28 September 1993 (47th Sitting) (see Doc. 6903, report of the Social, Health and Family Affairs Committee, rapporteurs: Mrs Robert and Mr Daniel).
   Text adopted by the Assembly on 28 September 1993 (47th Sitting).

women and children who are the main losers in the war. They have suffered and witnessed barbaric acts and are liable to pass on a hatred which has devastated them. The rights of the child, a recent achievement of the international community, have been trodden underfoot.

7.   The Assembly, therefore, urges the governments of the member and non-member states grouped together in the Council of Europe:

i.   to take the requisite action on the declarations made at the New York World Summit for Children in 1990, by subscribing to the principle of "First Call for Children", according to which meeting the essential needs of children must be a top political priority when resources are allocated and must be taken fully into account when various policies are devised, and to undertake, as appropriate, to ratify and apply the provisions of the United Nations Convention on the Rights of the Child;

ii.   to express their support for this principle at the summit of heads of state and government (to be held on 8 and 9 October 1993 in Vienna) and to focus their discussions at the next Conference of European Ministers responsible for Family Affairs (Paris, 13-15 October 1993) on this central issue;

iii.   to undertake to protect children from the scourge of war and to condemn the barbaric practice in recent armed conflicts of using women and children as targets and human shields, as well as the widespread use of anti-personnel mines, particularly those resembling toys, of which the main victims are children;

iv. if the conflict in the former Yugoslavia continues, to take, in consultation with specialised organisations and NGOs, the immediate measures needed to ensure that the children and women of Bosnia-Herzegovina are given the food, water, heating, medical care and treatment and psychosocial help which are vital for their survival, that is to say, to ensure in all cases freedom of access for humanitarian relief and to secure observance for "havens of peace and safety" for the children;

v.   to accompany the measures imposing embargoes and other sanctions on the warring parties with the humanitarian arrangements needed to protect the lives and health of the most vulnerable group of civilians, especially children;

vi. to introduce, at a European level, a co-ordinating structure to provide information on immediately available medical facilities (for example, the number of beds reserved for emergency treatment for children in each country) and to develop mutual assistance between hospitals in order to promote the rebuilding of hospitals, donations in kind and personnel support in the former Yugoslavia;

vii. to ensure that rape victims, both women and children, receive the necessary medical care, psychological support and legal aid, not least in host countries;

viii. to provide the appropriate emergency medical, psychological and educational aid for children who have witnessed or suffered cruelty, inhuman or degrading acts or the loss of their loved ones;

ix. in the facilities for accommodating displaced persons, and refugee camps in particular, to help the women to feel useful by providing them with opportunities to engage in occupations and receive education and vocational training and allowing them to retain their active role, notably in performing their everyday family duties and housework;

x. to supply the children of the former Yugoslavia affected by the conflict with a minimum of education and the educational and play material (books, toys, etc.) which is vital for children's development;

xi. to develop, particularly for children, programmes of education in peace, tolerance and democracy;

xii. to assist in the initial and further vocational training of local personnel, especially those responsible for children, and to give them the moral support and psychological help needed for overcoming the burnout syndrome.

8. The Assembly launches an urgent appeal to the governments of the states grouped together in the Council of Europe and to the European Community to contribute financially to humanitarian relief, to relax the conditions placed on the grant of subsidies allocated to the various humanitarian organisations at work in the former Yugoslavia and to increase the size of the subsidies, so that needs can be effectively met.

9. It invites the governments of Council of Europe member states to make optimum use of the instrument constituted by the Council of Europe's Social Development Fund by means of a special aid account, so that immediate practical steps can be taken to meet the manifold needs emerging from the conflict in the former Yugoslavia.

10. The Assembly also invites governments not to overlook the risk that similar conflicts might break out in or around Europe, to continue discussion on humanitarian action in cases of armed conflict and to devise a concerted European strategy, so as to take timely steps to develop and reinforce, in every country, all the peace forces in society.

11. The Assembly invites the international community to review and adapt the humanitarian law governing the protection, in cases of armed conflict, of civilians, notably women and children, in keeping with human rights and the rights of the child.

12. Finally, the Assembly condemns the inhuman actions of all the warring factions, and calls upon Bosnians, Croats and Serbs to behave like civilised persons and not like animals, and furthermore demands that the principles of international humanitarian law be strictly observed by all concerned in every respect.

Committee of Ministers

Resolution (52) 72
Protection of children in the event of war

(Adopted by the Ministers' Deputies on 22 December, 1952)

The Committee of Ministers,

Having regard to Recommendation 29 (1952) of the Consultative Assembly on the protection of children in the event of war;

Having regard, in particular to paragraph i. of this Recommendation,

Recommends that member governments:

i. take as soon as possible all the necessary steps to ratify the Geneva Convention of 12th August, 1949, concerning the protection of civilians in time of war;

ii. take appropriate measures to provide the protection advocated in that Convention in close collaboration with the National Red Cross Societies, private and public humanitarian bodies, and the International Red Cross Committee.

Resolution (68) 37
Laws and regulations designed
to compensate family commitments

(Adopted by the Ministers' Deputies on 29 November 1968)

The Committee of Ministers,

Considering that the aim of the Council of Europe is to achieve a greater unity between its members for the purpose, among others, of facilitating their social progress;

Considering that under Articles 16 and 17 of the European Social Charter the Contracting Parties undertake to promote the economic, legal and social protection of family life by such means as social and family benefits, fiscal arrangements, promotion of family housing, benefits for the newly married, and any other appropriate means;

Considering that social progress in Europe can be attained in particular by the harmonisation of legislation and social practice and by the abolition of discrimination in the social field on the grounds of nationality;

Noting that this aim cannot be attained by all the member states of the Council of Europe whether they are Contracting Parties to the European Social Charter or not, without an appropriate family policy apt to meet the needs of families both through economic and financial measures designed to compensate for the burdens which they must bear and through adequate organisation of all other services to enable the family as a whole and its members to develop to the full within the community;

Taking note of the Social Committee's study on economic and financial laws and regulations designed to compensate for family commitments;

Considering that, while certain economic measures in favour of the family are taken in all member states, the nature and extent of these measures vary considerably but that in many respects there are possible ways of making progress, due regard being given to economic and social factors or traditions peculiar to each of the member states,

A. Recommends that governments of member states determine their family policy in regard to compensation for family commitments in accordance with the following:

I. Principles governing compensation for family commitments

A family dimension should be added to social policy as a whole. Measures to compensate for family commitments should be designed to secure adequate living conditions and means during the entire family life and in particular for its founding and development without undermining family responsibility. Such measures should pursue in particular the four goals set out below:

1.   An income for the family:

– regular money payments covering at least part of the expenditure entailed in running a family, and in particular by payment of family allowances;

– *ad hoc* benefits, in money or in kind, intended to help families in specific circumstances, for example at the time of birth;

– granting other social security benefits according to family needs;

– tax concessions based on the number of children where this is consistent with the principles governing the national relief systems;

– reducing expenses through special measures such as certain reductions of education costs, reduced fares, lower rates for power supply etc.

2.   Improved living conditions for families:

– assisting young couples settling into their first home;

– a housing policy geared to family requirements.

3.   Improved cultural facilities for families by means of:

– an education policy giving equal opportunity to all children;

– a socio-cultural equipment policy corresponding to the needs of families.

4.   Protection of mothers by means of:

– a policy of equal treatment for mothers, whether they are solely housewives or have some additional occupation;

– appropriate measures to obviate the need for mothers of young children to take up employment for financial reasons.

These measures should take account of the general economic trend, having regard in particular to its effect upon family standards.

II. Family allowances

1.   Family allowances should be paid until the statutory school-leaving age. They should continue to be paid or replaced by other corresponding allowances up to a higher age limit determined by the national legislation in respect of children pursuing their studies or undergoing vocational training.

2.   For children who are disabled or suffering from a chronic disease and who are incapable of earning a living wage, allowances should be paid either until the time such a child is entitled to receive other benefits provided for handicapped persons at least equivalent to the above-cited allowances or until a higher age limit than the usual one, to be determined by national legislation.

3.   All working sections of the population should receive family allowances or corresponding benefits. Equality of treatment should be granted to aliens, refugees and stateless persons. Family allowances for a claimant's children who usually reside abroad should be paid under conditions and within limits to be agreed upon by the member states concerned.

4.   Benefits should not in principle depend on the income or wealth of the family.

5.   Benefits should be paid at least from the second child onwards.

III. Setting up and housing of families

1.   Young couples

Steps should be taken to assist newly-married couples (by means for instance of low-interest loans, encouragement of pre-marriage saving etc.) to settle in their homes.

2.   Family housing

Measures such as the following should be taken to promote family housing:

a.   Families should be assisted in purchasing their own flats or houses by means of scaled facilities (bonuses, tax concessions, loans), taking into consideration the number of children;

b.   Low-interest loans and/or subsidies should be granted for the building of family housing (flats and one-family houses) so that the rent plus the other charges may be within the means of the family;

c.   Rents should be adjusted to the family income and the number of children by means of rent allowances or rent rebates when the rent of a flat or one-family house plus additional charges exceeds what a family can reasonably afford;

d.   Special measures of assistance in favour of co-operative housing should be considered.

IV. Social security

All members of the family should be covered by social security benefits in all appropriate contingencies.

V. Education

1.   The cost of educating children during the period of compulsory schooling should be reduced to a minimum, particularly by such measures as:

a.   free schooling, reduced tuition fees (or none at all) (cf. Article 10 (4) of the Social Charter);

b.   free school books (or other educational supplies);

c. award of scholarships and allowances, particularly in the case of children having to live in a place other than their parents' residence in order to attend school;

d. reduced fares for schoolchildren where transport is indispensable or refund of such fares;

e. free or cheap school meals.

2. Where children are pursuing their studies or undergoing vocational training, appropriate allowances should be granted.

VI. Aid to parents

1. *a.* All mothers should be entitled to free or reimbursable medical examination during pregnancy;

b. Fees payable to establishments (crèches, kindergartens, infant schools, etc.) looking after children during the daytime should be reduced, at least for certain income groups;

2. *a.* All mothers employed outside the home should be allowed a reasonable period of leave before and after confinement;

b. An employed mother should be compensated for loss of earnings by means of an adequate allowance paid during maternity leave;

c. Appropriate measures should be developed to assist working mothers to combine in the best possible manner their family duties and an outside occupation, either through direct help or by providing special protection schemes in favour of the women concerned;

d. Home-aid services should be envisaged to help the mother or another member of the family who takes the place of the mother when she is unable to take care of the family owing to sickness, rest cure or recreation leave. Financial aid should be granted when the family means are inadequate.

VII. Family holidays and other facilities

1. Steps should be taken to encourage family holidays.

2. Consideration should also be given to special travel facilities in favour of large families, for example reduced fares of every kind.

VIII. Equipment and services for families

Adequate equipment and services should be provided or sponsored to meet family needs, such as nursery-schools, day-care centres, boarding schools and home-aid services.

B. Emphasises that nothing in the present resolution may be construed as preventing any member state from taking measures more favourable than those recommended above.

C. Invites the governments of member states to keep it informed every three years of the action taken by them on this resolution.

Resolution (70) 15
Social protection of
unmarried mothers and their children

(Adopted by the Ministers' Deputies on 15 May 1970)

The Committee of Ministers of the Council of Europe,

Taking the Intergovernmental Work Programme of the Council of Europe into consideration;

Having regard to the contents of the report presented by the experts responsible for making a study on the social and legal protection of unmarried mothers and their children;

Considering paragraph 17 of Part I of the European Social Charter, as expanded by Article 17 of Part II of the same, which lays down the right of mothers and children, irrespective of marital status and family relations, to appropriate social and economic protection;

Convinced that the health, the satisfactory bringing-up and the future of every child are functions of the possibilities given to his mother to provide him with a welcoming home and of the social and psychological situation created by society;

Underlining that in order to avoid any segregation appropriate social work must not be exclusively provided for unmarried mothers and their children;

Believing however that appropriate social and medical measures for pregnant women on their own contribute to a diminution of accidents during pregnancy, of still birth and of infantile mortality, the levels of which are particularly high in their case;

Believing that for combining their professional duties with their family responsibilities, single mothers have a particular need for the amenities and services foreseen for helping all mothers,

Recommends the governments of the member states:

I. To promote and encourage help and assistance for single pregnant women and mothers who are on their own with the following aims:

1. To provide them with all the information they need, to give them advice on the action to be taken and to put them in touch with the appropriate social and medical services;

2. To provide the pregnant woman with medical care, when advisable combined with social measures as mentioned in the following;

3. To ensure in particular that the pregnant woman may obtain psychological and social casework help so as to:

a. help her to accept her pregnancy and her future role as a mother;

b. reassure her by preparing with her plans for the future, *inter alia* concerning her working situation, possible vocational training, housing situation and perhaps placement of the child;

Such casework should be entrusted to qualified social workers, helped if necessary by psychologists. In all events, teamwork (grouping in particular social workers, physicians, psychologists, legal experts, psychiatrists) is desirable and, where necessary, continued guidance should be given;

4. To provide, if necessary, the pregnant woman with possibilities for temporary accommodation facilities, where both her physical and her mental health are attended to, in conditions guaranteeing privacy and independence;

5. To provide her with all necessary assistance, and, taking into account the legislation in force on social security and labour protection, in particular:

a. to help her to keep her employment when it does not entail any risk for herself or the baby;

b. to provide her with possibilities to perform less arduous work or to cease working in the interests of her health or that of the baby, and

c. to secure her economic support during the pregnancy and after the delivery;

6. To arrange for confinement free of charge if need be, to take place in good psychological and health conditions, preferably in hospital;

7. To make help available in establishing paternity and obtaining payment of such financial contributions as the father would have to make to herself and her child; for example the introduction of a system of advances, financed by the authorities, would provide a guarantee of regular payment so far as maintenance allowances are concerned;

8. To help the mother, if necessary, to be established in suitable employment after the birth:

a. either in her former work,

b. or by enabling her to obtain the necessary professional qualifications, or to complete training or studies previously entered into;

9. To help her, if necessary, in finding suitable housing for herself and her child:

a. either, particularly for young inexperienced mothers without means, in temporary boarding homes for mothers and babies where the former may be prepared for their role as mothers and also for the exercise of a professional activity, conditions guaranteeing privacy and independence,

b. or in individual accommodation;

In this respect the public authorities should make provision, in the implementation of their social housing policy, for flats suited to small family units, without these being in any way segregated;

10. To guarantee her and her child the same benefits as those to which other families, fulfilling the same conditions, are entitled with regard to social security and all other advantages available for families;

11. To ensure that sufficient services and facilities be organised to enable her to work outside the home:

a. day nurseries whose opening hours should be adapted to the needs of the mothers;

b. supervision and recreational facilities for children of school age outside school hours as well as during school holidays, (e.g. day centres, canteens, holiday camps);

c. domiciliary assistance (e.g. home help services and baby sitting), *inter alia*, in cases of sickness;

These facilities and services are useful for all families but they are all the more necessary for mothers on their own, who are usually compelled to fulfil at the same time family and professional tasks. They should be made available at a reasonable cost or even free of charge in cases of need;

12. To facilitate access for her and her child to family holiday homes where available, in order to enable them to spend holidays together;

II. To ensure the effectiveness of measures described under I by the following methods:

1. To make widely known the social and medical institutions and bodies which have as their object the protection of mother and child; teaching in schools and information in youth organisations should play a major role in this respect;

2. To encourage pregnant women to make use of those institutions and bodies, and to ensure that they would be made welcome;

3. To encourage doctors, midwives and members of para-medical professions as well as teachers and social workers to draw the attention of pregnant women who are on their own to the bodies mentioned above, and to advocate their use;

4. To ensure that at the local level, individuals or families in difficulty have at their disposal a service or a person capable of giving them information, of providing them with guidance and of obtaining effective co-operation between all the services and bodies concerned with social protection (such as the social services, medico-social services, social security offices, employment services etc.) which may have a role to play in solving the case under consideration;

5. To stimulate as far as possible modern mass communication media (radio, television, press) to make public opinion aware of the problems of

unmarried mothers and their children and to seek to obtain a greater comprehension of those problems by society, with a view to doing away with prejudice against them and to securing their acceptance on an equal footing with other families;

6. To undertake or encourage social research on the situation of unmarried mothers and the consequences of this situation in today's society;

7. To include in educational curricula preparation for family life and instruction relating to male and female responsibilities, particularly so far as procreation is concerned;

8. To bring about the use of non-discriminatory terminology with regard to the mothers and children in question.

Resolution (77) 33
on placement of children

(Adopted by the Committee of Ministers on 3 November 1977,
at the 27th meeting of the Ministers' Deputies)

The Committee of Ministers,

Considering that the aim of the Council of Europe is the achievement of greater unity between its members for the purpose of safeguarding and realising the ideals and principles which are their common heritage and of facilitating their economic and social progress;

Bearing in mind the United Nations Declaration of the Rights of the Child and especially its second, fifth and sixth principles;

Bearing in mind Articles 16 and 17 of the European Social Charter, concerning the right of families to social, legal and economic protection and the right of mothers and children to social and economic protection;

Bearing in mind the conclusions of the 13th Conference of European Ministers responsible for Family Affairs held in 1973;

Realising that children who grow up in environments that do not meet their fundamental physical, emotional, intellectual and social needs are put in jeopardy of their lifelong welfare;

Affirming that preventive measures in the widest possible sense should remain the first strategy to avert this danger;

Aware that in spite of these measures many children will continue to need temporary or long-term placement outside their families;

Anxious to ensure that placement of children is carried out in the best possible circumstances,

Recommends the governments of member states:

I.   General principles

1.   To recognise that all arrangements for placement should be based on the following principles:

1.1. The need for placement should be avoided as far as possible through preventive measures of support for families in accordance with their special problems and needs;

1.2. A request for placement should be considered as a warning signal of a difficult family situation; consequently efforts to meet the child's needs should always be related to an understanding of the problems of his family and arrangements for the child should as a rule be coupled to specific arrangements for helping the parents;

1.3. The arrangements made for the child (including a decision to leave him in his family or to place him) should try to ensure the highest possible degree of satisfaction of his developing emotional needs and his physical wellbeing as well as any preventive medical educational or other care necessary to meet any special problems he may have;

These arrangements should provide, as far as possible and when this is in the best interests of the child:

– maintenance of links to his family;

– stability of care and bonds of affection, taking into account the child's developmental stage in regard to the formation of emotional attachments;

– respect of his individuality;

– a cultural and social environment which is appropriate and acceptable to society;

– integration into a local community and preferably the same one as the family's;

– for adolescents, opportunities for assuming responsibility, for achieving independence and for taking up adult roles;

1.4. The decisions about the child's placement should normally be taken after advice given by a multidisciplinary team; similar advice should be available at each review;

1.5. A plan for the child should be drawn up based on an assessment of the family, of the child himself and of the possible solutions available, in the light of the objectives mentioned above;

This plan should incorporate in particular:

– a decision on the best initial mode of placement for the child;

– a review of the child's situation after a period which will vary according to age and individual circumstances (being shorter in the case of very young children), but which should not normally exceed six months, after which there should be further reviews at regular intervals;

1.6. Long-term placement of very young children in residential units should be avoided as much as possible; thus adoption in the light of the European Convention on the Adoption of Children should be facilitated and encouraged to the greatest possible extent.

II. Policy

2. To ensure in the framework of their policies for family welfare that placement decisions are taken according to sound procedures and in a favourable context, in particular by:

A. *Family support*

2.1. Considering, in the framework of general economic and social policies, the implementation of measures to assist all families in rearing children well; and developing more specific measures of family policy such as preparation at school of children of both sexes for home and family life;

2.2. With a view to reducing the need for residential care on the sole grounds of handicap, providing the families of children with physical or mental handicaps with the necessary emotional support, with financial allowances, and also with technical, medical and educational support in decentralised forms; such support could, for example, be provided through day care facilities, services in the home, schemes for reducing parental burdens, transport services, material aid;

2.3. Providing facilities for the special assistance of families with acute psycho-social problems affecting the development of the child;

B. *Management of placements*

2.4. Encouraging the participation in the management of a child's placement of the following:

– the service or organisation responsible for the placement, i.e. the placement agency;

– the parents;

– the child, who should be given an opportunity to discuss his situation progressively as he matures in understanding;

– those caring for the child (foster parents or staff of residential units);

– social and other workers concerned with the family;

– personnel of the statutory preventive public health services;

– pre-school and school personnel, paediatricians, psychologists, and any other specialists involved;

2.5. Ensuring that the professional staff involved in the management of the placement work, as far as possible, as a multidisciplinary team;

C. *Organisation*

2.6. Subjecting all organisations responsible for placement to strict regulation and supervision, to ensure the maintenance of high professional standards;

2.7. Integrating the organisations responsible for the placement of children with those responsible for assisting families or ensuring their closest co-operation in each case; and securing the decentralisation of responsibility in different organisations and services necessary to achieve co-operation at local level, so as to create areas of responsibility which can be better supervised;

2.8. Ensuring that financial arrangements do not establish an accidental bias towards the choice of one particular form of placement;

2.9. Generally seeing that the organisation responsible for placement is capable of adaptation to new techniques and knowledge;

D. Modes of placement

2.10.   With a view to enabling them to match each placement to individual needs, making available to placement agencies an array of modes of placement from foster homes to various kinds of therapeutic care in residential homes (examples are given in the appendix);

2.11.   Progressively providing the best possible geographical distribution of places so as to facilitate maintenance of links to the natural family and to promote co-operation with the biological parents, unless considered undesirable for the child;

2.12.   Progressively making support services (psychologists, psychiatrists, specialised equipment, etc.) equally available to all staff of all types of residential units and to foster parents;

2.13.   Promoting foster care as being frequently the best mode of temporary placement, especially for young children and therefore ensuring:

– education of the public on the value of foster care;

– the development of schemes for recruiting foster parents;

– careful selection of ordinary and specialised foster parents to be based, *inter alia*, on the assessment of each member of the household;

– thorough preparation of foster parents including discussion on child development, the problems of foster children and the specific situation of the child to be placed with them;

– definition of the obligations and rights of parents in whose care children are placed and the requirements they must satisfy;

2.14.   Providing for strict control of fostering arrangements and making fostering, especially private fostering, conditional upon notification and licensing;

2.15.   Discouraging, with a view to its elimination, illegal fostering by promoting general measures of support for families and extending the authorised machinery for placement;

2.16.   Providing for the development of small family-type residential units for children when fostering is not possible, and in consequence:

a.   progressively running down larger residential institutions;

b.   ensuring that all residential units, including any larger institutions retained for the time being:

– are organised in sub-units of a family type;

– receive children of mixed ages and both sexes;

– have mixed staff to provide identification objects of both sexes;

– provide opportunities for keeping siblings together;

– encourage co-operation with biological parents;

– provide opportunities for experiments whereby parents and children can live together for a short time within the unit;

– provide special units for adolescents when needed;

c. encouraging the running of all residential units in close contact with the surrounding community, all personnel being considered as members of the caring team and the children being encouraged, according to their capacity, to participate in the running of the units;

E. *Staff and training*

2.17. Recognising that the staff of placement agencies and of residential units are faced with an extremely delicate and laborious task, for which they must be suitably selected and trained, especially in child development and family social work;

2.18. Ensuring that the staff of placement agencies will be adequately trained and experienced in making placement decisions;

2.19. Ensuring that the training of the staff of placement agencies, of residential units and of field-workers include work in multidisciplinary teams, and also with parents, foster parents and children; considering to this end introducing a common element into the initial training of different disciplines and facilitating inter-disciplinary joint discussion groups as part of in-service training;

2.20. Providing a basic preparatory training with particular emphasis on knowledge of children for all foster parents using individual and group methods, and more extensive training for certain kinds of foster parents;

2.21. Providing for the continuous training of all staff of residential units as a means of improving their professional knowledge and of giving them psychological support; providing to this end, *inter alia*, training courses for all the staff of a unit at the same time, reliefs for living-in staff and resources for regular staff meetings;

2.22. Providing for the further training of foster parents using individual and group methods as a source of psychological support and emphasising the importance of knowledge of child development;

2.23. Ensuring that the training of foster parents takes place with the participation of the ordinary child care team as well as of any necessary specialists.

III. Research

3. Having due regard to the principles of confidentiality and privacy in respect of those concerned;

3.1. To encourage active research and evaluation on all modes of placement;

3.2. To promote further research on a local, national and international basis as well as the international exchange of information on problems of placement such as:

- the extent of and trends in needs of placement;

- the effects of different placement modes especially long-term placements;

- direct and indirect costs of various modes of placement.

IV. Others

4.1. To acknowledge, in the field of child welfare, the need to promote consultation and co-operation among bodies associated with social welfare, health, educational and legal matters, as well as among the professional groups concerned;

4.2. To encourage associations of foster parents;

4.3. To encourage communication with children so that their wishes and feelings may be taken into account so far as is practicable in policies of placement.

Appendix to Resolution (77) 33

List of placement modes

(The following list is not exhaustive, but indicates a variety of measures which can be made available).

a.   Closer supervision and support of the child in its own family;

b.   Appropriate daycare placements (can be combined with a);

c.   Placement in the extended family (i.e. a supervised placement by an authorised organisation as distinct from care arrangements made spontaneously on the sole responsibility of the parents);

d.   Ordinary foster care (for which selection, preparation and continued support are nonetheless needed);

e.   Specialised foster care (implies a more intensive training to deal with particular problems of the foster children and generally an increased remuneration);

f.   "Seasonal" residential units (implies that the child returns home for part of the year);

g.   Short-stay residential units for whole families;

h.   Small residential units where the staff (generally a couple) are permanently resident and the children are within the range of an ordinary family in number and, as far as possible, in age distribution; often known as "family group homes";

i.   Specialised residential units (say of about twenty-five children) with special facilities (psychiatric, pedagogical, technical) for the treatment or care of a particular category of children; such units should be organised in sub-units of type h;

j.   Placement of adolescents in small, mainly self-governing communities of their own age group, under light but skilled supervision, or in a flat of their own.

Recommendation No. R (79) 17
concerning the protection of children against ill-treatment

(Adopted by the Committee of Ministers on 13 September 1979
at the 307th meeting of the Ministers' Deputies)

The Committee of Ministers, under the terms of Article 15.*b* of the Statute of the Council of Europe,

1.   Considering that the aim of the Council of Europe is the achievement of greater unity among its members for the purpose of safeguarding and realising the ideals and principles which are their common heritage and of facilitating their economic and social progress;

2.   Bearing in mind the United Nations' Declaration on the Rights of the Child, and especially its second and ninth principles;

3.   Bearing in mind Article 17 of the European Social Charter concerning the rights of mothers and children to appropriate social and economic protection;

4.   Bearing in mind Recommendation 561 (1969) of the Consultative Assembly of the Council of Europe;

5.   In the light of the report on the causes and prevention of child abuse prepared at the request of the Social Committee;

6.   Reaffirming the generally accepted principle that the rights of parents, guardians and custodians over children may and should be subjected to the necessary restraints to prevent serious and avoidable harm to the children;

7.   Reaffirming that this principle should be applied through effective intervention on the part of public authorities;

8.   Confirming that physical or emotional ill-treatment or neglect of children by those responsible for their care is a serious problem in most member states;

9.   Considering also that such child abuse may be the most extreme manifestation of a wider problem of family disorder and often society as a whole;

10.   Noting that the long-term effects of the abusive home environment are frequently disastrous for the child's growth, his learning capacities, his personality development as well as his future behaviour as a parent and thus costly for society in the long run;

11.   Regretting that, despite this fact, there is ignorance, indifference and even resistance within society to the acknowledgement of the extent and

gravity of the phenomenon and that it is often regarded as a problem for the authorities and not for the individual;

12. Noting that the search for a long-term solution to this problem requires a dual strategy, consisting of effective measures of immediate intervention, detection and management, and secondly a policy of prevention;

13. Noting the initiatives taken in several member states and in non-member states to develop systematic and co-ordinated methods in the prevention and management of child abuse, and their positive results;

14. Anxious therefore, in view of the urgency of the problem, to promote the general application of such methods to combat the problem in member states;

15. Anxious to encourage research and projects intended to obviate the lack of data presently available and the inadequacy of experience in this field, as well as to adapt measures taken to the newly acquired knowledge;

16. Stressing that effective prevention and management of the problem requires the fullest co-ordination and co-operation between the health, social and other agencies,

I.   Recommends that the governments of member states take all necessary measures to ensure the safety of abused children, who for the purposes of this recommendation are those subjected to physical injury and those who are victims of neglect, deprivation of affection or mental cruelty likely to jeopardise their physical, intellectual and emotional development, where the abuse is caused by acts or omissions on the part of persons responsible for the child's care or others having temporary or permanent control over him;

     To this effect, it invites them to:

1.   foster a better awareness of the extent and gravity of the problem, in particular by encouraging public education campaigns in order to spread information on child abuse as a social phenomenon, on its causes, its signs and the measures which are being taken or could be taken to combat it;

2.   with a view to ensuring, in the most effective way, prevention, detection and management of cases of child abuse, improve the organisation of the child welfare and protection system, taking into account the principles and suggestions mentioned at Appendix I;

3.   promote co-ordination, knowledge and understanding among services and among persons belonging to the various professional groups involved in child protection, in order to facilitate a multidisciplinary approach;

4.   promote research into the problem giving priority within available resources to studies on schemes for prediction and prevention and for early identification and management; formulate specific definitions on child abuse, and consider research along the lines indicated at Appendix II;

5.   keep child protection legislation constantly under review in order to ensure that it conforms to the guidelines set forth in the present recommen-

dation and, if appropriate, adapt it according to developments in understanding of the problem of child abuse;

II. Invites the governments of member states to inform the Secretary General of the Council of Europe every five years of the steps they have taken to implement the present recommendation.

Appendix I to Recommendation No. R (79) 17

Principles and suggestions to be considered

1. *Prevention*

In order to ensure effective prevention it would be appropriate:

a.   to improve general socio-economic conditions and to develop measures for family welfare giving special consideration to those population groups which are economically and socially at a disadvantage;

b.   to develop family planning services with a view to enabling couples to avoid unwanted pregnancies;

c.   to encourage all measures likely to contain violence in society;

d.   to research into the most effective ways of preparing young people for parenthood, including the provision of courses at school and use of the mass media for teenagers and the public in general;

e.   to ensure, especially during the first pregnancy, that all parents have adequate opportunities to learn and discuss methods of child rearing appropriate to the various stages of development and are encouraged to do so;

f.   to devote particular attention to the perinatal period in order to promote the establishment of emotional bonds between the parents and the newborn child by:

- ensuring a good preparation for childbirth and parenthood for both parents,
- emphasising support and understanding for the mother in labour and discouraging the excessive use of emotionally traumatising practices at the time of birth, which might affect the mother's attitude towards the child,
- encouraging rooming-in in the maternity wards,
- promoting parents' self-confidence and competence in handling their baby, avoiding over-emphasis on the acquisition of technical skills,
- favouring and promoting breast-feeding, where appropriate, by educating parents and persons who are likely to advise mothers,
- recognising the important role of the father *vis-à-vis* both the mother and the newborn child, for example by giving the father the opportunity to participate at the childbirth and by giving consideration to providing for childbirth leave without loss of income for him;

g.   when low birthweight or sick newborn babies, particularly handicapped babies, are in special care units, to encourage maximum contact between parents and infants and especially to ensure support and counselling by nurses, doctors and others;

h.   to ensure that there exists a comprehensive preventive child health care system capable of following, by regular checks, the progress of every pre-school child, paying special attention to:

   i.   continuity of health care;

   ii.   ways of improving the take-up of services by families prone not to make full use of them;

i.   to establish a mechanism, or extend research, for predicting vulnerable families at an early stage in the antenatal and perinatal period;

j.   to give special care and support to vulnerable families with parenting problems in the early stages of the child's life;

k.   since many parents concerned have unrealistic expectations about child development and bearing in mind that the majority have not had a good model of parenting themselves and have great difficulty in understanding how to achieve a warm family relationship, to pay very special attention to:

i.   teaching these parents to understand the needs and behaviour of young children at different stages of development;

ii.   understanding and treating marital problems, giving psychological help where necessary;

iii.   relieving environmental stresses which often coexist.

2. *Detection*

In order to reach the main objective, i.e. the detection of all cases of child abuse at an early stage, it would be appropriate:

a.   to give the public information about reporting systems which it can use with discretion, so that the people around a child at risk may take effective measures;

b.   to encourage the public and especially those most likely to meet ill-treated children to assist in the detection of cases of abuse;

c.   to take such measures as are necessary to enable persons subject to professional secrecy to disclose cases of ill-treatment or neglect of minors, on the basis of established procedures and in a manner consistent with professional ethics, *inter alia* by the enactment of legislative provisions for this purpose or encouraging the adoption of similar provisions in codes of professional conduct.

3. *Management*

a.   The priority objective should be the interruption of ill-treatment and the prevention of further abuse in every detected case;

b.   As a subsidiary objective, it should be endeavoured to maintain as far as practicable the child in his family by effective measures of support and treatment of the whole family unit;

c.   It would be appropriate to ensure the use at local level, within the existing institutions for child welfare, of procedures making it possible to take action as soon as a case has been reported or detected, and providing in every case for immediate medical and psycho-social investigation by a multidisciplinary team and, if appropriate, legal intervention;

d.   Procedures should be made available, subject to due process of law, both for short-term emergency removal of a child from its family to a place of safety and for partial or total deprivation of parental rights or of the exercise of those rights for a period or permanently, the criterion for the decision being the best interests of the child, assessed, where possible, after a thorough multidisciplinary psycho-social study of the child, its parents and the whole family;

e.   Regular assessment of the long-term growth and development of the child can be used as a sign of the total family well-being as well as alerting professional staff to its own need for special treatment, training or care;

f.   Steps should be taken to ensure the continuity and coherence of management and the adequate co-ordination of the parties involved.

4. *Training of personnel*

With a view to ensuring an adequate training of the personnel in the various professional groups dealing with the protection of children against ill-treatment, it would be appropriate:

a.   to favour a systematic approach to such training and to stimulate studies and experiments to determine the most appropriate content of such training, the teaching methods as well as the preparation of the necessary teaching aids;

b.   to make such training an integral part of the formal training of all workers likely to be involved in the detection, management and prevention of child abuse;

c. to provide opportunities for in-service training and for regular refresher courses, in the light of the rapid developments of knowledge in the field;

d. to ensure that the training programmes of all paediatricians, school doctors, general practitioners and child psychologists, as well as of other members of the medical and para-medical professions likely to come across the problem, will enable them to recognise cases of child abuse at an early stage;

e. to ensure that social workers, teachers, members of the police and all professional workers likely to come across cases of child abuse will be taught to recognise signs of it;

f. to make known to all the professional workers referred to in d and e the steps to be taken in the presence of a suspected case;

g. to emphasise the need for a multidisciplinary approach in this training, as a means of breaking down any barriers to co-operation between disciplines and professions;

h. to ensure the co-operation of all bodies or services responsible for the training of all relevant professions, of the management for child abuse and of the teams, if any, especially concerned with child abuse attached to local paediatric units;

i. to introduce a new awareness of the concept of responsibility into training for medical and social personnel as well as into information for the public at large.

Appendix II to Recommendation No. R (79) 17

Subjects of research

i. The evaluation of schemes for predicting families needing special help to prevent abnormal ways of child rearing.

ii. The evaluation of schemes for the best means of providing this early intensive help and counselling.

iii. The evaluation of the various family support systems on a long-term basis, once abuse has been recognised, e.g. extra health visiting, counselling, home-help services, day foster care, substitute grand-mothers, crisis nurseries, day nurseries, twenty-four-hour assistance.

iv. Carefully controlled follow-up studies on the later development and personality of children who have been abused.

v. The evaluation of various forms of substitute family care, in terms of the child's overall personality development.

vi. The establishment of guidelines for estimating the relative safety of the home before returning the child.

vii. The study of various ways in which the existing law may be more effectively used for the protection of children.

viii. Statistical data on the problem and research into the lives of people committing child abuse.

ix. Action research programmes on measures of prevention, detection and management.

Recommendation No. R (80) 12 concerning marriage guidance and family counselling services

(Adopted by the Committee of Ministers on 27 June 1980
at the 321st meeting of the Ministers' Deputies)

The Committee of Ministers, under the terms of Article 15.*b* of the Statute of the Council of Europe,

1.   Recalling the report presented by the experts responsible for conducting a study entitled "Marriage guidance and family counselling in Europe", published in 1975;

2.   Taking into account the rights and principles set forth in the European Social Charter, in particular the right of the family to economic, legal and social protection, stated under Article 16;

3.   Recognising that the family is a basic institution in society and that it must be given particular attention;

4.   Aware of the fact that drastic economic and social changes, as well as political and ideological movements and the new sets of values and patterns of behaviour which govern emotional and sexual relationships have generated problems in marriage stability;

5.   Realising that the disturbances observed in marriage and family relationships may result in serious psychological and other consequences, both for the adults and for the children concerned;

6.   Noting that in the majority of member states people confronted with difficulties of a confidential family nature are increasingly seeking help in the form of advice from specialist services,

Recommends the governments of member states:

a.   to recognise the importance of services providing counselling, to ensure a more stable emotional, individual and family equilibrium, and

b.   to encourage the development of these services on the following lines:

A.   *Services*

1.   These services should be adapted to the social, economic and cultural contexts of each country; thus no one type of service can be universally recommended.

2.   These services should be offered in a form covering, as far as possible, the intimate personal problems of their clients.

3. Since these services should be easily accessible to all, proper geographical distribution should be ensured.

4. Services should be accurately publicised in terms designed to reach the most varied socio-economic groups among the population.

5. The quality of services offered should be constantly improved and interviewing techniques revised in order to adapt them to the evolution of social behaviour. The methods, form and organisational content of these services should be adapted to the specific requirements of the different social strata.

6. The services offered should be available not only to couples, but also to persons separated or divorced from each other, single parents and other single people and young people.

7. Marriage guidance, family counselling and family planning services, whenever separated, should co-operate closely.

Co-operation on a continuing basis should also be established, if need be, between these services and the bodies providing personal social and medical support.

8. Clients should have the assurance that their privacy would be protected both in respect of the service consulted, which shall treat all information in confidence, and of the public authorities. The position of counsellors in relation to confidentiality should be examined.

9. The services concerned should also carry out information and educational work, making use whenever appropriate of sex education, discussion groups, courses on the dynamics of the couple and information sessions on parent/child relationships.

10. The possibility of using the mass media, in particular radio and television broadcasts, should be explored.

B. *Staff*

1. The greatest care should be taken over both selection and training of the staff employed in these services.

2. Training and selection should take different forms depending on the work to be done by the applicants and on their basic training. Marriage guidance or family counselling should be undertaken only by qualified persons.

3. As a high degree of emotional stability and self control are essential in this type of work, criteria for selection should be carefully defined, with emphasis on human qualities, including respect for the individual, readiness to help and the necessary skill in establishing human relationships.

4. Training should be designed, in the first place, to develop these natural abilities, and, in the second, to encourage acquisition of the appropriate skills.

5. Theoretical training, where appropriate, may be accompanied by practice in the field in whatever services this may be necessary.

6.   Arrangements should be made to provide, as far as possible, the counsellors with guidance; discussions for the purpose of providing guidance should be so organised that the relations established with clients can be studied on the basis of actual cases.

7.   Permanent education and training should be developed through the use of in-service training, educational leave programmes and interdisciplinary meetings.

8.   The experience of marriage and family counsellors could possibly be used within the framework of the reconciliation procedures provided for in certain legislative systems for divorce.

C.   *Research*

Research should be encouraged with a view to:

1.   evaluating the potential demand for services of this kind, their effectiveness and their suitability to the setting in which they operate;

2.   determining clients' motivations and wishes, so as to discover why members of certain socio-professional categories generally make less use of these services;

3.   ascertaining the cause of family problems.

Recommendation No. R (81) 3
concerning the care and education of children from birth to the age of eight[1]

(Adopted by the Committee of Ministers on 23 January 1981 at the 328th meeting of the Ministers' Deputies)

The Committee of Ministers, under the terms of Article 15.*b* of the Statute of the Council of Europe,

Considering that the aim of the Council of Europe is to achieve a greater unity between its members and that this aim is to be pursued, in particular, through common action in the social and cultural fields;

Bearing in mind the United Nations' Declaration on the Rights of the Child (1959);

Having regard to Recommendation 874 (1979) of the Assembly on a European Charter on the Rights of the Child;

Having regard to the Declaration on the care and education of the child from birth to eight adopted by the Conference on the theme "From birth to eight: young children in European Society in the 1980s", which was organised by the Council for Cultural Co-operation in Strasbourg from 17 to 20 December 1979;

Recalling that this conference was one of the Council of Europe contributions to the International Year of the Child (1979);

Considering the importance of the care and education of children from birth to eight,

Recommends that the governments of member states:

a. take account, in their policies on the care and education of young children, of the principles set out in Section I of the appendix hereto and take the measures concerning their implementation set out in Section II of the appendix.

b. ensure that this recommendation is distributed as widely as possible among interested persons and bodies.

---

1. In accordance with Article 10.2.*c* of the Rules of Procedure for the meetings of the Ministers' Deputies, the Representatives of Ireland and of the United Kingdom approved the adoption of this text but reserved the right of their governments to comply with it or not.

Appendix to Recommendation No. R (81) 3

I. Principles concerning the care and education of the child from birth to eight

A. *The rights of the child*

The child must enjoy the fundamental rights as set out in the United Nations Declaration on the Rights of the Child, as well as the right to develop his physical, emotional, intellectual, social and spiritual potential to the full and to be respected as an individual in his own right.

The child will normally depend primarily on his family to recognise and secure these rights. The family operates within a wider social framework from which it should be able to obtain the support it needs to fulfil its obligations. In providing such support, care should be taken not to undermine parental responsibilities towards the child.

All services with a contribution to make to the development of young children – especially health, education and social services – should work with, and through, the family to provide continuity of experience for the child.

B. *The care and education of young children*

The care and education of pre-school children should fulfil the following criteria. They should:

– meet the child's need for security and affection and social life, including leisure activities, with other children and adults;

– provide the conditions for good physical and mental health;

– stimulate the child's creative and intellectual development and his capacity for expression;

– help the child to become integrated into his environment and to cope with life, and encourage the child's independence, initiative and free play;

– respect the child's cultural and psychological identity and recognise his uniqueness and individuality;

– open up both family and pre-school circles to the wider society to enable the child to meet other people of all ages.

Educational provision should be made available for all children whose parents wish them to have it during at least two years preceding the start of primary school. The lack of financial means should not be a barrier to children who need such educational provision.

Support services – including health, social services and education – have an important role to play in the development of all children, but the form of provision should take account of their particular needs, which differ according to their stage of development, their personal capacities and their cultural backgrounds:

i.   children who live in urban areas have great need of care and education owing to living conditions in towns: lack of space, pollution of various kinds, dangers in the streets, parents' absence (time spent at work plus travelling time);

ii.   children who live in rural and sparsely populated areas are more difficult to cater for. It is therefore necessary to find untraditional and flexible solutions to bring pre-school education to these children;

iii.   children who live in circumstances of extreme socio-economic deprivation have special needs;

iv.   children of cultural minorities, whether native or immigrant, should receive an education which promotes their integration into the regional or national community, as a basis for mutual enrichment;

v.   handicapped children should, whenever necessary, have available to them establishments which meet their special needs.

In association with the child care and child psychological services, health services should operate within pre-school care and education provision to detect, assess and treat handicapping conditions.

C. *People and agencies participating in the care and education of young children*

All those contributing to the care and education of young children (including the family in the widest sense, the community and self-help groups, volunteers, teachers) should be able to benefit from the findings of up-to-date research and knowledge of developments in the concept of early education and, whenever appropriate, to participate in such research.

Professionals need initial training supplemented by in-service training. Both should be of the highest possible quality.

II. Role of member states

Taking into account the importance of care and education of children from birth to eight in the European society of the 1980s, member states should:

1.   organise the care and education of young children, in close co-operation with parents, as a means of complementing family up-bringing and as a first stage in life-long learning. This should be done by:

– providing adequate funds;

– improving family, social and labour legislation;

– planning education systems in such a way as to maintain continuity and to educate children to become creative and innovatory adults;

2.   prepare parents and future parents for the responsibilities inherent in the education of young children;

3.   assume responsibility or provide support for organisations and institutions caring for young children, especially for those children whose need is most obvious;

4.   promote and encourage research and the training of staff in order to provide children with care and education, under the best possible conditions, supervised by highly qualified staff, who, as far as possible, should operate in multidisciplinary teams;

5.   ensure that the various national, regional and local administrations co-ordinate family and child care services to guarantee continuity of experience for the child.

Recommendation No. R (84) 24
on the contribution of social security to preventive measures

*(Adopted by the Committee of Ministers on 7 December 1984
at the 378th meeting of the Ministers' Deputies)*

The Committee of Ministers, under the terms of Article 15.*b* of the Statute of the Council of Europe,

1. Considering that the aim of the Council of Europe is to achieve a greater unity between its members, notably for the purpose of facilitating their social progress;

2. Considering that the development and improvement of preventive measures will facilitate social progress in Europe;

3. Recalling the rights and principles regarding prevention set forth in the European Social Charter, especially in Articles 3, 7, 11, 14, 15 and 17 of Part II;

4. Having regard to the standards of social security protection laid down in the European Code of Social Security and the Protocol thereto and, in particular, the preventive measures prescribed in these instruments in the fields of medical care, occupational hazards and unemployment;

5. Convinced that prevention is vitally important not only to individual health, well-being and fulfilment but also to community welfare;

6. Convinced that, in view of the humanitarian, social and financial implications of the risks inherent in modern living and working conditions, social security should make a greater contribution to preventive measures, particularly by developing fundamental and applied research in this field, where such measures are not the responsibility of other institutions or bodies;

7. Considering that the development of preventive measures is, by reducing such risks or lessening their impact, likely to reduce social security expenditure;

8. Being of the opinion that, even in those fields where preventive measures do not substantially reduce expenditure, they are justified on humanitarian and social grounds;

9. Considering it desirable, lastly, that the right to preventive measures be recognised as part of the right to social security,

Recommends that the governments of member states:

– create conditions to encourage the development of preventive measures in the framework of social security, where such measures are not the responsibility of other institutions;

– to this end, put into practice the principles and measures set out in Parts A and B respectively of the appendix to this recommendation.

Appendix to Recommendation No. R (84) 24

For the purpose of this recommendation:

– the term "prevention" applies to any measure aimed at preventing the occurrence of a contingency covered by social security;

– the expression "controlling the consequences" applies to any measure aimed at preventing an aggravation of the condition or situation of the person concerned resulting from the occurrence of such a contingency;

– the expression "rehabilitation and compensation" applies to any measure which will alleviate the social and financial consequences of the occurrence of such a contingency, particularly rehabilitation.

A. General policy principles

1.   Social security should have sufficient resources to develop preventive measures in all fields within its responsibility. The possibility of earmarking special financial resources for preventive measures to be taken by social security should also be studied.

2.   For the various contingencies it covers, social security should be concerned not only to remedy and compensate but also to meet the cost of appropriate preventive measures.

3.   Easier access to health care facilities and improvement in the procedure for the award of social security benefits should be encouraged in order to facilitate the development of measures in all fields to prevent and control the consequences of contingencies that have arisen and rehabilitate and compensate the persons concerned.

4.   Preventive measures should be systematically reviewed in order better to assess their cost-effectiveness.

5.   Social security should help to promote medical and social research into preventive measures so as to be in possession of material of a nature to facilitate informed decisions regarding prevention. In particular, it is necessary to compile and keep up to date statistics for all branches of social security and to harmonise them in order to facilitate comparison between member states.

6.   Informing and educating the public, especially by means of consciousness-raising campaigns, should be among the priority activities of social security. Information services could be set up within social security institutions.

7.   Social security could also offer its support – financial in particular – to other bodies involved in prevention.

8.   Lastly, the preventive work of social security institutions should be fully co-ordinated with that of the public authorities, local government and other bodies.

B. Specific measures

9.   In the fields named below the following measures could be promoted:

Health

10. Paying particular attention to promoting health, in particular through health education programmes (at school, at work and in the community) because of the positive influence of such education on the contingencies covered by social security. Health education may allow each individual to become aware of the possibilities he

95

has of improving his health or preventing certain diseases and hence of directly influencing his living and working conditions.

11. Encouraging members of the public to comply with the preventive measures recommended by the national health authorities, by offering appropriate facilities.

12. Studying the possibility of introducing preventive health measures involving incentives, for example the granting of financial advantages to people who voluntarily undergo preventive examinations.

13. Ensuring that preventive examinations are geared more specifically to sections of the populations which are at risk.

14. Encouraging the development of preventive measures as part of ordinary, and in particular preventive, health care.

15. Reinforcing medical examinations during pregnancy and improving health and social aid for expectant mothers and mothers on their own.

16. Facilitating access to health care facilities by reducing or abolishing the proportion of the costs borne by the protected persons, subject to the funds available, notably in the case of serious illness, by developing the third-party-payment system or by promoting prevention-oriented health centres and their satisfactory geographical distribution.

17. Giving priority to functional and occupational rehabilitation measures for the sick, accident victims and invalids.

Occupational hazards

18. Promoting the prevention of occupational injuries and diseases, in particular by informing and advising firms, alerting and training workers and visiting firms.

19. Encouraging firms to develop and perfect their job safety measures, for instance by financial action (advances to employers), by means of a rating system (adjustment of contribution rates or insurance premiums according to the number of accidents in the firm and to the effort it has made at prevention) or by means of consciousness-raising campaigns.

20. Assisting with the organisation of occupational health services, with particular reference to Resolution (72) 5 on the harmonisation of measures to protect the health of workers in places of employment.

21. Promoting occupational redeployment for workers particularly exposed to occupational injuries and diseases and, where appropriate, fostering the occupational rehabilitation of victims of work accidents or occupational diseases and compensating for loss of earnings arising from the occurrence of such contingencies.

22. Co-ordinating these preventive measures with those of other bodies in charge of prevention in this sphere (in particular labour inspectorates).

Unemployment

23. Developing measures to prevent and control the consequences of unemployment and to rehabilitate and compensate the persons concerned, in accordance with the principles and guidelines set out in Recommendation No. R (82) 8 on employment policy and the protection of workers against the effects of unemployment.

Old age

24. Contributing to the development of measures to prevent and control the consequences of old age and to rehabilitate and compensate the persons concerned, such

measures to be based on the aims and measures set out in Resolution (70) 16 on social and medico-social policy for old age.

25. Adjusting pension scheme arrangements to meet the needs of people who wish either to stop work gradually, or to stop work completely before reaching pensionable age, or to continue working after pensionable age when the economic and social situation permits, having regard to the provisions of Resolution (76) 32 on social security measures to be taken in favour of pensioners and persons remaining in activity after pensionable age.

26. Promoting preparation-for-retirement measures so as to prevent social, psychological and physiological problems resulting from a sudden transition from working life to retirement, having regard to Resolution (77) 34 on preparation for retirement.

27. Encouraging appropriate preventive examinations with a view to ensuring that old people remain as active as possible, both physically and mentally.

28. Promoting a policy of allowing old people to continue to live in their own homes and integrating them into society, with a view to forestalling deterioration in their usual way of life and admission to hospital, by means of welfare measures for the benefit of old people (home helps, home medical care, home visiting services, meals-on-wheels).

29. Helping to organise residential facilities for old people, who, for financial, social or medical reasons, cannot remain in their usual surroundings.

Family welfare

30. Paying particular attention to the specific needs of certain categories (for instance, large and single-parent families) by increasing where necessary the benefits awarded to them or by setting up special services.

31. Considering the possibility of making the working hours of people bearing direct family responsibilities more flexible, without thereby adversely affecting the social security benefits to which they would be entitled (more part-time work, parental or family leave, shortening of the working week).

32. Investigating the possibility of conferring direct social security rights on persons looking after children at home, where they do not already enjoy such rights, taking into account Resolution (75) 28 on social security for women at home.

33. Promoting social services to assist families (family aid services, crèches, child-minding centres, social centres).

34. Considering, where appropriate, arranging for maintenance obligations to be met by social security institutions in cases where the principal person liable defaults, subject to the possible subrogation of the said institutions in respect of the rights of the persons concerned.

Recommendation No. R (85) 4
on violence in the family[1]

(Adopted by the Committee of Ministers on 26 March 1985
at the 382nd meeting of the Ministers' Deputies)

The Committee of Ministers, under the terms of Article 15.*b* of the Statute of the Council of Europe,

Considering that the family is the basic organisational unit of democratic societies;

Considering that the defence of the family involves the protection of all its members against any form of violence, which all too often occurs among them;

Considering that there is violence in any act or omission which prejudices the life, the physical or psychological integrity or the liberty of a person or which seriously harms the development of his or her personality;

Considering that such violence affects, in particular, children on the one side and women on the other, though in differing ways;

Considering that children are entitled to special protection by society against any form of discrimination or oppression and against any abuse of authority in the family and other institutions;

Considering that the same is true of women in so far as they are subject to certain *de facto* inequalities which hamper the reporting of any violence of which they are victims;

Having regard in this respect to its Resolution (78) 37 on the equality of spouses in civil law;

Having regard also to its Recommendation No. R (79) 17 concerning the protection of children against ill-treatment;

Having regard to the proceedings of the Council of Europe's 4th Criminological Colloquy, on the ill-treatment of children in the family;

Having regard to Recommendation 561 (1969) of the Consultative Assembly of the Council of Europe, on the protection of minors against ill-treatment,

---

1. When this recommendation was adopted, the Representative of the United Kingdom, in application of Article 10.2.*c* of the Rules of Procedure for the meetings of the Ministers' Deputies, reserved the right of her Government to comply or not with Article I.5 of the recommendation.

Recommends that the governments of member states:

I. With regard to the prevention of violence in the family:

1. alert public opinion to the extent, seriousness and specific characteristics of violence in the family with a view to obtaining its support for measures aimed at combating this phenomenon;

2. promote the dissemination among families of knowledge and information concerning social and family relations, early detection of potentially conflictual situations and the settlement of interpersonal and intra-family conflicts;

3. provide appropriate professional training for all those responsible for intervening in cases of violence in the family, particularly those who, because of their functions, are in a position to detect such cases or deal with the victims thereof;

4. arrange for and encourage the setting up, and support the work, of agencies, associations or foundations whose aim is to help and assist the victims of violent family situations, with due respect for the privacy of others;

5. set up administrative departments or multidisciplinary boards with the task of looking after victims of violence in the family and with powers to deal with such cases.

Their powers might include the following:

– to receive reports of acts of violence in the family;

– to arrange for medical examinations at the victim's request;

– to help, care for and advise the various parties involved in cases of violence in the family and to that end to carry out social inquiries;

– to pass on, either to the family and children's courts or to the prosecuting authorities, information which the department or board deems should be submitted to one or another of those authorities;

6. impose strict rules on these departments or boards concerning the divulging of information to which they have access in the exercise of their powers;

II. With regard to the reporting of acts of violence in the family:

7. circulate specific information on the advisability and feasibility for persons who become aware of cases of violence in the family of reporting them to the competent bodies, particularly those mentioned in paragraphs 4 and 5 above, or of directly intervening to assist the person in danger;

8. consider the possibility of removing the obligation of secrecy from the members of certain professions so as to enable them to disclose to the bodies mentioned in paragraph 5 above any information concerning cases of violence in the family;

III. With regard to state intervention following acts of violence in the family:

9.   take steps to ensure that, in cases of violence in the family, the appropriate measures can be quickly taken, even if only provisionally, to protect the victim and prevent similar incidents from occurring;

10. take measures to ensure that, in any case resulting from a conflict between a couple, measures are available for the purpose of protecting the children against any violence to which the conflict exposes them and which may seriously harm the development of their personality;

11. take measures to ensure that the victim's interests are not prejudiced by interference between civil, administrative and criminal measures, it being understood that criminal measures should be taken only as a last resort;

12. review their legislation on the power to punish children in order to limit or indeed prohibit corporal punishment, even if violation of such a prohibition does not necessarily entail a criminal penalty;

13. study the possibility of entrusting cases of violence in the family only to specialist members of prosecuting or investigating authorities or of trial courts;

14. take steps to ensure that, as a general rule, a psycho-social inquiry is carried out into such cases and that, particularly on the basis of the findings of the inquiry and in accordance with criteria that take account of the interests of the victim as well as the children of the family, the prosecuting authority or the court is able to propose or take measures other than criminal ones, especially when the suspect or accused agrees to submit to the supervision of the competent social, medico-social or probation authorities;

15. do not institute proceedings in cases of violence in the family unless the victim so requests or the public interest so requires;

16. take measures to ensure protection against any external pressures on members of the family giving evidence in cases of violence in the family. In particular, minors should be assisted by appropriate counsel. Moreover, the weight of such evidence should not be diminished by rules relating to the oath;

17. consider the advisability of adopting specific incrimination for offences committed within the family.

Recommendation No. R (87) 6
on foster families[1]

(Adopted by the Committee of Ministers on 20 March 1987
at the 405th meeting of the Ministers' Deputies)

The Committee of Ministers, under the terms of Article 15.*b* of the Statute of the Council of Europe,

Considering that the aim of the Council of Europe is to achieve a greater unity between its members, *inter alia*, by promoting the adoption of common rules in legal matters;

Recognising that the law should protect the welfare of children;

Recognising that it is normally in a child's interests to remain with his family of origin and that an improvement in support for these families would ensure that the need for fostering is reduced;

Considering that it is possible to improve the legal systems relating to the fostering of children in order to promote the development of the personality of the child and to protect his person and his moral and material interests;

Considering that an improvement of the situation of foster parents might contribute to the welfare of children;

Realising that consideration might be given to the effects of fostering in other contexts such as social and other benefits;

Having regard to Resolution (77) 33 on the placement of children and Recommendation No. R (84) 4 on parental responsibilities,

Recommends the governments of member states to include in their legislation, rules on foster families based on the principles set out in the appendix to this recommendation.

---

1. When this recommendation was adopted, and in application of Article 10.2.*c* of the Rules of Procedure for the meetings of the Ministers' Deputies, the Representatives of Denmark and Norway reserved the right of their Governments to comply or not with Principle 5 of the appendix to the recommendation.

Appendix to Recommendation No. R (87) 6

For the purposes of this recommendation, a fostering occurs when a child is entrusted, otherwise than with a view to adoption, to a couple or an individual ("foster parents") who takes care of the child for more than a short time or for an undetermined time and who does not have legal custody of the child and who is not a parent.

Principle 1

1.   National legislation should provide a system of supervision of foster parents in order to ensure that they provide the necessary moral and material conditions for the proper development of the child, in particular by means of their personal qualities, especially their ability to bring up the child, and their housing conditions.

National legislation may provide that such supervision does not apply where the fostering is with a close relative.

2.   The supervision should be based:
   – on information given by the foster parents to the competent authority, or
   – on an authorisation system, or
   – on any other means which would enable this objective to be attained, for example a system of official approval of persons who regularly receive children.

3.   In any event the competent authority should intervene and provide support where the interests of the child so require.

Principle 2

The personal relationships of the child with his family of origin should be maintained and information concerning the well-being of the child should be given to that family, provided that this is not detrimental to the essential interests of the child.

Principle 3

The foster parents should be presumed to have the power to exercise, on behalf of the legal representatives of the child, those parental responsibilities which are necessary to care for the child in day-to-day or urgent matters.

Principle 4

As far as possible before any important decision is taken concerning the person of the child, the foster parents should be given the opportunity to express their views.

Principle 5

After a foster child has become integrated into the foster family, in particular after a substantial period of fostering, the foster parents should be able to apply, subject to any conditions specified by national legislation, to a judicial or other competent authority, for power to exercise certain parental responsibilities including, where appropriate, legal custody.

Principle 6

Where the child has been integrated into the foster family, in particular after a substantial period of fostering, then, if the person or the authority which made the fostering wishes to terminate it and the foster parents oppose the termination, it is for the judicial or other competent authority to take a decision.

Principle 7

1.   Before any decision is taken by the competent authority under Principles 5 and 6, the parents and the foster parents should be given the opportunity to express their views. The child should be consulted if his degree of maturity with regard to the decision so permits.

2.   The authority should base its decision primarily on the interests of the child, taking account in particular of the links between the child, his parents and his foster parents. This decision should be taken without undue delay.

Principle 8

Agreements relating to the fostering of a child may not derogate from the principles set out in this recommendation.

Recommendation No. R (87) 20
on social reactions to juvenile delinquency

*(Adopted by the Committee of Ministers on 17 September 1987
at the 410th meeting of the Ministers' Deputies)*

The Committee of Ministers, under the terms of Article 15.*b* of the Statute of the Council of Europe,

Considering that young people are developing beings and in consequence all measures taken in their respect should have an educational character;

Considering that social reactions to juvenile delinquency should take account of the personality and specific needs of minors and that the latter need specialised interventions and, where appropriate, specialised treatment based in particular on the principles embodied in the United Nations Declaration of the Rights of the Child;

Convinced that the penal system for minors should continue to be characterised by its objective of education and social integration and that it should as far as possible abolish imprisonment for minors;

Considering that measures in respect of minors should preferably be implemented in their natural environment and should involve the community, in particular at local level;

Convinced that minors must be afforded the same procedural guarantees as adults;

Taking account of earlier work by the Council of Europe in the field of juvenile delinquency and in particular of Resolution (78) 62 on juvenile delinquency and social change and the conclusions of the 14th Criminological Research Conference on "Prevention of juvenile delinquency: the role of institutions of socialisation in a changing society";

Having regard to the United Nations Standard Minimum Rules for the Administration of Juvenile Justice (the Beijing Rules),

Recommends the governments of member states to review, if necessary, their legislation and practice with a view:

I. *Prevention*

1. to undertaking or continuing particular efforts for the prevention of juvenile maladjustment and delinquency, in particular:

a. by implementing a comprehensive policy promoting the social integration of young people;

b. by providing special assistance and the introduction of specialised programmes, on an experimental basis, in schools or in young peoples' or sports' organisations for the better integration of young people who are experiencing serious difficulties in this field;

c. by taking technical and situational measures to reduce the opportunities offered to young people to commit offences;

II. *Diversion – mediation*

2.   to encouraging the development of diversion and mediation procedures at public prosecutor level (discontinuation of proceedings) or at police level, in countries where the police has prosecuting functions, in order to prevent minors from entering into the criminal justice system and suffering the ensuing consequences; to associating Child Protection Boards or services to the application of these procedures;

3.   to taking the necessary measures to ensure that in such procedures:

– the consent of the minor to the measures on which the diversion is conditional and, if necessary, the co-operation of his family are secured;

– appropriate attention is paid to the rights and interests of the minor as well as to those of the victim;

III. *Proceedings against minors*

4.   to ensuring that minors are tried more rapidly, avoiding undue delay, so as to ensure effective educational action;

5.   to avoiding committing minors to adult courts, where juvenile courts exist;

6.   to avoiding, as far as possible, minors being kept in police custody and, in any case, encouraging the prosecuting authorities to supervise the conditions of such custody;

7.   to excluding the remand in custody of minors, apart from exceptional cases of very serious offences committed by older minors; in these cases, restricting the length of remand in custody and keeping minors apart from adults; arranging for decisions of this type to be, in principle, ordered after consultation with a welfare department on alternative proposals;

8.   to reinforcing the legal position of minors throughout the proceedings, including the police investigation, by recognising, *inter alia*:

– the presumption of innocence;

– the right to the assistance of a counsel who may, if necessary, be officially appointed and paid by the state;

– the right to the presence of parents or of another legal representative who should be informed from the beginning of the proceedings;

– the right of minors to call, interrogate and confront witnesses;

– the possibility for minors to ask for a second expert opinion or any other equivalent investigative measure;

– the right of minors to speak and, if necessary, to give an opinion on the measures envisaged for them;

   – the right to appeal;

   – the right to apply for a review of the measures ordered;

   – the right of juveniles to respect for their private lives;

9. to encouraging arrangements for all the persons concerned at various stages of the proceedings (police, counsel, prosecutors, judges, social workers) to receive specialised training on the law relating to minors and juvenile delinquency;

10. to ensuring that the entries of decisions relating to minors in the police records are treated as confidential and only communicated to the judicial authorities or equivalent authorities and that these entries are not used after the persons concerned come of age, except on compelling grounds provided for in national law;

IV. *Interventions*

11. to ensuring that interventions in respect of juvenile delinquents are sought preferably in the minors' natural environment, respect their right to education and their personality and foster their personal development;

12. to providing that intervention is of a determined length and that only the judicial authorities or equivalent administrative authorities may fix it, and that the same authorities may terminate the intervention earlier than originally provided;

13. when residential care is essential:

   – to diversifying the forms of residential care in order to provide the one most suited to the minor's age, difficulties and background (host families, homes);

   – to establishing small-scale educational institutions integrated into their social, economic and cultural environment;

   – to providing that the minor's personal freedom shall be restricted as little as possible and that the way in which this is done is decided under judicial control;

   – in all forms of custodial education, to fostering, where possible, the minor's relations with his family:

     - avoiding custody in places which are too distant or inaccessible;

     - maintaining contact between the place of custody and the family;

14. with the aim of gradually abandoning recourse to detention and increasing the number of alternative measures, to giving preference to those which allow greater opportunities for social integration through education, vocational training as well as through the use of leisure or other activities;

15. among such measures, to paying particular attention to those which:

   – involve probationary supervision and assistance;

– are intended to cope with the persistence of delinquent behaviour in the minor by improving his capacities for social adjustment by means of intensive educational action (including "intensive intermediary treatment");

– entail reparation for the damage caused by the criminal activity of the minor;

– entail community work suited to the minor's age and educational needs;

16. in cases where, under national legislation, a custodial sentence cannot be avoided:

– to establishing a scale of sentences suited to the condition of minors, and to introducing more favourable conditions for the serving of sentences than those which the law lays down for adults, in particular as regards the obtaining of semi-liberty and early release, as well as granting and revocation of suspended sentence;

– to requiring the courts to give reasons for their prison sentences;

– to separating minors from adults or, where in exceptional cases integration is preferred for treatment reasons, to protecting minors from harmful influence from adults;

– to providing both education and vocational training for young prisoners, preferably in conjunction with the community, or any other measure which may assist reinsertion in society;

– to providing educational support after release and possible assistance for the social rehabilitation of the minors;

17. to reviewing, if necessary, their legislation on young adult delinquents, so that the relevant courts also have the opportunity of passing sentences which are educational in nature and foster social integration, regard being had for the personalities of the offenders;

V. *Research*

18. to promoting and encouraging comparative research in the field of juvenile delinquency so as to provide a basis for policy in this area, laying emphasis on the study of:

– prevention measures;

– the relationship between the police and young people;

– the influence of new crime policies on the functioning of legal systems concerned with minors;

– specialised training for everyone working in this field;

– comparative features of juvenile delinquency and young adult delinquency, as well as re-education and social integration measures suitable for these age-groups;

– alternatives to deprivation of liberty;

– community involvement in the care of young delinquents;

– the relationship between demographic factors and the labour market on the one hand and juvenile delinquency on the other;

– the role of the mass media in the field of delinquency and reactions to delinquency;

– institutions such as a youth ombudsman or complaints board for the protection of young people's rights;

– measures and procedures of reconciliation between young offenders and their victims.

Recommendation No. R (90) 2
on social measures
concerning violence within the family[1]

(Adopted by the Committee of Ministers on 15 January 1990
at the 432nd meeting of the Ministers' Deputies)

The Committee of Ministers, under the terms of Article 15.*b* of the Statute of the Council of Europe,

1. Considering that the aim of the Council of Europe is the achievement of greater unity among its members for the purpose of safeguarding and realising the ideals and principles which are their common heritage and of facilitating their economic and social progress;

2. Bearing in mind the right to respect for private and family life as defined in Article 8 of the European Convention on Human Rights;

3. Bearing in mind the right of the family to social, legal and economic protection, and the rights of mothers and children to appropriate social and economic protection, as defined in Articles 16 and 17 of the European Social Charter;

4. Bearing in mind the Declaration on equality between women and men, adopted by the Committee of Ministers at its 83rd Session (16 November 1988);

5. Bearing in mind Recommendation No. R (84) 4 of the Committee of Ministers on parental responsibilities;

6. Bearing in mind Recommendation 561 (1969) of the Assembly of the Council of Europe on the protection of minors against ill-treatment;

7. Bearing in mind Recommendation No. R (79) 17 of the Committee of Ministers concerning the protection of children against ill-treatment;

8. Bearing in mind the proceedings of the Council of Europe's 4th Criminological Colloquy, on the ill-treatment of children in the family (1979);

9. Bearing in mind Recommendation No. R (87) 21 of the Committee of Ministers on assistance to victims and the prevention of victimisation;

10. Having regard to Recommendation No. R (85) 4 of the Committee of Ministers on violence in the family;

---

1. When this recommendation was adopted, the Representative of Denmark, in application of Article 10.2.*c* of the Rules of Procedure for the meetings of the Ministers' Deputies, reserved the right of her Government to comply or not with paragraphs 6 of Section A and 46 of Section B of the appendix to the recommendation.

11. Having regard to the conclusions of the Council of Europe's Colloquy on violence within the family: measures in the social field (Strasbourg, 25-27 November 1987);

12. Recognising that the problem of violence in the family calls for measures to be taken at national and international level;

13. Noting that violence within the family occurs at all levels of society and in all countries, rich or poor, with no regard, for instance, to family structures, ethnic origin, age, language, religion, political or other opinion, national or social origin, or property;

14. Acknowledging that social and economic pressures on families contribute to violent behaviour;

15. Noting the need to identify the other factors contributing to violence, to prevent violence in the family and to consider social measures to remedy violence in the family when it has already taken place;

16. Considering the need for a change in the consciousness of the whole of society, whereby everyone would recognise the unacceptability of the phenomenon of violence both in the family and in society as a whole;

17. Recognising the general importance of the non-violent settlement of conflicts and the discouragements of the misuse of power;

18. Believing that trends towards the democratisation of the family, implying respect for members of the family as individuals with equal rights and equal opportunities, can help to discourage violence;

19. Bearing in mind the importance of adequate financial resources for carrying out planned and proposed measures in the social field,

Recommends that the governments of member states take or, where appropriate, encourage the general preventive measures and the specific measures mentioned in the appendix to the present recommendation.

Appendix to Recommendation No. R (90) 2

Section A: General preventive measures

1. The family, a fundamental unit of society, should be supported by all possible means.

2. The rights of individuals should be recognised and respected, with particular attention being paid to those of the weaker members of the family.

3. Full equality should be implemented between the sexes; this involves equal education, equal opportunities for work and decision-making, and equal opportunities for economic independence and personal growth.

4. Social and economic pressures should be relieved in areas such as social welfare, health, housing and urban planning, the world of work, culture, education.

5. The extent, seriousness and negative consequences of violence within the family should be accurately established. The public should be extensively informed about them, and about the principles of non-violent settlement of conflicts, the non-acceptance by society of the misuse of power and the possibilities of treatment. To this end, education and the media should be properly used.

6. The justification of violence in the media should be limited by all the means possible in a democratic society. The media should be invited to collaborate (via professional codes of conduct for instance) in such a policy.

7. Adequate housing and urban policies which can prevent potentially explosive situations within the family as well as in the wider community should be undertaken. The specific needs of the elderly, of families (in particular those with many children), of young people and of certain underprivileged groups should be given high priority.

8. Social and economic protection on an independent basis should be assured for those caring full-time at home for young children, an elderly parent or a disabled relative, in order to support carers in what can be conditions of constraint and conflict.

9. Everything necessary should be done to reconcile family life with working life, with particular attention being paid to, on the one hand, the provision, quality and accessibility of child day-care facilities, family support services and social security, and, on the other hand, on a voluntary basis, part-time work, flexible arrangements of working hours and parental leave.

10. Research should be undertaken to identify those family situations which lead to an increased number of dangerous conflicts, in order to prevent or resolve potentially violent situations.

11. In the absence of adequate research on the special situation of disabled members of the family, governments should promote and/or subsidise studies on this subject, as well as considering in depth to what extent the present recommendation can be applied to this particularly vulnerable group.

Section B: Specific measures

I. *Information*

1. Non-sensationalist information campaigns should be encouraged on the part of the media, schools and other agencies that influence the public at large. Such campaigns could include information on work in women's shelters, on crisis intervention centres, on parental responsibilities and on agencies to which children can turn.

2.   Information concerning the causes, identification and prevention of family violence must be adapted to those to whom it is addressed: professional people, children, young adults, parents, etc.

3.   Adequate means should be found for providing victims, particularly first-time
victims, with information concerning crisis intervention methods, such as crisis telephone numbers and the addresses of shelters and self-help groups.

II. *Detection of violence*

4.   The public in general and professionals dealing with families in particular should
be made aware of the need to detect and make an early diagnosis of cases of violence
within the family. This can be achieved by information campaigns for the general
public and by special information campaigns aimed at specific categories of professionals.

III. *Reporting violence*

5.   The community as a whole should be encouraged to act responsibly and report
cases of violence in the family to authorities empowered to help or change the situation. This applies particularly to neighbours, friends, workers in day-care and other
institutions and teachers, who have to overcome an understandable reticence in the
matter.

6.   All cases of violence reported at hospitals, social services, or by the police should
be directed to the social services or to relevant courts (for instance, family courts,
where they exist), with the informed consent of the adult victim of violence or in
accordance with other guarantees laid down by domestic law, in order that the necessary steps to safeguard the person in danger can be taken. Guidelines for reporting
should be developed.

7.   Whenever the social services are not informed, for example because of professional secrecy, this should not suppress the need to assist individuals in danger.

8.   The conditions in which victims of violence within their family disclose their pain-
ful experiences, whether to social, medical, or judicial authorities, should be improved. Facilities should exist for victims to be given support by a social worker or a
confidant in addition to any legal representation that might be appropriate.

IV. *Help and therapy for the whole family*

9.   Practical services that should be available for all members of the family include,
apart from social welfare services in general:

   - telephone lines (for emergency calls and for counselling),
   - crisis services, where possible with a twenty-four hour service,
   - counselling centres.

Steps should be taken to co-ordinate these various services.

10.   The therapy adopted for the treatment of victims of violence, especially sexual
abuse, whether individual therapy or therapy for the family as a whole, should be
adapted to each case.

11.   The creation of self-help groups for victims and self-help groups for perpetrators
should be widely encouraged and supported.

12.   A combination of professional individual therapy and self-help groups should be
used wherever possible, since experience shows such a combination to be effective.

V. *Measures for children*

13.   The good care and upbringing of children should be promoted. This includes the training of young parents both before and after the birth of their children, and the provision of advisory services.

14.   The importance should be emphasised of the general condemnation of corporal punishment and other forms of degrading treatment as a means of education, and of the need for violence-free education.

15.   Particular attention should be paid by the social and health services to individuals and families known to be particularly at risk as far as violence against children is concerned.

16.   The specific problems that may be encountered in families where there are step-children, or foster children or disabled children should be taken into consideration.

17.   In order to achieve continuity in the treatment of the family, which is one of the great challenges when working with child abuse, ways of working should be developed that integrate the authority of the members of the various professions concerned.

18.   When the interests of an abused child are in conflict with those expressed by its parents, the child's interests should in principle have priority. When there is a need to protect the child by removing it from its family, for a short or long term, that should not be considered as an end in itself but as a provisional part of an overall family treatment approach for the interests of both parties. Work with the family should continue, regardless of the child's removal.

19.   A wide spectrum of treatment offers should be developed:

  – emotional support for the child as well as the parents,

  – help with socio-economic stress factors,

  – treatment of parent/child interaction and marital relationships,

  – work towards improving the family's social network.

VI. *Measures for women*

20.   Women who are victims of violence within the family should be given co-ordinated and comprehensive assistance, including, if necessary, financial assistance in accordance with national legislation. Specific responsibility for particular tasks in dealing with violence against women should be assigned to public authorities in association, where necessary, with non-governmental organisations.

21.   If legal possibilities for removing an abusive spouse exist, they should be used to allow the abused woman and her children to remain at home.

22.   Where a victim of violence was previously financially dependent on the violent person, financial assistance should be made available, if needed, to enable the victim and children to become independent. This measure should not discharge the perpetrator from his financial responsibilities.

23.   There should be general and sufficient provision of possibilities of finding accommodation in a hostel for battered women (shelter). The aim of shelters for battered women is to provide rapid help for women and children in danger. Before being provided with accommodation in a hostel for battered women, the persons concerned should, where possible, be given counselling.

24.   Victims of violence should not themselves be expected to meet the capital and recurrent costs of shelters. Public authorities should, in appropriate circumstances and according to national legislation, subsidise these shelters.

25.   Each crisis centre and shelter for abused women should have its own policy concerning the disclosure of its address and the acceptance or non-acceptance of visitors. If the reuniting of the family is considered possible, supervised meetings between the family members in the shelter can be of help. In some countries, however, experience shows that shelters function more effectively if outside people have no access to them. Abused women must be entirely free to decide whether or not they want to return to their partners.

26.   Once a battered woman has been admitted to a shelter, she should, if she so wishes, be adequately helped by social workers, psychologists, lawyers and other qualified persons, including experienced voluntary workers who can help in particular with practical and administrative questions concerning the woman and, as appropriate, her children. An important element can also be mutual assistance and the exchange of experiences with other battered women in the shelter.

27.   When a battered woman leaves a shelter, proper after-care should be provided, preferably by a social worker who can visit the woman, on request, in her home and take care of her problems.

28.   Self-help groups should be established, whereby women who have left a shelter meet each other regularly and help each other in order to avoid isolation. Informal networks should be set up for the exchange of information and ideas between shelters and self-help groups.

VII.   *Measures for old people*

29.   There is a particular lack of knowledge of the extent of violence against old people. As a first step, research should be undertaken or promoted and information programmes should be carried out.

30.   An effective family policy for old people (including day-centres, community services, home care services, respite care) should be set up in order to relieve pressure on families and thus contribute to the reduction of factors leading to violence.

31.   The situation of frail old people (in particular as to the respect of their rights) who have been placed in an institution or host family in return for payment should be the subject of special attention in order to avoid possible abuse by members of their family who have remained in contact with them.

32.   In order to avoid old people being "excluded" from their community, appropriate housing and living conditions should be promoted by governments and local authorities.

33.   Close members of the family should have access to information and counselling about specific problems that can arise when caring for old people.

34.   The strengthening of awareness and competence among health and social workers who are called on to assist elderly victims of abuse should be seen as crucial. When designing adequate services for abused old people, existing health and social services should be considered responsible for dealing with the problem.

35.   Measures envisaged should include the removal of the abused old person from the scene of violence as well as family counselling, preferably with the agreement of the person concerned but, failing that, by taking coercive action against the perpetrator.

VIII. *Measures for the perpetrators*

36.   Help-oriented measures for perpetrators should be encouraged after a court appearance and when the due process of law has taken its course. These might include self-help groups of offenders and psychotherapy in or out of prison.

37.   The social services should maintain contact with perpetrators whose families have left them, to find out their needs, discuss their problems and give them counselling and help.

38.   Research on therapeutic methods and other measures which could have a positive influence on perpetrators should be promoted.

IX. *Education*

39.   The establishment of programmes for the prevention of physical, emotional and sexual abuse should be encouraged in schools. This should be done by setting up committees in competent education authorities, with membership drawn from the field of education and those who work in the area of child abuse, as well as from among the parents and, where appropriate, from voluntary organisations. Special training should be provided for the members of such committees.

40.   Educational programmes starting at the pre-school level should take into account changes in society, including increased attention to childhood, positive perceptions of old age and the changing roles of women and men. Positive aspects of human relationships and moral values, and of human love, affection and sexuality should be outlined and discussed before issues of violence and sexual abuse are raised. Specific courses on partnership and parental responsibilities should include the learning of non-violent conflict resolution.

X. *Social workers*

41.   When confronted by problems of violence, social workers should preferably work in multidisciplinary teams together with all the professions concerned; this is particularly important when there is a question of reporting family violence to the authorities.

42.   In the course of their everyday work, social workers should be provided with help in the form of supervision and further training to enable them to clarify their own values and to distinguish within different examples of family violence, what concerns the victims and what concerns the perpetrators of the violence.

43.   Initial and in-service training of social workers, workers in day-care and other institutions, medical personnel, magistrates, police and teachers should include the learning of multidisciplinary and inter-institutional work.

XI. *Role of voluntary associations*

44.   Competent voluntary organisations can make an important contribution to the prevention and remedying of violence in the family. They should be recognised, encouraged and financially supported in their work by the public authorities, in accordance with the provisions set out in Recommendation No. R (85) 9 of the Committee of Ministers on voluntary work in social welfare activities. The best possible co-operation between the various public services and the voluntary organisations and workers should be ensured.

45.   In order to satisfy the particular demands made by the prevention and treatment of violence in the family, it is highly desirable that voluntary workers be properly selected, trained and supervised.

XII. *Financial implications*

46.   National, regional, and local authorities should take the appropriate steps for the provision of proper financing of the programmes and measures implemented in the framework of this recommendation.

Recommendation No. R (90) 14
on the preparation of an information brochure
on the social security rights and obligations
of migrant workers and of their families

*(Adopted by the Committee of Ministers on 18 June 1990
at the 442nd meeting of the Ministers' Deputies)*

The Committee of Ministers, under the terms of Article 15.*b* of the Statute of the Council of Europe,

Considering that it is the aim of the Council of Europe to achieve a greater unity between its members, particularly in order to promote their social progress;

Considering that the social security protection of migrant workers and their families is one of the essential tasks of the Council of Europe, as is evidenced particularly by the adoption of various international instruments, such as the European Social Charter and especially its Article 12, paragraph 4, the European interim agreements on social security, the European Convention on Social Security and its supplementary agreement, and the European Convention on the Legal Status of Migrant Workers;

Conscious of the difficulty of providing completely adequate information on the social security rights and obligations of migrant workers and their families, owing to the multiplicity and complexity of the applicable provisions at both the national and international levels;

Considering that the effective application of these social security instruments depends also on the information made available to migrant workers, and those principally dealing with them, on the rights and obligations of migrant workers as well as on the means to exercise the former and comply with the latter;

Conscious of the need to improve the information available to those who are insured and in particular to migrant workers and their families concerning their social security rights and obligations;

Considering that refugees and stateless persons should also be included in this effort to provide information;

Considering the usefulness of providing migrant workers and their families, if possible in their mother tongue, as well as those dealing with migrant workers, with a model information leaflet on the social security rights and obligations of migrant workers and their families,

Recommends that the governments of the member states ensure the dissemination, to all the persons and authorities concerned, of information on the rights and obligations of migrant workers and their families, following, where possible, the outline of the brochure appended to this recommendation.

Appendix to Recommendation No. R (90) 14

*Outline of the brochure on the social security rights
and obligations of migrant workers and their families*[1]

Part A

General description of the national social security system of ...

I.   *Introduction*

Short description of the brochure.

II.   *General themes*

    a. Brief general description of the national social security system

    b. Arrangements for contributing to the financing of the general scheme

    c.   Conditions for joining the social security system – Steps to be taken

    d. Possible remedies in the event of refusal, suspension or discontinuation of social security benefits or disagreement with a decision taken by a social security institution or department – Return of benefits wrongly received

    e. Useful information (address and telephone number of institutions or government departments responsible for each branch and of social security information centres)

    f. Brief enumeration of bilateral and multilateral instruments that have been ratified

    (Although each state may adjust the arrangement of the information according to the specific needs of its social security system, it would nevertheless be desirable to provide relevant information corresponding to each of the headings below.)

III.   *Detailed description of the national system*

1.   *Medical care* (benefits in kind)

    a. Contingency covered

    b. Persons protected

    c. Benefits provided. Extent of the cover according to the type of care (for example, local practitioner, hospital care, dental care, pharmaceutical products). Duration of the provision of benefits

    d. Conditions (for example, qualifying period)

    e. Arrangements for the provision of benefits (for example, waiting period, sharing of medical costs)

    f. Formalities. Practical details of benefits provided

2.   *Sickness benefit* (cash benefits)

    a. Contingency covered

    b. Persons protected

    c. Benefits provided (method of calculation, duration of the provision of benefits)

    d. Conditions (for example, qualifying periods)

---

1. For easier reading and accessibility, this information could be provided in separate leaflets for each benefit or branch of social security.

     e. Arrangements for the provision of benefits (for example, waiting period)

     f. Formalities

3. *Unemployment benefit*

     a. Contingencies covered (total unemployment, partial unemployment)

     b. Persons protected

     c. Benefits provided (method of calculation, duration of the provision of benefits)

     d. Conditions (for example, qualifying period)

     e. Arrangements for the provision of benefits (for example, waiting period)

     f. Formalities

4. *Old-age benefit*

     a. Contingency covered

     b. Persons protected

     c. Benefits provided (method of calculation)

     d. Conditions of entitlement (for example, qualifying period, cessation of gainful employment)

     e. Formalities

5. *Employment injury benefit*

     a. Contingencies covered

     b. Persons protected

     c. Benefits provided (method of calculation, duration of the provision of benefits: for example, cash benefits, benefits in kind, other benefits, special benefits for vocational rehabilitation and retraining, preventive measures)

     d. Conditions (for example, qualifying period)

     e. Arrangements for covering the cost of medical care

     f. Formalities

6. *Family benefit*

     a. Contingency covered

     b. Persons protected

     c. Benefits provided (method of calculation, duration of the provision of benefits: for example, amount of family allowance, other types of benefit)

     d. Conditions (for example, residence conditions and qualifying period)

     e. Formalities

7. *Maternity benefit*

     a. Contingencies covered

     b. Persons protected

     c. Benefits provided (for example, medical care – amount of cost-sharing by the beneficiary, if applicable, maternity grants – method of calculation)

     d. Conditions (for example, qualifying period, residency conditions)

     e. Formalities – Arrangements for covering the cost of medical care

8. *Invalidity benefit*

     a. Contingencies covered

     b. Persons protected

    c. Benefits provided (method of calculation). Supplementary benefits (for example, rehabilitation, vocational retraining)

    d. Conditions (for example, qualifying period)

    e. Formalities

9. *Survivor's benefit*

    a. Contingency covered

    b. Persons protected (for example, survivors, male or female, children)

    c. Benefits provided (method of calculation)

    d. Conditions (for example, qualifying period, qualifying age, qualifying period of marriage)

    e. Formalities

Part B

Description of the protection generated by the different international instruments for the co-ordination of social security in the framework of relations between ... and ...

Medical care

    a. Enumeration of instruments that have been ratified

    b. Contingencies covered. Details concerning the contingencies covered by the different instruments

    c. Persons protected. Details concerning the persons protected by the different instruments

    d. Types of benefit. Details concerning the types of benefit covered by the different instruments

    e. Conditions for award. Details concerning conditions for award laid down in the different instruments

    f. Length of period over which benefits are provided and provision abroad. Details concerning the length provided by the different instruments

    g. Administrative aspects

The other branches should be set out in a similar manner.

Recommendation No. R (91) 2
on social security for workers without professional status (helpers, persons at home with family responsibilities and voluntary workers)[1]

(Adopted by the Committee of Ministers on 14 February 1991 at the 452nd meeting of the Ministers' Deputies)

The Committee of Ministers, under the terms of Article 15.*b* of the Statute of the Council of Europe,

Considering that the aim of the Council of Europe is to achieve greater unity between its members for the purpose, *inter alia*, of facilitating their social progress;

Considering that strengthening the social security protection of workers without recognised professional status, persons at home with family responsibilities and persons undertaking work of a social character on a voluntary basis is one way of facilitating social progress;

Noting that, in spite of the progress made in making social security benefits generally available to the populations of the member states, people in these categories are not adequately protected in all the member states in a manner consistent with the social and economic position which they occupy in our societies;

Bearing in mind the provisions of its own Resolution (75) 28 on social security for women at home and of its Recommendations No. R (85) 9 on voluntary work in social welfare activities;

Considering that the protection of people in these categories can be improved only by progressively giving them personal rights to social security benefits;

Recalling, as regards protection for other unpaid persons, the principles and guidelines set out in its recommendations No. R (86) 5 on making medical care universally available and No. R (87) 5 on making old-age and invalidity benefits generally available,

---

1. When this recommendation was adopted and in application of Article 10.2.*c* of the Rules of procedure for the meetings of the Ministers' Deputies;
– the Representatives of Belgium and Germany reserved the right of their Governments to comply or not with the recommendation as a whole;
– the Representative of Greece reserved the right of his Government to comply or not with Section A, Sub-heading *b*, of the appendix to the recommendation.

Recommends that the governments of member states, in accordance with the guidelines appended to this recommendation, progressively take the measures needed to ensure that:

– persons working in family businesses without recognised professional status,

– persons at home with family responsibilities for young children, or dependent disabled or old persons, and

– persons doing voluntary work

may enjoy social security protection. Their protection can be realised by derived rights or, more particularly, by the acquisition of personal rights.

Appendix to Recommendation No. R (91) 2

A. *Persons without recognised professional status participating in the professional activities of self-employed workers*

a. *Personal scope*

1.   The recommendation applies to members of the self-employed worker's family who habitually participate, under the conditions laid down by national law, in the activities of self-employed workers by performing either the same or ancillary tasks, and who are not compulsorily protected in respect of this activity by social security schemes covering employees or the self-employed. These people shall be designated as "helpers" for the purposes of this recommendation.

2.   The recommendation applies to helpers participating in any independent activity, in particular a commercial industrial, craft, agricultural or professional activity.

b. *Material scope*

3.   Helpers should, under appropriate conditions, benefit from compulsory social security protection equivalent or similar to that enjoyed by the self-employed worker in whose activity they participate.

4.   In member states where compulsory insurance does not yet exist for helpers, this objective may be achieved progressively: initially, measures could be taken to ensure that those concerned can become voluntarily affiliated under prescribed procedures to a social security scheme.

c. *Financing*

5.   Protection for helpers should be financed either by their own contribution, taking into account their contributory capacity, or by those of the economic unit represented by the self-employed worker and his helpers, taking into account its contributory capacity, or by taxation or by a combination of these systems.

B. *Persons at home with family responsibilities for young children, disabled or old persons*

a. *Personal scope*

6.   The recommendation applies to persons at home devoting themselves in a family context to bringing up young children or caring for dependent disabled or old persons.

b. *Material scope*

7.   All the persons concerned should be covered by the branches of sickness/maternity (benefits in kind), invalidity, old-age and family benefits.

8.   Persons who interrupt or delay the start of their occupational activity, for a given period, to exercise family responsibilities in looking after young children or dependent disabled or old persons, should be given credit for the period in question, in accordance with prescribed procedures, for the purpose of entitlement to invalidity and old-age benefits, and the calculation of those benefits.

9.   Periods of part-time work should be considered as periods of full-time work in order to fulfil the qualifying period required for entitlement to sickness/maternity, old-age and invalidity benefits and family benefit when part-time work is chosen in order to exercise family responsibilities in looking after young children or dependent disabled or old persons. Old-age, invalidity and family benefits should be brought up

to the level that full-time occupational activity would give them during the period in question.

10. Persons who refrain from engaging in an occupational activity to devote themselves for a given period in a family context to bringing up young children or caring for dependent disabled or old persons should be given credit for the period in question, in accordance with prescribed procedures, for the purpose of entitlement to invalidity and old-age benefits, and the calculation of those benefits.

c. Amount of benefits

11. The amount of the benefits should correspond to the standards laid down by the Council of Europe's social security instruments, particularly the European Code of Social Security (revised).

d. Financing

12. The protection of the persons concerned should be financed:

– either by their own contributions, taking account of their contributory capacity;

– by all the members of the scheme;

– by taxation; or

– by a combination of those systems.

C. Persons undertaking work of a social character on a voluntary basis

a. Personal scope

13. The recommendation applies to persons voluntarily undertaking activities or providing services of a social or socio-cultural character, either in the framework of organisations of social or socio-cultural value or as individuals.

14. The member states shall determine the conditions which a person must satisfy in order to be regarded as a voluntary worker, particularly when the voluntary activity is undertaken on an individual basis.

b. Material scope

15. Persons doing voluntary work within an organisation of recognised social or socio-cultural value should be compulsorily insured against all the risks covered by the branches of sickness (medical care), old-age, employment injury, family benefit, invalidity and survivors' benefit.

16. The same protection should be offered on a voluntary basis to persons doing voluntary work who are not working within an organisation.

c. Financing

17. The protection of persons doing voluntary work should be financed:

– either by personal contributions;

– by contributions from organisations of recognised social or socio-cultural value, in the case of voluntary workers working within an organisation;

– by contributions from public (local, regional or national) authorities. It is desirable that protection against occupational hazards be entirely financed in this way; or

– by a combination of those systems.

d. *Protection in the event of international travel*

18. When voluntary workers travel internationally either in or outside Europe, they should enjoy adequate protection under the provisions of domestic legislation or, if necessary, under appropriate instruments of social security or by any other adequate means.

e. *Amount of benefits*

19. The amount of benefits should correspond to the standards laid down by the Council of Europe's social security instruments, particularly the European Code of Social Security (revised).

Recommendation No. R (91) 11
concerning sexual exploitation, pornography and prostitution of, and trafficking in, children and young adults

(Adopted by the Committee of Ministers on 9 September 1991 at the 461st meeting of the Ministers' Deputies)

The Committee of Ministers, under the terms of Article 15.*b* of the Statute of the Council of Europe,

Considering that the well-being and interests of children and young adults are fundamental issues for any society;

Considering that sexual exploitation of children and young adults for profit-making purposes in the form of pornography, prostitution and traffic of human beings has assumed new and alarming dimensions at national and international level;

Considering that sexual experience linked to this social phenomenon, often associated with early sexual abuse within the family or outside of it, may be detrimental to a child's and young adult's psychosocial development;

Considering that it is in the interests of member states of the Council of Europe to harmonise their national legislation on sexual exploitation of children and young adults in order to improve the co-ordination and effectiveness of action taken at national and international level with a view to tackling this problem;

Having regard to Recommendation 1065 (1987) of the Parliamentary Assembly of the Council of Europe on the traffic in children and other forms of child exploitation;

Recalling Resolution No. 3 on sexual exploitation, pornography and prostitution of, and trafficking in, children and young adults of the 16th Conference of European Ministers of Justice (Lisbon, 1988);

Recalling Recommendation No. R (85) 4 on violence in the family, Recommendation No. R (85) 11 on the position of the victim in the framework of criminal law and procedure, Recommendation No. R (87) 20 on social reactions to juvenile delinquency and Recommendation No. R (87) 7 concerning principles on the distribution of videograms having a violent, brutal or pornographic content;

Bearing in mind the Convention for the Protection of Human Rights and Fundamental Freedoms (1950) and the European Social Charter (1961);

Bearing also in mind the United Nations Convention on the Rights of the Child (1989),

I.   Recommends that the governments of member states review their legislation and practice with a view to introducing, if necessary, and implementing the following measures:

A. *General measures*

a. *Public awareness, education and information*

1.   make appropriate documentation on sexual exploitation of children and young adults available to parents, persons having minors in their care and other concerned groups and associations;

2.   include in the programmes of primary and secondary school education information about the dangers of sexual exploitation and abuse to which children and young adults might be exposed, and about how they may defend themselves;

3.   promote and encourage programmes aimed at furthering awareness and training for those who have functions involving support and protection of children and young adults in the fields of education, health, social welfare, justice and the police force in order to enable them to identify cases of sexual exploitation and to take the necessary measures;

4.   make the public aware of the devastating effects of sexual exploitation which transforms children and young adults into consumer objects and urge the general public to take part in the efforts of associations and organisations intervening in field;

5.   invite the media to contribute to a general awareness of the subject and to adopt appropriate rules of conduct;

6.   discourage and prevent any abuse of the picture and the voice of the child in an erotic context;

b. *Collection and exchange of information*

7.   urge public and private institutions and agencies dealing with children and young adults who have been victims of any form of sexual exploitation, to keep appropriate statistical information for scientific purposes and crime policy, while respecting anonymity and confidentiality;

8.   encourage co-operation between the police and all public and private organisations handling cases of sexual abuse within the family or outside of it and of various forms of sexual exploitation;

c. *Prevention, detection, assistance*

9.   urge police services to give special attention to prevention, detection, and investigation of offences involving sexual exploitation of children and young adults, and allocate to them sufficient means towards that end;

10.   promote and further the creation and operation of specialised public and private services for the protection of children and young adults at risk in order to prevent and detect all forms of sexual exploitation;

11. support public and private initiatives at local level to set up helplines and centres with a view to providing medical, psychological, social or legal assistance to children and young adults who are at risk or who have been victims of sexual exploitation;

d. *Criminal law and criminal procedure*

12. ensure that the rights and interests of children and young adults are safeguarded throughout proceedings while respecting the rights of the alleged offenders;

13. ensure throughout judicial and administrative proceedings confidentiality of record and the respect for privacy rights of children and young adults who have been victims of sexual exploitation by avoiding, in particular, the disclosure of any information that could lead to their identification;

14. provide for special conditions at hearings involving children who are victims or witnesses of sexual exploitation, in order to diminish the traumatising effects of such hearings and to increase the credibility of their statements while respecting their dignity;

15. provide under an appropriate scheme for compensation of children and young adults who have been victims of sexual exploitation;

16. provide for the possibility of seizing and confiscating the proceeds from offences relating to sexual exploitation of children and young adults;

B. *Measures relating to pornography involving children*

1. provide for appropriate sanctions taking into account the gravity of the offence committed by those involved in the production and distribution of any pornographic material involving children;

2. examine the advisability of introducing penal sanctions for mere possession of pornographic material involving children;

3. ensure, particularly through international co-operation, the detection of firms, associations or individuals, often linked with two or more countries, using children for the production of pornographic material;

4. envisage informing the public, in order to raise awareness, of the implementation of penal policy, the number of prosecutions and convictions in cases involving child pornography, while ensuring the anonymity of the children concerned and of the alleged offenders;

C. *Measures relating to the prostitution of children and young adults*

1. increase the material and human resources of welfare and police services and improve their working methods so that places where child prostitution may occur are regularly inspected;

2. encourage and support the setting up of mobile welfare units for the surveillance of, or establishment of contact with, children at risk, particularly street children, in order to assist them to return to their families, if possible,

and, if necessary, direct them to the appropriate agencies for health care, training or education;

3. intensify efforts with a view to identifying and sanctioning those who foster or encourage the prostitution of children or young adults, or who profit from it, on the one hand, and of the customers of child prostitution, on the other;

4. create or develop special units within the police and, if necessary, improve their working methods, in order to combat procuring of children and young adults;

5. dissuade travel agencies from promoting sex tourism in any form, especially through publicity, in particular by instituting consultations between them and the public services;

6. give priority to vocational training and reintegration programmes involving children and young adults who are occasionally or habitually prostituting themselves;

D. *Measures relating to the trafficking in children and young adults*

1. supervise the activities of artistic, marriage and adoption agencies in order to control the movement within, or between countries, of children and young adults, to prevent the possibility that they will be led into prostitution or other forms of sexual exploitation;

2. increase surveillance by immigration authorities and frontier police in order to ensure that travel abroad by children, especially those not accompanied by their parents or their guardian, is not related to trafficking in human beings;

3. set up facilities and support those existing, in order to protect and assist the victims of traffic in children and young adults.

II. International aspects:

Recommends that the governments of member states:

1. examine the advisability of signing and ratifying if they have not done so:

– the United Nations Convention for the Suppression of the Traffic in Persons and the Exploitation of the Prostitution of Others (1950);

– the Hague Convention on Jurisdiction, Applicable Law and Recognition of Decrees relating to Adoptions (1965);

– the European Convention on the Adoption of Children (1967);

– Convention No. 138 concerning Minimum Age for Admission to Employment, of the International Labour Organisation (1973);

– the United Nations Convention on the Rights of the Child (1989);

2. introduce rules on extraterritorial jurisdiction in order to allow the prosecution and punishment of nationals who have committed offences concerning sexual exploitation of children and young adults outside the

national territory, or, if applicable, review existing rules to that effect, and improve international co-operation to that end;

3. increase and improve exchanges of information between countries through Interpol, in order to identify and prosecute offenders involved in sexual exploitation, and particularly in trafficking in children and young adults, or those who organise it;

4. establish links with international associations and organisations working for the welfare of children and young adults in order to benefit from data available to them and secure, if necessary, their collaboration in combating sexual exploitation;

5. take steps towards the creation of a European register of missing children.

III. Research priorities:

Recommends that the governments of member states promote research at national and international level, in particular in the following fields:

1. nature and extent of various forms of sexual exploitation of children and young adults, especially with a cross-cultural view;

2. nature of paedophilia and factors contributing to it;

3. links between adoption and sexual exploitation;

4. links between sexual abuse within the family and prostitution;

5. characteristics, role and needs of the consumers of child prostitution and child pornography;

6. evaluation studies of vocational training and reintegration programmes concerning youth involved in prostitution;

7. structure, international networks, interconnections and earnings of the sex industry;

8. links between the sex industry and organised crime;

9. possibilities and limitations of the criminal justice system as an instrument of prevention and repression of various forms of sexual exploitation of children and young adults;

10. epidemiology, causes and consequences of sexually transmitted diseases in children and young adults, and analysis of their links with sexual abuse and exploitation.

Recommendation No. R (92) 2
on making family benefits generally available[1]

(Adopted by the Committee of Ministers on 13 January 1992
at the 469th meeting of the Ministers' Deputies)

The Committee of Ministers, under the terms of Article 15.*b* of the Statute of the Council of Europe,

Considering that the aim of the Council of Europe is to achieve a greater unity between its members for the purpose, *inter alia*, of facilitating their social progress;

Considering that generalisation of family benefits constitutes a means of furthering social progress in Europe;

Recalling that, in its Declaration on Human Rights of 27 April 1978, the Committee of Ministers resolved to explore the possibilities of extending individual rights, particularly in the social field, requiring protection by European conventions or other suitable means;

Bearing in mind the right to social security, part VII of the European Code of Social Security as amended by the Protocol thereto, part VII of the European Code of Social Security (revised), as well as the provisions of the Committee of Ministers Resolution (68) 37 on the laws and regulations designed to compensate family commitments and Resolution (70) 15 on the social protection of unmarried mothers and their children;

Noting that, despite the progress achieved, social security systems needed to adapt more fully to the new patterns of family life and to the changing structure of households in order to ensure the welfare of children;

Considering that it lies with member states through their social legislation to promote the welfare of families with dependent children and to ensure that they enjoy a decent standard of living, respecting always the principle of equality of treatment between men and women;

Noting that the concept of family benefits can include within the different member states a number of various benefits in kind or in cash;

---

1. When this recommendation was adopted and in application of Article 10.2.*c* of the Rules of procedure for the meetings of the Ministers' Deputies;
– the Representative of Germany reserved the right of his Government to comply or not with the recommendation as a whole;
– the Representative of Italy reserved the right of his Government to comply or not with paragraph 9 of the appendix to the recommendation;
– the Representative of Spain reserved the right of his Government to comply or not with paragraphs 3, 9 and 10 of the appendix to the recommendation.

Considering that for the purposes of this recommendation priority attention should be given to basic family benefits, namely family allowances,

Recommends that the governments of the member states:

1. in cases where there is no provision for family benefits, create a family benefit scheme, comprising, during an initial period, at least the granting of family allowances;

2. extend progressively the right to family allowances to cover all children residing in each member state in accordance with the guiding principles contained in the appendix (part A) to the present recommendation;

3. set the amount of these family allowances at a sufficiently high level to contribute substantially to the standard of living of the family, in accordance with the guiding principles contained in the appendix (part B) to the present recommendation, and also to contribute to guaranteeing an average minimum subsistence level for children;

4. to progressively make all existing family benefits generally available.

Appendix to Recommendation No. R (92) 2

Part A

Guiding principles for the granting of family benefits covered by the present recommendation

Objectives

1.   The fundamental objective of family benefits should be to ensure the welfare of children and the economic stability of their families.

Method of payment

2.   Family allowances should comprise periodical cash payments for the benefit of each child.

Entitlement to benefits

3.   Notwithstanding the method of financing, family allowances should be granted to all children residing in the territory of the member state.

4.   Family benefits should be granted as provided in the following circumstances:

   a.   at least until the end of the child's compulsory schooling or until the age of 16 years,

   b.   until the age of 18 for so long as the child is receiving further education or vocational training on a full-time basis and is not in receipt of an adequate income determined by national legislation.

Financing of family benefit schemes

5.   The progressive extension of the entitlement to family benefits should be facilitated by endowing the appropriate institutions with sufficient financial resources to achieve this objective.

6.   Where contributions are levied they should take account of the contributory capacity of the contributors, to avoid placing too heavy a burden on those with few means.

7.   Each member state should guarantee optimum solidarity in the financing of family benefits, in particular in favour of those in the lowest income groups.

The recipient of family benefits

8.   The recipient of family benefits should be the person actually responsible for the child, or the child when he or she reaches the age of majority.

Part B

Guiding principles concerning the level of family benefits covered by the present recommendation

9.   *a.* Family allowances should be set at a level which relates directly to the actual cost of providing for a child and should represent a substantial contribution to this cost.

   b. Provision should be made for the adjustment of family benefits in order to take into account changes in the cost of providing for children or in the general cost of living.

c. Those states meeting the minimum standard laid down in Article 49.*b* of the European Code of Social Security (revised) are considered to be implementing the provisions with regard to the level of benefits provided for in this recommendation.

10. *a.* Family allowances at the minimum rate should be granted regardless of means.

b. Benefits above the amount which results from the application of the principle mentioned in paragraph 9 may, however, be subject to a means test.

Recommendation No. R (93) 2
on the medico-social aspects of child abuse

(Adopted by the Committee of Ministers on 22 March 1993 at the 490th meeting of the Ministers' Deputies)

The Committee of Ministers, under the terms of Article 15.*b* of the Statute of the Council of Europe,

Considering that the aim of the Council of Europe is to achieve a greater unity between its members, in particular by the adoption of common rules on matters of common interest;

Recognising the right of all children to live in conditions favourable to their proper development and to grow up free from physical abuse, sexual abuse, emotional abuse, neglect and other forms of child abuse;

Noting that child abuse is a phenomenon which in recent years has given rise to considerable concern in member states;

Having regard to Recommendation No. R (79) 17 concerning the protection of children against ill-treatment, Recommendation No. R (85) 4 on violence in the family and Recommendation No. R (90) 2 on social measures concerning violence within the family;

Bearing in mind the United Nations convention on the Rights of the Child;

Recognising the need for policies designed to prevent child abuse, while taking into account the need for protection of privacy of all persons concerned, and the respect of confidentiality,

Recommends the governments of the member states:

1.   to adopt a policy which aims to secure the child's welfare within his/her family;

2.   to establish a system for the effective prevention, identification, notification, investigation, assessment, intervention, treatment, and follow-up of cases of child abuse on a multidisciplinary basis, which specifies clearly the roles and responsibilities of the various agencies involved;

3.   to take to this end the measures appearing in the appendix to this recommendation.

Appendix to Recommendation No. R (93) 2

1. *Prevention*

1.1 To develop, implement, monitor and evaluate a programme of preventive policies at primary, secondary and tertiary levels nationally and locally in respect of child abuse.

1.2. At a primary level:

a. to promote, through public information campaigns of various kinds (for example TV, radio, press, leaflets, posters) and other measures, societal awareness of children's rights to a life free from neglect, physical, emotional and/or sexual abuse, of the harmful consequences of child abuse and of positive, non-abusive modes of child-rearing;

b. to establish socio-economic conditions and health and social welfare services which strengthen the capacity of all families to support and care for their children;

c. to emphasise the rights of all children and young persons to freedom from abuse and the need to change patterns of upbringing and behaviour which threaten this;

d. to minimise levels of violence within society and the resort to violence in child-rearing practices.

1.3. At the secondary and tertiary levels: to develop, implement, monitor and where appropriate review preventive programmes to prevent child abuse taking account of local conditions and structures of service delivery. These may include:

a. the preventive measures outlined in Recommendation No. R (49) 17 concerning the protection of children against ill-treatment and Recommendation No. R (90) 2 on social measures concerning violence within the family;

b. the provision of playgroups, nurseries, child health care and other social welfare services to meet the material, psychosocial and medical needs of children and promote their proper development;

c. the provision of accessible, non-stigmatising services to help and support parents experiencing problems with child-rearing;

d. the implementation of educational programmes for children concerning their right to a life free from abuse, emphasising body awareness, assertiveness training and their right to say no;

e. publicity concerning sources of help (for example, telephone helplines, sheltered homes for children experiencing problems of neglect or abuse).

2. *Detection and notification*

2.1. Designate an agency (or agencies) or an individual at the appropriate level, available twenty-four hours a day, to receive notifications of abuse.

2.2. Encourage professionals (for example, teachers, doctors, social workers, nurses and others in contact with children) to notify the designated agency if they have reasonable grounds to believe that a child has been abused, is being abused or where there is a strong suspicion of abuse, or clear grounds for believing that it is likely to occur.

2.3. Advise professionals that in respecting ethical codes and legal rules of confidentiality, account should be taken of the fact that in such circumstances the designated agency should be notified.

2.4. Consider indemnity from legal proceedings to persons summoned as witnesses who, *bona fide* and with care, report abuse or a reasonable suspicion of child abuse.

2.5. Take measures to advise members of the community, for example, of the existence and signs of child abuse and of the availability of services to help children and families through public information campaigns in the media, and the distribution of leaflets, etc. in health clinics, libraries, etc.

2.6. Take steps to promote the responsible reporting of lay concerns that a child may be being abused, with safeguards where required for the anonymity of those making such reports.

2.7. Ensure that the person who has reported is informed of the appropriate steps taken as far as legal and moral codes of confidentiality permit.

2.8. Establish services (such as telephone helplines) for victims of abuse and other persons wishing to report their concerns.

3.   *Investigation and assessment*

3.1. Establish at the appropriate level services available twenty-four hours a day, with powers and resources to provide, within an appropriate time-scale, for:

 a. the multidisciplinary investigation of notifications of child abuse;

 b. psychosocial assessment of the needs of children and their families for practical assistance and support, therapy, legal measures of protection, etc.;

 c. medical assessment, psychosomatic and physical, of the child according to the nature of the concerns and the type of abuse;

 d. emergency or long-term legal measures for the protection of the child if required;

 e. the taking at any moment of urgent measures including placement in sheltered homes.

3.2. Ensure that in intervention in all cases of child abuse the best interests of the child shall be the primary consideration and that when services are made available to abused children and their families, they are sensitive to the child's age, wishes, understanding, gender and to his/her ethnic, cultural, religious and linguistic background, and to special needs, such as disability.

3.3. Implement policies which aim, whenever possible, to work in partnership with the child's parents and to secure the child's welfare within his/her own family, through the provision of appropriate help and support.

3.4. See to it that children are informed of the nature of concerns about them, of their rights and of the actions which will be taken to investigate the concerns.

3.5. Ensure that – except where this would be contrary to the best interests of the child – parents are informed of the concerns about their child and of their rights to participate in decision-making and of appeal.

3.6. Ensure that in cases where children are separated from their parents, strenuous efforts are made to maintain links between the child and his/her parents as far as possible and consistent with the welfare of the child.

3.7. See to it that children are appropriately represented and that their views are sought and taken into account, having regard to their age and understanding.

3.8. Make arrangements, where appropriate, for medical assessment of the child to be undertaken in suitable premises by personnel with training, skill, experience and aptitude in the identification of child abuse and in working with children. Any medical examination should be carried out within a time-scale appropriate to each case. In some circumstances, urgency is required.

3.9. Restrict any medical examinations to the minimum number and the least intrusive approach required to help establish whether child abuse has occurred, to secure the requisite treatment and, where necessary, to document clinical evidence which may be used, as appropriate, in legal proceedings for the protection of the child or the prosecution of abusers.

3.10. Ensure that in any police investigations and subsequent criminal proceedings the welfare and interests of the child are paramount. This includes sensitivity to the child's needs in interviews and in the courts when children are called as witnesses, and ensuring that any delays are kept to a minimum and do not prejudice the child's right to receive help.

3.11. Adopt practices which encourage the sharing of information between the various professionals involved in investigation and assessment and which acknowledge the need to respect the confidentiality of the information shared; this may be achieved through holding a multidisciplinary case conference convened within an agreed time-scale, at which reports from all those involved in the investigation and assessment are presented and a plan drawn up for the welfare and protection of children, for their families and, where appropriate, for the abuser(s).

4.   *Follow-up intervention, treatment and review*

4.1. Following investigation and assessment, to base all help, intervention and treatment for abused children upon a written plan designed to meet the needs of the child and his/her family, including any siblings, in the short, medium or long term. The plan may include, *inter alia*, the provision of financial and material aid, services such as day care, respite care or rehousing, therapy, counselling or support for the child and for his/her family; the need for services for the child and his/her family should be assessed whether the child is maintained at home or whether separation is deemed to be necessary.

4.2. Appoint a key worker for each case to consult with and co-ordinate all services or institutions involved with the child and the family and to ensure the implementation of the plan for the welfare and protection of the child and his/her family.

4.3. Establish policies which guarantee that appropriate help and support are provided, that judicial or administrative decisions taken promote the child's welfare and development and are made with all reasonable speed to a time-scale consistent with the child's needs and understanding.

4.4. Establish procedures at the appropriate level for the periodic review and follow-up of cases of abuse to monitor the implementation of the plans for the welfare and protection of the child and of his/her family. Central to such procedures is the involvement of a person (who may be the key worker or an independent advocate) whose role is to represent the child's interests and to act as advocate or guardian of the child's welfare, having regard to the child's needs, wishes and feelings.

4.5. Establish arrangements to facilitate the closure of cases, following multidisciplinary review, recovery of the victim and of the authors of abuse, and in circumstances in which services are no longer required for the welfare or protection of the child and his/her family.

4.6. Implement measures in respect of those who abuse children, whether through criminal prosecutions, therapy or a combination of treatment programmes with legal sanctions. Responses to abusers will be affected by consideration of, *inter alia*, the needs of the children concerned, the nature of the abuse, assessment of the abusers, their reactions and attitude to the abuse, the opportunities and prospects for treatment and rehabilitation as well as the requirements of the criminal justice system.

5. Training

5.1. Ensure that there is adequate training of the personnel in the various professional groups involved with the prevention of child abuse and the protection of children against abuse and, in particular, to:

a. require bodies responsible for basic qualifying courses for doctors, community nurses, social workers, teachers, police officers, child psychologists, the legal profession and any others likely to come across cases of child abuse, to include coverage of the topic of child abuse and child protection in the formal curriculum;

b. make known to all personnel who work with children their roles and responsibilities, and those of other professionals, with respect to the notification of suspected cases and the actions to be taken thereafter and ensure that all personnel are aware of the needs of children and of the legislation, policies, and procedures for securing the welfare and protection of abused children and their families, and for respecting confidentiality in the medical and all other fields;

c. ensure that professionals involved in the investigation and assessment of child abuse, in intervention and therapy with abused children, their families or abusers and in civil or criminal legal proceedings in connection with child abuse, are fully trained and appropriately experienced;

d. require those who are closely involved with cases of child abuse to undertake specialised training in the skills of communicating with children who are or may have been abused; and to have the necessary professional qualification, as well as involvement, availability and stability (families cannot be helped in a fragmentary and piecemeal fashion);

e. provide opportunities for in-service and post-qualifying training to keep professionals informed of developments and trends in work with abused children, their families and with abusers;

f. provide opportunities for multidisciplinary training, to increase understanding and co-operation between the many disciplines involved;

g. provide opportunities for those closely involved with cases of child abuse so as to examine their own responses to the issues and to explore the specific challenges of work with abused children, their families and with abusers;

h. monitor and evaluate training programmes in the field of child abuse to increase knowledge of appropriate content, teaching materials and methods.

6. Research

6.1. To promote research on a comparative basis between the member states to analyse the various systems for meeting the needs of children and their families and responding to child abuse and to compare and contrast their effectiveness for the children and families concerned.

6.2. To develop programmes of research on the topic of child abuse, in particular giving priority to:

a. the evaluation of different approaches to the prevention of child abuse;

b. the evaluation of different systems for the involvement of children and parents in decision-making and for the protection of their rights;

c. the evaluation of different approaches to treatment and intervention in direct work with children, families and abusers;

d. the identification of patterns and trends in child abuse to help target prevention and intervention.

7. *Financial implications*

7.1. To take appropriate steps at national, regional and local levels to ensure the provision of proper financing of the programmes and measures to be implemented within the framework of this recommendation.

Recommendation No. R (94)14
on coherent and integrated family policies[1]

*(Adopted by the Committee of Ministers on 22 November 1994
at the 521st meeting of the Ministers' Deputies)*

The Committee of Ministers, under the terms of Article 15.*b* of the Statute of the Council of Europe,

Considering that the aim of the Council of Europe is the achievement of greater unity among its members, for the purpose of safeguarding and realising the ideals and principles which are their common heritage and of facilitating their economic and social progress;

Considering the European Convention on Human Rights and recalling in particular the right to respect for private and family life as defined in Article 8;

Considering the European Social Charter and recalling the right of the family to social, legal and economic protection as defined in Article 16;

Bearing in mind the Declaration on equality between women and men, adopted by the Committee of Ministers at its 83rd Session (16 November 1988);

Bearing in mind Recommendation 1074 (1988) of the Parliamentary Assembly of the Council of Europe on family policy;

Bearing in mind Recommendation No. R (92) 2 of the Committee of Ministers on making family benefits generally available;

Taking note of the final communiqués of the sessions of the Conference of European Ministers responsible for Family Affairs;

Bearing in mind the rich diversity of work already completed by the Council of Europe relating to questions affecting families;

Taking into account the United Nations Convention on the Rights of the Child;

On the occasion of the International Year of the Family 1994 proclaimed by the United Nations;

---

1. When Recommendation No. R (94) 14 was adopted, and in application of Article 10.2.c of the Rules of Procedure for the meetings of the Ministers' Deputies, the Representative of the Netherlands declared that he accepted this recommendation reserving however the right to apply its provisions, as appropriate, to single persons and people living together, and provided that measures to assist families with children do not harm the interests of other categories.

Taking note of the interaction between the family and political, economic and social evolution;

Recognising that the family takes on different forms within the same society, or within the lifespan of a single individual, thus creating different stages of family life cycles;

Recognising that the interests of families in all sectors of society and areas of policy call for a better co-ordination of all social policies involved – for example those affecting young people, elderly people, and disabled people, as well as health, employment, vocational training, social protection, consumer protection, culture, migration, environment, housing, education, media, traffic and tourism – in order to give families better living conditions and to improve their human relations;

Recognising that the dramatic changes in family structures create a need for coherent and integrated family policies, followed by appropriate measures, to promote balanced legal, social and economic treatment for families, helping them to discharge their functions and thus to live in dignity;

Recommends that member governments support the implementation of coherent and integrated family policies on the basis of the following principles: consultation, co-ordination, efficiency and flexibility; these principles to be applied across the board, at local, regional and national level, as appropriate.

Appendix to Recommendation No. R (94) 14

Basic principles

At the dawn of the twenty-first century, family policies must support families in present-day society, giving them the protection and assistance which they need to discharge their functions in society. The full potential of all families, and particularly the poorest families, must be promoted, so that they can exercise both their responsibilities and their independence in a manner consistent with the dignity which belongs to every human being.

1.   Regardless of its form and diversity, the family remains a fundamental unit of society; it plays the primary role in socialisation.

2.   The family also plays the primary role in promoting solidarity between the generations and with the weakest members of the community, as well as genuine partnership between the couple. Parents are primarily responsible for bringing up their children according to the basic values of a democratic society. High priority must be given to education and mediation services making it possible to resolve any family conflicts.

3.   Within families, the rights of each member must be taken into account.

4.   The family must be a place where equality, including legal equality, between women and men is especially promoted by sharing responsibility for running the home and looking after children, and, more specifically, by ensuring that mother and father take turns and complement each other in carrying out their respective roles.

5.   The public authorities should promote the harmonious reconciliation of family life and working life.

6.   Family policies must take into account the plurality of family structures and their specific needs.

7.   Children should be prepared for independent, responsible and caring citizenship by having their rights and needs taken into account within the family. They should be educated and adequately informed about their rights and duties.

8.   The public authorities should make the necessary provision to enable children to help themselves to have access to their rights, and are entitled to intervene in the private family domain, in accordance with the law, when the child is in danger within it. They need to be aware of the responsibilities and difficulties involved in respecting as far as possible the integrity of the family unit, whilst also identifying and deciding on appropriate action in those cases where the child's rights are violated by family members.

9.   Government policies should take account of the costs involved in bringing up children.

10.   In order for older family members to enjoy a dignified and secure old age, it is particularly necessary to respect their capacity to stay independent, to continue to take their own decisions and to remain a part of the community.

11.   Governments have a special responsibility to protect families at times of economic crisis, particularly by introducing both preventive and assistance measures to achieve a significant reduction in the number of families living in poverty, while fully respecting their dignity.

12.   The public authorities should create conditions conducive to the well-being and autonomy of families, particularly by providing appropriate day-care, medical, social, educational and cultural services.

13. Families should be given the possibility of forming or joining associations, so that they can convey their views on family issues to the authorities and suggest measures which they consider in their interest.

14. The concept inherent to this recommendation is defined as follows:

 i. The significance of preventive family policy must be emphasised: a family may need guidance, counselling and services at different stages of its life, by means of which its vulnerability can be greatly diminished.

 ii. The concept for a coherent and integrated family policy is that the role of the public authorities is to create the circumstances conducive to the emergence of a family unit in which the individual can develop in safety, self-respect and solidarity, enjoying fundamental rights, in a legal, social, cultural and economic context. Special needs of different types of families at various stages of family life cycles must be allowed for here.

 iii. The concept of a coherent and integrated family policy must be applied in examining all stages of policy with reference to the interests of the family and all its members.

 iv. The objective is that a coherent and integrated family policy should function across administrative boundaries as a factor co-ordinating all action taken affecting families.

 v. In practice this means co-ordinating and reconciling the various sectors which affect members of families as citizens, for example social security, working life, education, environment, consumer interests, culture, housing, traffic, mass media, tourism.

Migration

Table of contents

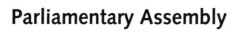

Parliamentary Assembly

Recommendation 841 (1978)[1]
on second generation migrants

The Assembly,

1. Considering that halting immigration in most labour-seeking countries has stabilised the foreign population in those countries;

2. Recognising that, as a consequence, second generation migrants, who were either born in the immigration country or entered it at a very early age, constitute a demographic factor of growing importance;

3. Considering that this situation presents novel features in that most of the young migrants retain the nationality of their parents and acquire a double socio-cultural identity;

4. Believing that this causes difficulties for second generation migrants with regard to their education and vocational training, and to their legal status in the immigration country;

5. Conscious that the socio-cultural development of migrants' children is closely linked with that of the migrant family as a whole;

6. Considering that specific measures should be taken on behalf of second generation migrants to complement the general measures taken with regard to young persons and to migrant workers;

7. Noting that, in the industrial countries, migrant workers frequently occupy unskilled or semi-skilled jobs, which leave them more vulnerable to the employment crisis, and that the social environment to which they belong scarcely makes for successful schooling or guidance of ensuing generations;

8. Deploring the continuing failure of member states to inform the Secretary General of the Council of Europe of action taken on resolutions of the Committee of Ministers, as they are required to do by the resolutions themselves;

9. Considering that any policy on migrant workers and their families must be based on an adequate knowledge of the phenomenon of migration,

10. Recommends that the Committee of Ministers ask the governments of the members states concerned:

---

1. *Assembly debate* on 30 September 1978 (13th Sitting) (see Doc. 4205, report of the Committee on Populations and Refugees).
   Text adopted by the Assembly on 30 September 1978 (13th Sitting).

i.   to give more effective assistance to their nationals workings abroad, particularly in the matter of education and training;

ii. to promote full-time vocational training, providing immigrants with structured qualifications and courses to increase their skills;

iii. to guarantee harmonious family reunion for migrant workers, ensuring that the family unit can be genuinely reconstituted in the immigration country, and to implement Committee of Ministers Resolution (78) 33, on family reunion with regard to labour migration in Council of Europe member states;

iv. to strengthen legislation so as to eliminate discrimination, firstly between migrants and indigenous workers, and secondly among the different categories of migrants themselves;

v.   to make the efforts necessary to encourage participation by young migrants in the life of the host community;

vi. to make it easier for young migrants who so wish to acquire the nationality of the immigration country, when they have either been born or completed most of their schooling in it;

vii. to sign, and ratify where appropriate, the European Convention on the reduction of cases of multiple nationality and on military obligations in cases of multiple nationality, as well as the 1977 Additional Protocol;

11. Also recommends that the Committee of Ministers prepare and implement, in the framework of the Intergovernmental Work Programme, a series of co-ordinated measures to provide better protection for second generation migrants, and in particular:

i.   inform the Assembly, through the Secretary General, of action taken by member states to implement Resolution (72) 18, on methods of compiling statistics on the international migration of workers;

ii. set up a European centre for documentation and statistics on international migration, to work in close co-operation with centres in member states;

iii. ask the Standing Conference of European Ministers of Education to continue its periodic assessments of action taken by member states and international organisations concerning the education of migrants;

iv. approve the project prepared by the Council for Cultural Co-operation on the education and cultural development of migrants, which is due to commence in 1980;

v.   give priority, in this context, to the pedagogic problems involved in the education of children and young persons, and to the cultural development of adults;

vi. promote the training of teachers with special responsibility for the education of migrant children and young persons;

vii. prepare to inform the Assembly in 1981, through the Secretary General, of action taken by member states to implement Resolution (76) 11 on equal treatment for national and migrant workers with regard to vocational guidance, training and retraining;

viii. take action on the proposals of the Council of Europe Special Representative for National Refugees and Over-Population on behalf of second generation migrants, and give priority, in this context, to the transition from schooling to vocational guidance and employment, while trying as far as possible to associate young persons in the taking of decisions concerning them;

ix. increase the specific budgetary resources allocated for experimental classes designed to foster the integration of migrant workers' children by means of a school system of the immigration country;

x. harmonise in a liberal manner the conditions for the issue by immigration countries of residence and work permits for young migrants reaching adulthood and/or working age;

12. Recommends that the Committee of Ministers study, again within the framework of the Inter-governmental Work Programme, the problems faced by second generation migrants in connection with military service and the advisability of introducing an alternative, such as community service in the immigration country;

13. Further recommends that the Committee of Ministers urge the member countries of the European Economic Community to apply effectively EEC Council Directive No. 486, of 25 July 1977, on the education of the children of migrant workers.

Recommendation 1066 (1987)[1]
on the social protection of migrant workers
and their families

The Assembly,

1.   Considering that the European Social Charter, the European Convention on Social Security and the European Convention on the Legal Status of Migrant Workers provide the necessary basis to guarantee proper social protection for migrant workers of whatever origin;

2.   Concerned nonetheless at the inequalities which are evident in the social protection of migrant workers living in Council of Europe member countries depending on their country of origin;

3.   Observing that the least well-off category of migrant workers in terms of social protection is that of workers from countries which are not members of the Council of Europe, especially if they are not covered by bilateral agreements;

4.   Recalling its Recommendation 915 (1981) on the situation of migrant workers in the host countries, in which it called upon the Committee of Ministers to invite the governments of member states to ratify the European Social Charter and the European Convention on the Legal Status of Migrant Workers;

5.   Regretting the fact that, despite that invitation, Belgium, Liechtenstein, Luxembourg, Malta, Portugal, Switzerland and Turkey are still not parties to the European Social Charter;

6.   Deploring also the fact that Austria, Belgium, Cyprus, Denmark, the Federal Republic of Germany, Greece, Iceland, Ireland, Italy, Liechtenstein, Luxembourg, Malta, Norway, Switzerland and the United Kingdom are not yet parties to the European Convention on the Legal Status of Migrant Workers;

7.   Emphasising that differences between social security systems in the member states constitute a major obstacle when it comes to guaranteeing effective social protection for the different categories of migrant workers;

8.   Conscious of the demographic importance in some member countries of the number of migrant workers from non-European countries;

---

1. *Assembly debate* on 7 October 1977 (17th Sitting) (see Doc. 5783, report of the Committee on Migration, Refugees and Demography).
   Text adopted by the Assembly on 7 October 1987 (17th Sitting).

9.   Observing that migrant workers very often have insufficient information about their rights and obligations in the field of social protection;

10. Considering that social protection for migrant workers in the host countries is not confined solely to the social security benefits which may be available to them, but also comprises other aspects, and especially legal aspects, which have a considerable bearing on living and working conditions;

11. Particularly concerned at the inadequate protection afforded to disabled migrants, who are all too often neglected in multilateral conventions and bilateral agreements, which leads to harmful consequences for second-generation migrants in the field of vocational training and access to employment;

12. Recalling that the repatriation programmes set up by certain host countries have not been successful;

13. Asserting that policies on assisted repatriation and resettlement in the countries of origin must be bases on the principle of maintenance of acquired rights or rights in course of acquisition, under the different social security systems, for migrant workers returning home;

14. Recalling that, in its Recommendation 1007 (1985) on the return of migrant workers to their country of origin, it called upon the Committee of Ministers to invite the governments of the host countries and the countries of origin to ratify the European Convention on Social Security and to conclude the social security agreements necessary to its implementation, so as to safeguard the maintenance of acquired rights and rights in course of acquisition by migrant workers in this field, and payments of benefits abroad,

15. Recommends that the Committee of Ministers:

    i.   embark upon activities designed to harmonise the social security systems in the member states and, above all, to speed up the adoption of the European Code of Social Security (revised), in order to lessen the existing differences and ensure a number of minimum benefits to all migrant workers of whatever origin;

    ii. take into account particularly the specific needs of disabled migrants when embarking upon any activity relating to the social protection of migrant workers and their families;

    iii. take into account the demographic importance of the number of migrant workers originating from non-European countries when considering what measures could appropriately be taken to adapt social security systems to their needs;

    iv. encourage member states to endeavour to harmonise the different bilateral agreements on migrant workers in the framework of legal co-operation within the Council of Europe;

    v.   invite the states which are not members of the Council of Europe but which have numerous nationals settled in member countries to accede to the European Convention on Social Security, in order to guarantee proper social protection for the migrant workers from those states;

vi. encourage, both within the Council of Europe and in the member states, any steps designed to keep migrant workers and their families better informed about social security questions;

vii. examine the possibility of preparing an outline instrument, open to non-member states, setting out the measures needed to safeguard the rights of migrant workers when they return to their country of origin;

viii. invite the government of the host countries and the countries of origin concerned by the repatriation of migrant workers, where they have not yet acceded to the European Convention on Social Security or are not bound by bilateral agreements, to co-operate in transferring workers' and employers' social security contributions made in the host countries to the institution responsible for social security in the country of origin;

ix. invite countries of origin, where no relevant social security agreements exist, to take a unilateral decision having the effect of accepting periods of insurance completed by their nationals abroad as equivalent to national periods entitling the workers concerned to social security rights;

x. invite those governments of member states which have not yet done so to sign and ratify the European Social Charter, the European Convention on Social Security and the Supplementary Agreement for its application, and the European Convention on the Legal Status of Migrant Workers;

xi. invite the governments of member states to take steps as soon as possible to put into effect the provisions of Recommendation No. R (79) 7 of the Committee of Ministers, concerning the speeding up of payment of mixed career pensions.

Recommendation 1093 (1989)[1]
on the education of migrants' children

The Assembly,

1. Having regard to its Recommendation 786 (1976) on the education and cultural development of migrants, and its Recommendation 1089 (1988) on improving community relations (European Days "Enjoying our diversity");

2. Welcoming the many activities being carried out in the field of the education and cultural development of migrants by the Council of Europe through the Council for Cultural Co-operation (CDCC) and the European Committee on Migration (CDMG), and by the European Community;

3. Considering that the resolution on migrants' education, adopted by the Standing Conference of European Ministers of Education (Dublin, May 1983), and Committee of Ministers Recommendation No. R (84) 18 on the training of teachers in education for intercultural understanding, notably in a context of migration, set out the principles on which coherent national policies for meeting migrants' educational and cultural needs should be based;

4. Observing, however, that despite the agreement over pedagogical principles for intercultural education, there are still divergences between host countries and countries of origin when it comes to the practicalities of the education of migrants' children;

5. Considering that the lack of standardisation of statistical data concerning, in particular, migrants' children and their education constitutes a major obstacle to co-operation between member states in this field;

6. Convinced that if the education of migrants' children is to be successful, account must be taken not only of the needs of this particular group of pupils but also of those of the school as a whole, which undergoes radical changes when young foreigners arrive;

7. Emphasising the need to shift away from the models of linguistic and cultural assimilation that have been prevalent in education so far;

8. Underlining, therefore, the need to introduce the language of the country of origin into the education system of the host countries, in line with the

---

1. *Assembly debate* on 31 January 1989 (19th Sitting) (see Doc. 5994, report of the Committee on Migration, Refugees and Demography, Rapporteur: Mrs Bourdara; and Doc. 6002, opinion of the Committee on Culture and Education, Rapporteur: Mrs Hennicot-Schoepges).
   Text adopted by the Assembly on 31 January 1989 (19th Sitting).

aim of a multilingual school, which has repeatedly been promoted by the Council of Europe and the European Community;

9.   Affirming that intercultural education is the only way of making use of the valuable asset represented by the presence of young migrants in schools;

10. Pointing out that the aim of intercultural education is to prepare all children, indigenous and migrant, to life in the pluricultural society;

11. Convinced that the adoption of an intercultural approach to education minimises the adaptation problems migrants' children experience if the migrants decide to return to their countries of origin;

12. Considering that the success of an intercultural policy depends to a large extent on a teacher training policy centred on the intercultural approach;

13. Underlining the need to create in each country the preconditions for all social groups to participate actively in the social, economic, cultural and collective life of the society;

14. Firmly supporting the current Council of Europe activities in the field of intercultural education;

15. Welcoming the follow-up given by the Committee of Ministers to the request from the European Ministers of Education to hold in 1989 a multidisciplinary conference on the educational and cultural aspects of community relations,

16. Recommends that the Committee of Ministers:

    a. promote consultation and co-ordination between education officers in the host countries and the countries of origin, so as to avoid the divergences that occur when the principles governing the education of migrants' children are put into practice;

    b. strengthen the research programmes and educational innovations that aim at the implementation of intercultural education for all children, in all sectors of the educational system;

    c. promote, within the context of intercultural education, activities including modern techniques in the field of teacher training;

    d. encourage educational exchanges at all levels of education and the setting up of a relationship between schools and migrant families;

    e. take the necessary steps to standardise statistical data concerning the education of migrants' children, in order to improve co-operation between member states in this field;

    f.   invite also representatives of migrants' associations, as well as teachers' associations, to attend the multidisciplinary conference on the educational and cultural aspects of community relations to be held in 1989;

    g. substantially improve the dissemination, in the member states, of information about Council of Europe activities in the field of migrants' education;

h. invite the member states to encourage the development of new structures and mechanisms that are geared to the management of migrants' children's linguistic and cultural diversity and complexity;

i. ensure that the Council of Europe works closely together with the European Community in this field.

Committee of Ministers

Resolution (70) 35
School education for the children of migrant workers

(Adopted by the Ministers' Deputies on 27 November 1970)

The Committee of Ministers,

I.   Having regard to the recommendation submitted to it by the Council of Europe Special Representative for National Refugees and Over-Population, following studies that have been carried out and in the light of the opinion expressed by his Advisory Committee on school education for the children of migrant workers;

II.   Considering that the instruction and education of children is an inalienable right which may be claimed even in difficult circumstances, such as those engendered by international migrations;

III.   Conscious of the necessity of ensuring, in their own interests, that the children of migrant workers do not lose their cultural and linguistic heritage and that they benefit from the culture of the receiving country;

IV.   Considering that efforts made by emigration and immigration countries to facilitate school education for the children of migrant workers will promote their adaptation or integration and consequently that of their parents;

V.   Considering that in this matter close collaboration between the relevant departments of the European member states to promote educational and cultural integration is in conformity with the aims defined in Article I of the Statute of the Council of Europe,

Recommends that governments of member states:

A – Guarantee, by means of legislation or regulation, exercise of the right of migrant workers' children to school education;

B – Take appropriate measures for the attainment of the following objectives:

1.   To improve the information given to families before departure about the educational facilities and requirements in the immigration country, and to provide on arrival advice and assistance in connection with enrolment in schools for those of compulsory school age;

2.   To provide for the children of migrant workers who do not emigrate with the head of the family the opportunity of starting or completing their compulsory education in their country of origin and possibly to provide free schooling and school equipment for them, for example in maintained or state schools;

3. To ensure that the responsible emigration services and school authorities advise the families of migrant workers to obtain, before a child's departure, standard records providing information on its school career and health, to assist in the assessment of its level of scholastic attainment;

4. To ensure that the appropriate local services, and where appropriate, the employers of migrant workers, inform the school authorities concerned without delay of the arrival of children of school age;

5. Possibly to establish, if need be, in co-operation with the authorities of the countries concerned, in areas where a sufficient number of migrant workers' families live, special classes of courses designed to assist the gradual integration of the children into the normal classes of the country of immigration, in particular by helping them to learn the language of the country; children of migrant workers should be taught in special classes or attend special courses for the shortest time strictly necessary;

6. To promote, after a period of adaptation appropriate to each child, full integration into normal classes in order to develop mutual understanding; with this in mind, immediate integration into the school in certain subjects such as drawing, physical training, handicrafts etc., should be encouraged as far as possible;

7. To see to it that, where practicable (and except for special classes or courses), compulsory classes do not contain dissimilar pupil groups in numbers likely to prejudice the teaching both of the children of migrant workers and of the native children;

8. To encourage, with the assistance of public and private bodies in the receiving country, the organisation of assisted and supervised study periods after school, in order to provide the necessary educational help for children who do not receive it at home;

9. To admit migrant workers' children, on the same basis as other children, to holiday camps and establishments for children below school age, and grant them scholarships, exemptions and other facilities;

10. To encourage migrant workers to take part in the life of their children's school;

11. To encourage teachers in the receiving country who have the children of migrant workers in their charge to acquire an adequate knowledge of teaching programmes in the countries of origin of such pupils;

12. To encourage and assist teachers in the countries of origin to follow courses in the receiving countries and vice versa, in order to promote understanding of the cultural and educational systems of these countries;

13. To promote, in the emigration countries, and also in the receiving countries, if the appropriate authorities agree, the training of specialist teachers to educate the children of migrant workers abroad, in the civilisation and language of their country of origin;

14. To encourage co-operation between the educational authorities in the emigration and immigration countries in order to promote such instruction, and award to the children who receive it certificates or diplomas drawn up in their mother tongue and stating the level attained;

15. To promote reintegration into school education of children of migrant workers who return to their country of origin;

16. For the purposes of admission to educational establishments to encourage a liberal attitude in relation to the equivalence of certificates and diplomas which testify to a sufficient level of education; and to ensure that migrant workers' children who have obtained such certificates or diplomas are enabled, on returning to their countries of origin, to enjoy all opportunities for their school career on the same basis as other pupils having pursued their studies abroad;

C – Report to the Council of Europe every four years on measures taken to give effect to this resolution.

Resolution (74) 14
on the situation of migrant workers
and their families in Europe

(Adopted by the Committee of Ministers on 21 May 1974
at the 232nd meeting of the Ministers' Deputies)

The Committee of Ministers,

Considering that the aim of the Council of Europe is to achieve greater unity between its members in order to safeguard and promote the ideals and principles which are their common heritage, and to facilitate their economic and social progress;

Noting the efforts deployed in the matter of migration by the Council of Europe and other international organisations;

Considering that the integration of migrant workers and their families into the society of the host countries needs to be facilitated;

Believing that, to alleviate the economic causes of migratory movements, the European states, acting in a spirit of solidarity, should do their utmost to promote the development of certain regions suffering from underemployment or unemployment;

Considering the extent assumed by the problem of clandestine migrant workers and the harmful effects of this phenomenon, both from the point of view of social standards and of the human dignity of migrant workers;

Conscious of the hardships which recessions, throughout the economy and in particular sectors, may impose upon workers in general and migrant workers and their families especially, both in their employment and in their private life;

Taking into account the belief expressed by the European Ministers of Labour at the Rome Conference in November 1972, that in the field of the protection of migrant workers and their families still greater progress could be made both in emigration and immigration countries,

Invite the governments of member states:

a. to give their full support to the Council of Europe's action in defence of the fundamental human rights, especially those of the worker, including the migrant worker;

b. to ensure that migrant workers in a situation of lawful employment, in a country of immigration, are placed on an equal footing with national workers where working and living conditions are concerned;

c. to encourage, at European level, international co-operation and co-ordination of action in order to achieve the most effective protection of migrant workers and their families;

d. to ensure that the clandestine introduction and exploitation of foreign manpower are prevented by all appropriate means, particularly by imposing effective penalties on those responsible for such practices;

e. to promote:

– participation of migrant workers and their families in the local community life of the immigration countries and in particular, to take the steps necessary to provide the most satisfactory schooling for the children of migrant workers in the host countries;

– a solution to the problem of housing to make family reunion possible by means of a programme of international co-operation which also takes account of the possibility of making wider use of the Council of Europe Resettlement Fund;

f. to promote the creation of new jobs in regions with a labour surplus, in particular by the transfer of capital or industry;

g. to provide facilities, as necessary, for vocational and linguistic preparation for migrant workers before their departure from their home countries;

h. to take the necessary action to prevent the consequences of economic crises, whether general or sectorial, from falling unduly on migrant workers lawfully employed and their families; in particular, in case of economic recession, to afford to migrant workers lawfully employed treatment not less favourable than that given to national workers, within the framework of national legislation.

Resolution (76) 12
on the school career and health record for children
attending school abroad[1]

*(Adopted by the Committee of Ministers on 10 March 1976
at the 255th meeting of the Ministers' Deputies)*

The Committee of Ministers,

Whereas the aim of the Council of Europe is to achieve a greater unity between its members, which aim shall be pursued, *inter alia*, by common action in social and cultural matters;

Bearing in mind the principle in the European Social Charter of 18 October 1961 that migrant workers who are nationals of one of the Contracting Parties, as well as their families, have a right to protection and assistance in the territories of other Contracting Parties;

Having regard to the difficulty which children moving from one state to another or returning to their countries of origin have in fitting into school systems with different administrative and teaching arrangements, as well as to the attendant risks for their school careers;

Having regard to its resolution (70) 35 on school education for the children of migrant workers, by which member governments were requested, among other things, "to ensure that the responsible emigration services and school authorities advise the families of migrant workers to obtain, before a child's departure, 'standard records' providing information on its school career and health, to assist in the assessment of its level of scholastic attainment" (point B. 3);

Convinced of the desirability of promoting the European standardisation of means of providing such information, at both the educational and the administrative level,

Recommends that member governments:

a. ask their respective school authorities to use, for a three-year trial period, the appended school career and health record for children attending school abroad, the text of which is appended to this resolution;

b. take steps to ensure that the record is filled in by the appropriate school authority in the country of emigration and delivered to the appropri-

---

1. When it was adopted, the Representative of Austria, referring to Article 10.2.c of the Rules of Procedure for the meetings of the Ministers' Deputies, reserved his government's right to comply with the text of the resolution or not.

The Representative of Switzerland, who abstained in the vote, made the same reservation.

ate school authority in the country of immigration as soon as the child arrives at its new school;

c. co-operate with the consular authorities of other member states and with any other interested organisation in order to facilitate the use of the record;

d. inform the Secretary General of the Council of Europe, on the expiry of the three-year trial period, of their experience in using the record and of any changes they consider necessary or desirable to its contents.

Appendix to the Resolution (76) 12

Record issued on ....

.... (1)

**School career and health record
for children attending school abroad** (2)
(to be completed by the school authorities
responsible for the child's education) (1)

....

.... (1)

Child's surname
.... (1)

Forenames
.... (1)

Sex
.... (1)

Date of birth
.... (1)

Place of birth
.... (1)

Nationality
.... (1)

Mother tongue
.... (1)

Religion (optional)
.... (1)

....

....

....

....

....

....

....

....

---

(1) Space for translation into the language of the country to which the child is going.
(2) A model of this record, which is available in English, French, German, Greek, Italian, Dutch, Swedish and Turkish may be obtained upon request from the Secretariat General of the Council of Europe, 67006 STRASBOURG CEDEX, FRANCE.

For the attention
of school authorities

The school career record describes the child's knowledge and aptitudes, as well as his or her general state of health, at a given time.

It is designed to be used during the period of compulsory schooling and is intended to facilitate the educational assimilation of children in a new milieu, in the various immigration countries or upon their return to their home country, on the assumption that all necessary educational provision will be made in the country of arrival.

Head teachers must carefully scrutinise any entry which may be damaging to the holder of this record. The information contained in the school career and health record must not be used as a means of challenging the principle of equality of opportunity or of limiting the child's chances of educational and social integration in the host country.

Entries should be made in the language of the country in which the school issuing the record is situated and in the language of the country to which the child is going.

The school authorities in the host country should endeavour to co-operate closely with the consular authorities of the country of origin, and with any other department or authority concerned with reception arrangements for foreigners, in all matters relating to the practical use of this record, and help which parents may need in arranging for their children to be transferred.

A. Situation on leaving (last class attended)

Name and address of school ....
....

School year 19... - 19...

Type of education (primary, secondary, other) .... Class attended .... (1)

| 1 | 2 | 3 | 4 | 5 | 6 | 7 | 8 | 9 | 10 | | | |

Subjects studied (delete as appropriate)	Number of years studied	Number of hours each year	Assessment of pupil's proficiency (show by a cross)			
			very good	good	fair	poor
1. Language of instruction (.................................) a- oral expression						
b- reading						
c- written expression						
d- spelling						
2. Other languages including that of the home country a- (.................................) (oral expression)						
(written expression)						
b- (.................................) (oral expression)						
(written expression)						
c- (.................................) (oral expression)						
(written expression)						
3. Proficiency in mathematics - modern						
- traditional						
4. Proficiency in other subjects and abilities including artistic activities a- biology						
b- history (and civics)						
c- geography						
d- physics						
e- drawing						
f-						
g- .... (2)						
5. a- physical education						
b- sport						

Additional observations (3)
....
....
....

(1) Place a cross in the appropriate box; use empty boxes if compulsory schooling exceeds 10 years.
(2) These spaces can also be used to indicate knowledge of the culture and civilisation of the home country.
(3) To be completed only where necessary and, where possible, translated into the language of the country to which the pupil is going.

174

B. Personal characteristics (last school attended)

	Evaluation (show by a cross)			
	very good	good	fair	poor
1. Tidiness, carefulness				
2. Diligence				
3. Other remarks				

C. Previous schooling (including pre-school education)

Country	School year	Schooling (show by a cross)														
		Pre-school			Compulsory schooling (1)											
		1st	2nd	3rd	1st	2nd	3rd	4th	5th	6th	7th	8th	9th	10th		
	19../19..															
	19../19..															
	19../19..															
	19../19..															
	19../19..															
	19../19..															
	19../19..															
	19../19..															
	19../19..															
	19../19..															
	19../19..															
	19../19..															
	19../19..															

(1) Place a cross in the appropriate box; use empty boxes if compulsory schooling exceeds 10 years.

D. Particulars of the child's family

1. *Parents or other persons responsible for the child* (1)

Surname	....
Forenames	....
Date of birth	....
Occupation	....
Surname	....
Forenames	....
Date of birth	....
Occupation	....

2. *Family situation*

Forenames and
ages of brothers
and sisters

....
....
....
....

(1) State the relationship to the child, whether blood or otherwise (e.g. guardian).

School stamp ....

Date .... 19 ....

Teacher's signature

....

Head teacher's signature

....

E. State of health (1)

Immunisations	Type of serum	Date	Date	Date	Date	Immunity as a result of illness
1. Smallpox						
2. Whooping cough						
3. Diphtheria						
4. Tetanus						
5. Poliomyelitis						
6. Tuberculosis						
7. Typhoid						
8. German measles						
9. Trivalent vaccine (DTC)						
10.						
11.						
Tuberculin tests						
Illness						
1.						
2.						
3.						

Physiological condition (2)	

1. *Motor capacity*
  – motor co-ordination
  – lateralisation
  – lateral dominance
	3. *Hearing*
	tested (3) yes ☐ no ☐
	normal (3) yes ☐ no ☐

2. *Eyesight* tested (3) yes ☐ no ☐ normal (3) yes ☐ no ☐	4. *Handicaps* (4)

(1) To be completed by a medical practitioner (if possible the school doctor); will be sent separately as confidential information.
(2) To be completed where possible. This information will remained confidential.
(3) Place a cross in the appropriate box.
(4) State the degree of handicap.

The Council of Europe

The idea of the school career record came from the Council of Europe.

The Council of Europe was founded by ten nations on 5 May 1949, as the first European political institution, with the first international parliament; today, with eighteen member countries,[1] it is the European organisation with the widest geographical representation.

The Council of Europe, which has its headquarters at Strasbourg, was set up "to achieve a greater unity between its members for the purpose of safeguarding and realising the ideals and principles which are their common heritage and facilitating their economic and social progress".

1. Austria, Belgium, Cyprus, Denmark, the Federal Republic of Germany, France, Greece, Iceland, Ireland, Italy, Luxembourg, Malta, the Netherlands, Norway, Sweden, Switzerland, Turkey, the United Kingdom.

Resolution (78) 4
on social and economic repercussions on migrant workers of economic recessions or crises[1,2,3,4]

(Adopted by the Committee of Ministers on 2 February 1978 at the 282nd meeting of the Ministers' Deputies)

The Committee of Ministers,

Bearing in mind the aims of the European Social Charter concerning the effective exercise of the right to work and the right of migrant workers and their families to protection and assistance;

Having regard to the various Council of Europe social security agreements, viz. the 1953 Interim Agreements on Social Security, the 1953 Convention on Social and Medical Assistance and the 1972 European Convention on Social Security;

Considering that the rise in the rate of unemployment among migrant workers during economic recessions may be leading to a massive return of those migrant workers to their countries of origin, thus aggravating the unemployment situation and related problems in those countries;

Considering that the application of certain measures proposed in Resolution (69) 7 on the "return of migrant workers to their home country" in particular those concerning information, vocational training, transfer of savings, return journey and education of children on their return to their country of origin, is of particular value at times of economic crises or recessions;

Conscious of the special hardships which recessions throughout the economy may impose upon migrant workers and their families, both in their employment and in their family life;

Seeing that, in view of the particular position of migrant workers in times of economic recession, it is desirable that specific measures in their favour should be included in bilateral or multilateral agreements;

---

1. This resolution applies to migrant workers regularly employed.
2. When this resolution was adopted, the Representative of the United Kingdom, acting in accordance with Article 10.2.c of the Rules of Procedure for the meetings of the Ministers' Deputies, reserved the right of this government to comply with it or not.
3. When this resolution was adopted, the Representative of the Federal Republic of Germany, acting in accordance with Article 10.2.c of the Rules of Procedure for the meetings of the Ministers' Deputies, reserved the right of his government to comply or not with paragraphs II.1 and II.2.
4. When this resolution was adopted, the Representative of Belgium, acting in accordance with Article 10.2.c of the Rules of Procedure for the meetings of the Ministers' Deputies, reserved the right of this government to comply or not with paragraph II.6.

Noting that, while it is particularly important to take measures for the protection of migrant workers at the time when economic recessions or crises occur, other measures of a permanent nature such as preparation for the voluntary return of migrant workers to their home country and the drawing up of plans to facilitate their reintegration into the national economy should also be envisaged in order to minimise the difficulties arising out of such situations;

Bearing in mind that the recommendations adopted by the European Ministers of Labour at the conference held in Rome in November 1972 and the recommendations in Resolution (74) 14 call on the governments of member states to take the necessary action to ensure that migrant workers and their families do not particularly suffer from the consequences of economic crises for reasons linked to their own situations,

Recommends that the governments of member states:

I. General measures

1.   Ensure that migration policies are so framed that, in the employment field, migrant workers do not suffer more than other workers from the repercussions of an economic recession. Accordingly, cyclical fluctuations should not alter the principles of employment policy regarding foreign workers lawfully residing in countries where they are considered as an integral part of the national labour force;

2.   Encourage all measures designed to prevent discrimination between national workers and migrant workers both in the case of redundancy and, when possible under national legislation, in the case of subsequent re-engagement of migrant workers who have remained legally in the employing country, subject to the provisions of any existing bilateral or multilateral agreements;

3.   Take appropriate steps within the framework of national regulations on the employment of migrant workers, particularly in the fields of vocational training and retraining, to increase the occupational and geographical mobility of migrant workers who are out of work with a view to enabling them to find new jobs more easily, either in the receiving country or in their own countries;

4.   Take necessary measures to ensure that migrant workers, particularly those who have lost their jobs, are provided with social and administrative assistance to help them to exercise their rights;

5.   Encourage co-operation between immigration and emigration countries with a view to fostering the application of the measures recommended above.

II. Measures to be taken in cases of redundancy

1.   Ensure the uniform application of a definition of unemployment, as laid down by national legislation, to both national and migrant workers so that

the latter are placed on an equal footing with nationals as regards the rights and duties pertaining to unemployment;

2.   See to it that migrant workers have the same entitlement as national workers to any social assistance arrangements (such as unemployment assistance and any special allowances);

3.   Ensure application of the principles of Article IV of Resolution (74) 15 on equal treatment of national and migrant workers;

4.   Take steps to see that foreign workers made redundant have, subject to national regulation on residence and employment, the right to remain in the country of employment for at least as long as they are still entitled to unemployment benefit;

5.   Study the possibility of unemployed migrant workers who voluntarily return home being paid, taking into account national legislation, unemployment benefit or allowances in the countries of origin. Bilateral or multilateral agreements could be concluded, supplemented or ratified when they already exist, in order to continue to try to ensure that migrant workers are protected in this matter;

6.   Study the possibility of applying appropriate measures to ensure that, in the case of foreign workers who return to their countries of origin after being made redundant because of an economic recession and subsequently come back to the country of employment, their temporary absence from the latter does not count against them when their acquired rights or rights in the process of being acquired under its legislation are being assessed;

7.   Ensure, in accordance with paragraph IV.6.ii of Resolution (69) 7 and in the spirit of the current practice of certain countries, that a study is made of measures to facilitate the repatriation of both migrant workers made redundant as a result of an economic recession who wish to return to their countries of origin and of their families.

III. Measures to be considered by countries of origin on behalf of returning migrant workers

Ensure that the appropriate authorities improve the rehabilitation arrangements set up to receive returning migrants and take the following measures:

1. *Vocational training and retraining*

a. Facilitate the recognition of occupational qualifications and certificates in order to enable repatriates to use the skills they have acquired abroad;

b. Make arrangements – if necessary in co-operation with the employing countries – to offer repatriated migrant workers special courses for adapting their qualifications to the needs of their country of origin;

2. Re-employment

Encourage co-operation between the employment offices in the receiving and sending countries to facilitate the vocational reintegration of returning migrant workers into the professional life of their countries;

3. Social services

See to it that the appropriate measures are taken so that authorities in the sending countries are prepared to meet the demand for services and benefits likely to be made by returning migrant workers and their families;

4. Housing

Take into consideration certain national practices to make migrant workers residing abroad eligible on an equal footing with workers residing in the home country for the allocation, following their return to their countries, of housing constructed for workers as part of public social building schemes;

5. Children's education

a. Promote co-operation between the appropriate authorities in the receiving and sending countries to enable education authorities in the countries of origin to provide for the educational needs of children of returning migrant workers as far in advance of their return as possible;

b. Make use of the record for children attending school abroad, instituted by Resolution (76) 12, in order to facilitate the reintegration of returning children into the national school system;

6. Medical care

Take measures to waive or reduce any qualifying period of insurance, residence, employment or occupational activity laid down by national legislation for entitlement to free medical care or the refund of medical expenses in cases where such matters are not regulated by bilateral or multilateral conventions.

IV. Report to the Secretary General of the Council of Europe every five years on measures taken to give effect to this resolution.

Resolution (78) 33
on the reunion of families of migrant workers
in Council of Europe member states[1,2]

(Adopted by the Committee of Ministers on 8 June 1978
at the 289th meeting of the Ministers' Deputies)

The Committee of Ministers,

Considering that the family constitutes the basic unit of society and that the right to found a family and to share family life with its members should be safeguarded;

Stressing the grave nature of the social, human and moral problems which arise when the members of a family are separated;

Having regard to the provisions of Article 1 of the Statute of the Council of Europe and guided by Articles 16 and 19 of the European Social Charter, Articles 8 and 14 of the European Convention on Human Rights, Article 2 of the fourth Protocol to that Convention and Article 12 of the European Convention on the Legal Status of Migrant Workers;

Noting that the situation of migrant workers in the host country presents serious problems from the point of view of family reunion;

Recalling the recommendations contained in the Resolutions already adopted, and particularly in Resolutions (69) 8, (70) 35, (69) 7 and (74) 14 on low-cost housing, the schooling of migrant workers' children, the return to the home country, and the situation of migrant workers and their families in Europe, as well as those contained in Resolution (76) 12 on the school career and health record;

Considering that it is desirable, in order to facilitate the reuniting of migrant workers with their families, that the immigration and emigration states should take the measures listed below, while retaining those provisions already embodied in internal legislation and international agreements which are more favourable to migrant workers,

Recommends that the governments of member states:

---

1. When this resolution was adopted, the Representatives of the United Kingdom and of the Federal Republic of Germany, acting in accordance with Article 10.2.c. of the Rules of Procedure for the meetings of the Ministers' Deputies, reserved the right of their Governments to comply with it or not.
2. When this resolution was adopted, the Representative of Austria, acting in accordance with Article 10.2.c of the Rules of Procedure for the meetings of the Ministers' Deputies, reserved the right of her Government to comply with paragraph B.1.a or not.

A.   be guided, as regards the reuniting of migrant workers' families, by the following general principles:

1.   The reuniting of a migrant worker's family should be recognised in the internal legislation. With due regard for the preservation of public policy ("*ordre public*"), national security or morals, its exercise should not be made dependent on conditions which make it impossible;

2.   The administrative procedures concerning the admission of members of the family should be kept as simple as possible;

3.   The principle of freedom of departure and return for members of a migrant worker's family should be recognised in legislation of the emigration states;

B.   take the following specific measures:

1. *With regard to the admission of the members of migrant workers' families*

a.   Allow migrant workers to be joined by their spouse and dependent minor children and, when justified on humanitarian grounds, by dependent members of the family, particularly their ascendants and those of their spouse who are elderly and isolated in the country of origin, and consequently provide them with the necessary residence permits;

b.   Observe, for the purpose of family reunion, the following limits on conditions governing the admission of members of the family:

i.   When a waiting period is required, this should be reduced to a minimum and must not exceed twelve months, it being understood that measures should be taken to dispense with this conditions as soon as circumstances permit;

ii.   Housing quality requirements should be limited to those regarded as normal by national workers in the region where migrant workers are employed;

iii. When the family reunion is subject to conditions concerning the employment of the migrant worker, these can relate only to the capacity to provide for the needs of the family from stable and adequate resources, excluding unemployment benefit;

iv. If a medical examination is required for members of the family exercising the reunion, its sole purpose must be the detection of illnesses representing a danger to public health or public policy ("*ordre public*");

c.   Adopt the following specific measures to facilitate family reunion:

i.   When legislation or practice requires an application form, the migrant worker should be required to give only information relevant to family reunion;

ii.   To favour, in both the country of origin and the host country, any measures likely to reduce the travelling and settling-in expenses incurred by the members of the family when they are reunited;

d. Provide the members of the family with work permits in so far as the state and evolution of the labour market allow;

2. *With regard to the housing of the migrant worker's family*

Ensure for migrant workers the same access as national to low-cost accommodation. In addition, consider suitable unilateral, bilateral or international arrangements for financing such low-cost accommodation for migrant workers;

3. *With regard to information and assistance*

On a basis of co-operation between the country of origin and the receiving country, provide migrant workers, as far as possible in their mother tongue, with all relevant information on the conditions for family reunion and the formalities involved;

To this end, the competent public and private authorities should be given adequate means for:

i. Assisting the migrant worker to complete the administrative formalities for the admission of members of his family and the securing of accommodation (rentals, grants, loans and other facilities open to them);

ii. Providing the members of the family, before their departure for the host country, with free, direct and effective information on costs, travel and transport facilities, living conditions, health requirements and educational opportunities for the children and all necessary help in arranging their journey;

iii. Providing the members of the family, after their arrival in the host country, with relevant information, especially about social security benefits and social health services, school and vocational training systems, and in general with all necessary help in settling down and residence in the host country.

Recommendation No. R (84) 9
on second-generation migrants[1]

(Adopted by the Committee of Ministers on 20 March 1984
at the 368th meeting of the Ministers' Deputies)

The Committee of Ministers, under the terms of Article 15.*b* of the Statute of the Council of Europe,

1.   Considering that the aim of the Council of Europe is the achievement of greater unity between its members with a view to promoting, *inter alia*, their economic and social development;

2.   Noting that for the purpose of this recommendation second-generation migrants are considered to be children born in the host country of immigrant foreign parents, who have accompanied them or who have joined them under family reunion and who have accomplished there a part of their education or vocational training;

3.   Noting that second-generation migrants in host countries are in a particular situation, which differs from that of the other migrants of foreign origin, by reason of numerous links they have with them, the lengthy period they may have lived there, their possible familiarity with the habits, customs and culture of the countries in question and the extent to which they may have become integrated in the society there;

4.   Noting that at the same time they may retain close links with their countries of origin;

---

1. When this recommendation was adopted, the Representatives of Liechtenstein, Switzerland and the United Kingdom, in application of Article 10.2.*c* of the Rules of Procedure for meetings of the Ministers' Deputies, reserved the right of their governments to comply with it or not.

The Representative of Austria, in application of Article 10.2.*c* of the Rules of Procedure for meetings of the Ministers' Deputies, reserved the right of his government to apply the provisions of it only to minors of foreign nationality who were born in Austria, or who had accompanied their parents to Austria, or who had joined them and who had accomplished the major part of their compulsory education in Austria and completed it there. As far as minors who had accompanied their parents to Austria or who have joined them there are concerned, they should have entered Austria before 1 September 1982. Furthermore, he reserved the right of his government to comply or not with paragraphs I.*a-c*, II (3rd sub-paragraph) and III.b of the recommendation.

The Representative of the Federal Republic of Germany, in application of Article 10.2.*c* of the Rules of Procedure for meetings of the Ministers' Deputies, reserved the right of his government to comply or not with paragraphs I.*a*, I.*b*, II (1st and 3rd sub-paragraphs) and IV.*h* of the recommendation.

The Representative of Norway, in application of Article 10.2.*c* of the Rules of Procedure for meetings of the Ministers' Deputies, reserved the right of his government to comply or not with the last sentence of paragraph I.*b*.

5. Noting that second-generation migrants account for almost half the total immigrant population in certain countries;

6. Considering that a great number of them belong to the working population and that, in certain countries, they represent a large proportion of those seeking employment among the foreign population and in the numbers attending establishments dispensing elementary education;

7. Stressing the importance of the contribution by migrants to the economic, social, cultural and, in most cases, demographic development of host countries;

8. Considering that further action is required to encourage respect for the cultural identity of migrants in general and second-generation migrants in particular and to develop schemes designed to make the public more aware and informed of the culture, economy and society of the countries of origin of second-generation migrants;

9. Realising the value of progressively harmonising European administrative standards and regulations concerning the residence and employment of young foreigners and having regard, in this connection, to the provisions on residence and employment in the European Social Charter and the European Convention on the Legal Status of Migrant Workers;

10. Aware of the need for young second-generation migrants to receive assistance with occupational and social reintegration in the country of origin in the event of voluntary return;

11. Considering that the special situation of second-generation migrants may necessitate specific measures concerning their education and cultural development;

12. Noting the necessity and importance of close co-operation between host countries and countries of origin of the parents of second-generation migrants in these matters;

13. Having regard to Assembly Recommendation 841 on second-generation migrants,

Recommends that the governments of member states:

I. As regards residence:

a. lay down provisions guaranteeing residential stability for second-generation migrants and their spouses not possessing the nationality of the host country;

b. ensure that expulsion orders against second-generation migrants who have lived for a considerable time in the host country are issued only on account of offences punished by law courts or in exceptional cases relating in particular to national security and public policy. In this connection, consideration should be given to the occupational and family situation of the person concerned as well as his having been born in the host country and the fact that his family live and work there. A second-generation migrant against whom an expulsion order has been issued should have, in principle, the opportunity of lodging an appeal having suspensive effect with the judicial authorities;

c. guarantee, in accordance with the relevant regulations, that, in cases of temporary absence from the host country, second-generation migrants' rights acquired or being acquired through their birth, schooling or occupational activity shall be maintained when they return to that country;

II. As regards employment:

– guarantee to second-generation migrants vocational training which is incorporated in a general educational system offering real social advancement;

– endeavour to ensure that, to this end, action relating to information, vocational guidance, training and retraining as well as international co-operation, as outlined in Resolution (76) 11 concerning migrant workers, is taken;

– take measures assuring equal treatment between young nationals and young second-generation migrants as regards access to employment and genuine social and professional advancement, and to grant work permits if necessary;

a. *Information*

Develop and adapt to second-generation migrants' needs facilities dispensing information on employment, vocational training and educational opportunities;

b. *Guidance*

Organise, adapt or develop, if they already exist, vocational guidance schemes consisting of courses and interviews which take account of the specific aptitudes and needs of second-generation migrants and enable them to take advantage of the job opportunities offered to them;

c. *Pre-vocational training*

Consider the appropriateness of providing pre-vocational training – whenever possible in the languages of the countries of origin – beyond the compulsory school-leaving age for the following categories:

1. second-generation migrants with insufficient command of the spoken and written language of the host country who, despite attending beginners' or remedial classes, are unable to enter the vocational training system,

2. young people who have failed to obtain any school-leaving qualifications.

This pre-vocational training should enable those concerned to receive suitable vocational training;

d. *Vocational training*

Foster, in the same conditions as for nationals, access by second-generation migrants to vocational training centres and institutions providing preparation for employment, in the light of their capacities and aspiration; arrangements for teaching the language of the host country, which is necessary for the social and occupational integration of such migrants, should be provided or improved in this connection;

e. *Equivalence of qualifications*

Try to ensure that countries of origin and host countries recognise the equivalence of education and vocational certificates and qualifications, at least within the framework of bilateral agreements;

f. *International co-operation*

Promote co-operation between countries of origin and host countries to enable second-generation migrants to maintain links with the parents' country of origin and find appropriate employment if they return there;

Envisage where possible, following the conclusion of bilateral agreements, the organisation of visits or courses in parents' countries of origin, so that second-generation migrants can take free and fully-informed decisions on whether to return to the parents' country of origin or remain in the host country;

III. As regards acquisition of the nationality of the host country or resumption of the nationality of origin:

a. provide all the information needed by parents and second-generation migrants on the conditions in which nationality may be acquired and lost, and also on the consequences thereof, as well as reinstatement of nationality of origin and the procedures to be followed;

b. do everything that is necessary and possible to ensure that procedures for acquisition of nationality or reinstatement of nationality of origin are as simple and speedy as possible, and charges are as limited as possible, and do not exceed administrative costs;

c. ensure, within the framework of international agreements, that young migrants holding the nationalities of two or more member states are subject to national service or military service obligations in only one state;

IV. Recommendations on education and culture

a. promote, as far as possible, the education and cultural development of second-generation migrants, acting when appropriate in bilateral co-operation;

b. recognise the importance of intercultural education[1] in education;

---

1. Interculturalism advocates the integration of migrants into the receiving society and the defence and respect of the value of their languages and cultures as well as supplying the means for attaining these objectives.

c. develop appropriate measures for pupils from different cultural backgrounds, when assessing their abilities and knowledge;

d. encourage the co-ordination of educational objectives and, as far as possible, the mutual recognition of study and training undertaken in other countries to facilitate mobility;

e. promote the development of coherent policies in the educational, social and cultural fields according to second-generation migrants' needs, while obtaining the support and participation of host communities;

f. foster the integration of migrant girls and women in education and vocational training, in order to enable them to be fully involved in the life of the community;

In the receiving country:

g. promote the socio-occupational integration of young migrants through the educational system;

h. give full value to the culture of the parents' country of origin by integrating, possibly in co-operation with the country of origin, the teaching of the language and culture of the country of origin into ordinary school curricula;

i. promote the intercultural training of indigenous teachers, teachers from countries of origin, education officials and adult educators, and encourage the production of suitable teaching aids, in co-operation, where possible, with countries of origin;

j. promote the development of cultural activities, mainly through associations, to enable second-generation migrants to express their own cultural identity and to establish friendly contacts with the local population, and participate in local cultural life;

In the country of origin:

k. promote, with a view to the training of teachers and information of the population, knowledge of the living conditions and of the culture in the host countries;

l. consider means and take appropriate measures to help young returning migrants or their families to reintegrate and participate in local cultural life in such a way that they can make the best use of the cultural, linguistic and social experience acquired abroad.

Recommendation No. R (90) 14
on the preparation of an information brochure
on the social security rights and obligations
of migrant workers and of their families

(Adopted by the Committee of Ministers on 18 June 1990
at the 442nd meeting of the Ministers' Deputies)

The Committee of Ministers, under the terms of Article 15.*b* of the Statute of the Council of Europe,

Considering that it is the aim of the Council of Europe to achieve a greater unity between its members, particularly in order to promote their social progress;

Considering that the social security protection of migrant workers and their families is one of the essential tasks of the Council of Europe, as is evidenced particularly by the adoption of various international instruments, such as the European Social Charter and especially its Article 12, paragraph 4, the European interim agreements on social security, the European Convention on Social Security and its supplementary agreement, and the European Convention on the Legal Status of Migrant Workers;

Conscious of the difficulty of providing completely adequate information on the social security rights and obligations of migrant workers and their families, owing to the multiplicity and complexity of the applicable provisions at both the national and international levels;

Considering that the effective application of these social security instruments depends also on the information made available to migrant workers, and those principally dealing with them, on the rights and obligations of migrant workers as well as on the means to exercise the former and comply with the latter;

Conscious of the need to improve the information available to those who are insured and in particular to migrant workers and their families concerning their social security rights and obligations;

Considering that refugees and stateless persons should also be included in this effort to provide information;

Considering the usefulness of providing migrant workers and their families, if possible in their mother tongue, as well as those dealing with migrant workers, with a model information leaflet on the social security rights and obligations of migrant workers and their families,

Recommends that the governments of the member states ensure the dissemination, to all the persons and authorities concerned, of information on the rights and obligations of migrant workers and their families, following, where possible, the outline of the brochure appended to this recommendation.

Appendix to Recommendation No. R (90) 14

*Outline of the brochure on the social security rights
and obligations of migrant workers and their families*[1]

Part A

General description of the national social security system of ...

I.   *Introduction*

Short description of the brochure.

II.   *General themes*
   a.   Brief general description of the national social security system
   b.   Arrangements for contributing to the financing of the general scheme
   c.   Conditions for joining the social security system – steps to be taken
   d.   Possible remedies in the event of refusal, suspension or discontinuation of social security benefits or disagreement with a decision taken by a social security institution or department – return of benefits wrongly received
   e.   Useful information (address and telephone number of institutions or government departments responsible for each branch and of social security information centres)
   f.   Brief enumeration of bilateral and multilateral instruments that have been ratified

   (Although each state may adjust the arrangement of the information according to the specific needs of its social security system, it would nevertheless be desirable to provide relevant information corresponding to each of the headings below.)

III.   *Detailed description of the national system*

1.   *Medical care* (benefits in kind)
   a.   Contingency covered
   b.   Persons protected
   c.   Benefits provided. Extent of the cover according to the type of care (for example, local practitioner, hospital care, dental care, pharmaceutical products). Duration of the provision of benefits
   d.   Conditions (for example, qualifying period)
   e.   Arrangements for the provision of benefits (for example, waiting period, sharing of medical costs)
   f.   Formalities. Practical details of benefits provided

2.   *Sickness benefit* (cash benefits)
   a. Contingency covered
   b. Persons protected
   c. Benefits provided (method of calculation, duration of the provision of benefits)
   d. Conditions (for example, qualifying periods)
   e.   Arrangements for the provision of benefits (for example, waiting period)
   f.   Formalities

3.   *Unemployment benefit*
   a.   Contingencies covered (total unemployment, partial unemployment)

---

1. For easier reading and accessibility, this information could be provided in separate leaflets for each benefit or branch of social security.

  b. Persons protected
  c. Benefits provided (method of calculation, duration of the provision of benefits)
  d. Conditions (for example, qualifying period)
  e. Arrangements for the provision of benefits (for example, waiting period)
  f. Formalities

4. *Old-age benefit*
  a. Contingency covered
  b. Persons protected
  c. Benefits provided (method of calculation)
  d. Conditions of entitlement (for example, qualifying period, cessation of gainful employment)
  e. Formalities

5. *Employment injury benefit*
  a. Contingencies covered
  b. Persons protected
  c. Benefits provided (method of calculation, duration of the provision of benefits: for example, cash benefits, benefits in kind, other benefits, special benefits for vocational rehabilitation and retraining, preventive measures)
  d. Conditions (for example, qualifying period)
  e. Arrangements for covering the cost of medical care
  f. Formalities

6. *Family benefit*
  a. Contingency covered
  b. Persons protected
  c. Benefits provided (method of calculation, duration of the provision of benefits: for example, amount of family allowance, other types of benefit)
  d. Conditions (for example, residence conditions and qualifying period)
  e. Formalities

7. *Maternity benefit*
  a. Contingencies covered
  b. Persons protected
  c. Benefits provided (for example, medical care – amount of cost-sharing by the beneficiary, if applicable, maternity grants – method of calculation)
  d. Conditions (for example, qualifying period, residency conditions)
  e. Formalities – arrangements for covering the cost of medical care

8. *Invalidity benefit*
  a. Contingencies covered
  b. Persons protected
  c. Benefits provided (method of calculation). Supplementary benefits (for example, rehabilitation, vocational retraining)
  d. Conditions (for example, qualifying period)
  e. Formalities

9. *Survivor's benefit*
  a. Contingency covered
  b. Persons protected (for example, survivors, male or female, children)
  c. Benefits provided (method of calculation)
  d. Conditions (for example, qualifying period, qualifying age, qualifying period of marriage)
  e. Formalities

Part B

Description of the protection generated by the different international instruments for the co-ordination of social security in the framework of relations between ... and ...

Medical care
 a.   Enumeration of instruments that have been ratified
 b.   Contingencies covered. Details concerning the contingencies covered by the different instruments
 c.   Persons protected. Details concerning the persons protected by the different instruments
 d.   Types of benefit. Details concerning the types of benefit covered by the different instruments
 e.   Conditions for award. Details concerning conditions for award laid down in the different instruments
 f.   Length of period over which benefits are provided and provision abroad. Details concerning the length provided by the different instruments
 g.   Administrative aspects

The other branches should be set out in a similar manner.

Health

Table of contents

Parliamentary Assembly

Commmittee of Ministers

Parliamentary Assembly

Recommendation 989 (1984)[1]
on the fight against drug abuse and trafficking

The Assembly,

1.   Considering with dismay that the use of drugs, both narcotics and psychotropic substances, is still on the increase in the majority of the member countries;

2.   Noting that in the member states of the Council of Europe over the last few years there has been a major rise in the sale of cocaine, wider availability of heroin, the price of which has fallen, and an unprecedented increase in the use of cannabis which has benefited from the laxity of public opinion in some countries;

3.   Also noting that traditional narcotics have been joined by the dramatic appearance of new forms of abuse, such as multiple drug addiction, psychotropic drugs used for other than their therapeutic purpose, and the inhalation of glues, ether and solvents such as trichloroethylene;

4.   Alarmed by the fact that the average age of users is continuing to fall and ranges often from 13 to 16;

5.   Noting that a large number of national and international bodies are studying means to control drugs, are carrying out experiments and are trying to take effective action, but that, unfortunately, the results obtained, in the form of penal action, reintegration or prevention, are very limited in comparison with the resources invested;

6.   Considering that, as regards co-ordination both on the national level (between the various departments such as medical officers, judges, social services and police) and on the European level (research, customs co-operation, the exchange of information, the establishing of common criteria), the position is far from satisfactory, and that, as a general rule, both theoretical and practical activities are conducted in isolation in each country with increasing duplication and waste of resources;

7.   Recalling that over the last fifteen years the Council of Europe has made significant efforts in this field which have resulted in numerous recommendations by the Assembly and the Committee of Ministers, the most recent of which are Recommendation No. R (82) 5, on the prevention of drug addic-

1. *Assembly debate* on 27 September 1984 (10th and 11th Sittings) (see Doc. 5276, report of the Committee on Social and Health Questions, Doc. 5283, opinion of the Legal Affairs Committee, and Doc. 5284, opinion of the Committee on Culture and Education).
   Text adopted by the Assembly on 27 September 1984 (11th Sitting).

tion and the particular role of health education, and Resolution (73) 6, on the penal aspects of drug abuse;

8. Noting that:

i. since this work started, it has been possible to begin a dialogue between the member states and to obtain some practical results, but it has not been possible to make any joint assessment of the effectiveness of preventative measures;

ii. it has proved impossible to produce comparable data to facilitate an exchange of national experiences;

iii. the preventative and educational approach is not sufficiently advanced, at least in some countries, compared with traditional control methods;

iv. finally, some striking differences have come to light as regards the punitive approach;

9. Considering that the Committee of Ministers' decision of 1980 to integrate the "Pompidou Group" (Co-operation Group to combat drug abuse and illicit trafficking in drugs) – set up in 1971 to enable close multidisciplinary co-operation – into the Council of Europe, as the Assembly had asked in Recommendation 843 (1978), is a step forward;

10. Welcoming the final declaration of the 7th Ministerial Conference of the Pompidou Group Ministers and its positive outcome;

11. Noting with satisfaction the recent decision of the Spanish Government to join in the Pompidou Group, thus bringing the number of members to fourteen;

12. Believing that the problem of drugs, like that of violence, is linked to wider problems of modern society such as increasing stress, unemployment, leisure time or uncertainty about values;

13. Recalling its Recommendation 963 (1983), on cultural and educational means of reducing violence,

14. Recommends that the Committee of Ministers draw up, as part of its medium-term plan, a consistent multidisciplinary strategy for the fight against drug abuse and trafficking, using all the resources of the Council of Europe and paying particular attention to the following proposals:

A. *Action against drug trafficking*

i. To reaffirm that it should be a punishable offence to traffic in both "hard" and "soft" drugs, seeing that whilst the former certainly have a more devastating effect, the latter, because they are easier to obtain and to use, considerably increase the number of users and lower their average age, thus adding a quantitative dimension to the problem; each country's legislation should differentiate between both types of trafficking and provide for the punishment of the offenders in both cases;

ii.   To step up measures to combat large-scale drug trafficking, in particular :

a. by stressing the international dimension of this trafficking and the proven links with the networks of arms trafficking and terrorism and, being extremely concerned by the evidence that large sums of money made by selling drugs illegally are being used to finance international terrorism, by taking steps to encourage strong international efforts to stop the destabilising effects of this traffic ;

b. by intensifying the co-operation between the national authorities by improving the exchange of information on the flow of international capital associated with drugs and, more generally, on detecting, freezing and confiscating drug traffickers' financial assets ;

c. by examining, in specific cases, the possibility of stopping and searching vessels suspected of drug trafficking outside territorial waters, without losing sight of the provision of Article 108 of the United Nations Convention on the Law of the Sea which provides that "all states shall co-operate in the suppression of illicit traffic in narcotic drugs and psychotropic substances engaged in by ships on the high seas contrary to international conventions" ;

iii.   To consider urgently ways of countering the wave of glue, solvent and ether inhalation, for example by forbidding the sale of these products to minors without the express permission of their parents, by informing shopkeepers and encouraging them to co-operate with parents and the police ;

B.   *Prevention, treatment and reintegration*

i.   To implement specific measures to achieve the declared objective of Committee of Ministers Recommendation No. R (82) 5 : primary prevention as a priority policy with a view to improved health education so that young people adopt a healthy way of life ;

ii.   To accompany policies to combat such problems as drugs or violence by long-term positive strategies, preparing young people to play a constructive and creative role in democratic society and encouraging the continued cultural development of adults ;

iii.   To consider within this context integrating these problems into the programmes and curricula of educational establishments and community groups, the focus of the information being to make young people aware of their responsibilities for their own well-being, but also the penal consequences resulting from it ;

iv.   To organise training schemes for those in the education, health, social services and legal professions, in order to make these gradually more complementary, a situation which does not at present exist between teachers and families, judges and doctors, police and the social services ;

v.   To pay particular attention to the information that should be given to the general public, in order to change tolerant attitudes towards drugs, and to parents and children in recognising early symptoms of drug abuse ;

vi.   To put more emphasis on the useful role which could be played in combating drug abuse by the mass media ;

vii. To examine the development of therapeutic communities where young people receive help from teams with sufficient training to do an all-round job, encompassing health, psychological and social requirements and capable of listening actively to young people in difficulties, since these latter frequently reject traditional institutions, such as psychiatric centres, for example;

viii. To find a middle way between the extreme positions of compulsory treatment for every young user under 18, on the one hand, and on the other, a method of therapy which relies excessively on voluntary attendance; this new approach might, for example, lie in a suspension or remission of sentence if the user agrees to treatment;

ix. To improve the co-operation among the different authorities of the countries that produce and consume drugs, having in mind that an important amount of psychotropic and somniferous products exported to developing countries produce drug addiction;

15. Recommends that the Committee of Ministers invite the member states who have not already done so to join the "Pompidou Group", and show the political will to transform this Group into a real European centre for co-ordination, selection and implementation of methods of assessment; it could also provide systems of exchanging information, of liaison between researchers and experts, and for the transfer of specialised documentation and publications – in this context it would be necessary to provide a periodical review to be sent to those working in this field;

16. Recommends that the Committee of Ministers invite the governments of the member states to act together in the international organisations which are preparing worldwide programmes, and to ensure that the various measures planned correspond with the general spirit of the North-South dialogue, as, for instance, the proposal concerning the diversification and substitution of farming production from which natural drugs are extracted;

17. Recommends that the Committee of Ministers invite the governments of the member states to implement in full the appropriate recommendations adopted by the Committee of Ministers as listed in Appendix I to this recommendation;

18. Reiterates its recommendation to the Committee of Ministers to invite the governments of the member states who have not already done so to sign and ratify the conventions listed in Appendix II to this recommendation;

19. Recommends that the Committee of Ministers invite the governments of member states to encourage multidisciplinary epidemiologic studies, with the clear purpose of trying to find the relationship, if any, between the different types of drug and psychotrope consumption and sociological studies about distribution of drugs, detecting epidemic zones of great risk for the population, and factors of risk in specific groups of population.

Appendix I to Recommendation 989 (1984)

– Resolution (78) 11 on response of diplomatic and consular services of member states to the problems of their nationals abroad caused by their misuse of drugs;

– Resolution (78) 12 on measures in the field of information and education to be possibly undertaken by member states directed to the problems of young people who travel to areas where drugs are readily available ;

– Recommendation No. R (80) 10 on measures against the transfer and safe-keeping of funds of criminal origin;

– Recommendation No. R (82) 5 concerning the prevention of drug dependence and the special role of education for health;

– Recommendation No. R (82) 6 concerning the treatment and resocialisation of drug dependants.

Appendix II to Recommendation 989 (1984)

a. United Nations Conventions:

    i. Single Convention on Narcotic Drugs of 1961 ;

    ii. Protocol of 1972 modifying this Convention;

    iii. 1971 Convention on psychotropic substances;

b. Council of Europe Conventions:

    i. European Convention on Extradition of 1957 and its Protocols of 1975 and 1978;

    ii. European Convention on Mutual Assistance in Criminal Matters (1959) and its Protocol of 1978 ;

    iii. European Convention of 1970 on International Validity of Criminal Judgments;

    iv. European Convention of 1972 on the Transfer of Proceedings in Criminal Matters;

c. Convention of the Council for Customs Co-operation on mutual administrative assistance for the prevention, investigation and repression of customs offences, so-called Nairobi Convention which came into force in 1980, and in particular Appendix 10 on assistance with regard to the prevention of smuggling narcotics and psychotropic substances.

Recommendation 1153 (1991)[1]
on concerted European policies for health

1.   Health is a prerequisite for quality of life as well as an integral component of the social, economic and cultural development of the individual. Health promotion is an ambitious aim to be pursued by the adoption of common action.

2.   The right of all people to health protection is recognised in the Social Charter of the Council of Europe (Article 11) and many other of that treaty's provisions concern the health of the whole population, such as those on working conditions (Articles 2 and 3), social security benefits (Article 12), social and medical assistance (Article 13) or social protection of elderly persons (Article 4 of the Protocol to the Charter).

3.   Much work has already been done by the Council of Europe on hygiene and health education, health care and meeting the challenges of epidemics, new technologies and living conditions, in accordance with its humanist and ethical principles.

4.   The preamble to the World Health Organisation's Constitution states that "the enjoyment of the highest obtainable standard of health is one of the fundamental rights of every human being"; a great effort of co-ordination has been made between the Council of Europe and the WHO Regional Office for Europe in matters of common interest, and joint activities are undertaken.

5.   Close contacts must be maintained, and harmonised co-operation continued, between the Council of Europe and the World Health Organisation to promote the "health for all" policy adopted at world level by WHO and, in particular, the "European strategy of health for all by the year 2000", adopted at European regional level.

6.   Endorsing the ideas behind this strategy, the Assembly accordingly calls on the governments of Council of Europe member states to ensure that the principles and objectives of the above-mentioned strategy are borne in mind in the preparation and implementation of health policies and legislation. This effort should concentrate more especially on:

   i.   development and improvement of measures, especially primary measures, for the prevention of illness, and substantial reduction of accidents, particularly accidents at work, at home and on the roads;

---

1. *Assembly debate* on 26 April 1991 (8th Sitting) (see Doc. 6403, report of the Social, Health and Family Affairs Committee, Rapporteur: Mrs Helgadottir).
   Text adopted by the Assembly on 26 April 1991 (8th Sitting).

ii. health promotion and education, not least by media awareness campaigns emphasising the impact of lifestyle and behaviour on health and fitness and developing an individual sense of responsibility for one's own health and that of others;

iii. a multisectoral approach to health protection and promotion – for example in the field of nutrition;

iv. quality and effectiveness of health care;

v. equal access to health care, including to new techniques, treatment and products;

vi. development of research in the health field.

7.   The Assembly recommends that the Committee of Ministers draw on this strategy in the Council of Europe's work on concerted European health policies and focus the future activities on:

i.   the close links between health and environment, and the duty of all societies to avoid all kinds of health risks related to the environment and to regulate their activities so that air, water, foodstuffs and workplaces do not endanger the individual's health;

ii. education for health, in schools and in the community as a whole;

iii. *a.* mental health, especially amongst young people;

    b. the need for research on special health problems of old age such as Alzheimer's disease;

    c. improvement of care for the dependent old and chronically ill, with a special concern for the severe lack of nursing staff;

    d. development of palliative medicine and appropriate care of the dying;

    e. active participation in joint efforts at European and international levels to combat Aids;

iv. giving health priority in various sectors of activity, so as to make possible co-ordination of efforts for health promotion;

v.   the issue of healthy housing according to income and family size, and the opportunity of including a right to decent housing among the social rights recognised in the Social Charter of the Council of Europe and its protocol;

vi. continuous efforts to combat effectively addiction to and dependence on drugs, alcohol and tobacco (bearing in mind that heavy tobacco smoking is on the increase amongst women, with accelerating lung cancer), in implementation of the various proposals already made by the Parliamentary Assembly on that subject;

vii. emphasising where necessary vaccinations for infants;

viii. formulating an adequate policy for prescribing medicines and preventing their excessive consumption or abuse;

ix. respecting the principles of the Declaration of Helsinki (revised) on clinical trials involving human subjects.

8.   The Assembly recommends moreover that the Committee of Ministers emphasise the "health" dimension in co-operation with the countries of Central and Eastern Europe. At a time when most of these countries are seeking to restructure their health services, it is urgently necessary to familiarise them with the policies adopted by the member states and with the Council of Europe's guidelines and work on such questions as emergency care, the training of health staff, the prevention of hospital infections, blood transfusion and organ transplants, and to associate them with these activities in a practical and immediate way by arranging courses, seminars and exchanges of experts for their benefit.

Recommendation 1169 (1991)[1]
on education for health and drugs misuse in the member states of the Council of Europe and the European Community

1.   The Assembly continues to be alarmed that drugs misuse remains a major problem for all West European countries and is already affecting the populations of Eastern Europe: estimates of world-wide sales of illegal drugs approach 1,3 thousand million dollars (1 thousand million ecus) per year.

2.   For many years, drug-taking has not been confined to certain vulnerable categories of people, but has spread to all sections of the population, involving more and more age-groups, and is now increasing in sport.

3.   In its Recommendation 1085 (1988) on the fight against drugs, endorsed by the Committee of Ministers, the Assembly advocated a "four-pronged" approach:

i.   to develop better ways to reduce drug production;

ii.   to improve international co-operation to tackle trafficking and allow the seizure of traffickers' assets;

iii.   to undertake urgently more and better action to reduce demand;

iv.   to increase the number and quality of treatment facilities, and to research new treatments and techniques.

4.   Since supply can never be effectively eliminated, drugs education, from an early age onwards, is the best form of prevention and demand reduction.

5.   With this in mind, the Assembly recommended an enhanced role for health education in preventing drug dependency earlier this year; it welcomes the resolution on health educaton in schools of the Council of Ministers of Education of the European Communities (23 November 1988), and the conclusions of the first World Ministerial Summit to Reduce Demand for Drugs (9-11 April 1990).

6.   Although all member countries are devoting increasing attention to preventive education as the best means of reducing demand for illegal drugs, education for health – including education about drugs misuse – still requires a higher priority and must be taught in schools in an overall, structured framework as part of the core school curriculum.

---

1. *Assembly debate* on 25 September 1991 (18th Sitting) (see Doc. 6472, report of the Social, Health and Family Affairs Committee, Rapporteur: Mr Rathbone).
   Text adopted by the Assembly on 25 September 1991 (18th Sitting).

7. Although common principles on health education can be agreed at European level, there must be room for adaptation to prevailing cultural and social circumstances. But national and international exchange of information on successful health educaton programmes can assist development of the most effective policies in drugs educaton and prevention programmes everywhere.

8. The proper way to position education for health courses is to integrate them within a multidisciplinary approach to social and health problems, encouraging students to recognise the benefits of a generally healthy and drug-free life style, including sport and other active recreational activities.

9. Education for health at an early age is essential. Before drug habits become a temptation or take root, children must experience preventive health educaton at both primary and secondary educational levels, especially in high-risk environments.

10. Education for health should not stop at school. Employers should take responsibility for informing employees about the adverse effects of legal and illegal drugs at home and at work; they should provide counselling for misusers, in particular in professions where safety is a key factor.

11. Opportunities should be provided for "re-education", training or retraining of former addicts to allow them to take up jobs rather than re-enter the drug misuse culture.

12. Training information and health education initiatives against the use of drugs in sport should be increased and particularly directed at trainers and doctors working with sportsmen.

13. Accordingly, the Assembly recommends that the Committee of Ministers:

    i. reaffirm that education for health is the most crucial element in reducing demand for drugs;

    ii. recognise the importance of devoting more money and resources to local, national and international programmes of education for health and drug misuse prevention, particularly among young people and in the world of sport;

    iii. recognise the important role that voluntary and non-governmental organisations have in initiating methods and materials for educaton for health in local communities;

    iv. urge all member governments immediately to enlarge and improve their education for health programmes, the drug misuse prevention content of them and the funding support given to them;

    v. progress as fast as possible with a comprehensive survey of good health educational practices and policies in all member countries, so that best practice at local and regional levels can be shared and acted upon;

    vi. promote further European pilot projects on drugs education within programmes of education for health in schools, among parents, professionals and voluntary organisations, and in the workplace;

vii. establish and support a means of systematic exchange of information between all member countries and those with special guest status, with a view to establishing and maintaining the most comprehensive and effective national and international strategies on education for health;

viii. encourage the highest possible level of co-ordination between public and private services, education establishments and voluntary groups;

ix. urgently seek better ways of financing a European investment fund for drugs education programmes in co-ordination with the Council of Ministers and the Commission of the European Communities;

x. ensure that all member states take action to implement the resolution on the role of education in the fight against drugs of the Council of Ministers of Education of the European Communities (3 December 1990), the resolution on reducing the demand for narcotic and psychotropic substances of the Council of Ministers of Health of the European Communities (29 November 1990), other relevant resolutions of the European Community and the Council of Europe, and the conclusions of the first World Ministerial Summit to Reduce Demand for Drugs (9-11 April 1990).

14. Furthermore, the Assembly requests the Committee of Ministers to report on actions taken to meet these recommendations, during the Assembly's 44th Session in 1992.

Committee of Ministers

Resolution AP (72) 3
on the rehabilitation of children suffering
from dysmelic syndromes

*(Adopted by the Committee of Ministers on 19 April 1972
at the 209th meeting of the Ministers' Deputies)*

The representatives on the Committee of Ministers of Belgium, France, the Federal Republic of Germany, Italy, Luxembourg, the Netherlands and the United Kingdom of Great Britain and Northern Ireland, whose governments are parties to the Partial Agreement in the social and public health field, and the Representative of Austria, whose government has participated in the activities of the Joint Committee on the Rehabilitation and Resettlement of the Disabled of the above-mentioned Partial Agreement since 11 September 1962,

1.   Having regard to the recommendation on the rehabilitation of children suffering from dysmelic syndromes, adopted by the Joint Committee on the Rehabilitation and Resettlement of the Disabled on 4 December 1971 ;

2.   Considering that, under the terms of its Statute, the aim of the Council of Europe is to achieve a greater unity between its members for the purpose of safeguarding and realising the ideals and principles which are their common heritage and facilitating their economic and social progress ;

3.   Having regard to the provisions of the Brussels Treaty signed on 17 March 1948 by virtue of which Belgium, France, Luxembourg, the Netherlands and the United Kingdom of Great Britain and Northern Ireland declared themselves resolved to strengthen the social ties by which they are already united ;

4.   Having regard to the Protocol modifying and completing the Brussels Treaty, signed on 23 October 1954 by the signatory states of the Brussels Treaty, on the one hand, and the Federal Republic of Germany and Italy, on the other hand ;

5.   Observing that the seven governments parties to the Partial Agreement, which have resumed, within the Council of Europe, the social work hitherto undertaken by the Brussels Treaty Organisation and then by Western European Union (which derived from the Brussels Treaty as modified by the Protocol mentioned at paragraph 4 above), as well as the Government of Austria, which participates in the activities of the Joint Committee on the Rehabilitation and Resettlement of the Disabled, have always endeavoured to be in the forefront of progress in social matters and also in the associated field of public health and have for many years undertaken action towards harmonisation of their legislation ;

6. Considering that the wave of dysmelia observed between 1958 and 1962 cannot be described as an exceptional catastrophe but rather as an occurrence likely to be provoked at any time in a similar form by a teratogenic agent;

7. Considering that the number of potential teratogenic substances is tending to increase;

8. Considering that prompt information at international level about any proliferation of malformations of the same type may promote identification and, if possible, elimination of the substance,

Recommend that the seven governments parties to the Partial Agreement and the Government of Austria take all necessary measures with a view to:

1. early detection, through national records, of a proliferation of certain kinds of malformation, the determination of their origin and the speediest possible elimination of the substance causing them;

2. in the event of a proliferation of malformations, preventing as far as possible, by means of an international exchange of statistical data and speedy international action at European level, other teratogenic lesions from occurring;

3. informing the public, more widely than in the past, of the dangers of the uncontrolled ingestion of drugs, particularly during pregnancy;

4. combating drug abuse generally;

5. ensuring the maximum safety of drugs by means of legislation and state control of its application;

6. providing pregnant women with the best possible medical care;

7. promoting teratological research;

8. quickly setting up, for the optimum rehabilitation of persons suffering from congenital malformations of a given type, specialised treatment centres providing in addition to medical treatment and technical aids, psychological assistance to parents and later to the growing child;

9. ensuring that the medical, scholastic, occupational and social rehabilitation of children suffering from congenital malformations form a coherent process.

Resolution (73) 1
on the social services for
physically or mentally handicapped persons

(Adopted by the Committee of Ministers on 19 January 1973
at the 217th meeting of the Ministers' Deputies)

The Committee of Ministers,

Considering that the aim of the Council of Europe is to achieve a greater unity between its members for the purpose among others, of facilitating their social progress,

Guided by the principles contained in the European Social Charter, and in particular Article 15 thereof, which deals with the right of physically or mentally handicapped persons to vocational training, rehabilitation and social resettlement;

Recalling that the treatment, rehabilitation and social resettlement of physically or mentally handicapped persons is of the utmost importance in furthering both the well-being of the individual and the interests of society;

Noting that there has been a growing understanding in the member states of the Council of Europe of the importance of promoting measures for medical and vocational rehabilitation;

Having taken note of the study on the social resettlement of physically or mentally handicapped persons published by the Council of Europe;

Having considered the work of the Joint Committee for the Rehabilitation and Resettlement of the Disabled (Partial Agreement),

I.   Recommends the governments of members states to take into account the following principles when framing their general policy towards the handicapped, this term meaning persons who for physical or mental reasons encounter difficulties in their daily life and/or are in need of special action in respect of education, training, employment, standard of living or social adaptation;

A.   General policy with regard to the handicapped

1.   The general objective of this policy should be to give handicapped persons every opportunity to be as much integrated as possible into society. Whatever the cause, type and degree of their handicap may be, the handicapped should be given all opportunities for their personal development and for maximum participation in the activities of the community.

2. Public authorities should ensure that the general policy is carried into effect and in particular that:

a. laws and regulations are formulated, and subsequently adapted to take account of scientific and technical progress in relation to the handicapped;

b. all action for the handicapped is encouraged, co-ordinated and planned so as to fulfil the aims of the general policy and to avoid overlapping;

c. funds are available for performing, promoting or supporting public or private activities for the benefit of the handicapped;

d. necessary supervision and control are exercised regarding bodies running services for the handicapped;

e. statistics, especially those concerning the current needs and existing facilities, are compiled at the national level and considered as a necessary basis for the development of action for the handicapped;

f. foundations and bodies are encouraged to adapt their activities and working methods to modern needs and knowledge and that new services are set up where this is deemed necessary;

g. there is close co-operation between public bodies, organisations of handicapped persons and organisations of parents of such persons and other interested organisations.

3. Efforts should be made in order to ensure that:

a. public services and general social services are instituted and developed with due consideration of the needs of the handicapped;

b. these services may be modified or supplemented whenever this is deemed appropriate;

c. special social services are established and measures taken for the benefit of the handicapped whenever necessary.

4. Action should be taken to ensure that the population is made fully aware of the problems of the handicapped with a view, amongst other things, to combating any prejudice.

Special attention should be paid to the following:

a. all mass media of communication, should – as far as compatible with principles generally accepted in member states – be utilised in information campaigns. Such campaigns should be concentrated more on the understanding of the problems of the handicapped than on appeal for generosity;

b. all activities likely to bring the handicapped into closer contact with the social environment should be promoted;

c. measures should be taken in order to create a climate favourable to the employment of handicapped persons particularly among employers and workers and their organisations;

d. handicapped persons and their families should be given full and accurate information on their rights and proper guidance on the services to which they can apply and the benefits to which they are entitled;

e. the staff of all public and private bodies dealing with handicapped persons, including, *inter alia*, social workers, medical, pedagogical and other professional groups, should be well informed of the special problems of handicapped persons.

B. Social services and measures for the handicapped

a. *General principles*

1. Measures should be taken to ensure the prevention, early identification and treatment of handicaps.

For this purpose, schemes for medical examinations of pregnant women, pre-school and school children and health visiting and other means should be provided and those concerned encouraged to make use of them.

Persons who in the course of their duties come into contact with problem cases should be encouraged to facilitate contacts between such persons and the services able to give them assistance.

2. Full attention should be given to the advantages of establishing close co-operation between doctors, psychologists, social workers, specialists in vocational guidance, technicians and other professional groups on a team work basis. The work of all professional groups involved should be co-ordinated so as to treat the case as a whole.

3. Medical treatment and rehabilitation measures should be co-ordinated and continuous.

4. Special attention should be paid to the particular needs of multihandicapped persons with regard to education and rehabilitation.

5. As a general rule, measures should be taken to enable handicapped persons to stay within their own social environment and, particularly, to live in their family circle. In cases where a placement in an institution is necessary, it should be ensured that close links are maintained with the family.

6. The process of rehabilitation should be based on full co-operation between the relevant service or body and the handicapped person and his family who should be well informed and be in full agreement with any steps planned.

7. Adequate special and further training should be given to all categories of staff – medical, pedagogical, social, technical etc. – called upon to take part in the process of rehabilitation; this training should include such broad knowledge as to enable a multidisciplinary approach to rehabilitation.

These staff should enjoy appropriate career opportunities and adequate remuneration.

8. Research into the causes of handicaps and research likely to bring about improvements in the techniques and methods used in this field should be undertaken both at a national level and by international co-operation.

b. *Services and measures*

1.   When a handicap is detected in a child the parents should be offered proper guidance and financial or other support with regard to the best possible treatment, care and education of the child. To this end home-help and other supportive services should be organised and parents should be offered the possibility of having the child admitted to an ordinary or special kindergarten or nursery school or similar facilities according to the individual need of the child.

2.   Priority should be given to the integration of handicapped children of pre-school and school age into the normal education system, but due attention should be paid to the importance of giving the child that placement within education systems which fulfils his individual needs at any time. Education in specialised schools or institutions should be resorted to if the ordinary education facilities cannot be adapted so as to meet the needs of the pupil in the best possible way.

3.   It should be ensured that educational programmes and medical and/or other therapy are combined where necessary.

4.   Vocational guidance services should be provided for both young and adult handicapped persons to help them to solve the problems related to the choice of a profession, account being taken of their interests, aptitudes, qualifications, their handicap and the labour market possibilities; this choice should never be regarded as final.

5.   Every effort should be made to integrate the handicapped into normal vocational training systems, including access to higher education, and to adapt the normal training systems to the special needs of the handicapped where necessary, this being done in close co-operation between the authorities responsible for normal training and those responsible for the special problems of handicapped persons.

If the existing facilities cannot be adapted so as to meet the special needs of certain handicapped in the best possible way, recourse should be made to special vocational training systems.

6.   Where the existing employment services do not meet the needs of the handicapped, it would be advisable either to call upon special placement officers or to set up commissions of specialists able to give advice on the most appropriate type of work.

7.   Particular arrangements should be made for giving support when the handicapped person has need for tools or other special equipment in his work.

8.   Financial measure, including measures in the field of taxation, should be taken to ensure that, in appropriate cases, sufficient support is given for enabling handicapped persons to become self-employed.

9.   It would be desirable for adequate opportunities for sheltered employment to be offered to those handicapped persons, who, by reason of the

type or the degree of their handicap, are unable, either for a long time or permanently, to work in the normal conditions of open employment.

Equally, to the extent that national conditions so require, public and private enterprises which have posts capable of being filled by persons suffering from a physical (or mental) handicap or disability should be encouraged to reserve a certain quota of jobs for handicapped workers.

10. During the rehabilitation period subsistence expenses should be sufficiently covered and special expenses arising from the handicap should be met.

All financial support given to the handicapped and his family during the rehabilitation process should be closely co-ordinated.

11. Attention should be paid to the problems of handicapped persons who are not able to take up employment but have attained or could attain a certain autonomy in their daily lives.

Special measure should be taken such as the establishment of day centres, in which the handicapped would be helped to take up various activities and through which the mentally handicapped who are not able to take up employment could have the opportunity of continuing stimulation, education and occupation, in order to make use of and develop their faculties. These special measures should also include the provisions of services intended to assist the handicapped in their own homes.

The handicapped person should be helped to lead an independent life by means of the provision of special services, such as home-help or "meals on wheels". It would be desirable to give handicapped persons living with their families the opportunity of staying in special short-stay homes, thus considerably relieving the family of its burden.

12. Measures should be adopted to ensure that structural barriers are removed as far as possible so as to enable handicapped persons to have easy access to public buildings, transport etc.

Technical and other aids required by the handicapped in their daily lives should be made available to them free of charge or at a low cost. Special attention should be paid to the needs of those handicapped who cannot avail themselves of public transport.

13. Particular efforts should be made as regards housing facilities offered to handicapped persons.

Preference should be given to housing them within the normal housing intended for the general population; where such accommodation is intended for the handicapped it should be especially adapted as necessary.

Accommodation such as hostels and similar facilities in which the handicapped persons could lead more independent lives than in institutions should be provided when appropriate.

Accommodation in institutions should only be resorted to if it is not possible for the handicapped to live in ordinary conditions; generally smaller institutions should be preferred to larger ones as long as they offer satisfactory staff and facilities.

14. The organisations interested in cultural activities, sport and leisure should be encouraged to take the particular needs of handicapped persons into account and to take steps to enable them to participate in these activities.

II. Invites the governments of member states to inform the Secretary General of the Council of Europe every five years of the action taken by them on this resolution.

Resolution (74) 6
on methods for improving dental health

(Adopted by the Committee of Ministers on 27 February 1974, at the 229th meeting of the Ministers' Deputies)

The Committee of Ministers,

Considering that the aim of the Council of Europe is to achieve a greater unity between its members and that this aim may be pursued, *inter alia*, by the adoption of common rules in the social field and, in particular, in the public health field;

Noting that the World Health Organisation defines health as "a state of complete physical, mental and social well-being" and aims at the attainment by all people of the highest possible level of health;

Considering that dental health is essential for the achievement of such a state of health;

Noting that dental disease is among the most widespread diseases in all age groups;

Considering that they now represent serious and costly burdens for the community and often a considerable physical, social and psychological handicap to the individual;

Considering that in most member states it is impossible to meet the dental health needs fully, owing to the high incidence of dental disease causing a shortage of dental personnel;

Considering that most people are not well informed about the effects of dental disease and of the possibilities of combating it by means of preventive measures;

Considering that organised preventive measures including the use of fluorides reduce the disease rate considerably and consequently reduce the cost of restorative dentistry,

I.   Recommends to governments of members states that they take into consideration the principles set out in Appendix A and take account in their laws and regulations of the recommendations enunciated in Appendix B to this resolution;

II.   Invites the governments of member states to inform the Secretary General of the Council of Europe every five years of the action taken by them in pursuance to this resolution.

Appendix A to Resolution (74) 6

General principles

1.   Dental caries and periodontal disease are among the most prevalent human diseases.

2.   Both diseases are in principle preventable entities, but unless preventive measures are planned and organised, they will have little impact on present incidence of the two diseases.

The bacterial factor

3.   Dental caries and periodontal disease have one decisive causative factor in common, i.e. the bacterial accumulations on the teeth and the gums, or the dental plaque.

The substrate factor (diet)

4.1. In dental caries the plaque bacteria act on carbohydrates producing acids, sucrose being the most important cariogenic sugar.

4.2. Periodontal disease is a destruction of the tooth supporting (periodontal) tissues caused primarily by the bacterial activity of the dental plaque, without the necessary mediation of sugar degradation and acid formation. Here the substrate factor is thus of minor significance in comparison with the bacterial factor.

4.3. Sucrose restriction in food is the most important preventive measure against dental caries. The excessive intake of cariogenic sugars and particularly the consumption of sweet products between meals is especially harmful.

Oral hygiene

5.   Oral hygiene procedures aim primarily at elimination of the bacterial factor. Rational and systematic cleaning of the teeth, immediately after meals, has the potential power to reduce incidence of caries and periodontal diseases to a large extent. Unfortunately these fundamental principles of oral hygiene are not regularly put into practice by the public and this accounts for the high rate of caries and for most of the periodontal diseases.

The host resistance factor

6.1. There are well-founded methods to improve tooth resistance to dental caries. No effective measures are known to improve the host resistance to periodontal disease.

6.2. Host resistance to dental caries is markedly increased by incorporation of fluoride into the tooth. The most effective preventive measure in regard to dental hygiene is without any doubt the fluoridation of drinking water. Nevertheless, when this cannot be put into practice, alternative measures exist.

Appendix B to Resolution (74) 6

A. Preventive measures against caries and periodontal diseases

With the view to promoting progress in dental health in the member states of the Council of Europe, the following recommendations should be given the fullest effect possible.

1.   In order to improve oral hygiene in a population the following measures should be taken:

   a.   Information to the public on the role and the importance of oral hygiene in dental health preservation and the consequences of neglect;

   b.   Teaching and dissemination of various oral hygiene methods to all individuals and repetition of this lesson as often as is judged necessary and practicable;

   c.   Teaching of self-evaluation procedures of oral hygiene (disclosing methods);

   d.   Orthodentic treatment in cases of malaligned teeth in order to eliminate retention of food articles, and to facilitate cleaning of teeth;

   e.   Regular dental inspections for early detection and treatment of dental caries, during which oral hygiene instruction should be renewed;

   f.   The reduction of taxes on oral hygiene products in order to make them available to the population as a whole;

   g.   The increase in dental manpower working in the field of dental health education.

2.   In order to fight against the harmful effects of sugars the following measures are recommended:

   a.   information to the public on the role and the importance for dental health of a correct and varied diet in view of the fact that such a diet tends to reduce the harmful effects of dental plaque. Stress should be placed on the consequences of bad eating habits;

   b.   prohibition of sale and consumption of confectionery products and sweet beverages containing cariogenic sugars in schools;

   c.   while ensuring a balanced diet in terms of glucides, limitation of the excessive consumption, especially by children, of sweets and confectionery products containing cariogenic sugars, by regulating as far as possible advertisements in favour of such products particularly in places frequented by children and adolescents and by considering the possibility of increasing taxation on such products;

   d.   encouragement of publicity regarding alternatives to sweet products as between-meal snacks.

3.   For the increase of host resistance the most effective preventive measure is without any doubt the fluoridation of drinking water. At present and on the basis of variations in water consumption according to ecological conditions, in particular the temperature, the recommended fluoride content of drinking water in temperate climates is about 1mg/litre. If this is not possible the following alternative or additional measures are recommended in order to increase host resistance:

   a.   fluoridation of kitchen salt;

   b.   regular supervised administration of fluoride in the form of tablets; the dosage should be adjusted to the quantity of fluoride intake from water and food and to the age of the individual;

   c.   mouth rinsings, tooth brushings, and topical applications with fluoride-containing solutions;

   d.   daily use of effective fluoride toothpaste.

Current preventive research

4.   Use of antimicrobial agents, enzymes, fissure sealants, phosphates and vaccines are being studied but it is not yet possible to pronounce on the effectiveness of such solutions.

B. Dental health education

5.   In order to improve the health of the public, it is necessary to obtain their enlightened co-operation. For this it is recommended:

a. to make extensive and regular use of the various oral, written, visual and audio-visual means of communication, particularly television, through the medium of appropriately designed programmes;

b. to give special attention to high-risk groups in the following priority order through arranging for:

    i.   the training of practitioners in preventive dentistry by:

       – introducing a sufficient number of hours of instruction on dental health education and prophylaxy in dental and in medical school curricula;

       – associating future practitioners, during their training, in epidemiological surveys and educational projects concerning dental health;

    ii.   the training of dental auxiliaries capable of assisting dental practitioners efficiently as well as other health personnel in the field of prevention;

    iii.   the supplying of free educational material to expectant mothers during a dental check-up which should be made during pregnancy;

    iv.   the provision of adequate information on dental health problems to mothers of pre-school children;

    v.   the provision of information on dental health problems to teachers and educators in order to enlist their co-operation;

    vi.   instruction in dental health to be included in school curricula;

    vii.   a dental inspection at least once a year, for children of pre-school and school age;

    viii. the impression upon the public of the fundamental importance of regular dental inspection and early treatment, the only way of preventing the spread of dental diseases and detecting serious disorders at an early stage.

6.   The following guidelines for a school dental education programme are recommended:

a.   Children of pre-school age, i.e. children in nursery schools: initiation in the problems of dental health by means of stories, games and pictures;

b.   Primary school children: lessons in health education specifically centred on dental problems comprising elementary knowledge of:

    i.   the two sets of teeth and their arrangement (number, shape, names);

    ii.   the part played by teeth in mastication, phonation and physical appearance;

    iii.   the salient characteristics of the main diseases which can threaten teeth;

    iv. the importance of dental hygiene for the preservation of dental health.

At this initiation stage, the role of the teachers is of primary importance.

c.   Secondary school children:

    i.   more detailed recapitulation of the elementary knowledge described above, as part of general health education; this instruction may be provided by non-specialist teachers;

    ii.   more thorough study of the main dental diseases with special reference to the action of dental plaque, to periodontal diseases, the development of dental caries and resultant complications, and the importance of correcting irregularities in dental occlusion;

iii. practical demonstrations of oral hygiene including toothbrushing and methods of control by the individual should be given at this stage of education;

iv. the notions of prevention through regular dental inspections and prophylaxy by means of fluoride should be further developed. Attention should be drawn to the importance of food hygiene as well as the part played by carbohydrates.

d. Post-compulsory secondary stage: at this stage, after a brief recapitulation of the previous instruction given, emphasis should be placed on the role of dental health in social relations (from the aesthetic point of view and as a factor in success). At this stage the notion of dental restoration should be introduced (advantages and disadvantages) and the economic aspects.

e. For a rational implementation of all these measures it is recommended:

i. to create special tooth brushing facilities within each school group;

ii. to create special mobile units for the use by all schools for the screening of dental diseases;

iii. to create dental offices within the larger school groups.

C. Priorities in the selection of high-risk groups

7. It should be recognised that the effect of most preventive measures becomes obvious only after a long period and that, in the meantime, therapeutic measures must be available.

8. When preventive measures are introduced it should be borne in mind that children and adolescents derive the greatest benefit from such measures and should consequently be considered as priority groups.

D. Utilisation of dental personnel

9. In view of the shortage of dental personnel and the unmet need and increased demand for dental care, it would be desirable:

a. to make the most efficient use of the dentist's training and skill by the use of adequate assistance and especially delegation of simpler work to auxiliaries in conformity with the regulations of the member states;

b. to encourage the training and use of such assistants by the creation or the increase of the number of training schools for such staff. Among dental auxiliaries, qualified dental hygienists having been employed successfully in the field of prevention, consideration should be given to increasing facilities for their training and employment especially in case of short-age of dental practitioners.

10. Dental health education being an important function and the responsibility of the whole dental team, it should be ensured that the dentist is its central member.

E. Provisions concerning preventive measures under health schemes, insurance-based or otherwise

11. Taking into account the advantages offered by preventive measures over restorative treatment in relation to general health, it is recommended that the provision of preventive measures by members of the dental team be included under health schemes, insurance-based or otherwise.

F. Epidemiological surveys and research

12. Improvement of the dental health of the population of member states calls for:

a. More research of the following types:

229

i. epidemiological:

– to map systematically and methodically, adopting internationally recognised terminology and standardised statistical methods, the geographical prevalence of caries, periodontal and dental disorders in general at national and international level:

– to promote more studies of the dietary habits of the population;

ii. research into the available manpower, equipment and funds;

b. More evaluations to be used as a basis for drawing up programmes whose efficacity and suitability would be reviewed at regular intervals;

c. More information on research and evaluations for the health services, professional associations, dental personnel and the general public in order to foster a greater sense of responsibility about health questions;

d. More comparisons of national and international results and needs, and better co-ordination of effort among countries, the authorities, the services and bodies responsible and the general public.

Resolution (76) 6
containing recommendations to governments
on prevention of accidents in childhood

(Adopted by the Committee of Ministers on 18 February 1976 at the 254th meeting of the Ministers' Deputies)

The Committee of Ministers,

Considering that the aim of the Council of Europe is to achieve a greater unity between its members and that this aim may be pursued, *inter alia*, by the adoption of common action in the social and public health fields;

Expressing considerable concern at the lack of noticeable changes in member states concerning the situation of accidents in childhood since the study undertaken in the framework of the 1970 co-ordinated medical research programme;

Considering that accidents in childhood still present considerable public health problems;

Considering that these accidents represent unnecessary costly burdens for the community and often a considerable physical, social and psychological handicap to the child and its family;

Considering the need for continuous action in the field of prevention of accidents in childhood on local, regional, national and international levels,

I.   Recommends governments of member states to implement as fully as possible the measures enumerated in Appendix A and to make use, when introducing these measures, of the model given in Appendix B;

II.   Invites the governments of member states to inform the Secretary General of the Council of Europe every five years of the action taken by them in respect of the present resolution.

Appendix A to Resolution (76) 6

With a view to promoting child safety in member states of the Council of Europe, the following measures should be taken:

I.   *Organisation*

1.   The possibility should be examined of setting up a national body (whether governmental or non-governmental) which might assume responsibility for, e.g.:

– problem analysis,
– policy decision,
– guidelines formulation.

2.   Such a national body should develop effective means of communication with local organisations (governmental or non-governmental) who could be responsible for, e.g.:

– collection of information,
– programme development,
– co-ordination of programme implementation,
– research.

3.   If a non-governmental body has been encouraged to serve as the agent of the government for this purpose, then means should be placed at its disposal to render it effective.

II.   *Study and research*

1.   Research related to child safety should be problem orientated or service orientated.

2.   It should be concerned not only with mortality but also rather with child accidents morbidity in respect of:

– different age groups,
– different locations,
– different agents.

3.   It should be developed to identify the consequences of injury in terms of long-term and permanent disability.

4.   It should be carried out to indicate cost effectiveness of child safety programmes.

5.   Such research should use modern epidemiological methods to ensure that ecological circumstances are taken into account.

III.   *Education and training*

1.   Health education should stress the importance of safety and to this end should emphasise the need for the training of the child, the parent and the teacher and also ensure the active participation in safety behaviour of the child at all ages.

Such programmes of education should constantly be related to psycho-motor development of the child because of the different risks faces by each age group.

2.   The responsibilities of doctors and nurses and other health personnel in the promotion of child safety should be clearly recognised and this fact should be incorporated into their training.

3.   School curricula should be designed in such a way to include appropriate instruction and practice throughout the school age in safety measures and life-saving procedures.

4.   Training measures which are developed to encourage the protection of the child should recognise the importance of active community participation in the implementation of programmes for child safety.

IV.   *Legislation and standardisation*

1.   Regulations should be constantly reviewed and developed. They should be related to changing patterns of life and to information derived from research and studies.

2.   A standard institution should be designated in each country with the means to assess the design and safety aspects of manufactured articles, indoors and outdoors environment, and to keep these standards under close review and to keep close contact in this respect with industry.

3.   Whenever possible these national standards should receive international acceptability.

V.   *Information services*

1.   Governments should give the widest possible distribution to all instances concerned with child safety of both the report prepared by the 1970 co-ordinated medical research team and the present resolution.

2.   Governments should indicate in addition to whom they would like the Council of Europe to distribute these publications.

Appendix B to Resolution (76) 6
Plan for a national programme of child safety

Model
The promotion of child safety
Model child accident prevention scheme

   Statistics

        Any national plan designed to prevent accidents must, to be successful, be based on accurate information regarding the causes, the incidence and the results of accidents. Statistical information relating to child accidents and their different causes must be continually available. It is probably practicable on a national scale only to consider mortality figures but these alone will indicate the size of the problem and, if publicised in an understandable form, will attract public awareness to avoidable childhood tragedies and risks which need not happen and could with thought and care so often be prevented. It is also desirable to plan local surveys in different parts of the country where, as well as the mortality figures which will already be known, valuable information will be obtained regarding the vulnerability of children to accidents and to the differing risks which they face. This combination of national mortality figures associated with local morbidity studies will provide a wealth of material upon which an effective plan of prevention can be based. Doctors will play a leading part in the accurate preparation of such data, for they see the victims of these accidents, and the validity of the information will depend greatly on their accurate reporting. It is then necessary, through the popular media of communication such as the radio and the press, to keep the public informed about such accidents so that they cannot claim ignorance of existing dangers and thus will be sympathetic to measures which are taken to reduce them.

Organisation

Government naturally has a leading role to play; however, it is important that government activity in accident prevention be co-ordinated. In some cases it may be appropriate for a single government department to be concerned; in others an inter-departmental co-ordinating committee may meet the need. It should be responsible for the collation of information and its distribution, the promotion of legislation, and the stimulation of action by local and regional authorities and by voluntary organisations. It would need to recognise that alone it would achieve little, but that indirectly through the agency of local statutory and voluntary authorities, and with the aid of national propaganda, it could make a substantial impact. At national level it will best achieve this result by establishing a committee widely representative of organisations which are involved.

Co-ordination

Local "weeks" devoted to accident prevention with exhibitions and talks in public meeting places and in schools and clinics can prove highly rewarding; an imaginatively prepared exhibition with an adequacy of simple colourful information, together with practical talks, can well excite more interest and response than the impersonal poster or the national radio programme. Such "weeks", perhaps at yearly intervals, could be devoted to different forms of childhood accident and their prevention.

This continuing local activity in the interests of promoting child safety will require the active support of local organisations and individuals and can best be created and maintained by the establishment of local representative committees who would work under the guidance of and in association with the local health authorities. The latter will turn for advice to their medical officers of health who rightly regard child safety as an important part of child health, but others should be equally involved. The architect, too, has responsibility to see that safe homes are designed for the protection as well as the comfort of their occupants. Then again the town planning officer has a duty to ensure that the environment which he is creating recognises the need for road safety, and has play spaces which are easily accessible, provide scope for adventure and are yet safe. Industry, too, has a concern with child safety, for management should recognise that its employees will be more effective and more contented in the knowledge that their children are being safely cared for during their time at work in the factory or the office.

Research

Local surveys of accident morbidity, which will need the co-operation of doctors and hospitals, will attract considerable local interest and will form the basis upon which local research can be conducted; research not only into the incidence of accidents and their causes but also into the effectiveness of the various forms of accident prevention which are practised. Research which enables an evaluation of methods of accident prevention is all-important; there is a tendency to believe that continuous propaganda on orthodox and traditional lines will achieve the best results, but it may well prove that the public becomes no longer receptive to such measures and that new, as yet untried, approaches will for a time prove far more rewarding. The other advantage of such local studies and research is that it will involve local people who may well prove more influential and effective than remote central departments and agencies; studies have shown that a locally based education programme of accident prevention, if maintained, can be highly successful. Local surveys should however be undertaken on a planned and co-ordinated basis in order to ensure that the results are nationally representative.

Legislation and standards

With advances in scientific knowledge, life for the individual and the family becomes more sophisticated and in some respects more dangerous; equipment in the home becomes more complicated and elaborate and road traffic becomes more congested and at the same time often travels at greater speeds. There is a limit to what goodwill and exhortation can achieve, and an appliance, even a child's toy, may prove to be so dangerous that to prevent further manufacture or to render it safe legislation may prove necessary; in the same way the speed of vehicles in heavily populated areas may need to be controlled by law more strictly. Many examples are to be found in different countries of necessary legislation which has proved to be effective, e.g. poisons control, but it should only be considered when all other measures have failed. The writing of "standards" for articles, appliances and building materials is now the accepted practice in many countries and some, e.g. colour of electric wiring, are internationally agreed. Legislation, if necessary, can sometimes be based on such standards.

Education and training

Finally, one comes to probably the most important form of accident prevention – education. It is not always clearly appreciated that the small child of pre-school age is rarely aware of the dangers that exist in and around his home and the importance of adequate supervision cannot be over-stressed. This is essentially the responsibility of the parents, who themselves may sometimes be ignorant of some of the risks, for it is equally important for them to teach the child about these hazards and at the same time to protect him as far as it is humanly possible from those which he cannot avoid unaided.

The child watches the adult and tends to learn from such experience, but the adult is not always the best teacher. The educational curriculum should include instruction in accident prevention and life saving since this is an important part of the process of growing to maturity – not always recognised. Teachers themselves need to be persuaded of the merit of this and should be able confidently to give instruction in this; for this purpose it needs to form part of their training and to be included in their own curriculum. There is no advantage in delaying this aspect of child education until a certain age is reached because, generally speaking, the earlier the age at which such instruction begins the more likely it is for the knowledge to be retained – and this feature of the educational system should continue throughout the school-days. Education does not stop there, because continuing health education should form a valuable part of every country's governmental programme and should be an important feature of the work of doctors, nurses and health visitors whether with individual patients or in their work in clinics and hospitals. The medical officer of health has an essential role. There is nevertheless a limit to the effect which they can achieve, and the assistance of the various means of dissemination of information on a large scale, such as the newspapers or the radio or television, should be sought. It is tempting to imagine that the public in any country can benefit from a mass of detailed instruction presented in the shortest possible time, but experience suggests that for most people one feature concerned with one aspect of child safety at a time, presented in the simplest terms, is more likely to be understood, learnt and retained. Health education, for its greatest success, requires the advice and experience of the medical officer of health, the teacher, the epidemiologist and the expert in ways of communication.

As the control of disease becomes firmer, as surgical skills become more far-reaching, as anaesthetics become more sophisticated and drugs more precise in their action, so accidents loom larger as a leading cause of death and disability. It thus becomes vitally necessary to develop and employ the most effective means of preventing them. Similar types of accident affect all age groups and thus similar means of protection can be equally successful, but too often children are the victims because of lack of supervision, training or sheer unawareness of the risks which they face. The government, the manufacturer, the parent, the teacher and the statutory authorities all bear a responsibility.

Resolution (78) 12
on measures in the field of information and education to be possibly undertaken by member states directed to the problems of young people who travel to areas where drugs are readily available[1]

*(Adopted by the Committee of Ministers on 3 March 1978
of the 284th meeting of the Ministers' Deputies)*

The Committee of Ministers,

Considering that the aim of the Council of Europe is to achieve greater unity between its members and that this aim can be pursued, *inter alia*, by the adoption of common action in the field of public health;

Considering that the misuse of, and illicit traffic in dependence-producing drugs constitutes a grave threat to both public health and to the mental and physical health of individuals affected;

Noting that certain young people who travel to areas where drugs, both natural and synthetic, are readily available may fall into the habit of drug abuse, or be introduced to new drugs or begin to traffic illicitly in dependence-producing drugs;

Noting that these developments pose particularly serious threats to the individuals concerned and to the communities to which they return;

Considering that action is necessary to provide greater assistance to young people who may be affected in this way;

Considering that epidemiological and clinical data on all aspects of the problem are needed, and that the results of the latest research into methods of treatment and prevention are not always sufficiently widely known to those with responsibilities in this field;

Considering that education in the problems caused by dependence-producing drugs has been found to be most effective when included in a broad framework of mental and physical health and social welfare;

Considering that the measures contemplated should not affect the right of everyone to leave the territory of the state of which he is a national and to return to it,

---

1. When this resolution was adopted, the Representative of Ireland acting in accordance with Article 10.2.c of the Rules of Procedure for the meetings of the Ministers' Deputies, reserved the right of his government to comply with it or not.

I.   Recommends that member governments:

1. adopt measures to enable them to keep themselves regularly informed on the regions where travellers are specially exposed to all the problems associated with dependence-producing drugs and of the character of those problems in each region;

2. consider how information about the special consequences that might arise from drug abuse or drug trafficking during travel to these regions can best be included in those parts of the syllabus of education of young people which deal with drugs and drug problems when there is a need for it;

3. encourage youth organisations and other interested voluntary organisations to include in a broad framework of mental and physical health and social welfare, information on drugs and drug problems covering the special problems of travel;

4. consider the best way of securing the inclusion of the information and education about drugs and drug problems to teachers and other educators, social workers and health personnel, special information about the consequences of drug abuse and drug trafficking and the possible establishment of possible refresher courses at regular intervals on these problems for the afore-mentioned personnel;

5. consider the desirability of publishing leaflets and/or posters drawing the attention of young people to the special problems of drug abuse during travel to certain regions, to be made available at passport offices, vaccination centres, customs posts and similar places;

6. seek to persuade travel agencies to provide information, when it is necessary, about the problems causes by dependence-producing drugs in certain regions in the same way as that provided about health matters generally;

7. consider the best way of securing the inclusion of epidemiological medico-social and clinical information about drug misuse and its treatment, with particular reference to young groups, in courses of education and making this information widely available to all other persons with professional responsibilities in this field and encouraging the wide dissemination of knowledge of prevention and treatment techniques, including the results of latest research;

II.   Invites the governments of member states to keep the Secretary General informed every five years of action taken in pursuance of this resolution.

Resolution (78) 61
on the role of the psychologist as a member of
a medical team caring for parents, children and adolescents

*(Adopted by the Committee of Ministers on 29 November 1978
at the 296th meeting of the Ministers' Deputies)*

The Committee of Ministers,

Considering that the aim of the Council of Europe is to achieve a greater unity between its members and that this aim can be pursued, *inter alia*, by the adoption of common standards in the social and public health fields;

Considering that the medico-social services caring for parents, children and adolescents have not developed uniformly in most member states of the Council of Europe;

Considering the interdependence between psycho-social and physical factors with regard to the health and the well-being of children and their parents, and the role which should be played by the psychologist in preventive and remedial action towards children, their families and their environment;

Considering the need for co-operation between professionals in different disciplines in view of the special psychological, physical and social needs of children and their parents;

Considering that the need for psychological care for parents, children and adolescents exceeds the present supply;

Considering the need for the development of a pure and applied psychological research to evaluate and to improve the effectiveness of the services provided for children, adolescents and their parents;

Considering psychologists should take part in the planning of medico-social services at both national and local levels with a view to improving the quality of such services;

Considering it is essential to associate psychologists in the planning of psychological elements of curricula for other health professions;

Considering that it is desirable to establish common basic standards for the training of psychologists in member states of the Council of Europe;

Considering the need to adopt measures relating to the organisation and operation of a comprehensive and integrated service for children, adolescents and parents;

Considering that it is desirable to harmonise national policies on the role of the psychologist as a member of a health team caring for parents, children and adolescents,

I. Recommends that the governments of member states consider, when adopting national legislation, regulations and practices, the principles mentioned in the Appendix to this resolution;

II. Invites the governments of member states to inform the Secretary General of the Council of Europe, at five-yearly intervals, of the action they have taken in pursuance of this resolution.

Appendix to Resolution (78) 61

Part I – Role and functions

1.   In medico-social services caring for parents, children and adolescents, psychologists have different roles depending on their training and the organisation peculiar to each country. Nevertheless, the nature of their tasks makes it necessary for them to work in multidisciplinary teams;

2.   Accordingly, in order to determine the area covered by psychologists, it is necessary to:

   a.   define their functions and roles according to the specific objectives they pursue in the context of the general services provided for parents, children and adolescents;

   b.   up-date and constantly reassess the psychologist's functions so that the qualitative and quantitative provision of psychological services can take account of research into social changes;

3.   At the present time, psychologists in the member states may undertake:

   a.   to assess the need of and resources for children, adolescents, their parents and their environmental background;

   b.   to offer direct assistance in various forms, ranging from specialised education to support counselling and treatment of children and adolescents, parents or the family unit;

   c.   to provide information and training and to supervise educational and therapeutic interactions;

   d.   to assume administrative duties and to take part in planning;

4.   The psychologist's contribution may therefore be:

a.   in the field of primary prevention

   i.   to inform parents, the public and the administrative authorities of the potential dangers associated with various social and interpersonal situations, in order to promote a greater awareness of the causes of mal-adjustments;

   ii.   to recall the fundamental values concerning human relations threatened by social and economic changes;

   iii.   to highlight the influence of family and other relationships on the emotional, intellectual and social aspects of the personality development;

   iv.   to take part in the preparation of programmes for family and health education and their implementation, and also research in that sector.

b.   in the field of secondary and tertiary prevention

   i.   to assess the situation with a view to participating in the drawing up of a programme of action and rehabilitation. This is a continuous process which may require modification as the results of the continuing assessment become available;

   ii.   to play a part in the life of the multidisciplinary team taking part in the preparation of programmes, in the supervision of their implementation and in the evaluation of their effectiveness;

   iii.   to provide a specifically psychological service for maladjusted children and adolescents and their families; this service must be considered as a direct therapeutic intervention;

5.   Psychologists should be able to draw the attention of the public authorities to problems encountered so that those responsible for public affairs become more aware

of the state of health and well-being of the population and thus take adequate steps to remedy the shortcomings detected in this way.

Part II – Education and training of psychologists

1.   All psychologists working with parents, children and adolescents should have a university education covering the theoretical aspects of psychology and including an introduction to the experimental methods and findings derived from scientific psychology. They should also have a good understanding of procedures used in evaluating evidence from experimental findings or field studies;

2.   In addition, professional psychologists should have a specialised knowledge of the relevant aspects of applied psychology acquired both from advanced formal teaching and supervised practical experience.

3.   Since psychology is a rapidly developing discipline professional psychologists should have the opportunity for continuing education and training to keep their knowledge up to date. This should be encouraged by employers providing study leave and financial support for attending courses at intervals;

4.   Programmes for advanced specialised training, theoretical as well as practical, should be available for psychologists, e.g. training in child psychotherapy, marital or family therapy or special behavioural techniques;

5.   Experience as well as advanced training increases the value of a psychologist's service to the clients. This implies that there should be a grading structure within the psychological profession itself which the employing authorities should recognise;

6.   For effective multidisciplinary team functioning it is essential for the psychologist to have some knowledge of the field of work of colleagues in other disciplines and to be aware of the limitations imposed by their own education and training.

7.   In order to facilitate interchange of personnel and co-operation, it is desirable to work towards a minimum common standard of educaton and training for psychologists in Council of Europe member states.

Part III – Status

Psychologists should have a status in conformity with their own professional responsibilities and the specific nature of their work.

This status should take into account the following elements:

1.   Considering the roles and functions defined in Part I above, it seems essential that the specific contribution made by psychologists to the team's work and their responsibilities shall be recognised by public administrations in all the Council of Europe member states.

2.   Psychologists should be free to select methods of assessment and treatment within the limits of their competence and within the limits of their professional code of ethics while respecting the medical responsibility of the doctor.

3.   Steps should be taken to define the minimum qualifications necessary in order that psychologists be able to participate in multidisciplinary teams working with children, adolescents and their parents.

4.   The codes of ethics and the limits given by national legislation and rules given by competent national authorities for psychologists and/or guidelines for professional practices in the member states of the Council of Europe should be harmonised and recognised.

5.   The possibility of authorisation to practise being granted to psychologists working in the health field by a central organisation, recognised by or under the control of the ministries concerned with health and social welfare.

Measures should be taken to recognise and protect the autonomy of this professional activity throughout the member states of the Council of Europe.

Part IV – Teaching and research

1.   *Teaching*

In assessing the psychologists' work it should be borne in mind that they devote a significant part of their time to teaching and training other psychologists and specialists in other disciplines.

2.   *Research*

Resources should be allocated for applied scientific research to evaluate techniques for assessment, treatment and the efficiency of psychological services provided for care of children, adolescents and their parents. This is vital if there are to be advances in the provision of health care.

Resolution AP (81) 4
on the education of schoolchildren, foodhandlers and consumers with regard to the hazards of microbiological contamination of food

(Adopted by the Committee of Ministers on 11 February 1981, at the 329th meeting of the Ministers' Deputies)

The Representatives on the Committee of Ministers of Belgium, France, the Federal Republic of Germany, Italy, Luxembourg, the Netherlands and the United Kingdom of Great Britain and Northern Ireland, these states being parties to the Partial Agreement in the social and public health field, and the Representatives of Austria, Denmark, Ireland and Switzerland, states which have participated in the public health activities carried out within the above-mentioned Partial Agreement since 1 October 1974, 2 April 1968, 23 September 1969 and 5 May 1964 respectively.

Considering that the aim of the Council of Europe is to achieve a greater unity between its members and that this aim may be pursued by common action in the social and public health field;

Having regard to the provisions of the Brussels Treaty signed on 17 March 1948, by virtue of which Belgium, France, Luxembourg, the Netherlands and the United Kingdom of Great Britain and Northern Ireland declared themselves resolved to strengthen the social ties by which they were already united;

Having regard to the Protocol modifying and completing the Brussels Treaty, signed on 23 October 1954 by the signatory states of the Brussels Treaty on the one hand and the Federal Republic of Germany and Italy on the other hand;

Observing that the seven states parties to the Partial Agreement which have continued within the Council of Europe the social work hitherto undertaken by the Brussels Treaty Organisation and then by Western European Union, which derived from the Brussels Treaty as modified by the Protocol mentioned in the fourth paragraph above, as well as Austria, Denmark, Ireland and Switzerland, which participate in Partial Agreement activities in the field of public health, have always endeavoured to be in the forefront of progress in social matters and also in the associated field of public health, and have for many years undertaken action towards harmonisation of their legislation;

Having regard to the recommendation on the education of schoolchildren, foodhandlers and consumers with regard to the hazards of microbiological contamination of food, adopted by the Partial Agreement Public Health Committee on 31 October 1980;

Being aware of the high incidence of foodborne disease resulting from the contamination of foodstuffs by certain micro-organisms;

Taking the view that there is a need to ensure that education in food hygiene is given to schoolchildren, foodhandlers and consumers,

I.   Recommend to the governments of the seven states parties to the Partial Agreement, as well as to the governments of Austria, Denmark, Ireland and Switzerland that they take all appropriate measures to further education in food hygiene following the principles set out hereafter;

1.   Basic education in general hygiene should be provided for young schoolchildren; older pupils should receive further instruction in domestic and food hygiene.

Basic education for younger children should deal first and foremost with personal and environmental hygiene. The primary aim should be to interest the child in the particular problems involved in health care.

Education for the older age group should deal specifically with matters relating to domestic and food hygiene. It should also deal with matters relating to the processing, preparation, storage and preservation of food.

2.   Persons professionally engaged in the handling of food, including its processing, presentation, packaging, storage, distribution, sale and delivery, should possess a basic knowledge of food hygiene.

Managerial and supervisory staff should have received formal training in food hygiene at recognised vocational training establishments to enable them to provide suitable instruction to their assistants. This instruction is especially important for new employees at the time of starting work.

The practice of requiring workers in certain food trades to attend special courses of instruction, covering in particular food hygiene, and to possess a certificate of proficiency should be extended.

3.   Consumers should be informed about the general and specific aspects of food hygiene.

Consumer education may be provided by adult education classes, the mass media and through consumer associations. Manufacturers should play a major role in consumer education through adequate labelling and by providing appropriate information on the storage and handling of their products.

Emphasis should be given to the hazards associated with home preservation of foods, especially non-acid foods, and attention drawn to the modes of transmission of hazardous organisms and their relevance to outbreaks of food poisoning.

4.   Education in hygiene should be given by competent, specially trained personnel, such as domestic science teachers, biology teachers,

dieticians, home economists and other professional food advisers. The relevant authorities should be asked to consider the particular needs of food hygiene education when planning their school curricula. Teaching methods and materials should be planned in consultation with health authorities.

Visual display materials should be used whenever possible to illustrate and reinforce formal and informal instruction.

II.   Invite the said governments to inform the Secretary General of the Council of Europe every five years of the action they have taken to implement this resolution.

Recommendation No. R (82) 4
on the prevention of alcohol related problems especially among young people

(Adopted by the Committee of Ministers on 16 March 1982 at the 344th meeting of the Ministers' Deputies)

The Committee of Ministers, under the terms of Article 15.*b* of the Statute of the Council of Europe,

Considering that the aim of the Council of Europe is to achieve greater unity among its members and that this aim can be pursued, *inter alia*, by the adoption of common regulations in the health field;

Recalling its Resolution (78) 46 on methods of treating alcoholism;

Considering the increasing incidence of problems connected with alcohol in member states;

Considering the direct harmful effects of alcohol misuse on the constitution of the human being during his development, on his learning capacity, his creativity and his health as well as the indirect effects of alcohol related problems, such as reduced efficiency at work, cost of treatment and rehabilitation of the people concerned, and their incidence on the family and society;

Considering in particular the trend towards a lowering of the age at which the consumption begins;

Considering that these phenomena are due to many factors (social, economic, legal, cultural, etc.) and that a comprehensive preventive policy is needed,

Recommends governments of member states to:

– adopt a comprehensive national policy on production, distribution and sale of beverages containing alcohol;

– co-ordinate such policy to the utmost extent with that of the other member states;

– take positive action in the field of the prevention of alcohol related problems;

– take account as far as possible of the measures outlined at the appendix to this recommendation.

Appendix to Recommendation No. R (82) 4

I. Introduction

1.   For the purposes of this recommendation, the term "young people" means the age-group ranging from conception to the early 20s, that is to say the age at which they enter the adult world.

2.   Several of the preventive measures set out below concern all age-groups, as alcohol consumption patterns of young people very often reflect those of adults, while others are selectively aimed at young people.

3.   The measures to be taken should concern:

i.   prevention and especially education for health, since the latter is likely to instil healthy living habits into young people which will influence their whole life;

ii.   the health and social implications of action affecting the consumption of alcohol.

4.   These measures should be integrated in a comprehensive, coherent and credible policy.

II. Measures to be taken in the field of education for health

5.   In general, education for health should aim to:

i.   make everyone aware of his responsibilities concerning the maintenance and promotion of health;

ii.   develop the individual's capacity to take informed decisions which affect his personal, family or social welfare;

iii.   encourage a positive attitude to individual initiative;

iv.   help each individual to fit into working life and society generally, so that in it he can express himself, make his own contribution and achieve fulfilment.

6.   To that end, consideration should be given to ways of:

6.1. *Setting in motion and co-ordinating an information policy*

In this respect it is recommended:

i.   that, in addition to permanent information, vigorous information campaigns be conducted on the problems related to alcohol consumption (accidents on the roads, at work and in the home, effects on family life, cost to society, etc.);

ii.   that this general information be made more specific for target groups, and in particular:

     − to inform all concerned, especially expectant mothers, of the dangers of alcohol consumption to the foetus (Lemoine and Jones syndrome);

     − to inform families, especially mothers, about young persons' extreme sensitivity to alcohol;

     − to stress how much children's behaviour is influenced by that of the family group which instils norms, stereotypes and patterns in the young.

6.2. *Setting the guidelines for health education on alcohol related problems*

In this connection, it would be advisable:

i.   that in schools, such education:

     − be taught in a positive way, be integrated in all aspects of the curriculum, and provide objective information;

– take account of the alcohol patterns of the socio-cultural context to which it is addressed;

– be backed up by active learning techniques and action at group level;

– form part of an overall conception of the various forms of non-therapeutic use of drugs and be included as well in education on nutrition;

– be aimed, if not at temperance, then, at least, at lowering the level of consumption of alcoholic beverages;

– include at the same time a programme aimed at the family and the community (occupational groups, key figures, opinion-makers, mediators, decision-takers, media);

– be supported from outside by a preventive, promotional and comprehensive policy (health, leisure);

ii.   in the military environment, to pursue information programmes after the training period in the field of education for health;

iii.   in the working environment:

– to display permanently information documents on alcohol related problems;

– to circulate regularly oral and written information on questions of gradual alcohol dependence, namely to middle management and control services, and in staff training courses, as is done in respect of employment injury.

6.3 *Setting the guidelines for the training of several professional groups in the field of alcohol related problems* (teachers, social workers, psychologists, sociologists, nurses, doctors, especially school health and occupational doctors, journalists, lawyers and penitentiary staff).

It would be advisable to train such personnel to detect situations which may give rise to alcohol related problems and in this connection:

– to pay special attention to young people who experience difficulties with adjustment, integration or adaptation to a different culture, who are resident in boarding schools, have family or school difficulties, or who live in depressed areas, in a drinking environment, or in families with economic difficulties (primary prevention);

– to identify as early as possible the signs of gradual alcohol dependence on the basis of clinical, biochemical or social indicators or of questionnaires (secondary prevention);

– to indicate the risk groups as much as possible without stigmatising a certain group as being potentially subject to alcohol related problems. Such labelling can have the undesirable side-effect of making a certain group identify itself with the stigma imposed on it, as a result of which the behaviour considered undesirable can possibly gain strength.

III. Medical and social measures

7.   Efforts should be made to encourage:

i.   the development of a co-ordinated leisure policy for young people (including the military) by offering them especially culture and sports activities so as to occupy their leisure time in a constructive way; leisure facilities and activities should be integrated in the local socio-cultural framework;

ii.   the promotion, especially in urban areas, of youth clubs and "out-reach" activities run by qualified staff;

iii.   financial support of voluntary organisations active in health promotion;

iv.   the development of consultation services for adolescents which should prefer- ably be separated from family services and organised in an attractive and informal way so as to encourage young people to seek help at an early stage; the active participation of adolescents in the organisation and management of such services should be strongly encouraged;

v.   the development of vocational guidance, employment and vocational training services with a view to preventing social exclusion;

vi.   the support both morally and financially of organisations combating alcohol related problems, especially if they participate actively in the framework of the objec- tives of a national programme;

vii.   the enhancement of awareness by the individual, family and community of alco- hol related problems and of the possible forms of individual and collective action in order to encourage their active participation in preventive measures;

viii.   an increase in the number of socio-medical services providing aid and treatment for alcoholics as recommended in Resolution (78) 46 of the Committee of Ministers on methods of treating alcoholism;

ix.   material aid to associations whose purpose is to help former alcoholics.

IV. General measures

8.   Such measures might include:

i.   making the campaigns against alcohol misuse and alcohol related problems one of the main objectives of health policy;

ii.   ensuring that alcoholic beverages are highly taxed so as to discourage consump- tion;

iii.   not authorising the sale of alcoholic beverages in recreational or sporting clubs during spectator events, competitions, etc.;

iv.   regulating sales of alcoholic beverages to young people especially in supermar- kets;

v.   prohibiting the sale of alcoholic beverages from machines;

vi.   banning special offers of alcoholic beverages;

vii.   enforcing measures limiting very strictly the quantity of alcohol per person to be bought in duty-free shops in airports, ports, on ships, etc.;

viii.   banning the sale of alcoholic beverages in petrol stations and in restaurants near main highways;

ix.   encouraging production and consumption of non-alcoholic drinks;

x.   lowering the alcoholic content of certain drinks and fixing a maximum alcoholic content for beer and cider;

xi.   making obligatory the availability of free drinking water in restaurants, bars, etc., as well as the inclusion of non-alcoholic beverages on menus;

xii.   regulating access and sale of alcoholic beverages to young people and to this end:

   – banning the sale of alcoholic beverages and access to public houses at least to young people under 16;

   – extending the ban on serving alcoholic drinks to pupils in secondary schools; they should be offered alternatives (milk, fruit juice) at reasonable prices;

   – banning the sale of alcoholic beverages in bars on university premises;

   – providing numerous drinking fountains in teaching establishments;

– regulating shops selling alcoholic drinks especially near teaching establishments frequented by young people;

– banning the employment of minors in public houses;

xiii. applying in full the recommendations of Resolution (73) 7 of the Committee of Ministers relating to the punishment of road traffic offences committed whilst driving a vehicle under the influence of alcohol; it is recommended to fix as low as possible the maximum amount of alcohol in the blood above which a driver shall be subject to prosecution.

V. Special measures to be taken at work place

9. Such measures might include:

i. prohibiting alcoholic beverages on the premises and making available at the same time non-alcoholic beverages; as regards work canteens and restaurants, the prohibition could be lifted after working hours or when a limited consumption is without danger for the person or his working environment;

ii. prohibiting all payment in kind in the form of alcoholic beverages;

iii. making supervisory personnel aware of the dangers of allowing inebriated employees to remain at the place of work.

VI. Measures concerning advertising

10. Efforts should be made to:

i. regulate advertising to avoid aiming it at the young or glamourising alcohol;

ii. create an awareness among the media, especially journalists and people from the world of entertainment, of the way in which favourable attitudes to the consumption of alcoholic beverages can influence young people;

iii. support advertising of non-alcoholic beverages.

VII. Measures to be taken in the field of research

11. Consideration should be given to ways of reviewing national research needs, and of co-ordinating strategies and disseminating relevant research findings.

12. It would further be advisable:

i. to study the social and psychological causes of consumption and dependence on alcohol in order to improve prevention and facilitate the detection of problems at an early stage;

ii. to establish in co-operation with the World Health Organisation:

– common statistical standards to ensure to ensure the comparability of data on consumption and disabilities;

– means of assessing prevention programmes;

iii. to develop studies on new non-alcoholic beverages.

Recommendation No. R (82) 5
concerning the prevention of drug dependence
and the special role of education for health

*(Adopted by the Committee of Ministers on 16 March 1982
at the 344th meeting of the Ministers' Deputies)*

The Committee of Ministers, under the terms of Article 15.*b* of the Statute of the Council of Europe,

Considering that the aim of the Council of Europe is to achieve a greater unity between its members and that this aim may be pursued, *inter alia*, by the adoption of a common approach in the health and social protection fields;

Recalling Recommendation No. (82) 6 on the treatment and resocialisation of drug dependants;

Recognising that on the one hand the prevalence of drug dependence has not decreased in member states, being either stabilised or still on the increase, despite the measures already taken, and that, on the other, in general the problem of changing attitudes to drugs remains unsolved;

Conscious of the risks involved in ignoring the many harmful consequences of experimentation with drugs, and of the supposedly recreational use of drugs;

Judging that prevention and early treatment programmes for those on the verge of dependence have proved difficult to implement because of the illicit nature and social stigmatisation of drug use, and that emphasis should be placed on the primary prevention of drug dependence applied to the whole population, especially by means of educaton for health programmes aimed at school children as the target group, so that they can learn to protect themselves against the dangers of a society where drugs exist or other harmful substances are commonly used, and aware also that tertiary drug dependence prevention programmes have not been developed to a sufficient extent;

Judging that, to reduce the demand for drugs, education for health should be related to the psychological and socio-cultural characteristics of each target group, and should impart a simple understanding of how the human body works, and which of its systems might be damaged by drug or other abuse;

Aware of the need to institute comprehensive education for health programmes which aim to promote a whole range of healthy attitudes and life-styles so that within each member state's socio-cultural context, individuals may each consciously choose the way of life best suited to their needs;

Realising that the traditional structure of school education may not encourage the institution of comprehensive, informal and non-authoritarian education for health, integrated in the school curriculum, and aimed at encouraging active pupil participation and the collaboration of parents and others in the community,

Recommends that governments of member states should:

– approach the problem of preventing drug dependence taking note that:

i. *primary prevention* should include, alongside legislation and controls to curb illicit drug trafficking and to regulate the supply of licit drugs, comprehensive education for health programmes with drug abuse prevention components;

ii. *secondary prevention* should include, as well as measures to detect at an early stage individuals or groups at high risk from drug abuse, educational and other forms of suasion designed to reduce the detected risk of abuse;

iii. *tertiary prevention* of drug dependence should comprise not only therapeutic services for dependants but also comprehensive measures to help them to become integrated in society and to achieve personal fulfilment;

iv. specific preventive measures must be accompanied by general social policy initiatives designed to deal with the problems often behind drug dependence; the break-up or weakening of the family's role in sustaining a sense of personal identity; unemployment among young people; educational systems which are ill-adapted to the modern world and to young persons' needs; the absence of adequate leisure facilities, particularly for the young in depressed urban areas;

– take the following measures to prevent drug dependence:

1. *Generally*

a. to ensure that adequate financial support is available for the primary prevention of drug dependence, more particularly for the provision of comprehensive education for health, for each age-group in schools and other educational establishments;

b. to ensure that a comprehensive education for health programme is established for each area or community, within and outside schools and other educational establishments;

c. to promote a partnership between all groups and individuals concerned at regional, provincial and community level, by co-ordinating and if necessary rearranging existing institutions and services so as to draw fully on each level's potential (parents, group leaders, etc.);

d. to undertake programmes to train health educators by, first, identifying those who can train and, second, by locating and where necessary giving training to the key workers in each community or area already able to share the tasks with others in a non-authoritarian setting, who are most likely to be found among teachers, members of primary health care teams, school health or public health officers, psychiatrists, young workers or social workers;

e. to include in all education for health programmes or projects experimental testing procedures, especially the evaluation of the impact of programmes, etc. on individuals' attitudes and their subsequent behaviour, particularly as regards drug use and abuse.

2. *In particular*

a. to set up educaton for health programmes which:

i. concentrate on school-age children and adolescents, and can be an integral part of school education, beginning at primary level and continuing at secondary level. Health education should not be taught as a separate school subject, but should be co-ordinated by a senior teacher and included in several areas of teaching, and in the general set of values upheld by the school among which the encouragement of sports and other leisure activities is also important;

ii. aim generally to encourage individuals to assume responsibility for their health as they grow up, by becoming adequately aware of health risks and benefits, and of what kind of life-style they should adopt to suit their personality;

iii. correspond to the actual needs of the group taught, are comprehensible, attractive and positive, illustrating opportunities rather than prohibiting certain behaviour; the educational staff should be objective in their approach and credible in their presentation, and pursue the following specific objectives:

– to enable individuals to improve their overall mental health, their social skills and their interpersonal relations;

– to raise their self-esteem and reduce any sense of alienation;

– to clarify each individual's values, demonstrating in what manner conflicts can arise between a person's values and reality;

– to encourage decision-making, active learning and the deliberate choice of a healthy way of life;

iv. do not single out drug abuse as a special problem, but simply include it in a list of activities which are dangerous (or merely futile). Drugs should be shown to be a seductive illusion in relation to what individuals want and need to develop their own personalities, and not as forbidden (but perhaps desirable) substances. All drugs should be dealt with, whether licit (including prescribed drugs) or illicit. The association between drug abuse and the other addictions (chiefly tranquillisers, solvents, alcohol and tobacco) should not be ignored;

v. consist in detailed teaching and active learning projects integrated into several subjects in the school curriculum, and if possible informal discussion groups based on school communities, involving non-teaching staff, parents, school health service personnel, etc. (a "health convention");

b. to establish the training and selection of education for health staffs, on the basis that such staff may either add this responsibility to their existing professional duties, or be full-time specialist workers in the drug-abuse field. Both types of staff need adequate training:

    i. teachers, social workers or others who take on specific responsibilities for health education generally with special reference to drug-abuse problems need:

    – clear guidance on the known risks to health, resulting from behavioural and social factors;

    – a satisfactory understanding of the psychosocial problems of children and adolescents;

    – some basic knowledge about drugs and their effects;

    – a good grasp of how to co-ordinate education for health programmes;

    ii. specialist workers in the field of drug-abuse prevention (mainly secondary and tertiary) need a multidisciplinary training to include:

    – a clear grasp of the respective aims of primary, secondary and tertiary prevention;

    – a profound understanding of psychological development and social interaction, particularly as regards adolescents and young people;

    – appropriate scientific knowledge about drugs;

    – a good understanding of the wider pressures exerted by society on the young;

    iii. the selection of staff should be based on these criteria:

    – ability to undertake multidisciplinary work;

    – wide experience of various patterns of individual and group behaviour;

    – special interest in and understanding of the problems of children and young people;

    – capacity to relate to young people in a non-authoritarian but well-defined manner, and to collaborate with teachers, parents, school health services, community services, etc.;

    iv. where drug-abuse prevention represents an additional work-load for a given professional (e.g. teacher, primary health care provider, social worker) special attention should be paid to the balance of the individual's working arrangements;

c. to assess education for health programmes; the measurement of their effects on health behaviour in the subsequent lives of children must take into account that they are at an experimental stage and are applicable to large populations of children at their primary and secondary school levels, forming part of a comprehensive education syllabus; such assessment would require a sequenced procedure which would take into consideration the following:

    i. an initial baseline statement on local community health needs which would generate and govern a relevant and acceptable health education programme suitable for a small-scale application to test its feasibility, should be undertaken;

ii. accepting that a health education programme necessarily focuses on life-styles affecting health, it would include teaching about the associated risk factors, attitudes to health care and enhancing motivation to change harmful habits and it would require a long-term follow-up mechanism if the efficacy of the programme is to be tested;

iii. that this long-term follow-up would need studies involving representative cohorts in the population in order to assess the effects of the programme and to assess the confounding effects of other variables;

iv. in parallel with the long-term follow-up studies, a facility which permits the adaptation of health education programmes to changes in local health needs would be necessary; this would require that the indicated change itself and the change of programme were effected in a standardised way;

d. (other general measures) to supplement education for health and other primary preventive measures by the implementation of a social policy which is designed:

i. to discourage recourse to psychotropic substances as a response to stress and other personal problems, in particular by using the mass media to devalue alcohol and drugs in the public eye and by giving doctors incentives to prescribe fewer drugs and to give more positive advice on how to live a healthy life;

ii. to assist families to help each other, particularly at times of stress or other difficulty for adolescents;

iii. to encourage the creation or renewal of integrated communities, in which, notably, schools and health and social services should reflect and respond to the cultural context of the community, promote social integration, enable people to lead an active and useful life, and especially to promote youth employment and facilitate access to training courses and opportunities for work experience to all young people who need them.

Recommendation No. R (88) 7
on school health education and the role and training of teachers

*(Adopted by the Committee of Ministers on 18 April 1988
at the 416th meeting of the Ministers' Deputies)*

The Committee of Ministers, under the terms of Article 15.*b* of the Statute of the Council of Europe,

Considering that the aim of the Council of Europe is to achieve a greater unity between its members and that this aim may be pursued, *inter alia*, by the adoption of a common approach in the health and social protection fields;

Recalling its Recommendation No. R (82) 4 on the prevention of alcohol-related problems especially among young people and its Recommendation No. R (82) 5 concerning the prevention of drug dependence and the special role of education for health, as well as the concerns which lay behind these two recommendations;

Considering that, in spite of the development of elaborate and specialised health systems combining general preventive measures and the availability of medical care services, numerous health problems continue to arise which do not respond to traditional preventive and curative measures;

Noting that the majority of these problems are linked to life-styles not conducive to health and that health education can contribute to avoiding them by promoting healthy attitudes and life-styles;

Noting that, alongside the central role of the family, the most appropriate structure for the introduction of health education is the school, as it regroups the young, the age-group which is most able to learn healthy behavioural patterns;

Conscious that the establishment of school health education programmes requires:

– guidelines for the planning and development of health education curricula;

– a clear definition of the role of the teacher in this field;

– basic, in-service and further training of all teachers to allow them to contribute within their field to the programmes in question,

Recommends that the governments of member states adopt a comprehensive policy for health education in schools, taking into account the matters contained in the appendix.

Appendix to Recommendation No. R (88) 7

1.   *Basic concepts*

1.1. Health is more than the absence of infirmity or illness, it is a quality of life comprising social, mental, moral and emotional as well as physical dimensions. It is a dynamic asset to be acquired, defended and constantly rebuilt throughout life.

1.2. Health education essentially consists in:

– providing better information on factors which influence health,

– elucidating the relationships which exist between health and the physical and psycho-social environment,

– developing individual, family and collective awareness and a sense of responsibility in relation to health,

– promoting responsible attitudes and ways of life conducive to health.

1.3. Health education at school implies that children and adolescents are confronted with formal and informal experiences enabling them to acquire attitudes and behaviour patterns which have a positive effect on their health, and are given the information and capacities required in order to make free decisions. It is different from other "taught" school subjects in that it is an interdisciplinary activity which has to permeate the whole of school life and extend into the outside community, and requires a personal commitment on the part of all those involved.

2.   *Objectives of school health education*

School health education should:

i.   at pre-primary level, promote the mental, social and emotional development of children within the pre-school environment, stimulating them to become aware of their bodies in relation to others and the environment; and encourage experience of, and active participation in, the decision-making process;

ii.   at primary level, allow pupils gradually to acquire knowledge of human growth and development, and awareness of the basic issues of the relationship between health and the environment;

iii.   at secondary level, enable young people to develop their knowledge of human growth and of physical, psychological and social development, and of factors which have a positive or negative effect on health; to appreciate positively this period of physical and psychological change to attain a proper measure of self-esteem; to learn to analyse attitudes and behaviour which have an effect on health, in order to facilitate active training in decision-taking.

3.   *Guidelines for the planning and development of a health education programme*

3.1. Health education programmes should take account of schoolchildren's social and cultural environment.

3.2. Programme planners should take account of:

i.   state of health needs and health-related behaviour as identified by children and young people themselves and by their parents;

ii.   state of health needs, as identified by doctors, practitioners and health inspectors;

iii.   the state of health needs and types of health-related behaviour as they are seen by the community in which the children and young people live and by that in which they might later live.

258

3.3. Through a participative process, planners should develop a school health programme reflecting identified needs and priorities. School health education programmes should be articulated on three levels:

3.3.1. The health-promoting curriculum, including an overt "taught" component and different approaches incorporated in all aspects of the curriculum;

3.3.2. The ethos established at school or health in school. It is necessary to ensure that life within the school is consistent with the aims of the health educaton programme; it should ensure physical and mental health and good social relations;

3.3.3. The various provisions of the school health and social services. Good coordination between the school and health and social services is necessary just as much to ensure the involvement of these services in the development of school health education programmes as in their implementation.

3.4. The health-promoting curriculum should take account of changes and developments occurring within the school population and its environment.

3.5. Health education issues should be taken up repeatedly at different levels of increasing complexity, according to the level of understanding of children and young people, so that they relate to their interests and needs (spiral development of curriculum).

3.6. As the objectives range from imparting knowledge to modifying behaviour, all methods might be considered, from the most classical to the most modern: traditional classes, discussion, group work, socio-educational activities, communication techniques, etc. Whatever methods are adopted, their effectiveness is influenced by the involvement and degree of commitment of the teacher.

4.   *Research and evaluation*

4.1. Research could give a better understanding of the perceptions of pupils, teachers, parents, social services and health service staff and representatives of the community with regard to health, and could help in the development of teaching materials designed to improve working conditions in the classroom and taking account of the most recent scientific data.

4.2. All components of the curriculum should be evaluated and the achievement of objectives assessed in a formative and summative way; teachers, pupils, parents, social and health service staff, and community representatives should all be involved in this process.

5.   *Training of teachers*

5.1. In view of its differences from other "taught" subjects, all teachers need to be prepared for working in the field of health education, whether they are to play a major or a minor role.

5.2. Teacher training should be organised for primary school teachers preferably at both initial training and in-service levels. Secondary school teachers should be introduced to health education during their basic training, and should have the opportunity to extend their knowledge during the course of their work.

6.   *Professional preparation of teachers*

6.1. In general, teachers should be:

    i. familiar with current theoretical bases of health education;

    ii. aware of national developments in the field both within the educational system and in the community at large.

6.2. During training, the following issues should be stressed:

    i.   the potential of the school as a forum for promoting the health of children individually and the "collective" health of the school community;

    ii. health education is not only concerned with giving information but involves the clarification of values, attitudes and beliefs with a possibility of multiple choice and is not free from ethical considerations;

    iii. health is multi-faceted and is influenced by decisions taken and policies adopted in a wide range of government sectors (for example health, social and economic fields);

    iv. health education needs to be seen as a democratic process where pupils are encouraged to seek out and use relevant information leading to appropriate decision-making in given situations.

6.3. Objectives to be pursued in the preparation of teachers for health education should include the following:

    i.   increasing knowledge about health; this should include social, emotional, moral and mental as well as physical components;

    ii. increasing understanding of the relationships between health and other components of the curriculum;

    iii. helping teachers and students to see that health educaton is an essential element in the development of personal skills and the personality;

    iv. demonstrating that health issues can be integrated into other aspects of the curriculum;

    v. demonstrating the importance of a variety of informal approaches which should be congruent with the formal health education curriculum;

    vi. helping teachers and students learn the use of methods appropriate to health education;

    vii. helping teachers recognise the role of others in education for health and of pupil counselling; they should be encouraged to call upon the expertise of teaching colleagues, members of the school health service, community groups, parents, etc.

6.4. The contents of training should ensure that all teachers, in the course of their professional preparation:

    i.   acquire a basic knowledge about and a sense of responsibility for creating a healthy school environment;

    ii. be made sensitive to the health needs of children;

    iii. obtain an insight into the basic growth and developmental processes of children;

    iv. acquire knowledge of the skills necessary to make independent decisions about one's own health;

    v. become familiar with the methodology to be used relevant to the cognitive and emotional elements of curriculum development;

    vi. become skilled in multidisciplinary work with colleagues in collaborative teaching strategies;

    vii. become able to co-operate with other significant individuals, systems and services.

6.5. Teachers who are identified as having specific roles in the school health education programmes, for example, co-ordinators, those involved in teaching particular parts of the curriculum or particular groups of children, need to have appropriate skills in addition of those of other teachers. They should be familiar with all aspects of the curriculum related to health. They should, in particular:

i. have special knowledge of how to develop comprehensive programmes and how to identify possible gaps;

ii. play appropriate roles in implementing the programme;

iii. be able to give advice to other teachers; and

iv. assess the achievement of objectives, evaluate both the appropriateness of the methods employed and the effectiveness of the curriculum in contributing to pupils' health.

7. *Organisation of teacher training*

7.1. Training colleges and other appropriate establishments, should gradually become organised in order to provide this type of training for teachers through multidisciplinary teams; in the absence of specialists, such colleges should appoint a co-ordinator to enlist specialists from a variety of disciplines from outside the college to ensure that the eclectic nature of health educaton is reflected in the teaching.

7.2. In-service training should be organised, preferably within the school, by co-ordinators belonging to the above institutions.

7.3. Training institutions responsible for the pre-service and in-service training of teachers should have at their disposal guidelines in the form of training documents which should be prepared at national level through co-operation between the health and education sectors. Such documents should contain:

i. a guide to the training including both method and content;

ii. all the necessary materials for teachers participating in the course.

7.4. In-service training should include examination of topical questions.

8. *Development of policies on health education*

8.1. In order to ensure impact throughout the school system, policies need to be developed. Such policies should:

i. ensure co-ordination at central, regional and local levels between the health and education sectors by means of co-ordinating committees supporting the introduction of health education in all school curricula;

ii. provide for the appointment of persons responsible at regional level for developing strategies within schools in close co-operation with the head teacher and, if necessary, the school co-ordinating committee;

iii. ensure that resources of time and materials are provided to support all those involved.

Recommendation No. R (92) 3
on genetic testing and screening for health care purposes[1]

(Adopted by the Committee of Ministers on 10 February 1992
of the 470th meeting of the Ministers' Deputies)

The Committee of Ministers, under the terms of Article 15.*b* of the Statute of the Council of Europe,

Considering that the aim of the Council of Europe is to achieve a greater unity between its members;

Having regard to the Convention for the Protection of Human Rights and Fundamental Freedoms of 4 November 1950 and the Convention for the Protection of Individuals with regard to Automatic Processing of Personal Data of 28 January 1981;

Having regard to the Recommendations of the Committee of Ministers No. R (90) 3 on medical research on human beings, No R. (90) 13 on prenatal genetic screening, prenatal genetic diagnosis and associated genetic counselling and No R. (92) 1 on the use of analysis of deoxyribonucleic acid (DNA) within the framework of the criminal justice system;

Bearing in mind that recent progress in the field of biomedical science has made it possible to obtain a greater knowledge of the human genome and the nature of genetic disorders;

Recognising the benefits and potential usefulness of these techniques not only for the individual, but also for the family and other relatives as well as the population as a whole;

Aware that the introduction of genetic testing and screening also arouses anxiety and that it is therefore desirable to give assurances as to their proper use;

Bearing in mind that rules governing the collection and use of medical data also apply to genetic data collected and used for health care purposes, including medical research;

---

1. When this Recommendation was adopted and in application of Rule 10.2.*c* of the Rules of Procedure of the Ministers' Deputies;
– the Representative of the Netherlands reserved the right of his government to comply or not with Principle 7 of the Recommendation;
– the Representative of Germany reserved the right of his government to comply or not with the words "and/or to avoid giving birth to affected offspring" in the third indent of sub-paragraph *a* of the paragraph on "Purpose, scope and definitions" of the Recommendation.

Recognising the need for education of the members of the health care professions and the general public about the importance of genetic factors to health and for including this subject in curricula for general and further education, both at school and at university level, and in professional training;

Considering that each country must determine its own special needs in order to develop the most appropriate services;

Recognising that it should be the goal for every country to offer its citizens equal opportunity of access to genetic testing and screening services;

Aware of the dangers of discrimination and social stigmatisation which may result from genetic information and determined to fight such phenomena,

Recommends that the governments of the member states:

a.   be guided in their legislation and policy by the principles and recommendations set out below;

b.   promote in their educational systems the teaching of human genetics.

Principles and recommendations

Purpose, scope and definitions

The purpose of this recommendation is to ensure respect for certain principles in the field of genetic testing and screening for health care purposes, including medical research.[1]

For the purposes of this recommendation:

a.   the term "genetic tests for health care purposes" refers to tests which serve:

– to diagnose and classify a genetic disease;

– to identify unaffected carriers of a defective gene in order to counsel them about the risk of having affected children;

– to detect a serious genetic disease before the clinical onset of symptoms in order to improve the quality of life using secondary preventive measures and/or to avoid giving birth to affected offspring;

– to identify persons at risk of contracting a disease where both a defective gene and a certain life-style are important as causes of the disease.

b.   the term "genetic diagnosis" refers to tests carried out to diagnose a presumed ailment on an individual or several members of a family, in the framework of a family study.

c.   the term "genetic screening" refers to genetic tests carried out on a population as a whole or a subset of it without previous suspicion that the tested individuals may carry the trait.[2]

---

1. Genetic testing and screening can be carried out at different levels, such as on chromosomes, genes (DNA), proteins, organs or a given individual, and can be complemented with aspects of the family history.
2. The essential distinction between genetic diagnosis and genetic screening is that the latter is not initiated by the individual who is its subject, but by the provider of the screening service.

I. *Rules for good practice in genetic testing and screening*

Principle 1 – Informing the public

a.   Plans for the introduction of genetic testing and screening should be brought in advance to the notice of individuals, families and the public.

b.   The public should be informed about genetic testing and screening, in particular their availability, purposes and implications – medical, legal, social and ethical – as well as the centres where they are carried out. Such information should start within the school system and be continued by the media.

Principle 2 – Quality of genetic services

a.   Proper education should be provided regarding human genetics and genetic disorders, particularly for health professionals and the paramedical professions, but also for any other profession concerned.

b.   Genetic tests may only be carried out under the responsibility of a duly qualified physician.

c.   It is desirable for centres where laboratory tests are performed to be approved by the state or by a competent authority in the state, and to participate in an external quality assurance.

Principle 3 – Counselling and support

a.   Any genetic testing and screening procedure should be accompanied by appropriate counselling, both before and after the procedure.

Such counselling must be non-directive. The information to be given should include the pertinent medical facts, the results of tests, as well as the consequences and choices. It should explain the purpose and the nature of the tests and point out possible risks. It must be adapted to the circumstances in which individuals and families receive genetic information.

b.   Everything should be done to provide, where necessary, continuing support for the tested persons.

II. *Access to genetic tests*

Principle 4 – Equality of access – non-discrimination

a.   There should be equality of access to genetic testing, without financial considerations and without preconditions concerning eventual personal choices.

b.   No condition should be attached to the acceptance or the undergoing of genetic tests.

c.   The sale to the public of tests for diagnosing genetic diseases or predisposition for such diseases, or for the identification of carriers of such diseases, should only be allowed subject to strict licensing conditions laid down by national legislation.

Principle 5 – Self-determination

a. The provision of genetic services should be based on respect for the principle of self-determination of the persons concerned. For this reason, any genetic testing, even when offered systematically, should be subject to their express, free and informed consent.

b. The testing of the following categories of persons should be subject to special safeguards:

– minors;

– persons suffering from mental disorders;

– adults placed under limited guardianship.

Testing of these persons for diagnostic purposes should be permitted only when this is necessary for their own health or if the information is imperatively needed to diagnose the existence of a genetic disease in family members.

The consent of the person to be tested is required except where national law provides otherwise.

Principle 6 – Non compulsory nature of tests

a. Health service benefits, family allowances, marriage requirements or other similar formalities, as well as the admission to, or the continued exercise of certain activities, especially employment, should not be made dependent on the undergoing of tests or screening.

Exceptions to this principle must be justified by reasons of direct protection of the person concerned or of a third party and be directly related to the specific conditions of the activity.

b. Only if expressly allowed by law may tests be made compulsory for the protection of individuals or the public.

Principle 7 – Insurance

Insurers should not have the right to require genetic testing or to enquire about results of previously performed tests, as a pre-condition for the conclusion or modification of an insurance contract.

III. *Data protection and professional secrecy*

Principle 8 – Data protection

a. The collection and storage of substances and of samples and the processing of information derived therefrom must be in conformity with the Council of Europe's basic principles of data protection and data security laid down in the Convention No. 108 of 28 January 1981 and the relevant recommendations of the Committee of Ministers in this field.

In particular in genetic screening and testing or associated genetic counselling, personal data may be collected, processed and stored only for the purposes of health care, diagnosis and disease prevention, and for research closely related to these matters, as outlined in Principle 5.

b.   Nominative genetic data may be stored as part of medical records and may also be stored in disease-related or test-related registers. The establishment and maintenance of such registers should be subject to national legislation.

Principle 9 – Professional secrecy

Persons handling genetic information should be bound by professional rules of conduct and rules laid down by national legislation aimed at preventing the misuse of such information and, in particular, by the duty to observe strict confidentiality. Personal information obtained by genetic testing is protected on the same basis as other medical data by the rules of medical data protection.

However, in the case of a severe genetic risk for other family members, consideration should be given, in accordance with national legislation and professional rules of conduct, to informing family members about matters relevant to their health or that of their future children.

Principle 10 – Separate storage of genetic information

Genetic data collected for health care purposes, as for all medical data, should as a general rule be kept separate from other personal records.

Principle 11 – Unexpected findings

In conformity with national legislation, unexpected findings may be communicated to the person tested only if they are of direct clinical importance to the person or the family.

Communication of unexpected findings to family members of the person tested should only be authorised by national law if the person tested refuses expressly to inform them even though their lives are in danger.

IV. *Research*

Principle 12 – Supervision

Research projects involving medical genetic data have to be carried out, in conformity with the standards of medical ethics, under the direct supervision of a responsible physician or, in exceptional circumstances, of a responsible scientist.

Principle 13 – Handling of data

a.   Samples collected for a specific medical or scientific purpose may not, without permission of the persons concerned or the persons legally entitled to give permission on their behalf, be used in ways which could be harmful to the persons concerned.

b. The use of genetic data for population and similar studies has to respect rules governing data protection, and in particular concerning anonymity and confidentiality. The same applies to the publishing of such data.

Recommendation No. R (93) 2
on the medico-social aspects of child abuse

(Adopted by the Committee of Ministers on 22 March 1993
at the 490th meeting of the Ministers' Deputies)

The Committee of Ministers, under the terms of Article 15.*b* of the Statute of the Council of Europe,

Considering that the aim of the Council of Europe is to achieve a greater unity between its members, in particular by the adoption of common rules on matters of common interest;

Recognising the right of all children to live in conditions favourable to their proper development and to grow up free from physical abuse, sexual abuse, emotional abuse, neglect and other forms of child abuse;

Noting that child abuse is a phenomenon which in recent years has given rise to considerable concern in member states;

Having regard to Recommendation No. R (79) 17 concerning the protection of children against ill-treatment, Recommendation No. R (85) 4 on violence in the family and Recommendation No. R (90) 2 on social measures concerning violence within the family;

Bearing in mind the United Nations Convention on the Rights of the Child;

Recognising the need for policies designed to prevent child abuse, while taking into account the need for protection of privacy of all persons concerned, and the respect of confidentiality,

Recommends the governments of the member states:

1.   to adopt a policy which aims to secure the child's welfare within his/her family;

2.   to establish a system for the effective prevention, identification, notification, investigation, assessment, intervention, treatment, and follow-up of cases of child abuse on a multidisciplinary basis, which specifies clearly the roles and responsibilities of the various agencies involved;

3.   to take to this end the measures appearing in the appendix to this recommendation.

Appendix to Recommendation No. R (93) 2

1. *Prevention*

1.1. To develop, implement, monitor and evaluate a programme of preventive policies at primary, secondary and tertiary levels nationally and locally in respect of child abuse.

1.2. At a primary level:

   a. to promote, through public information campaigns of various kinds (for example TV, radio, press, leaflets, posters) and other measures, societal awareness of children's rights to a life free from neglect, physical, emotional and/or sexual abuse, of the harmful consequences of child abuse and of positive, non-abusive modes of child-rearing;

   b. to establish socio-economic conditions and health and social welfare services which strengthen the capacity of all families to support and care for their children;

   c. to emphasise the rights of all children and young persons to freedom from abuse and the need to change patterns of upbringing and behaviour which threaten this;

   d. to minimise levels of violence within society and the resort to violence in child-rearing practices.

1.3. At the secondary and tertiary levels: to develop, implement, monitor and where appropriate review preventive programmes to prevent child abuse, taking account of local conditions and structures of service delivery. These may include:

   a. the preventive measures outlined in Recommendation No. R (49) 17 concerning the protection of children against ill-treatment and Recommendation No. R (90) 2 on social measures concerning violence within the family;

   b. the provision of playgroups, nurseries, child health care and other social welfare services to meet the material, psychosocial and medical needs of children and promote their proper development;

   c. the provision of accessible, non-stigmatising services to help and support parents experiencing problems with child-rearing;

   d. the implementation of educational programmes for children concerning their right to a life free from abuse, emphasising body awareness, assertiveness training and their right to say no;

   e. publicity concerning sources of help (for example, telephone helplines, sheltered homes for children experiencing problems of neglect or abuse).

2. *Detection and notification*

2.1. Designate an agency (or agencies) or an individual at the appropriate level, available twenty-four hours a day, to receive notifications of abuse.

2.2. Encourage professionals (for example, teachers, doctors, social workers, nurses and others in contact with children) to notify the designated agency if they have reasonable grounds to believe that a child has been abused, is being abused or where there is a strong suspicion of abuse, or clear grounds for believing that it is likely to occur.

2.3. Advise professionals that in respecting ethical codes and legal rules of confidentiality, account should be taken of the fact that in such circumstances the designated agency should be notified.

2.4. Consider indemnity from legal proceedings to persons summoned as witnesses who, *bona fide* and with care, report abuse or a reasonable suspicion of child abuse.

2.5. Take measures to advise members of the community, for example, of the existence and signs of child abuse and of the availability of services to help children and families through public information campaigns in the media, and the distribution of leaflets, etc. in health clinics, libraries, etc.

2.6. Take steps to promote the responsible reporting of lay concerns that a child may be being abused, with safeguards where required for the anonymity of those making such reports.

2.7. Ensure that the person who has reported is informed of the appropriate steps taken as far as legal and moral codes of confidentiality permit.

2.8. Establish services (such as telephone helplines) for victims of abuse and other persons wishing to report their concerns.

3. *Investigation and assessment*

3.1. Establish at the appropriate level services available twenty-four hours a day, with powers and resources to provide, within an appropriate time-scale, for:

    a. the multidisciplinary investigation of notifications of child abuse;

    b. psychosocial assessment of the needs of children and their families for practical assistance and support, therapy, legal measures of protection, etc.;

    c. medical assessment, psychosomatic and physical, of the child according to the nature of the concerns and the type of abuse;

    d. emergency or long-term legal measures for the protection of the child if required;

    e. the taking at any moment of urgent measures including placement in sheltered homes.

3.2. Ensure that in intervention in all cases of child abuse the best interests of the child shall be the primary consideration and that when services are made available to abused children and their families, they are sensitive to the child's age, wishes, understanding, gender and to his/her ethnic, cultural, religious and linguistic background, and to special needs, such as disability.

3.3. Implement policies which aim, whenever possible, to work in partnership with the child's parents and to secure the child's welfare within his/her own family, through the provision of appropriate help and support.

3.4. See to it that children are informed of the nature of concerns about them, of their rights and of the actions which will be taken to investigate the concerns.

3.5. Ensure that – except where this would be contrary to the best interests of the child – parents are informed of the concerns about their child and of their rights to participate in decision-making and of appeal.

3.6. Ensure that in cases where children are separated from their parents, strenuous efforts are made to maintain links between the child and his/her parents as far as possible and consistent with the welfare of the child.

3.7. See to it that children are appropriately represented and that their views are sought and taken into account, having regard to their age and understanding.

3.8. Make arrangements, where appropriate, for medical assessment of the child to be undertaken in suitable premises by personnel with training, skill, experience and aptitude in the identification of child abuse and in working with children. Any medical examination should be carried out within a time-scale appropriate to each case. In some circumstances, urgency is required.

3.9. Restrict any medical examinations to the minimum number and the least intrusive approach required to help establish whether child abuse has occurred, to secure the requisite treatment and, where necessary, to document clinical evidence which may be used, as appropriate, in legal proceedings for the protection of the child or the prosecution of abusers.

3.10. Ensure that in any police investigations and subsequent criminal proceedings the welfare and interests of the child are paramount. This includes sensitivity to the child's needs in interviews and in the courts when children are called as witnesses, and ensuring that any delays are kept to a minimum and do not prejudice the child's right to receive help.

3.11. Adopt practices which encourage the sharing of information between the various professionals involved in investigation and assessment and which acknowledge the need to respect the confidentiality of the information shared; this may be achieved through holding a multidisciplinary case conference convened within an agreed time-scale, at which reports from all those involved in the investigation and assessment are presented and a plan drawn up for the welfare and protection of children, for their families and, where appropriate, for the abuser(s).

4. *Follow-up intervention, treatment and review*

4.1. Following investigation and assessment, to base all help, intervention and treatment for abused children upon a written plan designed to meet the needs of the child and his/her family, including any siblings, in the short, medium or long term. The plan may include, *inter alia*, the provision of financial and material aid, services such as day care, respite care or rehousing, therapy, counselling or support for the child and for his/her family; the need for services for the child and his/her family should be assessed whether the child is maintained at home or whether separation is deemed to be necessary.

4.2. Appoint a key worker for each case to consult with and co-ordinate all services or institutions involved with the child and the family and to ensure the implementation of the plan for the welfare and protection of the child and his/her family.

4.3. Establish policies which guarantee that appropriate help and support are provided, that judicial or administrative decisions taken promote the child's welfare and development and are made with all reasonable speed to a time-scale consistent with the child's needs and understanding.

4.4. Establish procedures at the appropriate level for the periodic review and follow-up of cases of abuse to monitor the implementation of the plans for the welfare and protection of the child and of his/her family. Central to such procedures is the involvement of a person (who may be the key worker or an independent advocate) whose role is to represent the child's interests and to act as advocate or guardian of the child's welfare, having regard to the child's needs, wishes and feelings.

4.5. Establish arrangements to facilitate the closure of cases, following multidisciplinary review, recovery of the victim and of the authors of abuse, and in circumstances in which services are no longer required for the welfare or protection of the child and his/her family.

4.6. Implement measures in respect of those who abuse children, whether through criminal prosecutions, therapy or a combination of treatment programmes with legal sanctions. Responses to abusers will be affected by consideration of, *inter alia*, the needs of the children concerned, the nature of the abuse, assessment of the abusers, their reactions and attitude to the abuse, the opportunities and prospects for treatment and rehabilitation as well as the requirements of the criminal justice system.

5. Training

5.1. Ensure that there is adequate training of the personnel in the various professional groups involved with the prevention of child abuse and the protection of children against abuse and, in particular, to:

a. require bodies responsible for basic qualifying courses for doctors, community nurses, social workers, teachers, police officers, child psychologists, the legal profession and any others likely to come across cases of child abuse to include coverage of the topic of child abuse and child protection in the formal curriculum;

b. make known to all personnel who work with children their roles and responsibilities, and those of other professionals, with respect to the notification of suspected cases and the actions to be taken thereafter and ensure that all personnel are aware of the needs of children and of the legislation, policies, and procedures for securing the welfare and protection of abused children and their families, and for respecting confidentiality in the medical and all other fields;

c. ensure that professionals involved in the investigation and assessment of child abuse, in intervention and therapy with abused children, their families or abusers and in civil or criminal legal proceedings in connection with child abuse, are fully trained and appropriately experienced;

d. require those who are closely involved with cases of child abuse to undertake specialised training in the skills of communicating with children who are or may have been abused; and to have the necessary professional qualification, as well as involvement, availability and stability (families cannot be helped in a fragmentary and piecemeal fashion);

e. provide opportunities for in-service and post-qualifying training to keep professionals informed of developments and trends in work with abused children, their families and with abusers;

f. provide opportunities for multidisciplinary training, to increase understanding and co-operation between the many disciplines involved;

g. provide opportunities for those closely involved with cases of child abuse so as to examine their own responses to the issues and to explore the specific challenges of work with abused children, their families and with abusers;

h. monitor and evaluate training programmes in the field of child abuse to increase knowledge of appropriate content, teaching materials and methods.

6. Research

6.1. To promote research on a comparative basis between the member states to analyse the various systems for meeting the needs of children and their families and responding to child abuse and to compare and contrast their effectiveness for the children and families concerned.

6.2. To develop programmes of research on the topic of child abuse, in particular giving priority to:

a. the evaluation of different approaches to the prevention of child abuse;

b. the evaluation of different systems for the involvement of children and parents in decision-making and for the protection of their rights;

c. the evaluation of different approaches to treatment and intervention in direct work with children, families and abusers;

d. the identification of patterns and trends in child abuse to help target prevention and intervention.

7. Financial implications

7.1. To take appropriate steps at national, regional and local levels to ensure the provision of proper financing of the programmes and measures to be implemented within the framework of this recommendation.

Legal affairs

Table of contents

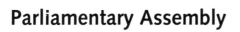

Parliamentary Assembly

Recommendation 869 (1979)[1]
on payment by the state of advances on child maintenance

The Assembly,

1.   Bearing in mind that the year 1979 was declared the "International Year of the Child" by the United Nations;

2.   Acknowledging, on the one hand, that in recent years the member states of the Council of Europe have made considerable efforts to improve the situation of children born out of wedlock and to alleviate the difficulties which illegitimacy can entail;

3.   Aware, on the other hand, that in many cases under-age children are brought up by one parent, whether because they were born out of wedlock or because their parents are separated or divorced, and that in such cases the persons liable for their maintenance often do not live under the same roof as they do;

4.   Aware also that special protection is needed for children whose situation is aggravated by the attempts frequently made by such persons to evade their maintenance obligations;

5.   Noting that the remedies provided for by law in these cases often prove ineffectual, and that even attachment is not always a guarantee that the full amount of the maintenance will be recovered, and that it will be paid on the due date;

6.   Having regard to the fact that one of the parents must consequently not only assume sole responsibility for the child's maintenance, but also for its education, which is an unbearable burden;

7.   Believing it to be desirable, therefore, that the state should pay advances on maintenance due, so that, if the full amount of maintenance owing in respect of a minor child cannot be recovered on the due date, the state will guarantee its subsistence and then recover the sums advanced from the debtor;

8.   Recalling that the European Conference on Family Law, held in Vienna in September 1977, proposed that the Council of Europe should recommend states to take action with a view to intervention, by way of an advance payment or on any other basis when the father or mother or one of them fail to discharge their maintenance obligations, and that a committee of experts of

---

1. *Text adopted by the Standing Committee,* acting on behalf of the Assembly, on 28 June 1979. See Doc. 4321, report of the Legal Affairs Committee.

the European Committee on Legal Co-operation has been instructed to examine this question,

9. Recommends that the Committee of Ministers should call on those governments of member states which have not already done so to bring their legislation into line with the principles approved by the Assembly and defined in the appendix to this recommendation.

Appendix to Recommendation 869 (1979)

Principles governing payment by the state of advances on child maintenance

1.　Advances on maintenance due are normally payable in respect of any under-age child habitually resident in the country paying them.

2.　Advances on maintenance are payable:

　　a.　if an action to recover maintenance, instituted during the three months preceding the application for an advance and based on a writ of execution (judgment or agreement approved by the guardian), has failed, or

　　b.　if a writ of execution cannot be obtained within three months of the instituting of proceedings to assert the child's right to maintenance, or

　　c.　if the place of residence of the debtor is not known.

3.　In the case of children born out of wedlock, advances may be paid without a writ of execution having been produced or before proceedings have been instituted to assert the child's right to maintenance.

4.　The amount of the advance paid may not exceed the sum decided on in the writ of execution, and shall at least be equal to the subsistence level laid down in the national legislation.

5.　The application for an advance may be filed by the child's legal representative, by the person who has custody of the child, or by the child himself.

6.　The child's legal representative and the person who has custody of the child should, as soon as they have knowledge of it, inform the state of any new ground for reducing the advances or ceasing payment thereof; anyone who fails to respect this rule may be required to refund any advance paid needlessly.

7.　The grant of advances does not release the maintenance debtor from his obligations under family law.

8.　The advances are conditional on surrender to the state of the equivalent amount from the child's estate.

Recommendation 874 (1979)[1]
on a European Charter on the Rights of the Child

The Assembly,

1.   Taking into account the reports of its Committee on Social and Health Questions on the legal position of the child and commercial exploitation, on child labour and medical care and on child abuse (Docs. 4376 and 4387);

2.   Recalling its Recommendation 561 of 1969 on the protection of minors against ill-treatment and noting with satisfaction that the Committee of Ministers has borne in mind the guidelines set out in that recommendation in the intergovernmental work of the Council of Europe;

3.   Recalling the European Convention on Human Rights and the European Social Charter;

4.   Bearing in mind the United Nations Declaration on the Rights of the Child, of 20 November 1959;

5.   Welcoming the decision of the United Nations to proclaim 1979 the International Year of the Child (IYC) and noting with appreciation the programmes initiated in developing countries by specialised United Nations agencies such as UNICEF;

6.   Expressing the earnest hope that IYC and the subsequent efforts will promote the legal protection of children, enhance awareness of their problems and needs and improve their living conditions in all regions of the world;

7.   Emphasising that a society's vitality depends on the possibilities it offers the younger generations for growth and development in safety, self-realisation, solidarity and peace;

8.   Aware of the fact that the vast majority of children are loved and cared for and also aware of the fact that the children in member states of the Council of Europe enjoy a better fate than those in developing countries, whose problems for daily survival, food and shelter are still acute;

9.   Convinced that there is still need for improvement of the children's situation also in Western Europe, in particular where there is poverty and social injustice;

---

1. *Assembly debate* on 3 and 4 October 1979 (9th and 10th Sittings) (see Doc. 4376, report of the Committee on Social and Health Questions).
   Text adopted by the Assembly on 4 October 1979 (10th Sitting).

10. Convinced that it must stress once again, on the occasion of the International Year of the Child, the importance of safeguarding children against abuse;

11. Considering that physical and psychological maltreatment of children is one of the most abhorrent abuses which takes place in any country;

12. Considering that abuse should not be taken as solely physical punishment inflicted upon children by parents, guardians or custodians but as a wider problem covering all physical and emotional ill-treatment, neglect and also denial of love and affection;

13. Considering that all member governments should give priority to legislation safeguarding children against abuse from parents or legal guardians, including the possibility in severe cases of removing the abused child from the custody of the abuser;

14. Bearing in mind the exposed situation in general of children, the existing exploitation of children and the sharp increase in the hard pornography industry, and taking into account that this industry represents a particularly vile way of profit-making;

15. Convinced that the public display of violence, criminality and terrorism in the mass media constitutes a permanent danger for youth;

16. Considering that there are in Europe too many families living in a state of extreme poverty, and that children of the fourth world more than others suffer from the lack of food, medical care, social provision and the inadequacy of the education system,

17. Recommends that the Committee of Ministers take without delay appropriate steps for the creation of a European Charter on the Rights of the Child which should be designed to give the maximum assistance to parents to fulfil their grave responsibilities, and take into account, *inter alia*, the following principles and guidelines:

I. General principles

a. Children must no longer be considered as parents' property, but must be recognised as individuals with their own rights and needs;

b. Government policies and programmes in member countries must take into account the importance for children of love and affection as much as their need for material assistance;

c. By ensuring the schooling of all children, and in particular of the most deprived children, educational programmes and upbringing in general in member countries should aim at:

- international solidarity and peace,
- education for democracy,
- co-operation and equality,
- equality of rights and of opportunities between sexes.

II. The legal position of the child

a. The rights of children in their environment should be safeguarded by creating for this purpose an official authority at community level;

b. The children's legal status in family and institutions ought to be co-ordinated and better unified;

c. The concept of "parental authority" must be superseded by "parental responsibility", and by clear description of children's rights as individual family members;

d. The children's legally defined rights to their own legal voice (official advocate) in cases of conflicts between parents, such as divorce and separation proceedings, must be improved, and based upon the principle that the interests of the child shall be regarded as paramount;

e. It should be confirmed that children, in time of war, should be given appropriate protection as provided by the Geneva Conventions of 1949 for the protection of victims of war.

III. Child abuse

a. Education for parenthood should be given during the last years at school both for boys and girls;

b. Consideration should be given to the needs of children whose mothers go out to work: where economic conditions force a mother to work to support her family, subsidised help should be available, such as local authority day care centres; and society should offer assistance so that one of the parents, when he or she so wishes, can devote himself or herself exclusively to the care and upbringing of the children without being subject to economic constraints;

c. Teachers and others in regular contact with children who often recognise that the family is going through stress should alert social services;

d. Legal provisions should encourage professionals connected with child care to contact social authorities when suspicion of abuse against children arises, and also encourage others to contact welfare authorities in such cases;

e. Steps should be taken in order to improve the co-operation between officials of all groups connected with child care, such as school teachers, nursery school teachers, psychologists, social workers, lawyers and police officers with regard to child abuse;

f. In the light of the importance of early diagnosis, existing knowledge on child abuse should be included as a compulsory part of the training for all groups of personnel dealing with children in all member countries.

IV. Prostitution and pornography

a. The fostering of healthy and responsible attitude to sexual behaviour by providing objective information on family, contraception and venereal diseases should be encouraged;

b. Particular attention should be paid to any connections between child prostitution and organised crime and narcotics, and to the fact that a liberal attitude towards the so-called "soft" drugs may have heavy negative consequences (see Recommendation 609 of the Assembly);

c. Strict laws and regulations should be adopted to abolish child pornography, and such laws and regulations should be harmonised among member states.

V. Child labour

Child labour, which is on the increase despite the persisting unemployment in member countries, must be regulated in a manner that protects the child against exploitation, against dangers to health and against practices which restrict its proper education and its physical, moral and mental development, by adopting in particular the following legal criteria:

a. Prohibition of full-time work under the age of 16 must become the objective in all member states and achieved within the next four years, and in the meantime all member states should accept and implement Article 7 of the European Social Charter fixing the minimum age for admission to employment;

b. The so-called "occasional work" or work in family businesses must be strictly regulated and must not interfere with the normal schooling and normal development of the child;

c. European standards for child labour minimum age requirements should also apply to European companies functioning abroad;

d. As parents are primarily responsible for child labour, the competent public authorities should inform the parents regularly of the existing legislation, risk and consequences of child labour.

VI. Social and medical protection

a. The rights of every child to life from the moment of conception, to shelter, adequate food and congenial environment should be recognised, and national governments should accept as an obligation the task of providing for full realisation of such rights;

b. The right to adequate care, including effective measures against disease and accidents, and adequate medical attention should be ensured;

c. All member governments should establish systems of obligatory free medical examination of children;

d. Due attention should be paid to protection against abuse of drugs, smoking and alcohol, and advertising for these products in broadcasting;

e. The right of handicapped children to be properly looked after and to be given adequate training and education should be guaranteed; urgent attention should be given to the problem of the child kept in long-stay hospitals; the organisation of voluntary visiting schemes should be considered, using media publicity and other methods.

VII. Sports

a. It should be ensured that high performance sports remain a voluntary undertaking, that no coercion of any sort be indulged in and that human dignity be respected at all times;

b. To reduce health hazards and educational disadvantages, regulations should be introduced in training methods and training periods;

c. Supervision should be exercised on the use of certain drugs which can prematurely stop growth or affect sexual development; drug detection tests during competitions ought to be increased;

d. The possibility for handicapped children to participate in sporting activities should be improved;

18. Further recommends that the Committee of Ministers consult the Parliamentary Assembly on the content of the proposed European Charter on the Rights of the Child.

Recommendation 1065 (1987)[1]
on the traffic in children and other forms of child exploitation

The Assembly,

1. Considering that children have the right to be brought up in a secure and humane way, and that society has an obligation to protect them and look after their interests;

2. Appalled by the international trade in children for such purposes as prostitution, pornography, slavery, illegal adoption, etc.;

3. Referring to its Recommendation 1044 (1986) on international crime, in which it recommends that the Committee of Ministers invite the governments of member states to co-operate in a study of and action against the trade in children;

4. Considering that children have the same right as all human beings to enjoy an environment which affords them security, health and physical integrity, and that they must be treated humanely, that society has a duty to provide them with protection, to monitor observance of their rights and to afford them equality of opportunity;

5. Bearing in mind its Recommendation 874 (1979) on a European charter on the Rights of the Child, covering a number of aspects ranging from legal status to medical and social protection;

6. Considering that it is essential that member states, as a matter of urgency, take the following measures:

a. sign and ratify, in so far as they have not yet done so, the following conventions:

i. the Convention for the suppression of the traffic in persons and the exploitation of the prostitution of others (United Nations Treaty Series No. 1342, opened for signature at Lake Success, New York, on 21 March 1950);

ii. the European Convention on the Adoption of Children (1967);

iii. the Hague Convention on jurisdiction, applicable law and recognition of degrees relating to adoption;

iv. Convention No. 138 of the International Labour Organisation, on the minimum age for employment;

---

1. *Assembly debate* on 6 October 1987 (15th Sitting) (see Doc. 5777, report of the Legal Affairs Committee).
   Text adopted by the Assembly on 6 October 1987 (15th Sitting).

v. the European Social Charter, with particular reference to Article 7 concerning the right of children and adolescents to protection;

b. support, in the United Nations General Assembly, the draft declaration on social and legal principles relating to the protection and welfare of children, with special reference to foster placement and adoption, nationally and internationally;

c. seek safeguards and improve all practices in the case of international adoptions, *inter alia*:

i. by the elaboration of a code of conduct and guidelines for individuals and agencies proposing to undertake the interstate movement of unaccompanied minors;

ii. by regulating that, in interstate adoption, placements should be made through competent authorities or agencies, with the application of safeguards and standards equivalent to those existing in respect of national adoption;

iii. by regulating that in no case should the placement result in improper financial gain for those involved;

d. promote and encourage a wide-ranging campaign of public information concerning the sale of and traffic in children, and the exploitation of child labour;

e. inform educators and youth of the rights of the child, and incorporate human rights education in school curricula at all levels;

f. promote the undertaking of judicious research programmes at national and international levels to analyse the forms, conditions and structures of the sale and traffic of children;

g. enact strict laws and regulations to combat child pornography and harmonise member states' relevant legislation;

h. promote and pursue a policy directed at meeting the needs of abandoned and street children;

i. condemn any policy of commercial and industrial competition based on exploitation of child labour, and ensure that the activities of national and international agencies working in the field of development are designed in such a way as to have a positive effect on the rights and interests of children throughout the world;

j. take measures to guarantee children working in conformity with Article 7 of the European Social Charter decent living and working conditions;

k. increase public surveillance of such children, for instance by improving the labour inspectorate, appointing ombudsmen to protect their rights, providing for education and training in the workplace, and introducing additional welfare measures concerning their health and diet,

7. Recommends that the Committee of Ministers instruct the European Committee on Crime Problems (CDPC) to study the traffic in children and other forms of exploitation of children as a priority matter in the light of the proposals made above.

Recommendation 1121 (1990)[1]
on the rights of children

The Assembly,

1. Recalling that a society's vitality depends on the opportunities it offers its younger generation for growth and development in safety, self-realisation, solidarity and peace;

2. Considering that children, that is human beings who have not attained their majority, are in need of special assistance, care and protection, and considering that the parents' primary responsibility needs to be reasserted and cannot be called into question;

3. Considering that children, for the full and harmonious development of their personality should grow up in an atmosphere of happiness, love and understanding;

4. Considering that the right of children to special protection imposes obligations on society and on the adults normally dealing with them such as parents, teachers, social workers, doctors and others;

5. Considering that, in addition to the right to be protected, children have rights they may independently exercise themselves – even against opposing adults;

6. Considering that parental powers and the authority of other adults on children are derived from a duty for protection and should exist only as long as they are necessary for the protection of the person and property of the child;

7. Considering that these powers decline as the child matures and that a child is subsequently able to exercise an increasing number of rights;

8. Considering that there is much uncertainty about the rights people under age have or may enjoy, and that it is highly desirable that all member states grant full legal capacity at the same age;

9. Considering that young persons, more and more frequently, travel, study and work abroad, and that, for this reason, coherent action and legislation are desirable in Council of Europe member states in respect of the rights of the child;

---

1. *Assembly debate* on 1 February 1990 (27th Sitting) (see Doc. 6142, report of the Committee on Legal Affairs and Human Rights, Rapporteur: Mrs Ekman; and Doc. 6150, opinion of the Social, Health and Family Affairs Committee, Rapporteur: Mr Bowden).
   Text adopted by the Assembly on 1 February 1990 (27th Sitting).

10. Welcoming the adoption of the Convention on the Rights of the Child by the General Assembly of the United Nations in November 1989;

11. Recalling its Recommendation 874 (1979) on a European Charter on the Rights of the Child, 1071 (1988) on child welfare and 1074 (1988) on family policy;

12. Recalling Recommendation No. R (88) 16 of the Committee of Ministers to member states on ratifying and improving the implementation of the conventions and agreements concluded within the Council of Europe in the field of private law, notably the conventions which protect the interests of the child,

13. Recommends that the Committee of Ministers:

A. Invite member states:

i. in so far as they have not yet done so, to sign and ratify:

   a. the European Social Charter (1961, European Treaty Series, No. 35), and, in particular, to accept Article 7 thereof on the protection of children and young people, Article 17 on the protection of mothers and children and Article 19, paragraph 6, on family reunion, and to ensure that the standards therein are fully enforced;

   b. the European Convention on the Adoption of Children (1967, European Treaty Series, No. 58);

   c. the European Convention on the Legal Status of Children Born out of Wedlock (1975, European Treaty Series, No. 85);

   d. the European Convention on Recognition and Enforcement of Decisions concerning Custody of Children and on Restoration of Custody of Children (1980, European Treaty Series, No. 105);

   e. International Labour Organisation (ILO) Convention No. 138 on the Minimum Age of Admission to Employment (1973);

ii. to envisage, if they have not yet done so, the appointment of a special ombudsman for children, who could inform them on their rights, counsel them, intervene and, possibly, take legal action on their behalf;

iii. to do whatever they can in favour of the rapid ratification and implementation of the United Nations Convention on the Rights of the Child;

B. Instruct the competent steering committees to examine the possibility of drawing up an appropriate legal instrument of the Council of Europe in order to complete the United Nations Convention on the Rights of the Child, and, in particular, to instruct the Steering Committee for Human Rights (CDDH) to consider the possibility of elaborating an additional protocol to the European Convention on Human Rights concerning the rights of the child;

C. Arrange for the above-mentioned European legal instrument to embody not only the civil and political rights of children but also their economic and social rights, and accordingly instruct the Steering Committee for Human Rights to collaborate with other committees in the various sectors concerned, such as the social and employment sectors;

D. Instruct the European Committee on Legal Co-operation (CDCJ), or another appropriate intergovernmental expert committee, to make a full study on the position of children in courts and on the acts a minor is entitled to accomplish before the age of full legal capacity, with a view to arriving at common European positions;

E. Convene a small group of highly competent independent experts to study how children may exercise the fundamental rights which have been granted to them by such international instruments as the European Convention on Human Rights and the European Social Charter;

F. Better inform children of the rights they have;

G. Establish co-ordination to ensure the systematic study of the rights of children and co-operation with other international organisations such as the European Community, the International Labour Organisation, the Hague Conference on Private International Law and non-governmental organisations.

Resolution 1011 (1993)[1]
on the situation of women and children
in the former Yugoslavia

1.   The Assembly refers in particular to Order No. 486 (1993) on the protection of human rights and the joint declaration of its Social, Health and Family Affairs Committee and Unicef (United Nations Children's Fund), adopted in Geneva on 24 June 1993.

2.   The conflict in the former Yugoslavia is marked by ethnic cleansing and barbarous violence against civilians, in particular women and children. The elementary rules and principles of the laws of war and the protective provisions of humanitarian law have been systematically flouted and violated.

3.   The international community has been powerless to provide an appropriate response, although the United Nations decision to set up an international court expresses its unwavering determination not to leave unpunished the war crimes and crimes against humanity committed during the conflict.

4.   Humanitarian action has shown its limitations; however, in spite of the difficulties encountered, an attempt has been made to offset the international community's shortcomings. Just tribute should be paid to the remarkable work performed by the various humanitarian organisations such as the UNHCR (Office of the United Nations High Commissioner for Refugees), Unicef, ICRC (International Committee of the Red Cross) and the NGOs (non-governmental organisations), and also to their staff, those women and men who devote themselves to helping others, often at the risk of their own lives.

5.   The current lack of subsidies means that this action may have to be discontinued, despite the increase in and diversification of the demand for humanitarian relief. Steps must be taken to continue to ensure the survival of civilian populations and also to treat the trauma caused by war, to reconstruct the vital infrastructure which has been destroyed and to give the population, especially the children, prospects of a future comprising something other than violence, hatred and revenge.

6.   In the last ten years, 90% of victims of armed conflict have been civilians; over one and a half million children have been killed, four million suffer from disabilities resulting from war, and a reported five million live in refugee camps. Moreover, in the conflict of the former Yugoslavia it is once again the

1. *Assembly debate* on 28 September 1993 (47th Sitting) (see Doc. 6903, report of the Social, Health and Family Affairs Committee, Rapporteurs: Mrs Robert and Mr Daniel).
    Text adopted by the Assembly on 28 September 1993 (47th Sitting).

women and children who are the main losers in the war. They have suffered and witnessed barbaric acts and are liable to pass on a hatred which has devastated them. The rights of the child, a recent achievement of the international community, have been trodden underfoot.

7. The Assembly, therefore, urges the governments of the member and non-member states grouped together in the Council of Europe:

i. to take the requisite action on the declarations made at the New York World Summit for Children in 1990, by subscribing to the principle of "First Call for Children", according to which meeting the essential needs of children must be a top political priority when resources are allocated and must be taken fully into account when various policies are devised, and to undertake, as appropriate, to ratify and apply the provisions of the United Nations Convention on the Rights of the Child;

ii. to express their support for this principle at the summit of heads of state and government (to be held on 8 and 9 October 1993 in Vienna) and to focus their discussions at the next Conference of European Ministers responsible for Family Affairs (Paris, 13-15 October 1993) on this central issue;

iii. to undertake to protect children from the scourge of war and to condemn the barbaric practice in recent armed conflicts of using women and children as targets and human shields, as well as the widespread use of anti-personnel mines, particularly those resembling toys, of which the main victims are children;

iv. if the conflict in the former Yugoslavia continues, to take, in consultation with specialised organisations and NGOs, the immediate measures needed to ensure that the children and women of Bosnia-Herzegovina are given the food, water, heating, medical care and treatment and psychosocial help which are vital for their survival, that is to say, to ensure in all cases freedom of access for humanitarian relief and to secure observance for "havens of peace and safety" for the children;

v. to accompany the measures imposing embargoes and other sanctions on the warring parties with the humanitarian arrangements needed to protect the lives and health of the most vulnerable group of civilians, especially children;

vi. to introduce, at a European level, a co-ordinating structure to provide information on immediately available medical facilities (for example, the number of beds reserved for emergency treatment for children in each country) and to develop mutual assistance between hospitals in order to promote the rebuilding of hospitals, donations in kind and personnel support in the former Yugoslavia;

vii. to ensure that rape victims, both women and children, receive the necessary medical care, psychological support and legal aid, not least in host countries;

viii. to provide the appropriate emergency medical, psychological and educational aid for children who have witnessed or suffered cruelty, inhuman or degrading acts or the loss of their loved ones;

ix. in the facilities for accommodating displaced persons, and refugee camps in particular, to help the women to feel useful by providing them with opportunities to engage in occupations and receive education and vocational training and allowing them to retain their active role, notably in performing their everyday family duties and housework;

x. to supply the children of the former Yugoslavia affected by the conflict with a minimum of education and the educational and play material (books, toys, etc.) which is vital for children's development;

xi. to develop, particularly for children, programmes of education in peace, tolerance and democracy;

xii. to assist in the initial and further vocational training of local personnel, especially those responsible for children, and to give them the moral support and psychological help needed for overcoming the burnout syndrome.

8. The Assembly launches an urgent appeal to the governments of the states grouped together in the Council of Europe and to the European Community to contribute financially to humanitarian relief, to relax the conditions placed on the grant of subsidies allocated to the various humanitarian organisations at work in the former Yugoslavia and to increase the size of the subsidies, so that needs can be effectively met.

9. It invites the governments of Council of Europe member states to make optimum use of the instrument constituted by the Council of Europe's Social Development Fund by means of a special aid account, so that immediate practical steps can be taken to meet the manifold needs emerging from the conflict in the former Yugoslavia.

10. The Assembly also invites governments not to overlook the risk that similar conflicts might break out in or around Europe, to continue discussion on humanitarian action in cases of armed conflict and to devise a concerted European strategy, so as to take timely steps to develop and reinforce, in every country, all the peace forces in society.

11. The Assembly invites the international community to review and adapt the humanitarian law governing the protection, in cases of armed conflict, of civilians, notably women and children, in keeping with human rights and the rights of the child.

12. Finally, the Assembly condemns the inhuman actions of all the warring factions, and calls upon Bosnians, Croats and Serbs to behave like civilised persons and not like animals, and furthermore demands that the principles of international humanitarian law be strictly observed by all concerned in every respect.

Opinion No. 186 (1995)[1]
on the draft European convention
on the exercise of children's rights

1. The Parliamentary Assembly has frequently dealt with the different aspects of children's welfare and their rights and has adopted a number of relevant texts in particular on child welfare and family policy; it is also examining a draft European convention on the exercise of children's rights.

2. The latest and most comprehensive Assembly text in this field is Recommendation 1121 (1990) on the rights of children. It was this recommendation that gave impetus to the Committee of Experts on Family Law (CJ-FA) in their work on a convention on the exercise of children's rights.

3. Recommendation 1121 (1990), drafted after the adoption of the 1989 United Nations Convention on the Rights of the Child, acknowledged the importance of this convention as the most complete international instrument on the children's rights and called upon Council of Europe member states ratify it.

4. However, the Assembly pointed out various gaps both in the substantive part and in the procedural mechanisms for the implementation of the United Nations convention. Consequently, the assembly suggested a multifaceted plan of action based on a thorough analysis of past accomplishments, failures and ongoing work.

5. The Assembly addressed several concrete proposals to the Committee of Ministers:

   i. It recommended that the Committee of Ministers instruct the competent steering committees to draw up an appropriate legal instrument of the Council of Europe to complete the United Nations Convention on the Rights of the Child and, in particular, to instruct the Steering Committee on Human Rights (CDDH) to consider the possibility of elaborating an additional protocol to the European Convention on Human Rights concerning the rights of the child (section B of Recommendation 1121 (1990));

   ii. Referring to the position of children in court, the Parliamentary Assembly voiced the view that children should be respected as individuals and should be granted the possibility to exercise an increasing number of rights independently, and even against opposing adults. To this end, the assembly invited the Committee of Ministers to instruct the European

---

1. *Assembly debate* on 25 April (10th Sitting) (See doc. 7270, report of the Committee on Legal Affairs and Human Rights, rapporteur: Mrs Jaani).
   Text adopted by the Assembly on 25 April 1995 (10th Sitting)

Committee of Legal Co-operation (CDCJ), or another appropriate intergovernmental expert committee, to make a full study on the position of children in courts and on the acts a minor is entitled to accomplish before reaching the age of full legal capacity, with a view to arriving at a common European position (section D of Recommendation 1121 (1991));

iii. Furthermore, the Assembly recommended that the Committee of Ministers convene a small group of highly competent independent experts to study how children may exercise the fundamental rights which have been granted to them by such international instruments as the European Convention on Human Rights and the European Social Charter (section E of Recommendation 1121 (1990)).

6. The draft European convention on the exercise of children's rights has been prepared by the Committee of Experts on Family Law (CJ-FA). It takes up only some of the Assembly proposals. It concentrates on the procedural rights of children in family proceedings affecting them and the promotion of the exercise of these rights.

7. The Assembly is convinced that the draft convention will strengthen the position of children in court and will promote the exercise of their procedural rights.

8. However, the Assembly is concerned that the draft convention leaves a broad margin of discretion to the contracting states regarding the choice of applicable provisions. Considering that the main purpose of this convention is to arrive at a common European position on the exercise of children's rights, the Assembly believes that a certain minimum of the procedural rights of children should be accepted by all states signatories to the convention.

9. Consequently, the Assembly recommends that the Committee of Ministers make the following amendments with a view to improving the draft convention:

i. *Article 1 (Scope and object of the convention)*

Change paragraph 4 as follows:

"Every state shall, at the time of signature or when depositing its instruments of ratification, acceptance, approval or accession by a declaration addressed to the Secretary General of the Council of Europe *accept that the convention shall apply to family proceedings concerning the residence of and access to children and shall* specify at least three *additional* types of proceedings before a judicial authority to which the convention is to apply."[1]

ii. *Article 11 (National bodies)*

– in paragraph 2, sub-paragraph *d*, replace "seek the views of" by "consult";

– add a new sub-paragraph e reading as follows:

---

1. Changes are given in italics.

"*e*. to intervene and, when necessary, take legal action on behalf of children";

iii.   *Article 15 (Establishment and functions of the Standing Committee)*

Add before sub-paragraph *a* the following new sub-paragraph:

"request Parties to the convention to produce reports at regular intervals on the application of the convention;"

iv.   *Article 16 (Members)*

– in paragraph 3, delete the second sub-paragraph;

– add the following new paragraph after paragraph 3:

"The United Nations Committee on the Rights of the Child shall attend the meetings of the Standing Committee as an observer."

10.   In addition, the Assembly suggests that the Committee of Ministers:

i.   consider including a definition of the concept "having sufficient understanding" in Article 2 of the draft convention;

ii.   consider elaborating a selection procedure for the members of the Standing Committee guaranteeing that this committee consist of highly competent and independent experts and that its procedures be transparent;

iii.   insert in the draft convention a non-discrimination clause, in particular concerning sex-discrimination.

11.   The Assembly further recommends that the Committee of Ministers:

i.   invite member states and non-member states which have participated in the elaboration of the convention according to the procedure provided for in Article 20, to sign and ratify the convention;

ii.   instruct the Steering Committee for Human Rights (CDDH) to continue its work on examining the possibility of elaborating an additional protocol to the European Convention on Human Rights concerning the rights of the child;

iii.   instruct other relevant committees of the Council of Europe to continue their work in the field of children's rights.

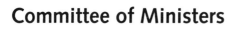

Committee of Ministers

Resolution (66) 25
Short-term treatment of young offenders of less than 21 years

(Adopted by the Ministers' Deputies on 30th April 1966)

The Committee of Ministers,

Considering the importance of developing effective measures against criminality manifested by young people;

Welcoming the attempts of governments to effect the reformation of young offenders under the age of 21 years without recourse to sanctions involving deprivation of liberty whenever that appears possible;

Recognising that nevertheless certain young offenders have to be detained in order to provide adequate treatment or a sanction appropriate to the offence;

Considering that certain young offenders need only a short period of treatment or that certain offences do not merit more than a short period of deprivation of liberty;

Recognising the serious disadvantages there can be when young offenders are required to serve short sentences of detention or imprisonment in establishments for adults,

Recommends that:

a. Whenever appropriate and possible, short-term methods of institutional treatment for young offenders should be used in reference to long-term methods;

b. Special establishments for such offenders should be set up which will provide a positive and suitable treatment for them, taking account of their age, stage of development, and individual needs so far as is possible in the limited time available;

c. Short-term treatment in special establishments for young offenders might be an alternative to or a complete substitute for ordinary short-term imprisonment. The choice made will influence the possibility of a special selection of offenders for this measure and affect the regimes to be adopted. Whatever conclusions are come to, care should be taken to exclude those offenders who, by reason of serious personal maladjustment, appear unsuitable for short-term methods of treatment;

d. Whatever balance between punitive and non-punitive approaches may be adopted as a starting point, there should be flexibility and experimentation in the regimes used in these establishments. The staff, which should include qualified social workers, should be specially selected for their capacity to work positively with young people. The possibility of providing post-institutional assistance should always exist;

   e. In order to promote the most efficient systems, it is desirable that basic statistical information be kept on offenders treated and that whenever possible research investigation should be used to evaluate the methods employed;

   f. Member states should consider the possibility of making arrangements which avoid so far as possible the serving of short prison sentences by young offenders in penal establishments taking adult offenders;

   Invites the governments to send reports to the Secretary General of the Council of Europe every three years informing him of the steps taken to implement these recommendations.

Resolution (72) 29
on the lowering of the age of full legal capacity

(Adopted by the Committee of Ministers on 19 September 1972
at the 213th meeting of the Ministers' Deputies)

The Committee of Ministers,

Considering that the aim of the Council of Europe is to achieve greater unity among its members, *inter alia*, by promoting the adoption of common rules in legal matters;

Noting that, whereas in the majority of member states the age of full legal capacity was established for a considerable period at 21 years, this age is now fixed below 21 in most member states;

Aware of the fact that under the laws of several member states minors of certain age enjoy special legal capacity to act independently in some important matters and that in fact in other states very similar results have been achieved by other means;

Believing that even though life today is more complex than formerly, the education gained during a prolonged compulsory schooling and the abundance of information available enable young people to meet the exigencies of life at an earlier age than before;

Recognising that the need of protecting young people is diminishing in importance as a result of measures designed to protect people of all ages in the economic field;

Believing that lowering the age of majority should encourage the development of a sense of responsibility in young people,

1. Recommends governments of member states to lower the age of majority below 21 years and, if they deem it advisable, to fix that age at 18 years, provided that states may retain a higher age of capacity for the performance of certain limited and specified acts in fields where they believe that a higher degree of maturity is required;

2. Recommends governments of member states especially those states where the age of majority may remain above 18 years, to consider the advisability of granting to certain minors capacity to carry out everyday transactions and to act independently in other appropriate fields;

3. Recommends governments of member states in which the lowering of the age of majority would substantially curtail the rights enjoyed by children under their parents' maintenance obligations, with the possible consequence

of depriving them of the necessary assistance for pursuing their education or training, to take appropriate measures to remedy such consequences;

4. Invites governments of member states to inform the Secretary General of the Council of Europe in due course of the action taken on the recommendation contained in this resolution.

Resolution (77) 13
on the nationality of children born in wedlock

(Adopted by the Committee of Ministers on 27 May 1977
at the 271st meeting of the Ministers' Deputies)

The Committee of Ministers,

Considering that the principle of the equality of a father's and a mother's rights concerning their joint children born in wedlock should entail in favour of such children the recognition of an equal right to acquire the nationality of their mother as well as that of their father;

Considering that it appears to be difficult to reach this goal in the near future and that it should therefore be achieved progressively,

Recommends to governments of member states:

1.   to grant their nationality at birth to children born in wedlock if their father or their mother possesses such nationality;

alternatively, to provide for these children up to the age of 22 facilities to acquire that nationality;

2.   to insert provisions in their internal legislation for the purpose of avoiding dual nationality resulting either directly or indirectly from descent or resulting from the place of birth.

To this end, they should, as minimum:

a. give the right to their nationals having another nationality to renounce their nationality;

b. permit their nationals having another nationality to make a declaration in favour of their nationality; consequently, to insert provisions according to which their nationals having made a declaration in favour of another nationality which they possess equally, shall lose their nationality automatically.

They may in addition provide that their nationals of more than 22 years of age, possessing equally another nationality, and who have not made a declaration in favour of one or the other of their nationalities, may be summoned according to the previous paragraph to make a declaration within a time-limit which shall not be shorter than six months for one or the other nationality and that they, failing to do so within that time-limit, shall automatically lose the nationality of the state which summoned them;

3. to inform each other reciprocally about declarations resulting in the acquisition, maintenance or loss of their nationality mentioned above as well as the modifications and the loss of nationality resulting from the application of the final sub-paragraph of paragraph 2 above.

Resolution (77) 33
on placement of children

*(Adopted by the Committee of Ministers on 3 November 1977
at the 277th meeting of the Ministers' Deputies)*

The Committee of Ministers,

Considering that the aim of the Council of Europe is the achievement of greater unity between its members for the purpose of safeguarding and realising the ideas and principles which are their common heritage and of facilitating their economic and social progress;

Bearing in mind the United Nations Declaration of the Rights of the Child and especially its second, fifth and sixth principles;

Bearing in mind Articles 16 and 17 of the European Social Charter, concerning the right of families to social, legal and economic protection and the right of mothers and children to social and economic protection;

Bearing in mind the conclusions of the 13th Conference of European Ministers responsible for Family Affairs held in 1973;

Realising that children who grow up in environments that do not meet their fundamental physical, emotional, intellectual and social needs are put in jeopardy of their lifelong welfare;

Affirming that preventive measures in the widest possible sense should remain the first strategy to avert this danger;

Aware that in spite of these measures many children will continue to need temporary or long-term placement outside their families;

Anxious to ensure that placement of children is carried out in the best possible circumstances,

Recommends the governments of members states:

I. General principles

1. To recognise that all arrangements for placements should be based on the following principles:

1.1. The need for placement should be avoided as far as possible through preventive measures of support for families in accordance with their special problems and needs;

1.2. A request for placement should be considered as a warming signal of a difficult family situation; consequently efforts to meet the child's needs should always be related to an understanding of the problems of his family and arrangements for the child should as a rule be coupled to specific arrangements for helping the parents;

1.3. The arrangements made for the child (including a decision to leave him in his family or to place him) should try to ensure the highest possible degree of satisfaction of his developing emotional needs and his physical wellbeing as well as any preventive medical, educational or other care necessary to meet special problems he may have;

These arrangements should provide, as far as possible and when this is in the best interests of the child:

– maintenance of links to his family;

– stability of care and bonds of affection, taking into account the child's developmental stage in regard to the formation of emotional attachments;

– respect of his individuality;

– a cultural and social environment which is appropriate and acceptable to society;

– integration into a local community and preferably the same one as the family's;

– for adolescents, opportunities for assuming responsibility, for achieving independence and for taking up adults roles;

1.4. The decisions about the child's placement should normally be taken after advice given by a multidisciplinary team; similar advice should be available at each review;

1.5. A plan for the child should be drawn up based on an assessment of the family, of the child himself and of the possible solutions available, in the light of the objectives mentioned above;

This plan should incorporate in particular:

– a decision on the best initial mode of placement for the child;

– a review of the child's situation after a period which will vary according to age and individual circumstances (being shorter in the case of very young children), but which should not normally exceed six months, after which there should be further reviews at regular intervals;

1.6. Long-term placement of very young children in residential units should be avoided as much as possible; thus adoption in the light of the European Convention on the Adoption of Children should be facilitated and encouraged to the greatest possible extent.

II. Policy

2. To ensure in the framework of their policies for family welfare that placement decisions are taken according to sound procedures and in a favourable context, in particular by:

A. *Family support*

2.1. Considering, in the framework of general economic and social policies, the implementation of measures to assist all families in rearing children well; and developing more specific measures of family policy such as preparation at school of children of both sexes for home and family life;

2.2. With a view to reducing the need for residential care on the sole grounds of handicap, providing the families of children with physical or mental handicaps with the necessary emotional support, with financial allowances, and also with technical, medical and educational support in decentralised forms; such support could, for example, be provided through day care facilities, services in the home, schemes for reducing parental burdens, transport services, material aid;

2.3. Providing facilities for the special assistance of families with acute psycho-social problems affecting the development of the child;

B. *Management of placements*

2.4. Encouraging the participation in the management of a child's placement of the following:

– the service or organisation responsible for the placement, i.e. the placement agency;

– the parents;

– the child, who should be given an opportunity to discuss his situation progressively as he matures in understanding;

– those caring for the child (foster parents or staff residential units);

– social and other workers concerned with the family;

– personnel of the statuary preventive public health services;

– pre-school and school personnel, paediatricians, psychologists, and any other specialists involved;

2.5. Ensuring that the professional staff involved in the management of the placement work, as far as possible, as a multidisciplinary team;

C. *Organisation*

2.6. Subjecting all organisations responsible for placements to strict regulation and supervision, to ensure the maintenance of high professional standards;

2.7. Integrating the organisations responsible for the placement of children with those responsible for assisting families or ensuring their closest co-operation in each case; and securing the decentralisation of responsibility in different organisations and services necessary to achieve co-operation at local level, so as to create areas of responsibility which can be better supervised;

2.8. Ensuring that financial arrangements do not establish an accidental bias towards the choice of one particular form of placement;

2.9. Generally seeing that the organisation responsible for placement is capable of adaptation to new techniques and knowledge;

D. *Modes of placement*

2.10. With a view to enabling them to match each placement to individual needs, making available to placement agencies an array of modes of placement from foster homes to various kinds of therapeutic care in residential homes (examples are given in the appendix);

2.11. Progressively providing the best possible geographical distribution of places so as to facilitate maintenance of links to the natural family and to promote co-operation with the biological parents, unless considered undesirable for the child;

2.12. Progressively making support services (psychologists, psychiatrists, specialised equipment, etc.) equally available to all staff of all types of residential units and to foster parents;

2.13. Promoting foster care as being frequently the best mode of temporary placement, especially for young children and therefore ensuring:
– education of the public on the value of foster care;
– the development of schemes for recruiting foster parents;
– careful selection of ordinary and specialised foster parents to be based, *inter alia*, on the assessment of each member of the household;
– thorough preparation for foster parents including discussion on child development, the problems of foster children and the specific situation of the child to be placed with them;
– definition of the obligations and rights of parents in whose care children are placed and the requirements they must satisfy;

2.14. Providing for strict control of fostering arrangements and making fostering, especially private fostering, conditional upon notification and licensing;

2.15. Discouraging, with a view to its elimination, illegal fostering by promoting general measures of support for families and extending the authorised machinery for placement;

2.16. Providing for the development of small family-type residential units for children when fostering is not possible, and in consequence:

a. progressively running down larger residential institutions;

b. ensuring that all residential units, including any larger institutions retained for the time being :
– are organised in sub-units of a family-type;
– receive children of mixed ages and both sexes;
– have mixed staff to provide identification objects of both sexes;
– provide opportunities for keeping siblings together;
– encourage co-operation with biological parents;
– provide opportunities for experiments whereby parents and children can live together for a short time within the unit;

312

– provide special units for adolescents when needed;

c. encouraging the running of all residential units in close contact with the surrounding community, all personnel being considered as members of the caring team and the children being encouraged, according to their capacity, to participate in the running of the units;

E. *Staff and training*

2.17.   Recognising that the staff of placement agencies and of residential units are faced with an extremely delicate and laborious task, for which they must be suitably selected and trained, especially in child development and family social work;

2.18.   Ensuring that the staff of placement agencies will be adequately trained and experienced in making placement decisions;

2.19.   Ensuring that the training of the staff of placement agencies, of residential units and of field-workers include work in multidisciplinary teams, and also with parents, foster parents and children; considering to this end introducing a common element into the initial training of different disciplines and facilitating inter-disciplinary joint discussion groups as part of in-service training;

2.20.   Providing a basic preparatory training with particular emphasis on knowledge of children for all foster parents using individual and group methods, and more extensive training for certain kinds of foster parents;

2.21.   Providing for the continuous training of all staff of residential units as a means of improving their professional knowledge and of giving them psychological support; providing to this end, *inter alia*, training courses for all the staff of a unit at same time, reliefs for living-in staff and resources for regular staff meetings;

2.22.   Providing for the further training of foster parents using individual and group methods as a source of psychological support and emphasising the importance of knowledge of child development ;

2.23.   Ensuring that the training of foster parents takes place with the participation of the ordinary child care team as well as of any necessary specialists.

III. Research

3.   Having due regard to the principles of confidentiality and privacy in respect of those concerned:

3.1. To encourage active research and evaluation on all modes of placement;

3.2. To promote further research on a local, national and international basis as well as the international exchange of information on problems of placement such as:

– the extent of and trends in needs of placement;

– the effects of different placement modes especially long-term placements;

– direct and indirect costs of various modes of placement.

IV. Others

4.1. To acknowledge, in the field of child welfare, the need to promote consultation and co-operation among bodies associated with social welfare, health, educational and legal matters, as well as among the professional groups concerned;

4.2. To encourage associations of foster parents;

4.3. To encourage communication with children so that their wishes and feelings may be taken into account so far as is practicable in policies of placements.

Appendix to Resolution (77) 33

List of placement modes

(The following list is not exhaustive, but indicates a variety of measures which can be made available.)

a. Closer supervision and support of the child in its own family;

b. Appropriate day-care placement (can be combined with a);

c. Placement in the extended family (i.e. a supervised placement by an authorised organisation as distinct from care arrangements made spontaneously on the sole responsibility of the parents);

d. Ordinary foster care (for which selection, preparation and continued support are nonetheless needed);

e. Specialised foster care (implies a more intensive training to deal with particular problems of the foster children and generally an increased remuneration);

f. "Seasonal" residential units (implies that the child returns home for part of the year);

g. Short-stay residential units for whole families;

h. Small residential units where the staff (generally a couple) are permanently resident and the children are within the range of an ordinary family in number and, as far as possible, in age distribution; often known as "family group homes";

i. Specialised residential units (say of about twenty-five children) with special facilities (psychiatric, pedagogical, technical) for the treatment or care of a particular category of children; such units should be organised in sub-units of type h;

j. Placement of adolescents in small, mainly self-governing communities of their own age group, under light but skilled supervision, or in a flat of their own.

Resolution (78) 62
on juvenile delinquency and social change

*(Adopted by the Committee of Ministers on 29 November 1978
at the 296th meeting of the Ministers' Deputies)*

The Committee of Ministers,

Having regard to the benefit to the Council of Europe member states of establishing common principles for the protection of young people and criminal policy concerning them;

Having regard to the fact that important changes are taking place in the contemporary society, associated in particular with the technological progress, urbanisation and development of the mass media;

Having regard to the fact that these changes affect interpersonal relationships, especially within families, and sometimes have adverse effects on the personal and social development of young people;

Considering that governments have much to gain by taking measures which make the best use of the positive aspects of social change and limit the undesirable consequences;

Considering that the social integration of young people is not in the first instance a task for judicial bodies but comes mainly within the scope of social policy and its development;

Considering that the following action is apt to influence favourably the socialisation of juveniles:

– improving housing conditions and social facilities for families with children, particularly in large housing estates, by making services and suitable accommodation available to promote the best possible development of young people;

– ensuring that there is an opportunity for all adolescents to have vocational training which corresponds to their interests and aptitudes;

– taking steps to ensure that young people are associated with the world of work and avoiding their unemployment for long periods;

– increasing measures of financial and social support for families with children, in particular the most disadvantaged ones; guaranteeing the care and safety of children;

– reviewing the school system so as to ensure that school meet the needs of each pupil and the requirements of modern life, and providing for the early detection of psychological and social difficulties among young people so that the latter can continue to be educated within the normal system;

– encouraging youth associations and organisations of sports and leisure-time activities which help to integrate their members into society;

– encouraging the mass media to take a greater and more constructive interest in the problems of young people by not perpetuating prejudices and stereotyped reactions in their respect,

Recommends the governments of member states to take account of the positive implications of the social measures mentioned above for the prevention of juvenile delinquency and the social integration of the young and to consider the possibility of taking the following measures in the field of criminal policy;

a. ensure the safeguarding of the fundamental rights of young people by their participation in all judicial and administrative measures which concern them;

b. review the sanctions and other measures applied to young people and increase their educative and socialising content;

c. keep to a minimum the sanctions and other measures which entail deprivation of liberty, and develop alternative methods of treatment;

d. provide for the abolition of large isolating institutions and their replacement by smaller establishments supported by the community;

e. attach special importance to assisting young people during periods of institutional treatment and in particular in the period of transition from institutional treatment to freedom outside;

f. review the law on minors in order to provide more effective assistance for young people at risk while avoiding marginalisation;

g. develop the community's participation in the implementation of measures aimed at young people in danger;

h. ensure that all the services available to young people in general are accessible to minors at risk;

i. co-ordinate the activities of all bodies concerned with assisting young people (social and educational services, police, courts, etc.);

j. involve families and volunteers in the work of the relevant professional teams;

k. develop the training and information of those concerned with the development of services and institutions with responsibility for young people in danger or young delinquents, in order to modify repressive attitudes;

Recommends the governments of member states to promote research in the field of social policy, in particular on the impact of preventive measures on the socialisation of families and young people as well as on the means of developing social solidarity;

Requests governments:

1. to ensure that this resolution, together with the explanatory report, is widely circulated within the appropriate bodies and departments;

2. to send a report every five years to the Secretary General of the Council of Europe on action taken on these recommendations.

Recommendation No. R (82) 2
on payment by the state of advances on child maintenance[1]

(Adopted by the Committee of Ministers on 4 February 1982
at the 343rd meeting of the Ministers' Deputies)

The Committee of Ministers, under the terms of Article 15.*b* of the Statute of the Council of Europe,

Considering that the aim of the Council of Europe is to achieve greater unity between its members, *inter alia* by promoting the adoption of common rules in legal matters;

Noting that a large number of children are brought up by only one of their parents and that often one of the persons who is responsible for meeting their needs (hereinafter referred to as the "debtor") does not live with them and does not comply with the maintenance obligation;

Considering that it is primarily the responsibility of parents to provide children with appropriate maintenance but that the state should intervene when they fail to do so;

Recollecting that the European Conference on Family Law, held at Vienna in September 1977, expressed the wish that states take necessary measures to intervene, either by way of advance payment or by any other method, when the father and mother or one of them fail to comply with their maintenance obligations;

Having regard to Recommendation 869 (1979) of the Consultative Assembly of the Council of Europe on payment by the state of advances on child maintenance;

Recognising the advantage of adopting common rules to enable states progressively to improve the rights of children in this field,

Recommends governments of member states:

1. to adopt, taking as a guide the principles contained in the appendix to this recommendation, a system of advance payment of maintenance to children when the debtor fails to comply with his obligation, or if they already have a system aiming at the same objective, to adapt it, if necessary, to the above-mentioned principles;

---

1. When this recommendation was adopted, the Representatives of Ireland and Italy, in application of Article 10.2.*c* of the Rules of Procedure for the meetings of the Ministers' Deputies, reserved the right of their Governments to comply with it or not.

2. to strengthen the means of recovering advances from a debtor resident in another state and, to this end, to facilitate the recognition and enforcement of decisions relating to maintenance obligations for children, where appropriate by ratifying the relevant international instruments.

Appendix to Recommendation No. R (82) 2

Principles

1.   Payments of advances on child maintenance will be made under a system set up by the state where a person who is under a legal obligation to pay maintenance, which has become enforceable by compulsory process, has failed to comply with his obligation. This system will apply to children habitually resident in the territory of the state and who are not living with the person liable to pay maintenance.

2.   The age of the child up to which payments will be made will be fixed by each state. In any event, the advance payment will be made until the end of the period of compulsory schooling.

3.   The advance payments may be refused if the child or the parent with whom he is living has sufficient financial resources to meet his needs.

4.   Advance payments may be limited to a sum fixed according to criteria laid down by each state.

5.   Advance payments will not release the debtor either from his obligations towards the state with regard to the sum advanced by the latter or from his obligations with regard to the child for any residual sum.

6.   Public authorities may recover advance payments from the debtor. Where they have the recognised power to do so they may also recover, on behalf of the maintenance creditor, the full sum required by a legal obligation which has become enforceable by compulsory process. Except in cases of double payment, the failure to recover from the debtor all or part of the advanced payments will not give a right to recover these advances from the child.

Recommendation No. R (84) 4
on parental responsibilities[1]

(Adopted by the Committee of Ministers on 28 February 1984
at the 367th meeting of the Ministers' Deputies)

The Committee of Ministers, under the terms of Article 15.*b* of the Statute of the Council of Europe,

Considering that the aim of the Council of Europe is to achieve a greater unity between its member states, *inter alia*, by promoting the adoption of common rules in legal matters;

Considering that it is possible to make improvements to the legal systems relating to parental responsibilities in order to promote the development of the personality of the child and to protect his person and his moral and material interests while guaranteeing legal equality between parents,

Recommends governments of members states to adapt, where necessary, their legislation to comply with the principles concerning parental responsibilities set out in the appendix to this recommendation.

---

1. When this recommendation was adopted and in application of Article 10.2.*c* of the Rules of Procedure for the meetings of the Ministers' Deputies,
– the Representatives of Denmark, Liechtenstein, Norway and the United Kingdom reserved the right of their Governments to comply or not with the first paragraph of Principle 9 as set out in the appendix to the recommendation ;
– the Representative of the Netherlands reserved the right of his Government to comply or not with Principle 11 as set out in the appendix to the recommendation.

Appendix to Recommendation No. R (84) 4

Principle 1

For the purposes of this recommendation:

a. parental responsibilities are a collection of duties and powers which aim at ensuring the moral and material welfare of the child, in particular by taking care of the person of the child, by maintaining personal relationships with him and by providing for his education, his maintenance, his legal representation and the administration of his property;

b. the terms "father", "mother", "parents" refer to persons having a legal filiation link with the child.

Principle 2

Any decision of the competent authority concerning the attribution of parental responsibilities or the way in which these responsibilities are exercised should be based primarily on the interests of the child. However, the equality between parents should also be respected and no discrimination should be made, in particular on grounds of sex, race, colour, language, religion, political or other opinion, national or social origin, association with a national minority, property, birth or other status.

Principle 3

When the competent authority is required to take a decision relating to the attribution or exercise of parental responsibilities and affecting the essential interests of the children, the latter should be consulted if their degree of maturity with regard to the decision so permits.

Principle 4

When the persons having parental responsibilities exercise them in a way which is detrimental to the essential interests of the child, the competent authority should take, of its own motion or on application, any appropriate measures.

Principle 5

Parental responsibilities for a child of their marriage should belong jointly to both parents.

Principle 6

In the case of a dissolution of a marriage or a separation of the parents, the competent authority requested to intervene should rule on the exercise of parental responsibilities. It should accordingly take any appropriate measures, for example by dividing the exercise of the responsibilities between the two parents or, where the parents consent, by providing that the responsibilities should be exercised jointly. In taking its decision, the authority should take account of any agreement concluded between the parents provided it is not contrary to the interests of the children.

Principle 7

1. Where the child is born out of wedlock and a legal filiation link is established with regard to one parent only, the parental responsibilities should belong to that parent.

2.   Where the child is born out of wedlock and a legal filiation link is established with regard to both parents, national law may provide that the parental responsibilities should be exercised:

a.   subject to the provisions of Principle 8:

i.   by the mother alone;

ii.   by the father alone, when a decision has been taken by the competent authority or when an agreement has been concluded between the two parents;

b.   according to the division between the two parents decided by the competent authority;

c.   jointly by both parents if they live together or if an agreement has been concluded between them.

Principle 8

In all cases both parents should be under a duty to maintain the child. The parent with whom the child does not live should have at least the possibility of maintaining personal relationships with the child unless such relationships would be seriously harmful to the interests of the child.

Principle 9

1.   Where the parental responsibilities are exercised jointly by both parents and one of them dies, these responsibilities should belong to the surviving parent.

2.   Where the parent who exercises alone some parental responsibilities dies, his responsibilities should be exercised by the surviving parent unless the interests of the child require any other measures.

3.   Where there is no longer any parent living, the competent authority should take a decision concerning the attribution of parental responsibilities. National legislation may provide that these responsibilities may be given to a member of the family or to a person designated by the last parent to die, unless the interests of the child require any other measures.

Principle 10

1.   Where parental responsibilities are exercised jointly by both parents, any decision affecting the interests of the child should be taken by the agreement of both.

2.   Where there is a disagreement and the matter is referred to the competent authority by one of the parents, this authority should insofar as the interests of the child so require, try to reconcile the parents, and if, this fails, take the appropriate decision.

3.   With regard to third parties, the agreement of both parents should be presumed except in cases where national law, having regard to the importance of the interests at stake, requires an express agreement.

Principle 11

Each parent should normally be informed of the exercise of the responsibilities which have not been given to him, to the extent desired by him, and in any event, when the essential interests of the child are affected.

Recommendation No. R (85) 4
on violence in the family[1]

(Adopted by the Committee of Ministers on 26 March 1985
at the 382nd meeting of the Ministers' Deputies)

The Committee of Ministers, under the terms of Article 15.*b* of the Statute of the Council of Europe,

Considering that the family is the basic organisational unit of democratic societies;

Considering that the defence of the family involves the protection of all its members against any form of violence, which all too often occurs among them;

Considering that there is violence in any act or omission which prejudices the life, the physical or psychological integrity or the liberty of a person or which seriously harms the development of his or her personality;

Considering that such violence affects, in particular, children on the one side and women on the other, though in differing ways;

Considering that children are entitled to special protection by society against any form of discrimination or oppression and against any abuse of authority in the family and other institutions;

Considering that the same is true of women in so far as they are subject to certain *de facto* inequalities which hamper the reporting of any violence of which they are victims;

Having regard in this respect to its Resolution (78) 37 on the equality of spouses in civil law;

Having regard also to its Recommendation No. R (79) 17 concerning the protection of children against ill-treatment;

Having regard to the proceedings of the Council of Europe's 4th Criminological Colloquy, on the ill-treatment of children in the family;

Having regard to the Recommendation 561 (1969) of the Consultative Assembly of the Council of Europe, on the protection of minors against ill-treatment,

---

1. When this recommendation was adopted, the Representative of the United Kingdom, in application of Article 10.2.*c* of the Rules of Procedure for the meetings of the Ministers' Deputies, reserved the right of her Government to comply or not with Article I.5 of the recommendation.

Recommends that the governments of member states:

I.   With regard to the prevention of violence in the family:

1.   alert public opinion to the extent, seriousness and specific characteristics of violence in the family with a view to obtaining its support for measures aimed at combating this phenomenon;

2.   promote the dissemination among families of knowledge and information concerning social and family relations, early detection of potentially conflictual situations and the settlement of interpersonal and intra-family conflicts;

3.   provide appropriate professional training for all those responsible for intervening in cases of violence in the family, particularly those who, because of their functions, are in a position to detect such cases or deal with the victims thereof;

4.   arrange for and encourage the setting up, and support the work, of agencies, associations or foundations whose aim is to help and assist the victims of violent family situations, with due respect for the privacy of others;

5.   set up administrative departments or multidisciplinary boards with the task of looking after victims of violence in the family and with powers to deal with such cases.

Their powers might include the following:

– to receive reports of acts of violence in the family;

– to arrange for medical examinations at the victim's request;

– to help, care for and advise the various parties involved in cases of violence in the family and to that end to carry out social inquiries;

– to pass on, either to the family and children's courts or to the prosecuting authorities, information which the department or board deems should be submitted to one or another of those authorities;

6.   impose strict rules on these departments or boards concerning the divulging of information to which they have access in the exercise of their powers;

II.   With regard to the reporting of acts of violence in the family:

7.   circulate specific information on the advisability and feasibility for persons who become aware of cases of violence in the family of reporting them to the competent bodies, particularly those mentioned in paragraphs 4 and 5 above, or of directly intervening to assist the person in danger;

8.   consider the possibility of removing the obligation of secrecy from the members of certain professions so as to enable them to disclose to the bodies mentioned in paragraph 5 above any information concerning cases of violence in the family;

III. With regard to state intervention following acts of violence in the family:

9. take steps to ensure that, in cases of violence in the family, the appropriate measures can be quickly taken, even if only provisionally, to protect the victim and prevent similar incidents from occurring;

10. take measures to ensure that, in any case resulting from a conflict between a couple, measures are available for the purpose of protecting the children against any violence to which the conflict exposes them and which may seriously harm the development of their personality;

11. take measures to ensure that the victim's interests are not prejudiced by interference between civil, administrative and criminal measures, it being understood that criminal measures should be taken only as a last resort;

12. review their legislation on the power to punish children in order to limit or indeed prohibit corporal punishment, even if violation of such a prohibition does not necessarily entail a criminal penalty;

13. study the possibility of entrusting cases of violence in the family only to specialist members of prosecuting or investigating authorities or of trial courts;

14. take steps to ensure that, as a general rule, a psycho-social inquiry is carried out into such cases and that, particularly on the basis of the findings of the inquiry and in accordance with criteria that take account of the interests of the victim as well as the children of the family, the prosecuting authority or the court is able to propose or take measures other than criminal ones, especially when the suspect or accused agrees to submit to the supervision of the competent social, medico-social or probation authorities;

15. do not institute proceedings in cases of violence in the family unless the victim so requests or the public interest so requires;

16. take measures to ensure protection against any external pressures on members of the family giving evidence in cases of violence in the family. In particular, minors should be assisted by appropriate counsel. Moreover, the weight of such evidence should not be diminished by rules relating to the oath;

17. consider the advisability of adopting specific incrimination for offences committed within the family.

Recommendation No. R (85) 7
on teaching and learning about human rights in schools

(Adopted by the Committee of Ministers on 14 May 1985
at the 385th meeting of the Ministers' Deputies)

The Committee of Ministers, under the terms of Article 15.*b* of the Statute of the Council of Europe,

Considering that the aim of the Council of Europe is to achieve a greater unity between its members for the purpose of safeguarding and realising the ideals and principles which are their common heritage;

Reaffirming the human rights undertakings embodied in the United Nations' Universal Declaration of Human Rights, the Convention for the Protection of Human Rights and Fundamental Freedoms and the European Social Charter;

Having regard to the commitments to human rights education made by member states at international and European conferences in the last decade;

Recalling:

– its own Resolution (78) 41 on "The teaching of human rights";

– its Declaration on "Intolerance: a threat to democracy" of 14 May 1981;

– its Recommendation No. R (83) 13 on "The role of the secondary school in preparing young people for life";

Noting Recommendation 963 (1983) of the Consultative Assembly of the Council of Europe on "Cultural and educational means of reducing violence";

Conscious of the need to reaffirm democratic values in the face of:

– intolerance, acts of violence and terrorism;

– the re-emergence of the public expression of racist and xenophobic attitudes;

– the disillusionment of many young people in Europe, who are affected by the economic recession and aware of the continuing poverty and inequality in the world;

Believing, therefore, that throughout their school career, all young people should learn about human rights as part of their preparation for life in a pluralistic democracy;

Convinced that schools are communities which can, and should, be an example of respect for the dignity of the individual and for difference, for tolerance, and for equality of opportunity,

I.   Recommends that the governments of member states, having regard to their national education systems and to the legislative basis for them:

a. encourage teaching and learning about human rights in schools in line with the suggestions contained in the appendix hereto;

b. draw the attention of persons and bodies concerned with school education to the text of this recommendation;

II.   Instructs the Secretary General to transmit this recommendation to the governments of those states party to the European Cultural Convention which are not members of the Council of Europe.

Appendix to Recommendation No. R (85) 7

Suggestions for teaching and learning about human rights in schools

1. *Human rights in the school curriculum*

1.1. The understanding and experience of human rights is an important element of the preparation of all young people for life in a democratic and pluralistic society. It is part of social and political education, and it involves intercultural and international understanding.

1.2. Concepts associated with human rights can, and should, be acquired from an early stage. For example, the non-violent resolution of conflict and respect for other people can already be experienced within the life of a pre-school or primary class.

1.3. Opportunities to introduce young people to more abstract notions of human rights, such as those involving an understanding of philosophical, political and legal concepts, will occur in the secondary school, in particular in such subjects as history, geography social studies, moral and religious education, language and literature, current affairs and economics.

1.4. Human rights inevitably involve the domain of politics. Teaching about human rights should, therefore, always have international agreements and covenants as a point of reference, and teachers should take care to avoid imposing their personal convictions on their pupils and involving them in ideological struggles.

2. *Skills*

The skills associated with understanding and supporting human rights include:

    i.   intellectual skills, in particular:

– skills associated with written and oral expression, including the ability to listen and discuss, and to defend one's opinions;

    – skills involving judgement, such as:

      - the collection and examination of material from various sources, including the mass media, and the ability to analyse it and to arrive at fair and balanced conclusions;

      - the identification of bias, prejudice, stereotypes and discrimination;

    ii. social skills, in particular:

    – recognising and accepting differences;

    – establishing positive and non-oppressive personal relationships;

    – resolving conflict in a non-violent way;

    – taking responsibility;

    – participating in decisions;

– understanding the use of the mechanisms for the protection of human rights at local, regional, European and world levels.

3. *Knowledge to be acquired in the study of human rights*

3.1. The study of human rights in schools will be approached in different ways according to the age and circumstances of the pupil and the particular situations of schools and education systems. Topics to be covered in learning about human rights could include:

    i.   the main categories of human rights, duties, obligations and responsibilities;

ii. the various forms of injustice, inequality and discrimination, including sexism and racism ;

iii. people, movements and key events, both successes and failures, in the historical and continuing struggle for human rights;

iv. the main international declarations and conventions on human rights, such as Universal Declaration of Human Rights and the Convention for the Protection of Human Rights and Fundamental Freedoms.

3.2. The emphasis in teaching and learning about human rights should be positive. Pupils may be led to feelings of powerlessness and discouragement when confronted with many examples of violation and negations of human rights. Instances of progress and success should be used.

3.3. The study of human rights in schools should lead to an understanding of, and sympathy for, the concepts of justice, equality, freedom, peace, rights and democracy. Such understanding should be both cognitive and based on experience and feelings. Schools should, thus, provide opportunities for pupils to experience affective involvement in human rights and to express their feelings through drama, art, music, creative writing and audiovisual media.

4.   *The climate of the school*

4.1. Democracy is best learned in a democratic setting where participation is encouraged, where views can be expressed openly and discussed, where there is freedom of expression for pupils and teachers, and where there is fairness and justice. An appropriate climate is, therefore, an essential complement to effective learning about human rights.

4.2. Schools should encourage participation in their activities by parents and other members of the community. It may well be appropriate for schools to work with nongovernmental organisations which can provide information, case-studies and firsthand experience of successful campaigns for human rights and dignity.

4.3. Schools and teachers attempt to be positive towards their pupils, and recognise that all of their achievements are important – whether they be academic, artistic, musical, sporting or practical.

5.   *Teacher training*

5.1. The initial training of teachers should prepare them for their future contribution to teaching about human rights in their schools. For example, future teachers should:

i. be encouraged to take an interest in national and world affairs;

ii. have the chance of studying or working in a foreign country or a different environment;

iii. be taught to identify and combat all forms of discrimination in schools and society and be encouraged to confront and overcome their own prejudices.

5.2. Future and practising teachers should be encouraged to familiarise themselves with:

i. the main international declarations and conventions on human rights;

ii. the working and achievements of the international organisations which deal with the protection and promotion of human rights, for example through visits and study tours.

5.3. All teachers need, and should be given the opportunity, to update their knowledge and to learn new methods through in-service training. This could include the study of good practice in teaching about human rights, as well as the development of appropriate methods and materials.

6.   *International Human Rights Day*

Schools and teacher training establishments should be encouraged to observe International Human Rights Day (10 December).

Recommendation No. R (87) 6
on foster families[1]

*(Adopted by the Committee of Ministers on 20 March 1987
at the 405th meeting of the Ministers' Deputies)*

The Committee of Ministers, under the terms of Article 15.*b* of the Statute of the Council of Europe,

Considering that the aim of the Council of Europe is to achieve a greater unity between its members, *inter alia*, by promoting the adoption of common rules in legal matters;

Recognising that the law should protect the welfare of children;

Recognising that it is normally in a child's interests to remain with his family of origin and that an improvement in support for these families would ensure that the need for fostering is reduced;

Considering that it is possible to improve the legal systems relating to the fostering of children in order to promote the development of the personality of the child and to protect his person and his moral and material interests;

Considering that an improvement of the situation of foster parents might contribute to the welfare of children;

Realising that consideration might be given to the effects of fostering in other contexts such as social and other benefits;

Having regard to Resolution (77) 33 on the placement of children and Recommendation No. R (84) 4 on parental responsibilities,

Recommends the governments of member states to include in their legislation rules on foster families based on the principles set out in the appendix to this recommendation.

---

1. When this recommendation was adopted, and in application of Article 10.2.*c* of the Rules of Procedure for the meetings of the Ministers' Deputies, the Representatives of Denmark and Norway reserved the right of their Governments to comply or not with Principle 5 of the appendix to the recommendation.

Appendix to Recommendation No. R (87) 6

For the purposes of this recommendation, a fostering occurs when a child is entrusted, otherwise than with a view to adoption, to a couple or an individual ("foster parents") who takes care of the child for more than a short time or for an undetermined time and who does not have legal custody of the child and who is not a parent.

Principle 1

1.   National legislation should provide a system of supervision of foster parents in order to ensure that they provide the necessary moral and material conditions for the proper development of the child, in particular by means of their personal qualities, especially their ability to bring up the child, and their housing conditions.

National legislation may provide that such supervision does not apply where the fostering is with a close relative.

2.   The supervision should be based:

   – on information given by the foster parents to the competent authority, or

   – on an authorisation system, or

   – on any other means which would enable this objective to be attained, for example a system of official approval of persons who regularly receive children.

3.   In any event the competent authority should intervene and provide support where the interests of the child so require.

Principle 2

The personal relationships of the child with his family of origin should be maintained and information concerning the well-being of the child should be given to that family, provided that this is not detrimental to the essential interests of the child.

Principle 3

The foster parents should be presumed to have the power to exercise, on behalf of the legal representatives of the child, those parental responsibilities which are necessary to care for the child in day-to-day or urgent matters.

Principle 4

As far as possible before any important decision is taken concerning the person of the child, the foster parents should be given the opportunity to express their views.

Principle 5

After a foster child has become integrated into the foster family, in particular after a substantial period of fostering, the foster parents should be able to apply, subject to any conditions specified by national legislation, to a judicial or other competent authority, for power to exercise certain parental responsibilities including, where appropriate, legal custody.

Principle 6

Where the child has been integrated into the foster family, in particular after a substantial period of fostering, then, if the person or the authority which made the fostering wishes to terminate it and the foster parents oppose the termination, it is for the judicial or other competent authority to take a decision.

Principle 7

1. Before any decision is taken by the competent authority under Principles 5 and 6, the parents and the foster parents should be given the opportunity to express their views. The child should be consulted if his degree of maturity with regard to the decision so permits.

2. The authority should base its decision primarily on the interests of the child, taking account in particular of the links between the child, his parents and his foster parents. This decision should be taken without undue delay.

Principle 8

Agreements relating to the fostering of a child may not derogate from the principles set out in this recommendation.

Recommendation No. R (87) 20
on social reactions to juvenile delinquency

(Adopted by the Committee of Ministers on 17 September 1987 at the 410th meeting of the Ministers' Deputies)

The Committee of Ministers, under the terms of Article 15.*b* of the Statute of the Council of Europe,

Considering that young people are developing beings and in consequence all measures taken in their respect should have an educational character;

Considering that social reactions to juvenile delinquency should take account of the personality and specific needs of minors and that the latter need specialised interventions and, where appropriate, specialised treatment based in particular on the principles embodied in the United Nations Declaration of the Rights of the Child;

Convinced that the penal system for minors should continue to be characterised by its objective of education and social integration and that it should as far as possible abolish imprisonment for minors;

Considering that measures in respect of minors should preferably be implemented in their natural environment and should involve the community, in particular at local level;

Convinced that minors must be afforded the same procedural guarantees as adults;

Taking account of earlier work by the Council of Europe in the field of juvenile delinquency and in particular of Resolution (78) 62 on juvenile delinquency and social change and the conclusions of the 14th Criminological Research Conference on "Prevention of juvenile delinquency: the role of institutions of socialisation in a changing society";

Having regard to the United Nations Standard Minimum Rules for the Administration of Juvenile Justice (the Beijing Rules),

Recommends the governments of member states to review, if necessary, their legislation and practice with a view:

I. *Prevention*

1. to undertaking or continuing particular efforts for the prevention of juvenile maladjustment and delinquency, in particular:

   a. by implementing a comprehensive policy promoting the social integration of young people;

b. by providing special assistance and the introduction of specialised programmes, on an experimental basis, in schools or in young peoples' or sports' organisations for the better integration of young people who are experiencing serious difficulties in this field;

c. by taking technical and situational measures to reduce the opportunities offered to young people to commit offences;

II. *Diversion – mediation*

2.   to encouraging the development of diversion and mediation procedures at public prosecutor level (discontinuation of proceedings) or at police level, in countries where the police has prosecuting functions, in order to prevent minors from entering into the criminal justice system and suffering the ensuing consequences; to associating Child Protection Boards or services to the application of these procedures;

3.   to taking the necessary measures to ensure that in such procedures:

– the consent of the minor to the measures on which the diversion is conditional and, if necessary, the co-operation of his family are secured;

– appropriate attention is paid to the rights and interests of the minor as well as to those of the victim;

III. *Proceedings against minors*

4.   to ensuring that minors are tried more rapidly, avoiding undue delay, so as to ensure effective educational action;

5.   to avoiding committing minors to adult courts, where juvenile courts exist;

6.   to avoiding, as far as possible, minors being kept in police custody and, in any case, encouraging the prosecuting authorities to supervise the conditions of such custody;

7.   to excluding the remand in custody of minors, apart from exceptional cases of very serious offences committed by older minors; in these cases, restricting the length of remand in custody and keeping minors apart from adults; arranging for decisions of this type to be, in principle, ordered after consultation with a welfare department on alternative proposals;

8.   to reinforcing the legal position of minors throughout the proceedings, including the police investigation, by recognising, *inter alia*:

– the presumption of innocence;

– the right to the assistance of a counsel who may, if necessary, be officially appointed and paid by the state;

– the right to the presence of parents or of another legal representative who should be informed from the beginning of the proceedings;

– the right of minors to call, interrogate and confront witnesses;

– the possibility for minors to ask for a second expert opinion or any other equivalent investigative measure;

– the right of minors to speak and, if necessary, to give an opinion on the measures envisaged for them;

    – the right to appeal;

    – the right to apply for a review of the measures ordered;

    – the right of juveniles to respect for their private lives;

9. to encouraging arrangements for all the persons concerned at various stages of the proceedings (police, counsel, prosecutors, judges, social workers) to receive specialised training on the law relating to minors and juvenile delinquency;

10. to ensuring that the entries of decisions relating to minors in the police records are treated as confidential and only communicated to the judicial authorities or equivalent authorities and that these entries are not used after the persons concerned come of age, except on compelling grounds provided for in national law;

IV. *Interventions*

11. to ensuring that interventions in respect of juvenile delinquents are sought preferably in the minors' natural environment, respect their right to education and their personality and foster their personal development;

12. to providing that intervention is of a determined length and that only the judicial authorities or equivalent administrative authorities may fix it, and that the same authorities may terminate the intervention earlier than originally provided;

13. when residential care is essential:

    – to diversifying the forms of residential care in order to provide the one most suited to the minor's age, difficulties and background (host families, homes);

    – to establishing small-scale educational institutions integrated into their social, economic and cultural environment;

    – to providing that the minor's personal freedom shall be restricted as little as possible and that the way in which this is done is decided under judicial control;

    – in all forms of custodial education, to fostering, where possible, the minor's relations with his family:

      - avoiding custody in places which are too distant or inaccessible;

      - maintaining contact between the place of custody and the family;

14. with the aim of gradually abandoning recourse to detention and increasing the number of alternative measures, to giving preference to those which allow greater opportunities for social integration through education, vocational training as well as through the use of leisure or other activities;

15. among such measures, to paying particular attention to those which:

    – involve probationary supervision and assistance;

– are intended to cope with the persistence of delinquent behaviour in the minor by improving his capacities for social adjustment by means of intensive educational action (including "intensive intermediary treatment");

– entail reparation for the damage caused by the criminal activity of the minor;

– entail community work suited to the minor's age and educational needs;

16. in cases where, under national legislation, a custodial sentence cannot be avoided:

– to establishing a scale of sentences suited to the condition of minors, and to introducing more favourable conditions for the serving of sentences than those which the law lays down for adults, in particular as regards the obtaining of semi-liberty and early release, as well as granting and revocation of suspended sentence;

– to requiring the courts to give reasons for their prison sentences;

– to separating minors from adults or, where in exceptional cases integration is preferred for treatment reasons, to protecting minors from harmful influence from adults;

– to providing both education and vocational training for young prisoners, preferably in conjunction with the community, or any other measure which may assist reinsertion in society;

– to providing educational support after release and possible assistance for the social rehabilitation of the minors;

17. to reviewing, if necessary, their legislation on young adult delinquents, so that the relevant courts also have the opportunity of passing sentences which are educational in nature and foster social integration, regard being had for the personalities of the offenders;

V. *Research*

18. to promoting and encouraging comparative research in the field of juvenile delinquency so as to provide a basis for policy in this area, laying emphasis on the study of:

– prevention measures;

– the relationship between the police and young people;

– the influence of new crime policies on the functioning of legal systems concerned with minors;

– specialised training for everyone working in this field;

– comparative features of juvenile delinquency and young adult delinquency, as well as re-education and social integration measures suitable for these age-groups;

– alternatives to deprivation of liberty;

– community involvement in the care of young delinquents;

– the relationship between demographic factors and the labour market on the one hand and juvenile delinquency on the other;

– the role of the mass media in the field of delinquency and reactions to delinquency;

– institutions such as a youth ombudsman or complaints board for the protection of young people's rights;

– measures and procedures of reconciliation between young offenders and their victims.

Recommendation No. R (88) 6
on social reactions to juvenile delinquency among young people coming from migrant families

*(Adopted by the Committee of Ministers on 18 April 1988
at the 416th meeting of the Ministers' Deputies)*

The Committee of Ministers, under the terms of Article 15.*b* of the Statute of the Council of Europe,

Drawing attention to the principles of the European Convention on Human Rights;

Having regard to the multinational and multiracial nature of most European societies today and the need for Council of Europe member states to make allowance for this when framing their policies;

Considering the need for each state to reduce, as much as possible, differences existing between nationals and non-nationals in the participation in the social life of the country of residence ;

Considering that any policy on juvenile delinquency necessarily entails taking measures to facilitate the social integration of young people in difficulty;

Considering that, of these young people, those coming from migrant families and in particular second-generation migrants deserve special attention;

Considering the need to prevent delinquent behaviour among the latter by giving them equal opportunities for self-fulfilment with the young among the indigenous population and enabling them to integrate themselves fully into the society of the country of residence;

Considering that special arrangements should be made to ensure that, when these young people come into contact with the system of justice for minors, the action taken is likely to foster their social integration;

Taking into account the work of the European Committee on Crime Problems in the sphere of juvenile delinquency and crime among migrants, namely: Resolution (75) 3 on the legal administrative aspects of criminality among migrant workers, Resolution (78) 62 on juvenile delinquency and social change, Recommendation No. R (84) 12 concerning foreign prisoners and Recommendation No. R (87) 20 on social reactions to juvenile delinquency,

Recommends the governments of member states to take the following measures in legislation and practice in order to avoid any discriminatory treatment of young people coming from migrant families in the juvenile justice system and within the policy of social integration of youth and to help those who have displayed delinquent conduct to derive the maximum benefit from the measures available under that system:

I. *Prevention*

1. To promote their access to all available institutions and social resources in order to enable them to acquire a social status equivalent to that of other young people; to this end, to give young migrants, in accordance with arrangements laid down in the legislation, the possibility of acquiring the nationality of the country of residence;

2. To promote their participation in all facilities for young people: youth clubs and associations, sports clubs and social services; in this framework, encourage organisations aiming at conserving the cultural heritage of these groups;

3. To offer adequate aid and assistance to these young people and their families when they are in social and family crisis situations;

4. To ensure, as far as possible, that schools which have a certain proportion of these young people among their pupils are provided with special facilities, such as a larger number of teachers sensitive to the questions of migrants and minorities, tuition in the language and civilisation of both the host country and the country of origin, extra support in school work;

5. To ensure, with a view to securing equality of opportunities, that compulsory school attendance is effective for girls as well as boys;

6. To promote the access of these young people, even at a later stage, to training and offer them information and assistance in obtaining and keeping employment.

II. *Police*

7. To insure that police services, which often constitute the fist point of contact with young people in difficulty, adopt a non-discriminatory attitude during these contacts, taking into account the cultural context in which these young people live;

8. To insure, consequently, that, in those departments of the police force responsible for juveniles, there are enough police officers having specialist training focused on the cultural values and standards of behaviour of the various ethnic groups with which they come into contact, including if possible police officers coming from a migrant background, and that all these officers may if necessary have recourse to interpreters;

9. To insure that those departments establish links with associations concerned with these young people, in particular in order to be able to give the latter adequate assistance and guidance.

III. *Juvenile justice and care system*

10. To ensure that these young people benefit equally with young nationals from innovations in the juvenile justice and care system (diversion, mediation, other new forms of intervention, etc.);

11. To ensure that persons handling cases of minors at the various stages in proceedings are able to communicate in a satisfactory manner with the young migrants on account either of their ethnic origin or of their specialist training;

12. To intensify and ameliorate the contacts between the agents of the criminal justice and care system and families of migrants or other persons from the minor's environment in order better to understand the problems of the minor and reach well-founded decisions; to this end, to secure also the assistance of associations concerned with these young people.

IV. *Interventions and measures*

13. To undertake an adequate review of the young person's personal and social circumstances, in order to avoid simplistic and automatic "cultural" explanations, based on cultural values and conflicts;

14. To avoid systematic placing of these young people in institutions by providing the necessary resources in order that non-custodial measures and alternatives to placement and imprisonment are accessible and effectively applied to these young people in the same way as the indigenous young people;

15. To ensure that educational and social staff are trained in the problems of these young people and include, if possible, members coming from migrant backgrounds, and they can have recourse to collaborators (professional or voluntary) or to associations with experience in this field;

16. To avoid grouping young people of the same origin in specialised institutions;

17. To ensure that religious convictions and practices, including food practices, of the groups concerned are respected in the course of these interventions;

18. To encourage the recruitment of foster families representative of the various communities existing in the national territory so that, if desirable, young people can be entrusted to families of the same cultural origin;

19. To avoid, in principle, the expulsion of second-generation migrants during their minority or later for offences committed during their minority.

V. *Research*

20. To promote research especially on the following subjects:

– perception of the juvenile criminal justice system by young migrants and young people belonging to ethnic or cultural minorities;

– problems of young people returning to the country of origin and measures to be taken to prevent their possible misadaptation and delinquency;

– social and ethnic discrimination and institutional practice;

– practice related to reporting facts concerning these groups to the criminal justice system;

– discrimination in the reporting of criminality of young migrants by the media;

– effects of democratic changes on the labour-market and impact on the position of migrants and the development of criminality;

– studies of victimisation of young migrants or young people belonging to minorities, especially by racial attacks;

– ethnic monitoring of recruitment and selection of staff working in the juvenile justice system.

Recommendation No. R (88) 16
on ratifying and improving the implementation
of the conventions and agreements concluded within
the Council of Europe in the field of private law, notably
the conventions which protect the interests of the child

(Adopted by the Committee of Ministers on 29 September 1988 at the 419th meeting of the Ministers' Deputies)

The Committee of Ministers, under the terms of Article 15.*b* of the Statute of the Council of Europe,

Having regard to Resolutions Nos. 2 and 4 adopted by the 16th Conference of European Ministers of Justice;

Considering that the conventions and agreements concluded within the Council of Europe in the field of private law constitute an essential basis to the achievement of a greater unity between the Council of Europe member states;

Considering that the more ratification these conventions and agreements attract, the more effective they will be;

Considering that the reasons for the lack of ratifications should be investigated with a view to seeking solutions to any obstacles;

Considering it important that the persons and bodies to whom these treaties apply should be able to make optimum use of the facilities thus offered to them;

Considering it particularly important that the member states take or reinforce measures which give effect to the best interests of the child and the interests of the family as a whole,

Recommends the governments of member states:

a.   to ratify the conventions and agreements concluded within the Council of Europe in the field of private law, notably the conventions which protect the interests of the child[1], if they have not yet done so;

b.   to take stock of ratifications of these conventions and agreements and analyse the reasons for any instances of non-ratification;

---

1. European Convention on the Adoption of Children (1967) (European Treaty, No. 58); European Convention on the Legal Status of Children Born out of Wedlock (1975) (European Treaty Series, No. 85) ; European Convention on Recognition and Enforcement of Decisions concerning Custody of Children and on Restoration of Custody of Children (1980) (European Treaty Series, No. 105).

c. to improve co-operation and the exchange of information between the central authorities designated in pursuance of some of these treaties in order to enable the persons and bodies concerned to avail themselves fully of the facilities made available to them;

d. to take appropriate measures to bring the existence and the functioning of these treaties to the knowledge of all those for whose benefit they are designed;

e. to seek the assistance of the Secretary General, if they wish in finding solutions to any problems that might have prevented such conventions and agreements from being ratified or fully implemented.

Recommendation No. R (91) 9
on emergency measures in family matters

(Adopted by the Committee of Ministers on 9 September 1991
at the 461st meeting of the Ministers' Deputies)

The Committee of Ministers, under the terms of Article 15.*b* of the Statute of the Council of Europe,

Having regard to the large number of family cases which require prompt action in order to prevent adverse or even irreversible consequences;

Noting that, in many cases, the courts and other competent authorities dealing with families matters do not succeed in providing rapid solutions where the interests of children and other persons in need of special protection and assistance are in serious danger;

Recognising that existing emergency measures do not always enable the courts and other competent bodies to deal satisfactorily with certain urgent cases and in particular with cases where children have been improperly removed or their welfare is in serious danger;

Considering that states should give great priority to emergency measures in family matters and provide sufficient resources to protect the interests of the family;

Agreeing that effective emergency measures should be widely available;

Noting that steps should also be taken to encourage the persons concerned and those acting on their behalf to seek prompt action to make use of the available emergency measures,

Recommends governments of member states to take all necessary steps to implement the following principles and ensure that effective emergency measures are available to the courts and other competent authorities dealing with family matters to protect children and other persons who are in need of special protection and assistance and whose interests are in serious danger.

Principle 1

Courts and other competent authorities dealing with family matters should have sufficient emergency powers and resources to protect children and other persons in need of special protection and assistance and whose interests are in serious danger.

Particular protection should be given to a child whose welfare is in serious danger owing to neglect or any other physical or mental ill-treatment or

347

who has been or may be improperly removed from a person entitled to custody.

Principle 2

These courts or competent authorities should be ready to act at any time in extremely urgent cases.

Principle 3

1. Simple and expeditious procedures should be available to ensure that decisions are reached very quickly. To this end, the following measures could be used:

 – lodging a request by simple application;

 – allowing a court or competent authority to act on its own motion;

 – provisional measures taken without a hearing;

 – using all modern communication technology to facilitate the introduction and conduct of any proceedings, the transmission of requests and exchanges of information between courts and other competent authorities and the different parties to the proceedings;

 – allowing the court or competent authority to play an active role in conducting the case and in calling for and taking evidence;

 – preventing any party from improperly delaying emergency measures.

2. National authorities should ensure that information on emergency measures is given to the public and to those to whom a person in need of such measures may turn for help.

3. Legal aid and advice should be provided rapidly when required.

4. Courts and other competent authorities should have the power to grant decisions which are immediately enforceable.

5. Courts and other competent authorities should be given sufficient powers to ensure that their decisions are rapidly enforced.

Principle 4

In family matters the existence of an international element should not be allowed to cause delay in giving a decision. To this end, states should ensure that simple and expeditious procedures are available.

In particular the following steps, in addition to those mentioned in Principles 1 to 3, should be taken where international co-operation between the courts or other competent authorities is required:

1. Any necessary assistance should be given to persons living abroad in applying for legal aid and advice and in providing translation, where appropriate.

2. These cases should be brought before the courts or other competent authorities without delay and dealt with rapidly.

3. Any necessary additional information from abroad concerning facts or law should be obtained quickly.

4. With a view to facilitating international co-operation in family matters, states should become parties to and apply effectively international instruments providing such co-operation and should consider withdrawing their reservations to such instruments where possible.

5. Where necessary, other forms of co-operation between states should be provided to ensure that emergency measures can be taken quickly.

6. In cases where the return of a child is sought, courts and other competent authorities :

    – make use of appropriate measures in order to trace the child ;

    – give a decision whenever possible within six weeks of the receipt of the complete application by the requested authority ; a decision to return the child should be enforceable.

Recommendation No. R (91) 11
concerning sexual exploitation, pornography and prostitution of, and trafficking in, children and young adults

(Adopted by the Committee of Ministers on 9 September 1991 at the 461st meeting of the Ministers' Deputies)

The Committee of Ministers, under the terms of Article 15.*b* of the Statute of the Council of Europe,

Considering that the well-being and interests of children and young adults are fundamental issues for any society;

Considering that sexual exploitation of children and young adults for profit-making purposes in the form of pornography, prostitution and traffic of human beings has assumed new and alarming dimensions at national and international level;

Considering that sexual experience linked to this social phenomenon, often associated with early sexual abuse within the family or outside of it, may be detrimental to a child's and young adult's psychosocial development;

Considering that it is in the interests of member states of the Council of Europe to harmonise their national legislation on sexual exploitation of children and young adults in order to improve the co-ordination and effectiveness of action taken at national and international level with a view to tackling this problem;

Having regard to Recommendation 1065 (1987) of the Parliamentary Assembly of the Council of Europe on the traffic in children and other forms of child exploitation;

Recalling Resolution No. 3 on sexual exploitation, pornography and prostitution of, and trafficking in, children and young adults of the 16th Conference of European Ministers of Justice (Lisbon, 1988);

Recalling Recommendation No. R (85) 4 on violence in the family, Recommendation No. R (85) 11 on the position of the victim in the framework of criminal law and procedure, Recommendation No. R (87) 20 on social reactions to juvenile delinquency and Recommendation No. R (87) 7 concerning principles on the distribution of videograms having a violent, brutal or pornographic content;

Bearing in mind the Convention for the Protection of Human Rights and Fundamental Freedoms (1950) and the European Social Charter (1961);

Bearing also in mind the United Nations Convention on the Rights of the Child (1989),

I. Recommends that the governments of member states review their legislation and practice with a view to introducing, if necessary, and implementing the following measures:

A. *General measures*

a. Public awareness, education and information

1. make appropriate documentation on sexual exploitation of children and young adults available to parents, persons having minors in their care and other concerned groups and associations;

2. include in the programmes of primary and secondary school education information about the dangers of sexual exploitation and abuse to which children and young adults might be exposed, and about how they may defend themselves;

3. promote and encourage programmes aimed at furthering awareness and training for those who have functions involving support and protection of children and young adults in the fields of education, health, social welfare, justice and the police force in order to enable them to identify cases of sexual exploitation and to take the necessary measures;

4. make the public aware of the devastating effects of sexual exploitation which transforms children and young adults into consumer objects and urge the general public to take part in the efforts of associations and organisations intervening in field;

5. invite the media to contribute to a general awareness of the subject and to adopt appropriate rules of conduct;

6. discourage and prevent any abuse of the picture and the voice of the child in an erotic context;

b. Collection and exchange of information

7. urge public and private institutions and agencies dealing with children and young adults who have been victims of any form of sexual exploitation, to keep appropriate statistical information for scientific purposes and crime policy, while respecting anonymity and confidentiality;

8. encourage co-operation between the police and all public and private organisations handling cases of sexual abuse within the family or outside of it and of various forms of sexual exploitation;

c. Prevention, detection, assistance

9. urge police services to give special attention to prevention, detection, and investigation of offences involving sexual exploitation of children and young adults, and allocate to them sufficient means towards that end;

10. promote and further the creation and operation of specialised public and private services for the protection of children and young adults at risk in order to prevent and detect all forms of sexual exploitation;

11. support public and private initiatives at local level to set up helplines and centres with a view to providing medical, psychological, social or legal assistance to children and young adults who are at risk or who have been victims of sexual exploitation;

d. Criminal law and criminal procedure

12. ensure that the rights and interests of children and young adults are safeguarded throughout proceedings while respecting the rights of the alleged offenders;

13. ensure throughout judicial and administrative proceedings confidentiality of record and the respect for privacy rights of children and young adults who have been victims of sexual exploitation by avoiding, in particular, the disclosure of any information that could lead to their identification;

14. provide for special conditions at hearings involving children who are victims or witnesses of sexual exploitation, in order to diminish the traumatising effects of such hearings and to increase the credibility of their statements while respecting their dignity;

15. provide under an appropriate scheme for compensation of children and young adults who have been victims of sexual exploitation;

16. provide for the possibility of seizing and confiscating the proceeds from offences relating to sexual exploitation of children and young adults;

B. *Measures relating to pornography involving children*

1. provide for appropriate sanctions taking into account the gravity of the offence committed by those involved in the production and distribution of any pornographic material involving children;

2. examine the advisability of introducing penal sanctions for mere possession of pornographic material involving children;

3. ensure, particularly through international co-operation, the detection of firms, associations or individuals, often linked with two or more countries, using children for the production of pornographic material;

4. envisage informing the public, in order to raise awareness, of the implementation of penal policy, the number of prosecutions and convictions in cases involving child pornography, while ensuring the anonymity of the children concerned and of the alleged offenders;

C. *Measures relating to the prostitution of children and young adults*

1. increase the material and human resources of welfare and police services and improve their working methods so that places where child prostitution may occur are regularly inspected;

2. encourage and support the setting up of mobile welfare units for the surveillance of, or establishment of contact with, children at risk, particularly street children, in order to assist them to return to their families, if possible,

and, if necessary, direct them to the appropriate agencies for health care, training or education;

3.   intensify efforts with a view to identifying and sanctioning those who foster or encourage the prostitution of children or young adults, or who profit from it, on the one hand, and of the customers of child prostitution, on the other;

4.   create or develop special units within the police and, if necessary, improve their working methods, in order to combat procuring of children and young adults;

5.   dissuade travel agencies from promoting sex tourism in any form, especially through publicity, in particular by instituting consultations between them and the public services;

6.   give priority to vocational training and reintegration programmes involving children and young adults who are occasionally or habitually prostituting themselves;

D. *Measures relating to the trafficking in children and young adults*

1.   supervise the activities of artistic, marriage and adoption agencies in order to control the movement within, or between countries, of children and young adults, to prevent the possibility that they will be led into prostitution or other forms of sexual exploitation;

2.   increase surveillance by immigration authorities and frontier police in order to ensure that travel abroad by children, especially those not accompanied by their parents or their guardian, is not related to trafficking in human beings;

3.   set up facilities and support those existing, in order to protect and assist the victims of traffic in children and young adults.

II. *International aspects*

Recommends that the governments of member states:

1.   examine the advisability of signing and ratifying if they have not done so:

– the United Nations Convention for the Suppression of the Traffic in Persons and the Exploitation of the Prostitution of Others (1950);

– the Hague Convention on Jurisdiction, Applicable Law and Recognition of Decrees relating to Adoptions (1965);

– the European Convention on the Adoption of Children (1967);

– Convention No. 138 concerning Minimum Age for Admission to Employment, of the International Labour Organisation (1973);

– the United Nations Convention on the Rights of the Child (1989);

2.   introduce rules on extraterritorial jurisdiction in order to allow the prosecution and punishment of nationals who have committed offences concerning sexual exploitation of children and young adults outside the

national territory, or, if applicable, review existing rules to that effect, and improve international co-operation to that end;

3.   increase and improve exchanges of information between countries through Interpol, in order to identify and prosecute offenders involved in sexual exploitation, and particularly in trafficking in children and young adults, or those who organise it;

4.   establish links with international associations and organisations working for the welfare of children and young adults in order to benefit from data available to them and secure, if necessary, their collaboration in combating sexual exploitation;

5.   take steps towards the creation of a European register of missing children.

III.   *Research priorities*

Recommends that the governments of member states promote research at national and international level, in particular in the following fields:

1.   nature and extent of various forms of sexual exploitation of children and young adults, especially with a cross-cultural view;

2.   nature of paedophilia and factors contributing to it;

3.   links between adoption and sexual exploitation;

4.   links between sexual abuse within the family and prostitution;

5.   characteristics, role and needs of the consumers of child prostitution and child pornography;

6.   evaluation studies of vocational training and reintegration programmes concerning youth involved in prostitution;

7.   structure, international networks, interconnections and earnings of the sex industry;

8.   links between the sex industry and organised crime;

9.   possibilities and limitations of the criminal justice system as an instrument of prevention and repression of various forms of sexual exploitation of children and young adults;

10. epidemiology, causes and consequences of sexually transmitted diseases in children and young adults, and analysis of their links with sexual abuse and exploitation.

Recommendation No. R (95) 6
on the application of the European Convention on Recognition and Enforcement of Decisions concerning Custody of Children and on Restoration of Custody Children

(Adopted by the Committee of Ministers on 7 February 1995
at the 582th meeting of the Ministers' Deputies)

The Committee of Ministers, under the terms of Article 15.*b* of the Statute of the Council of Europe,

Having regard to the European Convention on Recognition and Enforcement of Decisions concerning Custody of Children and on Restoration on Custody of Children, done at Luxembourg on 20 May 1980 and The Hague Convention on the Civil Aspects of International Child Abduction, done at The Hague on 25 October 1980;

Recognising that the right of access of parents is a normal corollary to the right of custody;

Realising that a delay in the repatriation of a child may occur when neither parent is able or willing to pay for the costs of the repatriation and may result in the child being placed in care until the repatriation can take place:

Noting that Principle 4 of Recommendation No. R (91) 9 on emergency measures in family matters provides that family cases should be brought before the courts or other competent authorities and dealt with without delay;

Agreeing on the need to resolve matters relating to the repatriation of children as soon as possible and in the best interests of the children themselves,

Recommends that governments of members states:

a. sign and ratify the European Convention on Recognition and Enforcement of Decisions concerning Custody of Children and The Hague Convention on the Civil Aspects of International Child Abduction as soon as possible if they have not already done so;

b. take necessary measures at a national and international level:

   i. to improve the operation of transfrontier access to children;

   ii. to secure the rapid return of a child in compliance with a court decision.

Education

Table of contents

Parliamentary Assembly

Committee of Ministers

Parliamentary Assembly

Recommendation 897 (1980)[1]
on educational visits and pupil exchanges
between European countries

The Assembly,

1.   Referring to the European Cultural Convention, which calls upon signatory states to facilitate the movement and exchange of persons;

2.   Considering that educational visits and school exchanges, if properly prepared and organised, constitute a direct and highly fruitful experience for young people in Europe, developing mutual understanding and a sense of belonging to a single civilisation, and also of their individuality;

3.   Believing that the importance of pupil exchanges is now recognised both nationally and internationally as being of educational, cultural and human value, but that more active support is needed from the public authorities;

4.   Wishing to enable all school children, irrespective of the financial situation of their families, to take advantage of these educational exchanges and visits;

5.   Stressing the importance of the organisation of study visits abroad, if possible during school time;

6.   Conscious of the growing cost of such exchanges and study visits, and of the difficult problems of insurance and legal liability to which they give rise;

7.   Recalling the activities of the Council of Europe and the Council for Cultural Co-operation relating to young people, and the proposals made by the European Association of Teachers at the course on "educational and school exchanges" organised at Sèvres in 1973;

8.   Referring to the conclusions of the 1977 Venice Colloquium on "pupil exchanges in the European Community", and to the proposals addressed in 1978 by the Commission of the European Communities to the Council in the context of Community action in the field of education;

9.   Considering that the hospitality offered by Greece, with the support of the Council of Europe, in summer 1978 to 1 000 school children from the Council for Cultural Co-operation countries, as also the similar Italian project for the summer of 1980, contribute to making the European idea better

---

1. *Text adopted by the Standing Committee*, acting on behalf of the Assembly, on 3 July 1980. See Doc. 4541, report of the Committee on Culture and Education.

known to the younger generation, and believing that other member states could follow this example;

10. Asserting that such school exchanges and educational visits should be as wide as possible, not limited to a restricted number of member states, and aware that a better balance should be struck between the states participating in these exchanges;

11. Noting that information on exchanges is generally incomplete and inadequately circulated,

12. Recommends that the Committee of Ministers:

A.   invite the governments of member states:

i.   to foster educational visits and school exchanges through support measures, especially financial, and to increase their range in order to include states whose languages are not widespread or not generally taught in schools beyond the national frontiers;

ii.   to encourage the inclusion of such visits and exchanges in school curricula;

iii.   to improve the content and availability of information, so as to make it more accessible to those interested;

B.   call upon the Council for Cultural Co-operation;

i.   to help circulate information about the various categories of exchanges at the European level;

ii.   to deal with the problem of school exchanges as a whole, in order to propose solutions on the European level;

iii.   to encourage the signatory states to the European Cultural Convention to follow the example set by the Greek and Italian Governments by taking turns on a regular basis to host visiting groups of European school children.

Recommendation 928 (1981)[1]
on the educational and cultural problems of
minority languages and dialects in Europe

The Assembly,

1.   Considering that respect for, and the balanced development of, all the European cultures, and of linguistic identities in particular, is very important to the development of Europe and the European idea;

2.   Considering that, in view of major differences in terms of population, sociological situation, standardisation of language, its use for private or official purposes, and opportunities for access to education and the mass media, each case must be dealt with on its merits, and that an across-the-board solution is not possible;

3.   Considering that the following principles should form the basis for the scientific, human and cultural treatment of each language:

– respect for scientific authenticity,

– the right of children to their own language,

– the right of communities to develop their own language and culture,

4.   Recommends that the Committee of Ministers consider whether it would be possible for governments of member states to implement the following measures in whatever manner is most appropriate:

   a. With regard to the scientific aspect, the gradual adoption, where applicable, alongside names that have come to be accepted, of correct toponymical forms based on the original language of each territory, however small;

   b. With regard to the human aspect, the gradual adoption of children's mother tongues for their education (use of dialects as the spoken language in pre-school education, and use of standardised mother-tongue language forms in primary education, the prevailing language of the country being then progressively introduced alongside the mother tongue);

   c. With regard to the cultural aspect, respect and official support for the local use of standardised minority languages, and for their current use in higher education and by the local mass media, in so far as this approach is favoured by the communities which speak them;

---

1. *Assembly debate* on 7 October 1981 (18th Sitting) (see Doc. 4745, report of the Committee on Culture and Education).
   Text adopted by the Assembly on 7 October 1981 (18th Sitting).

d. With regard to the political aspect, in all areas which have a language of their own and some degree of administrative structure within the state of which they are a part, the possibility of adoption of that language by those areas' authorities as the official or joint official language;

5. With regard to implementing in a European framework the proposals contained in paragraph 4.*a*, *b*, *c* and *d* above, recommends that the Committee of Ministers consider the feasibility of undertaking action for the purpose of gathering and disseminating information on developments in this field.

Resolution 874 (1987)[1]
on the quality and effectiveness
of school teaching

The Assembly,

1.　Having noted the report of its Committee on Culture and Education (Doc. 5670) and the hearing held by that committee on "The teacher in question" in Vaduz in May 1986;

2.　Convinced of the importance of the quality, relevance and effectiveness of school education as preparation of the individual for life in a competitive society and as a basic condition for our countries to keep pace with economic growth;

3.　Considering that education is a particularly effective way of improving inter-community relations and helping young people of immigrant origin to play a part in the society of the host community;

4.　Affirming the increasing importance of school education in the face of competing out-of-school pressures on young people and the decline of the educational role of the family;

5.　Believing that social change, technological development and the rise in unemployment make necessary the continual re-evaluation of school education (at primary and secondary levels), with regard to the optimal use of resources and the proper preparation of those involved in the teaching process;

6.　Noting that educational standards are changing rather than falling, and drawing attention to the professional skills required of the teacher in order to meet these changes;

7.　Believing that, to ensure the recruitment and maintenance of a teaching profession with the motivation, flair and competence required, considerable improvements should be made regarding:

　　i.　teachers' pay, status and conditions of employment;

　　ii.　teachers' working conditions (such as reduced class sizes and ability ranges);

　　iii.　initial and in-service training of teachers;

　　iv.　involvement of teachers in policy discussions affecting the school or curriculum;

---

1. *Assembly debate* on 30 January 1987 (28th Sitting) (see Doc. 5670, report of the Committee on Culture and Education).
　Text adopted by the Assembly on 30 January 1987 (28th Sitting).

v. introduction of new teaching methods on the basis of educational research;

8. Believing that, when designing syllabuses, consideration should be given to the fact that classes can include a large number, and sometimes a majority, of young people of immigrant origin;

9. Underlining the need also for a constructive partnership between teachers, parents and pupils, co-operation between schools and industry and trade unions, and the development of an interactive relationship between the school and the community;

10. Interested in possibilities of further encouraging the performance of teachers through assessment, merit pay and other differentials, but believing that this can only be negotiated when the more basic conditions have been met;

11. Believing that better use should be made of the pool of qualified teacher talent (especially when there are so many unemployed), for example to improve teacher-pupil ratios and to enable teachers to profit from in-service training without disrupting the curriculum;

12. Noting the decision of the Standing Conference of European Ministers of Education to take as the main theme of the 15th Session in Helsinki in May 1987 "New challenges for teachers and their education", and welcoming the considerable preparatory discussion this has involved in both non-governmental and intergovernmental bodies, and notably the 4th All-European Conference of Directors of Educational Research Institutions (Eger, Hungary, October 1986);

13. Recalling its Resolution 807 (1983) on European co-operation in the field of education, and 866 (1986) on East-West relations,

14. Invites the Standing Conference of European Ministers of Education;

a. to fulfil its role as an overview body on European co-operation in the field of education, by continuing to review and evaluate the activities of the international organisations concerned with a view to enabling governments to co-ordinate this work more effectively and more usefully;

b. in the context of ongoing European co-operation, to make proposals for specific activities to be carried out by the Council of Europe in such fields as:

   i. initial and in-service training of teachers;

   ii. assessment of the effectiveness of teaching and training;

   iii. intercultural education in the context of fostering better relations between children of migrant origin and the host community;

   iv. training of teacher trainers, school heads and education administrators;

   v. the development of teacher exchanges in Europe.

Recommendation 1111 (1989)[1]
on the European dimension of education

The Assembly,

1. Having regard to the European Cultural Convention (1954) which underlines the need for education to develop mutual understanding between the peoples of Europe, especially through the study of languages, history and civilisation;

2. Expressing its concern that education should prepare the individual for life in a democratic society by enabling him to carry out his duties and responsibilities as a citizen, introducing him to politics, and teaching him the fundamental principles and values at the root of our society, such as respect for human rights and democracy, as well as the tolerance and solidarity that result from a greater understanding and knowledge of others;

3. Recalling Recommendation No. R (83) 4 of the Committee of Ministers concerning the promotion of an awareness of Europe in secondary schools, and Resolution (85) 6 on European cultural identity;

4. Having noted the resolution of 24 May 1988 of the Council and Ministers of Education of the European Community, on the European dimension in education;

5. Regarding Europe, for the purposes of the European dimension of education, as extending to the whole of the continent and in no way synonymous with the membership of any particular European organisation;

6. Convinced that the rapidly improving relations with East European countries provide a crucial occasion for developing such a notion in education throughout the continent and for closer co-operation between the Council of Europe, the European Community and Unesco;

7. Welcoming the work of the Council for Cultural Co-operation with regard to the teaching of history, geography and modern languages, and its contribution to the development of a real European consciousness, but believing that this approach should be extended to other subjects such as economics, the environment, the visual arts, music and the sciences;

---

1. *Assembly debate* on 22 September 1989 (12th Sitting) (see Doc. 6113, report of the Committee on Culture and Education, Rapporteur: Mr Bassinet).
   Text adopted by The Assembly on 22 September 1989 (12th Sitting).

8.   Noting that, despite the emphasis placed by the Council of Europe on the European dimension of education, the idea has still to be more effectively integrated into teaching in practice;

9.   Stressing the need to include knowledge of other European countries in teacher training, and regretting the lack of means for enabling pupil exchanges between all parts of Europe;

10.   Believing that the new information technologies should be more fully exploited to develop international school links and projects, and that a wider use should be made of such activities as the European Schools' Day competition;

11.   Drawing attention also to the contribution that can be made to awareness of the European dimension by factors outside the formal school structure (such as the media or the fact of travelling), and wishing to associate those responsible, in particular in the fields of the media (written or broadcast) and of tourism, with the development of this dimension,

12.   Recommends that the Committee of Ministers further develop the European dimension of education in close concertation with the European Community and Unesco, where possible including Eastern Europe, and in particular:

a.   ensure more effective dissemination of information on current or completed activities undertaken by organisations involved in European cooperation in education, and more particularly the Council of Europe;

b.   encourage the European dimension in the training and in-service training of teachers, for example by promoting exchanges between teachers by increasing the number of Council of Europe bursaries, and by setting up in Strasbourg a European centre for teachers, along the lines of the European Youth Centre;

c.   give much greater emphasis to ongoing work on the teaching of history and modern languages, as well as launching programmes on geography and civics;

d.   initiate research into the European dimension in new subjects (such as economics, environmental education, the visual arts, music and the sciences), and encourage co-operation between pedagogical research and teacher-training institutions in Europe;

e.   encourage international networks of school links, making full use of the new information technologies as well as traditional methods;

f.   seek ways of associating those responsible for tourism, information and the media with the developing of strategies to enhance awareness of the European dimension, for instance by encouraging European publishing houses for teaching material.

Recommendation 1169 (1991)[1]
on education for health and drugs misuse in the member states of the Council of Europe and the European Community

1.   The Assembly continues to be alarmed that drugs misuse remains a major problem for all West European countries and is already affecting the populations of Eastern Europe: estimates of world-wide sales of illegal drugs approach 1,3 thousand million dollars (1 thousand million ecus) per year.

2.   For many years, drug-taking has not been confined to certain vulnerable categories of people, but has spread to all sections of the population, involving more and more age-groups, and is now increasing in sport.

3.   In its Recommendation 1085 (1988) on the fight against drugs, endorsed by the Committee of Ministers, the Assembly advocated a "four-pronged" approach:

   i.   to develop better ways to reduce drug production;

   ii.   to improve international co-operation to tackle trafficking and allow the seizure of traffickers' assets;

   iii.   to undertake urgently more and better action to reduce demand;

   iv.   to increase the number and quality of treatment facilities, and to research new treatments and techniques.

4.   Since supply can never be effectively eliminated, drugs education, from an early age onwards, is the best form of prevention and demand reduction.

5.   With this in mind, the Assembly recommended an enhanced role for health education in preventing drug dependency earlier this year; it welcomes the resolution on health educaton in schools of the Council of Ministers of Education of the European Communities (23 November 1988), and the conclusions of the first World Ministerial Summit to Reduce Demand for Drugs (9-11 April 1990).

6.   Although all member countries are devoting increasing attention to preventive education as the best means of reducing demand for illegal drugs, education for health – including education about drugs misuse – still requires a higher priority and must be taught in schools in an overall, structured framework as part of the core school curriculum.

---

1. *Assembly debate* on 25 September 1991 (18th Sitting) (see Doc. 6472, report of the Social, Health and Family Affairs Committee, Rapporteur: Mr Rathbone).
   Text adopted by the Assembly on 25 September 1991 (18th Sitting).

7.   Although common principles on health education can be agreed at European level, there must be room for adaptation to prevailing cultural and social circumstances. But national and international exchange of information on successful health educaton programmes can assist development of the most effective policies in drugs educaton and prevention programmes every- where.

8.   The proper way to position education for health courses is to integrate them within a multidisciplinary approach to social and health problems, encouraging students to recognise the benefits of a generally healthy and drug-free life style, including sport and other active recreational activities.

9.   Education for health at an early age is essential. Before drug habits become a temptation or take root, children must experience preventive health educaton at both primary and secondary educational levels, especial- ly in high-risk environments.

10. Education for health should not stop at school. Employers should take responsibility for informing employees about the adverse effects of legal and illegal drugs at home and at work; they should provide counselling for mis- users, in particular in professions where safety is a key factor.

11. Opportunities should be provided for "re-education", training or retraining of former addicts to allow them to take up jobs rather than re- enter the drug misuse culture.

12. Training information and health education initiatives against the use of drugs in sport should be increased and particularly directed at trainers and doctors working with sportsmen.

13. Accordingly, the Assembly recommends that the Committee of Ministers:

   i. reaffirm that education for health is the most crucial element in reducing demand for drugs;

   ii. recognise the importance of devoting more money and resources to local, national and international programmes of education for health and drug misuse prevention, particularly among young people and in the world of sport;

   iii. recognise the important role that voluntary and non-governmental organisations have in initiating methods and materials for educaton for health in local communities;

   iv. urge all member governments immediately to enlarge and improve their education for health programmes, the drug misuse prevention content of them and the funding support given to them;

   v. progress as fast as possible with a comprehensive survey of good health educational practices and policies in all member countries, so that best practice at local and regional levels can be shared and acted upon;

   vi. promote further European pilot projects on drugs education within programmes of education for health in schools, among parents, profession- als and voluntary organisations, and in the workplace;

vii. establish and support a means of systematic exchange of information between all member countries and those with special guest status, with a view to establishing and maintaining the most comprehensive and effective national and international strategies on education for health;

viii. encourage the highest possible level of co-ordination between public and private services, education establishments and voluntary groups;

ix. urgently seek better ways of financing a European investment fund for drugs education programmes in co-ordination with the Council of Ministers and the Commission of the European Communities;

x. ensure that all member states take action to implement the resolution on the role of education in the fight against drugs of the Council of Ministers of Education of the European Communities (3 December 1990), the resolution on reducing the demand for narcotic and psychotropic substances of the Council of Ministers of Health of the European Communities (29 November 1990), other relevant resolutions of the European Community and the Council of Europe, and the conclusions of the first World Ministerial Summit to Reduce Demand for Drugs (9-11 April 1990).

14. Furthermore, the Assembly requests the Committee of Ministers to report on actions taken to meet these recommendations, during the Assembly's 44th Session in 1992.

Recommendation 1202 (1993)[1]
on religious tolerance
in a democratic society

1.   The Assembly has already adopted a number of texts on related subjects and recalls in particular Recommendation 963 (1983) on cultural and educational means of reducing violence, Resolution 885 (1987) on the Jewish contribution to European culture, Recommendation 1086 (1988) on the situation of the Church and freedom of religion in Eastern Europe, Recommendation 1162 (1991) on the contribution of the Islamic civilisation to European culture and Recommendation 1178 (1992) on sects and new religious movements.

2.   Attention should also be drawn to the hearing on religious tolerance held by the Committee on Culture and Education in Jerusalem on 17 and 18 March 1992 and to the colloquy marking the 500th anniversary of the arrival of Jewish refugees in Turkey held on 17 September 1992 in Istanbul.

3.   Religion provides an enriching relationship for the individual with himself and his god, as well as with the outside world and the society in which he lives.

4.   Mobility within Europe and migratory movements to Europe have always resulted in the meeting of differing world views, religious beliefs as well as notions of human existence.

5.   This meeting of differing religious beliefs can lead to greater mutual understanding and enrichment, although it could also result in a strengthening of trends towards separatism and encourage fundamentalism.

6.   Western Europe has developed the model of secular democracy within which a variety of religious beliefs are in theory tolerated. History has shown, however, that such tolerance is also possible under a religious government (for example the Arabs in Spain and the Ottoman Empire).

7.   It is a matter of concern that in numerous countries there has been a renewed occurrence of xenophobia, racism and religious intolerance.

8.   Religion often reinforces, or is used to reinforce, international, social and national minority conflicts.

9.   There is a recognisable crisis of values (or rather the lack of them) in present-day Europe. The pure market society is revealed as inadequate as

---

1. *Assembly debate* on 2 February 1993 (23rd Sitting) (see Doc. 6732, report of the Committee on Culture and Education, Rapporteur: Mrs Fischer).
   Text adopted by The Assembly on 2 February 1993 (23rd Sitting).

was communism for well-being and social responsibility. The recourse to religion as an alternative has, however, to be reconciled with the principles of democracy and human rights.

10. In the context of current and future social trends and the growing pressures of multicultural communities, inadequate attention has so far been given to promotion of religious tolerance.

11. In each of the three main monotheistic religions a basis can be found for tolerance and mutual respect towards people with differing beliefs or towards non-believers. Every human being is viewed as the creation of the one God and, as such, is due the same dignity and the same rights, regardless of his convictions.

12. The question of tolerance between religions has to be further developed. The three monotheistic religions should be encouraged to give greater emphasis to those basic moral values that are essentially similar and tolerant.

13. European history shows that co-existence of Jewish, Christian and Islamic cultures when based on mutual respect and tolerance have contributed to the prosperity of nations.

14. The universal importance of religious freedom, as enshrined in Article 18 of the Universal Declaration of Human Rights and guaranteed in Article 9 of the European Convention on Human Rights, has to be reaffirmed. This freedom is rooted in the dignity of man and its realisation implies the realisation of a free, democratic society.

15. The secular state should not impose any religious obligations on its citizens. It should also encourage respect for all recognised religious communities and their relations with society as a whole.

16. The Assembly recommends that the Committee of Ministers call upon the governments of the member states, the European Community as well as the responsible authorities and organisations:

Legal guarantees and their observance

i.   to guarantee religious freedom, freedom of conscience and freedom of worship with specific reference to the rights indicated in the Assembly Recommendation 1086 (1988), paragraph 10;

ii.   to allow for flexibility in the accommodation of different religious practices (for example in dress, eating and observance of holy days);

Education and exchanges

iii.   to ensure that studies of religions and ethics are part of the general school curriculum, and to work towards a differentiated and careful depiction of religions in school books (including history books) and in classroom teaching with a view to achieving a better and deeper understanding of the various religions;

iv.   to emphasise that a knowledge of one's own religion or ethical principles is a prerequisite for true tolerance and that it might act also as a safeguard against indifference or prejudice;

v. to establish a "religious history school-book conference" consisting of a representative selection of theologians and philosophers for the purpose of compiling basic texts, documents and commentaries for teaching in schools;

vi. to make it possible to present to young people the ideas and deeds of living individuals of different religious beliefs as examples of religious tolerance in practice;

vii. to facilitate, in the framework of existing exchange programmes for secondary school students, university students or other young people, meetings and discussions with informed persons of differing beliefs;

viii. to promote inter-religious encounters and organisations that serve the purpose of furthering mutual understanding between religions and thereby peace and respect for human rights;

ix. to consider the provision of similar facilities for the religious schools of all recognised religions;

Information and "sensibilisation"

x. to ensure that fundamental religious texts and related literature are translated and made available in public libraries;

xi. to organise cultural projects on religious issues in the context of cultural promotion programmes;

Research

xii. to facilitate the development of a network of research institutes in Europe which would:

- collect, analyse and evaluate literature on religious tolerance;

- provide an information service with a good selection of this literature;

- organise workshops and research conferences on religious tolerance;

- serve as a competent and authoritative source of public information;

xiii. to stimulate academic work (seminars, degree courses, doctoral dissertations) in European universities on questions concerning religious tolerance.

Recommendation 1222 (1993)[1]
on the fight against racism, xenophobia
and intolerance

1.   The Assembly is deeply alarmed by the resurgence of racism, xenophobia and intolerance throughout Europe.

2.   It strongly condemns the resulting acts of violence committed in several Council of Europe member states.

3.   The Assembly is encouraged by the massive public response in many member states in favour of accepting and respecting the different cultures existing in Europe.

4.   The Assembly stresses the importance of addressing the root causes of racism, xenophobia and intolerance, and of applying existing national and international legal instruments to combat these phenomena.

5.   Action by national, regional and local authorities, as well as by non-governmental organisations, should further include prevention through education, support for the victims and protection and promotion of cultural diversity (as already stated in Recommendation 1206 (1993) on the integration of migrants and community relations).

6.   The Assembly underlines the role to be played by young people and therefore welcomes the Round Table held by its Committee on Culture and Education, in July 1993, between parliamentarians and youth representatives on "strategies to combat xenophobia".

7.   The Assembly also emphasises the crucial role that the media could play in presenting an open and tolerant society and in countering prejudice and hatred. Therefore, it invites the media to inform the public objectively of the dangers of racism, xenophobia and intolerance.

8.   It asks the advertising industry not to include commercials in films and/or television productions which encourage violence, brutality and racism.

9.   In certain member states, public opinion seems to be that the burden resulting from the application of the Geneva Convention of 1951 relating to the Status of Refugees is not fairly shared by all European countries. This belief contributes to the rise of xenophobia and racist sentiments.

---

1. *Assembly debate* on 29 September 1993 (49th Sitting) (see Doc. 6915, report of the Political Affairs Committee, Rapporteur: Mr Espersen; Doc. 6937, opinion of the Committee on Legal Affairs and Human Rights, Rapporteur: Mr López Henares; and Doc. 6935, opinion of the Committee on Culture and Education, Rapporteur: Mrs Err).
Text adopted by The Assembly on 29 September 1993 (49th Sitting).

10. The Assembly welcomes the suggestions by the Committee of Ministers that the forthcoming summit of heads of state and government, to be held in Vienna on 8 and 9 October 1993, result in an action plan of the Council of Europe against racism, xenophobia and intolerance.

11. The Assembly recommends that the Committee of Ministers include in the draft plan of action to be discussed at the summit the following:

i.   a European youth campaign enabling the young people of Europe to unite in a common struggle for European values;

ii.   an interdisciplinary comparative study in all Council of Europe member states on the root causes of racism, xenophobia and other manifestations of intolerance and exclusion as well as on the measures taken at national level, in order to lay down guidelines and common principles for a Europe-wide strategy;

iii.   the setting up of an independent group of experts which should:

   a.   monitor member states' compliance with international legal obligations;

   b.   exchange information and stimulate action at national, regional and local level;

   c.   consider communications addressed to it by non-governmental organisations;

   d.   report regularly to the Committee of Ministers, which should transmit these reports to the Assembly;

iv.   the creation, in close co-operation with the Office of the United Nations High Commissioner for Refugees, of a European refugee commission or forum to promote policies and measures which would be aimed at improving solidarity between member states as regards the consequences of receiving refugees and asylum-seekers;

v.   a decision to re-examine urgently the question of possible obstacles to acquisition of citizenship, in order to facilitate the integration of migrants, if under the national legislation of the host country the requirements of such acquisition are met;

vi.   specific measures to ensure effective communication and implementation of the plan and its objectives.

12. The Assembly also recommends that the Committee of Ministers call on the member states of the Council of Europe to:

i.   introduce or reinforce, as a matter of the utmost urgency, an active education and youth policy stressing the combat of intolerant, racist and xenophobic attitudes; special attention should be given to human rights education and language teaching;

ii.   support and fund activities by non-governmental organisations aimed at promoting tolerance and, where appropriate, initiate such action as the establishment of multi-cultural centres and the organisation of language courses for immigrants, training courses for youth leaders, multi-ethnic travel and other forms of cultural exchange;

iii.   set up national level organisations for the promotion of tolerance, with responsibility for encouraging dialogue between young people from immigrant and indigenous communities and for advising governments on the direction to be taken by their policies to promote tolerance;

iv.   ratify the United Nations International Convention on the Elimination of all Forms of Racial Discrimination and to accept the petition procedure provided for in Article 14 of the convention;

v.   ratify the International Covenant on Civil and Political Rights together with the optional protocol establishing a committee with the right to examine individual complaints;

vi.   ensure that interested lawyers and immigrant support organisations are aware of the provisions of the United Nations Convention on the Elimination of all Forms of Racial Discrimination, the International Covenant on Civil and Political Rights and the Council of Europe's Convention for the Protection of Human Rights and Fundamental Freedoms;

vii.   adopt legislation in line with the principles and guidelines to be drawn up by the Council of Europe for the punishment of persons initiating racist, xenophobic or anti-Semitic remarks or acts, as well as any act of discrimination of this kind perpetrated by the public authorities.

13. The Assembly recommends that the Committee of Ministers invite member states to promote, in the media, an active campaign against racist and xenophobic attitudes.

14. The Assembly also recommends that the Committee of Ministers invite the member states of the Council of Europe and the regional and local authorities to give priority to the means of combating racism and xenophobia.

Recommendation 1248 (1994)[1]
on education for gifted children

1.   The Assembly reaffirms education as a fundamental human right, and believes that it should, as far as possible, be appropriate to each individual.

2.   Whereas for practical purposes education systems must be set up as to provide adequate education for the majority of children, there will always be children with special needs and for whom special arrangements have to be made. One group of such children is that of the highly gifted.

3.   Gifted children should be able to benefit from appropriate educational conditions that would allow them to develop fully their abilities, for their own benefit and for the benefit of society as a whole. No country can indeed afford to waste talents and it would be a waste of human resources not to identify in good time any intellectual or other potentialities. Adequate tools are needed for this purpose.

4.   Special educational provision should, however, in no way privilege one group of children to the detriment of the others.

5.   The Assembly therefore recommends that the Committee of Ministers ask the competent authorities of the states signatory to the European Cultural Convention to take account of the following considerations in their educational policies:

    i.   legislation should recognise and respect individual differences. Highly gifted children, as with other categories, need adequate educational opportunities to develop their full potential;

    ii.   basic research in the fields of "giftedness" and "talent" and applied research, for instance to improve identification procedures, should be developed in parallel. Research on the "mechanisms of success" could help to tackle school failure;

    iii.   meanwhile, in-service teacher training programmes have to include strategies for identifying children of high ability or special talent. Information on gifted children should be made available to all those who deal with children (teachers, parents, doctors, social workers, ministries of education, etc.);

    iv.   provision for specially gifted children in a given subject area should preferably be arranged within the ordinary school system, from pre-school

---

1. *Assembly debate* on 7 October 1994 (31st Sitting) (see Doc. 7140, report of the Committee on Culture and Education, Rapporteur: Mr Hadjidemetriou).
   Text adopted by The Assembly on 7 October 1994 (31st Sitting).

education onwards. Flexible curricula, more chances of mobility, enriching supplementary material, audio-visual aids and project-oriented teaching styles are ways and techniques to foster the development of all children, whether highly gifted or not, and enable the identification of special needs at the earliest possible time;

v. the ordinary school system should be made flexible enough to enable the needs of high performers or talented students to be met;

vi. any special provision for highly gifted or talented students should be administered with discretion, to avoid the innate danger of labelling, with all its undesired consequences to society.

6. There is a need to clarify the notion of "giftedness" by an operational definition that is accepted and understandable in different languages. Therefore, the Assembly further recommends that the Committee of Ministers consider the setting-up of an *ad hoc* committee for this purpose including psychologists, sociologists, and educationalists of all relevant specialisations.

Recommendation 1281 (1995)[1]
on gender equality in education

1.   The Assembly believes that education for all girls and boys is a fundamental human right, regardless of gender, race, ethnic origin, family background or personal wealth.

2.   In line with its Recommendation 1229 (1994) on equality of rights between men and women, the Assembly asserts the importance of gender equality in education and believes that it should be guaranteed by the educational systems of all states party to the European Cultural Convention.

3.   It acknowledges the action already initiated by the Council of Europe on gender equality and in particular by the Standing Conference of European Ministers of Education (11th session in 1979 and 14th session in 1985) on gender equality in education and by the Steering Committee for Equality between Women and Men on participation of women in public and political life.

4.   The Assembly is however concerned that:

i.   co-education has led to more equality but in many countries there continue to be institutionalised and non-institutionalised forms of discrimination of girls and women;

ii.   traditional gender roles in education still strongly steer and reduce the choices of both sexes as regards education, occupation and lifestyles, thus reinforcing the male norms in division of family responsibilities and in the labour market, as well as their dominance in decision-making processes;

iii.   women and girls are still subject to sexual harassment and violence in society and in education.

5.   The Assembly believes therefore that strategies should be developed which create for girls and boys, women and men, *de jure* and *de facto* freedom of access to and freedom of choice in education including initial and further education, vocational training and adult education. Education should help them to develop their full potential, to preserve their personal integrity, to aim at economic independence and to participate fully in society and in political life.

6.   Girls and boys should be presented with positive role models of women of the past and present as a valid educational concept for removing stereo-

---

1. *Text adopted by the standing Committee*, acting on behalf of the Assembly, on 9 November 1995.
   See Doc. 7366, report of the Committee on Culture and Education, rapporteur: Baroness Gould of Potternewton.

types. Women as principals and decision-makers within a gender-balanced educational workforce can also be considered as important role-models.

7. Childbearing and motherhood have a considerable impact on women's activities. Knowledge of this, and also the sharing of responsibilities in the home and with the raising of children, should be a basic part of the school curriculum for boys and girls.

8. Gender equality in education can only be achieved by meeting the needs of employed women, especially those working in the educational fields, and by counteracting existing discrimination. The educational authorities of the member states should do all they can to achieve fixed and regular school timetables and provide mothers with support, such as child-oriented timetabling and provisions for personal choice of child care.

9. Gender equality in education must be part of an overall strategy for a more egalitarian and democratic society, considering that women of the past and present have contributed eminently to European culture and society and it is necessary to incorporate into education the knowledge that feminists have gathered on this contribution.

10. The Assembly acknowledges the significant contribution of the women's movement and feminist researchers and activists to human rights and gender equality in the educational field as well as in the political, social, cultural and economic fields and appreciates the expertise gathered in analysing and counteracting sexism and racism.

11. It believes that democracy can only be taught in schools in a democratic setting respecting the cultural plurality in Europe, and stressing the fundamental principle of equality between girls and boys, women and men, whatever differences there may be between them, their different viewpoints and experiences.

12. The Assembly, therefore, recommends that the Committee of Ministers ask the competent authorities of member states to promote education in human rights with a gender-sensitive approach and to take measures to accelerate *de jure* and *de facto* equality in education, promoting actively equal rights, equal chances and equal treatment in a gender-sensitive way of girls and boys, women and men, whether students or belonging to the workforce in education, and in particular to:

i.   create strategies for freedom of access to and freedom of choice in education, for girls and boys, women and men, including initial and further education, vocational training and adult education;

ii.   identify and spread good practice in gender sensitive education, for example by:

   a. revising teaching material and methods with a view to reinforcing non-discriminatory language and non-sexist teaching and to placing greater emphasis on equality and non-violence;

   b. revising stereotypes and role models for girls and boys, improving their self-images and providing them with positive role models while counteracting concepts of inequality and male violence;

c. better presentation of the importance of women in European history and culture;

d. taking greater consideration of the needs of girls and women and of boys and men for education in the fields of health, sex, family planning and parenthood;

e. directing attention in media education to non-sexist, non-racist and non-violent scenes, avoiding verbal and visual violence against girls and women;

iii. include gender sensitivity and the promotion of equality in all initial and in-service teacher training and in the training of vocational advisors;

iv. initiate gender-sensitive research, including the participation of researchers on feminism and migration;

v. improve the gender balance of teaching and administrative staff and school management;

vi. recognise the strategic and supportive role played by teachers and parents in the removal of discrimination, for example by improving communication between schools and parents especially for migrant girls, and by the provision of support services for working parents.

13. The Assembly further recommends that the Committee of Ministers:

i. place special emphasis on activities in the field of monitoring gender equality in education and provide in due course information on the situation within the area of the European Cultural Convention;

ii. expand international consultation and exchange of experiences with regard to legislation, educational programmes, studies or debates on topical problems relating to gender equality in education;

iii. initiate exchange programmes for teachers, students and researchers and increase the possibilities for training and research in gender-sensitive education, in both cases with due regard for gender-balance;

iv. instruct the European Commission against Racism and Intolerance to consider the dimension of gender equality in education in its work;

v. re-establish the former joint working party of the Steering Committees for Equality between Women and Men and the Council of Europe for Cultural Co-operation to study the effects of co-education and to organise subsequently an international policy-making conference.

Recommendation 1283 (1996)[1]
on history and the learning of history in Europe

1.   People have a right to their past, just as they have a right to disown it. History is one of several ways of retrieving this past and creating a cultural identity. It is also a gateway to the experiences and richness of the past and of other cultures. It is a discipline concerned with the development of a critical approach to information and of controlled imagination.

2.   History also has a key political role to play in today's Europe. It can contribute to greater understanding, tolerance and confidence between individuals and between the peoples of Europe – or it can become a force for division, violence and intolerance.

3.   Historical awareness is an important civic skill. Without it the individual is more vulnerable to political and other manipulation.

4.   For most young people, history begins in school. This should not simply be the learning by heart of haphazard historical facts; it should be an initiation into how historical knowledge is arrived at, a matter of developing the critical mind and the development of a democratic, tolerant and responsible civic attitude.

5.   Schools are not the sole source of historical influence and opinion. Other sources include the mass media, films, literature and tourism. Influence is also exercised by the family, peer groups, local and national communities, and by religious and political circles.

6.   The new communication technologies (CD-I, CD-ROM, Internet, virtual reality etc.) are gradually extending the range and impact of historical subjects.

7.   A distinction may be made between several forms of history: tradition, memories and analytical history. Facts are selected on the basis of different criteria in each. And these various forms of history play different roles.

8.   Politicians have their own interpretations of history, and some are tempted to manipulate it. Virtually all political systems have used history for their own ends and have imposed both their version of historical facts and their definition of the good and bad figures of history.

---

1. *Assembly debate* on 22 January 1996 (1st Sitting) (see Doc. 7446, report of the Committee on Culture and Education, rapporteur: Mr de Puig).
   Text adopted by the Assembly on 22 January 1996 (1st Sitting).

9. Even if their constant aim may be to get as close to objectivity as possible, historians are also well aware of the essential subjectivity of history and of the various ways in which it can be reconstructed and interpreted.

10. Citizens have a right to learn history that has not been manipulated. The state should uphold this right and encourage an appropriate scientific approach, without religious or political bias, in all that is taught.

11. Teachers and research workers should be in close contact to assure the continued updating and renewal of the content of history teaching. It is important that history keep pace with the present.

12. There should also be transparency between those working in all areas of history, whether in the school classroom, television studio or university library.

13. Particular attention should be given to the problems in central and eastern Europe which has suffered from the manipulation of history up to recent times, and continues in certain cases to be subject to political censorship.

14. The Assembly recommends that the Committee of Ministers encourage the teaching of history in Europe with regard to the following proposals:

i.   historical awareness should be an essential part of the education of all young people. The teaching of history should enable pupils to acquire critical thinking skills to analyse and interpret information effectively and responsibly, to recognise the complexity of issues and to appreciate cultural diversity. Stereotypes should be identified and any other distortions based on national, racial, religious or other prejudice;

ii.   the subject matter of history teaching should be very open. It should include all aspects of societies (social and cultural history as well as political). The role of women should be given proper recognition. Local and national (but not nationalist) history should be taught as well as the history of minorities. Controversial, sensitive and tragic events should be balanced by positive mutual influences;

iii.   the history of the whole of Europe, that of the main political and economic events, and the philosophical and cultural movements which have formed the European identity must be included in syllabuses;

iv. schools should recognise the different ways in which the same subjects are handled in different countries and this could be developed as a basis for interschool exchanges;

v. support should be given to the Georg Eckert Institute for International Textbook Research and Ministries of Education and educational publishers in member states should be asked to ensure that the institute's collection of textbooks is kept up-to-date;

vi. the different forms of history learning (textbook study, television, project work, museum visits, etc.) should be combined, without exclusive preference to any of them. New information technologies should be fully integrated. Proper educational (and academic) standards must be ensured for the material used;

vii. greater interaction should be fostered between school and out-of-school influences on young people's appreciation of history, for example by museums (and in particular history museums), cultural routes and tourism in general;

viii. innovatory approaches should be encouraged as well as continued in-service training, especially with regard to the new technologies. An interactive network of history teachers should be encouraged. History should be a priority subject for European teachers' courses organised within the framework of the Council for Cultural Co-operation in-service training programme for teachers;

ix. co-operation should be encouraged between teachers and historians, for example by means of the Education Committee of the Council for Cultural Co-operation's new project on learning and about teaching the history of Europe in the 20th century;

x. government support should be given to the setting up of independent national associations of history teachers. Their active involvement in the European history teachers' association Euroclio should be encouraged;

xi. a code of practice for history teaching should be drawn up in collaboration with history teachers as well as a European charter to protect them from political manipulation.

15. The Assembly supports freedom of academic research but would also expect professional responsibility as in the parallel field of broadcasting. The Assembly therefore recommends that the Committee of Ministers:

i. ask governments to assure continued financial support for historical research and the work of multilateral and bilateral commissions on contemporary history;

ii. promote co-operation between historians so as to help encourage the development of more open and more tolerant attitudes in Europe by taking account of different experiences and opinions;

iii. ensure that the right of historians to freedom of expression is protected.

16. European collaboration should be encouraged in the field of history. The Assembly recommends that the Committee of Ministers:

i. study the basic elements of the different histories of the peoples of Europe which, accepted by everyone, could be included in all European history textbooks;

ii. consider the possibility of establishing in member states an on-line library of history;

iii. encourage member states to establish national history museums on the lines of the German "House of History" in Bonn;

iv. promote multilateral and bilateral projects on history and history teaching and in particular regional projects between neighbouring countries.

Committee of Ministers

Resolution (52) 47
Exchange of teachers, students and young technicians among members of the Council of Europe

(Adopted by the Ministers' Deputies on 12th September 1952)

The Committee of Ministers,

Having considered Recommendation 18 of the Consultative Assembly,

Approves this Recommendation and

Further resolves:

1. to invite member governments to grant either directly or by means of exchanges, as great a number as possible of travelling scholarships to enable teachers, students and technicians to make educational visits abroad;

2. to invite each member government to take appropriate steps to enable its nationals to take part in international meetings, periods of study and courses on subjects of European interest;

3. to grant annually a number of Council of Europe travelling scholarships so as to enable nationals of member states to participate in international meetings, periods of study and courses of the kind mentioned in the previous paragraph;

4. to invite member governments to facilitate the exchange of workers and social workers, as also student employees for whom the International Association for the Exchange of Students for Technical Experience is not at present in a position to cater;

5. to offer Council of Europe travel grants to the persons mentioned in the preceding paragraph for study abroad, and to this end instructs the Secretariat General to collaborate with the international organisations concerned with exchanges of workers, such as the International Labour Organisation and the Secretariat of the Brussels Treaty Permanent Commission;

Requests member governments to inform the Secretary General of the action taken on this Recommendation.

Resolution (64) 11
Civics and European education

(Adopted by the Ministers' Deputies on 6th October 1964)

The Committee of Ministers,

Having noted the conclusions of the report on "Civics and European Education at the Primary and Secondary Level" published in the series *Education in Europe*;

Considering that the aim of civics is to provide a training in democratic citizenship and that its current objectives must therefore take account of the fact that today the individual is no longer a citizen of his own country only but also of Europe and the world;

Considering that, at a time when Europe is becoming a reality, it is the imperative duty of secondary education to inculcate into its pupils an awareness of European facts and problems;

Considering that the effective teaching of civics in the European countries is at present hampered by the lack of appeal of existing school courses and by the lack of preparation of the teachers;

Considering that the textbooks and basic material at present in use need to be adapted to the times;

Considering, finally that education in democratic citizenship is a continuous process, which should not be confined to a single subject of the curriculum but should permeate the whole course of education both inside and outside the school,

Resolves:

A. To recommend that governments, signatory or acceding to the European Cultural Convention:

1. draw up, with the above considerations in mind, a syllabus which can serve as a model for possible school curricula;

2. do everything within their power to ensure that all disciplines concerned – for instance history, geography, literature, modern languages – contribute to the creation of a European consciousness;

3. with a view to rendering the European aspect of civics teaching more interesting and consequently more effective, encourage the teaching profession to go beyond a purely static description of European institutions, by explaining their function in the light of the vital interdependence of the European peoples and of Europe's place in the world, and by attempting to

bring out the dynamic aspects of the European integration process and the concessions, indeed sacrifices, that it entails, and the political and cultural difficulties, even tensions, it may create;

4. promote methods of encouraging older pupils to take an active part in the study of current events and problems;

5. make or stimulate the making of, up-to-date documentation especially devised for educational purposes available to both teachers and pupils;

6. include in the general professional training course a preparation for the teaching of civics in a European context;

7. bear in mind that refresher courses are an excellent means of ensuring the up-to-datedness of teaching methods and material;

8. encourage collaboration between family and school in order to ensure the harmonious development of a civic consciousness among the young;

9. encourage the fullest use of broadcasting, television and other audio-visual aids in civic education;

B. To urge European and other international organisations to assume a certain responsibility for the desired improvements, for instance by providing special training courses, European reference material, audio-visual aids and other facilities referred to in the above-mentioned report.

Resolution (64) 12
Road safety education

(Adopted by the Ministers' Deputies on 6th October 1964)

The Committee of Ministers,

Considering that road safety education should be compulsory in all schools and classes during the period of compulsory schooling and beyond it;

Considering that it is not desirable, however, to make road safety education a separate subject, and that instruction should be given whenever the opportunity arises,

Resolves to recommend to governments:

– that such instruction should be given systematically;

– that a minimum number of hours should be stipulated for such instruction.

Resolution (69) 2
on an intensified modern language teaching programme for Europe

(Adopted by the Ministers' Deputies on 25 January 1969)

The Committee of Ministers,

Considering the Recommendation No. 40 (1968) of the Council for Cultural Co-operation concerning the teaching of modern languages;

Considering Recommendation 535 of the Consultative Assembly;

Having regard to the place given to modern languages in the European Cultural Convention;

Having regard to the importance of modern language teaching, as stressed by the European Ministers of Education at their 2nd and 3rd Conferences (Hamburg, April 1961 and Rome, October 1962);

Having regard to the Resolution No. 35 (1968) of the Council for Cultural Co-operation, calling for further efforts in this field, taking account of the recommendation of its Group of Co-ordinators and the suggestions made in the publication "Modern Languages and the World Today";

Believing:

– that if full understanding is to be achieved among the countries of Europe the language barriers between them must be removed;

– that linguistic diversity is part of the European cultural heritage and that it should, through the study of modern languages, provide a source of intellectual enrichment rather than be an obstacle to unity;

– that only if the study of modern European languages becomes general will full mutual understanding and co-operation be possible in Europe;

– that a better knowledge of modern European languages will lead to the strengthening of links and the increase in international exchanges on which economic and social progress in Europe increasingly depends;

– that a knowledge of a modern language should no longer be regarded as a luxury reserved for an élite, but an instrument of information and culture which should be available to all,

Expresses its satisfaction at the progress made since the "Major Project Modern Languages" was initiated;

Recommends to the governments of member states that an intensified programme be undertaken as follows:

1. In primary and secondary schools:

– Introduction to the maximum extent possible in existing national circumstances, of the teaching of at least one widely spoken European language to pupils from the age of about 10, with a view to extending such teaching as soon as possible to all boys and girls from about this age;

– Preparation of modern teaching materials for use in language courses making full and systematic use of audio-visual means;

– Development of language courses, making systematic use of television, radio and other audio-visual media in combination with modern study materials;

– Installation of special facilities for modern languages teaching, including well-stocked libraries and equipment enabling schools to take advantage of suitable radio and television programmes etc.;

– Revision of methods of assessment (tests, examinations ...) to give due prominence to auditory and oral skills;

– Systematic experimentation into the feasibility of introducing at least one widely spoken foreign language into the curriculum of all European school children at the earliest possible stage before the age of 10.

2. In institutions of higher and other forms of post-secondary education:

– Modernisation of courses of study for students who specialise in modern languages to ensure their proficiency in the present-day use of these languages and their acquisition of a sound knowledge of the civilisation of the country concerned;

– Installation of equipment to enable these students to practise their languages in the best possible conditions;

– Introduction or expansion, of arrangements for study visits (by means, where appropriate, of exchange or interchange) to foreign countries whose mother tongue is being studied:

– Provision of facilities (for instance, language centres) to cater for the general and professional needs of students who are not language specialists but who wish to learn, or to improve their command of, modern languages.

3. In adult education:

– The creation of proper facilities for "permanent education" in modern languages enabling all European adults to learn a language or languages of their choice in the most efficient way.

4. In initial and in-service training of modern languages teachers:

– Organisation, for all future and serving modern language teachers, of courses on recent developments in teaching methods, on such findings of linguistic science as are relevant to language teaching and on ways of using modern teaching apparatus efficiently;

– Promotion of arrangements for interchange or study visits abroad at regular intervals (for example, programmes allowing serving teachers to teach or study in the countries whose languages they teach);

– Provision of special training courses for modern language teachers entrusted with classes of adult learners.

5. In research:

(cf 1. sub-sections 5 and 2 above)

– Research into the factors affecting language acquisition, learning and teaching at all ages and with all categories of learner;

– Research into the development of the most suitable syllabuses, materials and methods of teaching for all categories of pupils and students;

– Definition of criteria of language proficiency leading to the production of tests for evaluating the results of language learning;

– Preparation of basic lists of words and structures of the European languages (spoken and written), to facilitate the construction of study materials appropriate to modern aims and methods of language teaching, and examination of the possibility of furthering the study of less widely known European languages;

– Analysis of the specialised language of science and technology, economics, etc.

Invites each government of member states as soon as possible,

– To nominate or create centres specialising in such fields as:

(i)   Systematic collection and distribution, to language teachers and others, of information on the findings of research having a bearing on modern language teaching;

(ii)   Documentation on the specialised use of languages particularly in science and technology;

(iii)   Techniques of testing proficiency in modern languages;

(iv)   Use of modern technical equipment for teaching languages;

– To examine whether any existing institutes or centres for modern languages could, with advantage, take over certain tasks of common European benefit;

– To appoint a "modern language correspondent" (a person or an institution or the existing governmental services dealing with the CCC) to be entrusted with the task of promoting the aims of the CCC and the realisation of its intensified European programme in modern languages;

– To promote co-operation with existing non-governmental organisations, in particular teachers' associations concerned with modern language teaching, and to further the establishment of such organisations wherever necessary;

– Invites other international governmental and non-governmental organisations, publishers and producers of equipment concerned with modern language teaching to assist in carrying out the intensified European programme in modern languages.

Resolution (70) 35
School education for the children of migrant workers

(Adopted by the Ministers' Deputies on 27 November 1970)

The Committee of Ministers,

I.   Having regard to the recommendation submitted to it by the Council of Europe Special Representative for National Refugees and Over-Population, following studies that have been carried out and in the light of the opinion expressed by his Advisory Committee on school education for the children of migrant workers;

II.   Considering that the instruction and education of children is an inalienable right which may be claimed even in difficult circumstances, such as those engendered by international migrations;

III.   Conscious of the necessity of ensuring, in their own interests, that the children of migrant workers do not lose their cultural and linguistic heritage and that they benefit from the culture of the receiving country;

IV.   Considering that efforts made by emigration and immigration countries to facilitate school education for the children of migrant workers will promote their adaptation or integration and consequently that of their parents;

V.   Considering that in this matter close collaboration between the relevant departments of the European member states to promote educational and cultural integration is in conformity with the aims defined in Article I of the Statute of the Council of Europe,

Recommends that governments of member states:

A – Guarantee, by means of legislation or regulation, exercise of the right of migrant workers' children to school education;

B – Take appropriate measures for the attainment of the following objectives:

1.   To improve the information given to families before departure about the educational facilities and requirements in the immigration country, and to provide on arrival advice and assistance in connection with enrolment in schools for those of compulsory school age;

2.   To provide for the children of migrant workers who do not emigrate with the head of the family the opportunity of starting or completing their compulsory education in their country of origin and possibly to provide free schooling and school equipment for them, for example in maintained or state schools;

3. To ensure that the responsible emigration services and school authorities advise the families of migrant workers to obtain, before a child's departure, standard records providing information on its school career and health, to assist in the assessment of its level of scholastic attainment;

4. To ensure that the appropriate local services, and where appropriate, the employers of migrant workers, inform the school authorities concerned without delay of the arrival of children of school age;

5. Possibly to establish, if need be, in co-operation with the authorities of the countries concerned, in areas where a sufficient number of migrant workers' families live, special classes of courses designed to assist the gradual integration of the children into the normal classes of the country of immigration, in particular by helping them to learn the language of the country; children of migrant workers should be taught in special classes or attend special courses for the shortest time strictly necessary;

6. To promote, after a period of adaptation appropriate to each child, full integration into normal classes in order to develop mutual understanding; with this in mind, immediate integration into the school in certain subjects such as drawing, physical training, handicrafts etc., should be encouraged as far as possible;

7. To see to it that, where practicable (and except for special classes or courses), compulsory classes do not contain dissimilar pupil groups in numbers likely to prejudice the teaching both of the children of migrant workers and of the native children;

8. To encourage, with the assistance of public and private bodies in the receiving country, the organisation of assisted and supervised study periods after school, in order to provide the necessary educational help for children who do not receive it at home;

9. To admit migrant workers' children, on the same basis as other children, to holiday camps and establishments for children below school age, and grant them scholarships, exemptions and other facilities;

10. To encourage migrant workers to take part in the life of their children's school;

11. To encourage teachers in the receiving country who have the children of migrant workers in their charge to acquire an adequate knowledge of teaching programmes in the countries of origin of such pupils;

12. To encourage and assist teachers in the countries of origin to follow courses in the receiving countries and vice versa, in order to promote understanding of the cultural and educational systems of these countries;

13. To promote, in the emigration countries, and also in the receiving countries, if the appropriate authorities agree, the training of specialist teachers to educate the children of migrant workers abroad, in the civilisation and language of their country of origin;

14. To encourage co-operation between the educational authorities in the emigration and immigration countries in order to promote such instruction, and award to the children who receive it certificates or diplomas drawn up in their mother tongue and stating the level attained;

15. To promote reintegration into school education of children of migrant workers who return to their country of origin;

16. For the purposes of admission to educational establishments to encourage a liberal attitude in relation to the equivalence of certificates and diplomas which testify to a sufficient level of education; and to ensure that migrant workers' children who have obtained such certificates or diplomas are enabled, on returning to their countries of origin, to enjoy all opportunities for their school career on the same basis as other pupils having pursued their studies abroad;

C – Report to the Council of Europe every four years on measures taken to give effect to this resolution.

Resolution (71) 29
on consumer education in schools

(Adopted by the Ministers' Deputies on 15 October 1971)

The Committee of Ministers,

1.   Having regard to Article 1 (*b*) of the Statute of the Council of Europe which provides for the pursuit of the aims of the Council

"by agreements and common action in economic, social, cultural, scientific, legal and administrative matters" ;

2.   Considering that the problems of European consumers are now virtually identical not least because of the ever increasing degree of economic integration ;

3.   Considering that the primary objective of the contemporary school is to provide general education to the population as a whole, thereby preparing the individual to play an active and enlightened role in society and also training him to deal with the actual problems he meets in everyday life not least as a responsible consumer ;

4.   Considering that the consumer has an important role to play in the economy, and by consequence in society, in the same way as has the producer and distributor, and that by exercising a free choice based on knowledge of the facts he will be able to make the best use of his resources – money, time, knowledge, ability – and that he will thereby contribute to the proper functioning of the economy in particular by stimulating effective and fair competition, and he will thereby similarly contribute to social and economic development ;

5.   Considering that the situation is not at present satisfactory for the consumer owing to his lack of the necessary knowledge and information and of other support in face of the increasing complexity of the technical, economic, legal social and cultural problems involved, and in face of the ever greater pressures he is exposed to from producers and distributors, particularly through advertising ;

6.   Considering that in order to remedy this situation consumer protection must start in school, thereby enabling the whole population to profit from the existing information and protection provided for by the law as well as from the assistance and means of action offered by public authorities, offered by consumer associations and other private bodies, or offered as the result of other private initiatives ;

7.   Considering that school children are not merely the consumers of tomorrow but are more actual consumers either in their own right or by influencing their parents' decisions ;

8.   Considering that the necessity of giving consumer education in schools is felt in all member states, and that the general principles of such education are commonly shared and correspond fully with the generally accepted aims of contemporary school education, even though national methods of implementation may take different forms as a result of differing habits of thought and of difference in economic, educational and other conditions;

9.   Having regard to the detailed proposals set out in the report on consumer education in schools, accompanying this resolution,

I.   Recommends to the governments of member states:

a. that they should take appropriate measures to encourage the provision of such consumer training to school children as will enable them to act as informed consumers throughout their lives;

b. that in implementing the provision of such consumer training full regard should be had to following specific recommendations:

i.   that, without ruling out the creation of a special subject when this appears desirable, consumer matters should, as far as possible, be introduced into the subjects at present being taught, with special emphasis on the development by pupils of an awareness and of a critical attitude towards these problems;

ii.   that consumer education should start in the very first years of school life, should be given in equal measure to all pupils – whether boys or girls, should in all circumstances continue during the whole period of compulsory education and should where possible continue thereafter;

iii.   that the training of teachers should be oriented towards consumer problems by including these matters in teacher training curricula and refresher courses, and where appropriate by also including these problems amongst those on which such teachers will be examined;

iv.   that school textbooks should be revised as necessary, that specialised equipment should be devised for teaching in this field, and that teachers' should be furnished with the necessary documentation and with indications of other appropriate sources of consumer information;

v.   that close co-operation should be encouraged and established between teachers' national educational authorities, consumer associations and other public or private bodies competent in consumer matters;

vi.   that the widest possible use of audio-visual aids, methods involving the active participation of the pupil, and mass communication media, such as radio and television, be encouraged in consumer education;

II.   Invites the governments of member states to keep it informed every three years of the action taken by them on this resolution.

Resolution (73) 19
on the Council of Europe higher education scholarship scheme

(Adopted by the Committee of Ministers on 13 April 1973 at the 220th meeting of the Ministers' Deputies)

The Committee of Ministers,

Recalling the proposal by the Government of the United Kingdom that its offer of fifty post-graduate fellowships for students from European countries might be developed under Council of Europe auspices;

Noting the welcome given to this offer and the statements of several governments that they would consider making provision for similar European scholarships;

Having received the opinion of the Council for Cultural Co-operation;

Expressing its appreciation to the governments which have already offered scholarships and being confident that in course of time their example will be followed by others,

Decides:

I.   A Council of Europe Higher Education Scholarships Scheme is hereby instituted.

II.   To be eligible for inclusion in this scheme, the scholarships offered by governments shall conform to the aims and criteria set out in the Appendix to this resolution.

III.   The Secretary General shall provide such administrative services as are required for the implementation of Sections III and IV of the Appendix to this resolution.

IV.   The Council for Cultural Co-operation is invited to convene in 1975, at the expense of the Cultural Fund, a meeting of those responsible for the scheme at national level, and thereafter to report to the Committee of Ministers and to make such recommendations for the revision and further development of the scheme as it considers appropriate in the light of experience.

Appendix to Resolution (73) 19

Aims, criteria and operation of the Council of Europe
higher education scholarships scheme

I. Aims

1.   To establish a system of scholarships which shall be both multilateral and specifically European. The scholarships, open to students from all member States of the Council for Cultural Co-operation[1] and possibly, at some future date to be agreed, from all European states, will complement those offered under bilateral cultural agreements; students from countries not linked by such agreements will profit particularly therefrom. The system is intended to enhance the development in Europe of a community of learning and research and to promote studies of benefit to European countries and to European unity.

2.   To encourage young people of the highest calibre to spend one, two or three post-graduate years in an educational institution of another member country. These years abroad should give scholars a deeper insight into the way of life and thought of the country whose guests they will be. As the scheme develops, the growing number of scholars will be in a position to make a significant impact in the Europe of the future.

Selectors should look for young men and women most likely to make a noteworthy contribution to society.

II. The criteria for scholarship offers to be included in the proposed system of Council of Europe scholarships

The scholarships offered shall conform to the above aims and:

1.   normally be tenable for a period of one to three years;

2.   be available only for post-graduate students (those who have already obtained a first degree; French term: *étudiants de troisième cycle; après la licence*);

3.   to be open initially to candidates from all member states of the Council for Cultural Co-operation;

4.   be administered by the national authorities (and not by the Council of Europe, whose role in the matter is depicted in Section III below), in accordance with the national regulations and circumstances.

III. The role of the Council of Europe

The role of the Council of Europe shall be as follows:

1.   lending its official auspices to the scheme;

2.   receipt of scholarships offers and examination as to whether they fit into the proposed scheme (but no involvement in the procedure of pre-selection and selection of candidates);

3.   assistance in announcing and advertising scholarships (in addition to national efforts to this effect);

---

1. The present members of the Council for Cultural Co-operation are the Members of the Council of Europe, plus Finland, the Holy See and San Marino.

4.   information of potential candidates (such as telling them to whom they must apply);

5.   analysis of the working of the scheme so that a suitable balance as regards geographical areas and disciplines is maintained (preparation of an analytical report every two years), and preparation of recommendations for improving the scheme;

6.   keeping a register of scholars;

7.   development of a model form for application and possibly of a model or standard certificate of completion of studies.

IV. Modalities of the Council of Europe's assistance

1.   *The offer*

Not later than November of the year preceding the academic year concerned, countries willing to offer scholarships under this scheme would inform the Secretary General of the Council of Europe of their intention to do so.

The communication should – if possible – contain the following details:

a.   the number of scholarships offered;

b.   the aims of these scholarships;

c.   the length of time for which they will be awarded;

d.   the type of studies or research for which they will be available (for example, if restricted to certain disciplines only or if priority is to be given to candidates wishing to work on particular topics);

e.   eligibility of candidates (requirements in respect of, for example, nationality, residence, age, first degree);

f.   language requirements;

g.   health requirements;

h.   emoluments (travel and subsistence expenses, tuition, laboratory and examination fees, grants for typing and binding theses, approved travel expenses within the host country, allowances for family members, etc.);

i.   social security (insurance in case of illness and accident);

j.   placing in universities (whether candidates can express a personal wish as to where they would like to be placed);

k.   accommodation available;

l.   conditions affecting residence and employment (can candidates leave the host country to go on holiday once or twice a year? Can they accept paid employment in the host country? Do they have to return to their home country once their period is over?);

m.   name and address of authority to which applications should be addressed and responsible for administration of the scholarships.

If there is a standard form for applications to be submitted, the country should attach a specimen of it.

2.   *Acceptance of offers*

The Secretariat of the Council of Europe will decide whether offers meet the agreed criteria, so that the scholarships available can be announced within the framework of the scheme. In cases of doubt, the members of the Council for Cultural Co-operation's Bureau may be consulted in writing. The decision is then communicated to the country concerned.

3. *The announcement of offers*

The Secretariat of the Council of Europe subsequently announces the fact that the country concerned will offer scholarships, informing in particular all authorities and persons contained in the mailing list of the Standing Conference on University Problems: countries may give the names and addresses of other bodies or persons to whom this information should be passed on as well. The announcement will also contain details of the offer as indicated above under IV.1.

4. *Register*

The Council of Europe will keep a register of scholars. Host countries will send in annual lists of candidates selected and of those who have successfully completed their period of study abroad.

Resolution (76) 12
on the school career and health record for children attending school abroad[1]

(Adopted by the Committee of Ministers on 10 March 1976 at the 255th meeting of the Ministers' Deputies)

The Committee of Ministers,

Whereas the aim of the Council of Europe is to achieve a greater unity between its members, which aim shall be pursued, *inter alia*, by common action in social and cultural matters;

Bearing in mind the principle in the European Social Charter of 18 October 1961 that migrant workers who are nationals of one of the Contracting Parties, as well as their families, have a right to protection and assistance in the territories of other Contracting Parties;

Having regard to the difficulty which children moving from one state to another or returning to their countries of origin have in fitting into school systems with different administrative and teaching arrangements, as well as to the attendant risks for their school careers;

Having regard to its resolution (70) 35 on school education for the children of migrant workers, by which member governments were requested, among other things, "to ensure that the responsible emigration services and school authorities advise the families of migrant workers to obtain, before a child's departure, 'standard records' providing information on its school career and health, to assist in the assessment of its level of scholastic attainment" (point B. 3);

Convinced of the desirability of promoting the European standardisation of means of providing such information, at both the educational and the administrative level,

Recommends that member governments:

a. ask their respective school authorities to use, for a three-year trial period, the appended school career and health record for children attending school abroad, the text of which is appended to this resolution;

b. take steps to ensure that the record is filled in by the appropriate school authority in the country of emigration and delivered to the appropri-

---

1. When it was adopted, the Representative of Austria, referring to Article 10.2.*c* of the Rules of Procedure for the meetings of the Ministers' Deputies, reserved his government's right to comply with the text of the resolution or not.
The Representative of Switzerland, who abstained in the vote, made the same reservation.

ate school authority in the country of immigration as soon as the child arrives at its new school;

c. co-operate with the consular authorities of other member states and with any other interested organisation in order to facilitate the use of the record;

d. inform the Secretary General of the Council of Europe, on the expiry of the three-year trial period, of their experience in using the record and of any changes they consider necessary or desirable to its contents.

Appendix to the Resolution (76) 12

Record issued on ....

.... (1)

School career and health record
for children attending school abroad (2)
(to be completed by the school authorities
responsible for the child's education) (1)

....

.... (1)

Child's surname
.... (1)   ....

Forenames
.... (1)   ....

Sex
.... (1)   ....

Date of birth
.... (1)   ....

Place of birth
.... (1)   ....

Nationality
.... (1)   ....

Mother tongue
.... (1)   ....

Religion (optional)
.... (1)   ....

---

(1) Space for translation into the language of the country to which the child is going.
(2) A model of this record, which is available in English, French, German, Greek, Italian, Dutch, Swedish and Turkish may be obtained upon request from the Secretariat General of the Council of Europe, 67006 STRASBOURG CEDEX, FRANCE.

For the attention
of school authorities

The school career record describes the child's knowledge and aptitudes, as well as his or her general state of health, at a given time.

It is designed to be used during the period of compulsory schooling and is intended to facilitate the educational assimilation of children in a new milieu, in the various immigration countries or upon their return to their home country, on the assumption that all necessary educational provision will be made in the country of arrival.

Head teachers must carefully scrutinise any entry which may be damaging to the holder of this record. The information contained in the school career and health record must not be used as a means of challenging the principle of equality of opportunity or of limiting the child's chances of educational and social integration in the host country.

Entries should be made in the language of the country in which the school issuing the record is situated and in the language of the country to which the child is going.

The school authorities in the host country should endeavour to co-operate closely with the consular authorities of the country of origin, and with any other department or authority concerned with reception arrangements for foreigners, in all matters relating to the practical use of this record, and help which parents may need in arranging for their children to be transferred.

A. Situation on leaving (last class attended)

Name and address of school ....
....

School year 19... - 19...

Type of education (primary,   Class attended .... (1)
secondary, other) ....

1	2	3	4	5	6	7	8	9	10			

Subjects studied (delete as appropriate)	Number of years studied	Number of hours each year	Assessment of pupil's proficiency (show by a cross)			
			very good	good	fair	poor
1. Language of instruction (..........................)						
a- oral expression						
b- reading						
c- written expression						
d- spelling						
2. Other languages including that of the home country						
a- (..........................)						
(oral expression)						
(written expression)						
b- (..........................)						
(oral expression)						
(written expression)						
c- (..........................)						
(oral expression)						
(written expression)						
3. Proficiency in mathematics						
- modern						
- traditional						
4. Proficiency in other subjects and abilities including artistic activities						
a- biology						
b- history (and civics)						
c- geography						
d- physics						
e- drawing						
f-						
g- .... (2)						
5. a- physical education						
b- sport						

Additional observations (3)
....
....
....

(1) Place a cross in the appropriate box; use empty boxes if compulsory schooling exceeds 10 years.
(2) These spaces can also be used to indicate knowledge of the culture and civilisation of the home country.
(3) To be completed only where necessary and, where possible, translated into the language of the country to which the pupil is going.

411

B. Personal characteristics (last school attended)

	Evaluation (show by a cross)			
	very good	good	fair	poor
1. Tidiness, carefulness				
2. Diligence				
3. Other remarks				

C. Previous schooling (including pre-school education)

Country	School year	Schooling (show by a cross)														
		Pre-school			Compulsory schooling (1)											
		1st	2nd	3rd	1st	2nd	3rd	4th	5th	6th	7th	8th	9th	10th		
	19../19..															
	19../19..															
	19../19..															
	19../19..															
	19../19..															
	19../19..															
	19../19..															
	19../19..															
	19../19..															
	19../19..															
	19../19..															
	19../19..															
	19../19..															

(1) Place a cross in the appropriate box; use empty boxes if compulsory schooling exceeds 10 years.

D. Particulars of the child's family

1. *Parents or other persons responsible for the child* (1)	
Surname	....
Forenames	....
Date of birth	....
Occupation	....
Surname	....
Forenames	....
Date of birth	....
Occupation	....
2. *Family situation*	
Forenames and	....
ages of brothers	....
and sisters	....
	....
	....

(1) State the relationship to the child, whether blood or otherwise (e.g. guardian).

School stamp ....

Date .... 19 ....

Teacher's signature

....

Head teacher's signature

....

E. State of health (1)

Immunisations	Type of serum	Date	Date	Date	Date	Immunity as a result of illness
1. Smallpox						
2. Whooping cough						
3. Diphtheria						
4. Tetanus						
5. Poliomyelitis						
6. Tuberculosis						
7. Typhoid						
8. German measles						
9. Trivalent vaccine (DTC)						
10.						
11.						
Tuberculin tests						
Illness						
1.						
2.						
3.						

Physiological condition (2)

1. *Motor capacity* – motor co-ordination – lateralisation – lateral dominance	3. *Hearing* tested (3) yes ☐ no ☐ normal (3) yes ☐ no ☐
2. *Eyesight* tested (3) yes ☐ no ☐ normal (3) yes ☐ no ☐	4. *Handicaps* (4)

(1) To be completed by a medical practitioner (if possible the school doctor); will be sent separately as confidential information.
(2) To be completed where possible. This information will remained confidential.
(3) Place a cross in the appropriate box.
(4) State the degree of handicap.

The Council of Europe

The idea of the school career record came from the Council of Europe.

The Council of Europe was founded by ten nations on 5 May 1949, as the first European political institution, with the first international parliament; today, with eighteen member countries,[1] it is the European organisation with the widest geographical representation.

The Council of Europe, which has its headquarters at Strasbourg, was set up "to achieve a greater unity between its members for the purpose of safeguarding and realising the ideals and principles which are their common heritage and facilitating their economic and social progress".

---

1. Austria, Belgium, Cyprus, Denmark, the Federal Republic of Germany, France, Greece, Iceland, Ireland, Italy, Luxembourg, Malta, the Netherlands, Norway, Sweden, Switzerland, Turkey, the United Kingdom.

Resolution (78) 12
on measures in the field of information and education to be possibly undertaken by member states directed to the problems of young people who travel to areas where drugs are readily available[1]

*(Adopted by the Committee of Ministers on 3 March 1978
of the 284th meeting of the Ministers' Deputies)*

The Committee of Ministers,

Considering that the aim of the Council of Europe is to achieve greater unity between its members and that this aim can be pursued, *inter alia*, by the adoption of common action in the field of public health;

Considering that the misuse of, and illicit traffic in dependence-producing drugs constitutes a grave threat to both public health and to the mental and physical health of individuals affected;

Noting that certain young people who travel to areas where drugs, both natural and synthetic, are readily available may fall into the habit of drug abuse, or be introduced to new drugs or begin to traffic illicitly in dependence-producing drugs;

Noting that these developments pose particularly serious threats to the individuals concerned and to the communities to which they return;

Considering that action is necessary to provide greater assistance to young people who may be affected in this way;

Considering that epidemiological and clinical data on all aspects of the problem are needed, and that the results of the latest research into methods of treatment and prevention are not always sufficiently widely known to those with responsibilities in this field;

Considering that education in the problems caused by dependence-producing drugs has been found to be most effective when included in a broad framework of mental and physical health and social welfare;

Considering that the measures contemplated should not affect the right of everyone to leave the territory of the state of which he is a national and to return to it,

---

1. When this resolution was adopted, the Representative of Ireland acting in accordance with Article 10.2.c of the Rules of Procedure for the meetings of the Ministers' Deputies, reserved the right of his government to comply with it or not.

I.   Recommends that member governments:

1.   adopt measures to enable them to keep themselves regularly informed on the regions where travellers are specially exposed to all the problems associated with dependence-producing drugs and of the character of those problems in each region;

2.   consider how information about the special consequences that might arise from drug abuse or drug trafficking during travel to these regions can best be included in those parts of the syllabus of education of young people which deal with drugs and drug problems when there is a need for it;

3.   encourage youth organisations and other interested voluntary organisations to include in a broad framework of mental and physical health and social welfare, information on drugs and drug problems covering the special problems of travel;

4.   consider the best way of securing the inclusion of the information and education about drugs and drug problems to teachers and other educators, social workers and health personnel, special information about the consequences of drug abuse and drug trafficking and the possible establishment of possible refresher courses at regular intervals on these problems for the afore-mentioned personnel;

5.   consider the desirability of publishing leaflets and/or posters drawing the attention of young people to the special problems of drug abuse during travel to certain regions, to be made available at passport offices, vaccination centres, customs posts and similar places;

6.   seek to persuade travel agencies to provide information, when it is necessary, about the problems causes by dependence-producing drugs in certain regions in the same way as that provided about health matters generally;

7.   consider the best way of securing the inclusion of epidemiological medico-social and clinical information about drug misuse and its treatment, with particular reference to young groups, in courses of education and making this information widely available to all other persons with professional responsibilities in this field and encouraging the wide dissemination of knowledge of prevention and treatment techniques, including the results of latest research;

II.   Invites the governments of member states to keep the Secretary General informed every five years of action taken in pursuance of this resolution.

Recommendation No. R (81) 3
concerning the care and education of children from birth to the age of eight[1]

(Adopted by the Committee of Ministers on 23 January 1981 at the 328st meeting of the Ministers' Deputies)

The Committee of Ministers, under the terms of Article 15.*b* of the Statute of the Council of Europe,

Considering that the aim of the Council of Europe is to achieve a greater unity between its members and that this aim is to be pursued, in particular, through common action in the social and cultural fields;

Bearing in mind the United Nations' Declaration on the Rights of the Child (1959);

Having regard to Recommendation 874 (1979) of the Assembly on a European Charter on the Rights of the Child;

Having regard to the Declaration on the care and education of the child from birth to eight adopted by the Conference on the theme "From birth to eight: young children in European Society in the 1980s", which was organised by the Council for Cultural Co-operation in Strasbourg from 17 to 20 December 1979;

Recalling that this conference was one of the Council of Europe contributions to the International Year of the Child (1979);

Considering the importance of the care and education of children from birth to eight,

Recommends that the governments of member states:

a. take account, in their policies on the care and education of young children, of the principles set out in Section I of the appendix hereto and take the measures concerning their implementation set out in Section II of the appendix.

b. ensure that this recommendation is distributed as widely as possible among interested persons and bodies.

---

1. In accordance with Article 10.2.*c* of the Rules of Procedure for the meetings of the Ministers' Deputies, the Representatives of Ireland and of the United Kingdom approved the adoption of this text but reserved the right of their governments to comply with it or not.

Appendix to Recommendation No. R (81) 3

I. Principles concerning the care and education of the child from birth to eight

A. *The rights of the child*

The child must enjoy the fundamental rights as set out in the United Nations Declaration on the Rights of the Child, as well as the right to develop his physical, emotional, intellectual, social and spiritual potential to the full and to be respected as an individual in his own right.

The child will normally depend primarily on his family to recognise and secure these rights. The family operates within a wider social framework from which it should be able to obtain the support it needs to fulfil its obligations. In providing such support, care should be taken not to undermine parental responsibilities towards the child.

All services with a contribution to make to the development of young children – especially health, education and social services – should work with, and through, the family to provide continuity of experience for the child.

B. *The care and education of young children*

The care and education of pre-school children should fulfil the following criteria. They should:

– meet the child's need for security and affection and social life, including leisure activities, with other children and adults;

– provide the conditions for good physical and mental health;

– stimulate the child's creative and intellectual development and his capacity for expression;

– help the child to become integrated into his environment and to cope with life, and encourage the child's independence, initiative and free play;

– respect the child's cultural and psychological identity and recognise his uniqueness and individuality;

– open up both family and pre-school circles to the wider society to enable the child to meet other people of all ages.

Educational provision should be made available for all children whose parents wish them to have it during at least two years preceding the start of primary school. The lack of financial means should not be a barrier to children who need such educational provision.

Support services including health, social services and education have an important role to play in the development of all children, but the form of provision should take account of their particular needs, which differ according to their stage of development, their personal capacities and their cultural backgrounds:

i.   children who live in urban areas have great need of care and education owing to living conditions in towns: lack of space, pollution of various kinds, dangers in the streets, parents' absence (time spent at work plus travelling time);

ii.   children who live in rural and sparsely populated areas are more difficult to cater for. It is therefore necessary to find untraditional and flexible solutions to bring pre-school education to these children;

iii.   children who live in circumstances of extreme socio-economic deprivation have special needs;

419

iv.   children of cultural minorities, whether native or immigrant, should receive an education which promotes their integration into the regional or national community, as a basis for mutual enrichment;

v.   handicapped children should, whenever necessary, have available to them establishments which meet their special needs.

In association with the child care and child psychological services, health services should operate within pre-school care and education provision to detect, assess and treat handicapping conditions.

C. *People and agencies participating in the care and education of young children*

All those contributing to the care and education of young children (including the family in the widest sense, the community and self-help groups, volunteers, teachers) should be able to benefit from the findings of up-to-date research and knowledge of developments in the concept of early education and, whenever appropriate, to participate in such research.

Professionals need initial training supplemented by in-service training. Both should be of the highest possible quality.

II. Role of member states

Taking into account the importance of care and education of children from birth to eight in the European society of 1980s, member states should:

1.   organise the care and education of young children, in close co-operation with parents, as a means of complementing family up-bringing and as a first stage in life-long learning. This should be done by:

    – providing adequate funds;

    – improving family, social and labour legislation;

    – planning education systems in such a way as to maintain continuity and to educate children to become creative and innovatory adults;

2.   prepare parents and future parents for the responsibilities inherent in the education of young children;

3.   assume responsibility or provide support for organisations and institutions caring for young children, especially for those children whose need is most obvious;

4.   promote and encourage research and the training of staff in order to provide children with care and education, under the best possible conditions, supervised by highly qualified staff, who, as far as possible, should operate in multidisciplinary teams;

5.   ensure that the various national, regional and local administrations co-ordinate family and child care services to guarantee continuity of experience for the child.

Resolution AP (81) 4
on the education of schoolchildren, foodhandlers and consumers with regard to the hazards of microbiological contamination of food

(Adopted by the Committee of Ministers on 11 February 1981, at the 329th meeting of the Ministers' Deputies)

The Representatives on the Committee of Ministers of Belgium, France, the Federal Republic of Germany, Italy, Luxembourg, the Netherlands and the United Kingdom of Great Britain and Northern Ireland, these states being parties to the Partial Agreement in the social and public health field, and the Representatives of Austria, Denmark, Ireland and Switzerland, states which have participated in the public health activities carried out within the above-mentioned Partial Agreement since 1 October 1974, 2 April 1968, 23 September 1969 and 5 May 1964 respectively.

Considering that the aim of the Council of Europe is to achieve a greater unity between its members and that this aim may be pursued by common action in the social and public health field;

Having regard to the provisions of the Brussels Treaty signed on 17 March 1948, by virtue of which Belgium, France, Luxembourg, the Netherlands and the United Kingdom of Great Britain and Northern Ireland declared themselves resolved to strengthen the social ties by which they were already united;

Having regard to the Protocol modifying and completing the Brussels Treaty, signed on 23 October 1954 by the signatory states of the Brussels Treaty on the one hand and the Federal Republic of Germany and Italy on the other hand;

Observing that the seven states parties to the Partial Agreement which have continued within the Council of Europe the social work hitherto undertaken by the Brussels Treaty Organisation and then by Western European Union, which derived from the Brussels Treaty as modified by the Protocol mentioned in the fourth paragraph above, as well as Austria, Denmark, Ireland and Switzerland, which participate in Partial Agreement activities in the field of public health, have always endeavoured to be in the forefront of progress in social matters and also in the associated field of public health, and have for many years undertaken action towards harmonisation of their legislation;

Having regard to the recommendation on the education of schoolchildren, foodhandlers and consumers with regard to the hazards of microbiological contamination of food, adopted by the Partial Agreement Public Health Committee on 31 October 1980;

Being aware of the high incidence of foodborne disease resulting from the contamination of foodstuffs by certain micro-organisms;

Taking the view that there is a need to ensure that education in food hygiene is given to schoolchildren, foodhandlers and consumers,

I. Recommend to the governments of the seven states parties to the Partial Agreement, as well as to the governments of Austria, Denmark, Ireland and Switzerland that they take all appropriate measures to further education in food hygiene following the principles set out hereafter;

1. Basic education in general hygiene should be provided for young schoolchildren; older pupils should receive further instruction in domestic and food hygiene.

Basic education for younger children should deal first and foremost with personal and environmental hygiene. The primary aim should be to interest the child in the particular problems involved in health care.

Education for the older age group should deal specifically with matters relating to domestic and food hygiene. It should also deal with matters relating to the processing, preparation, storage and preservation of food.

2. Persons professionally engaged in the handling of food, including its processing, presentation, packaging, storage, distribution, sale and delivery, should possess a basic knowledge of food hygiene.

Managerial and supervisory staff should have received formal training in food hygiene at recognised vocational training establishments to enable them to provide suitable instruction to their assistants. This instruction is especially important for new employees at the time of starting work.

The practice of requiring workers in certain food trades to attend special courses of instruction, covering in particular food hygiene, and to possess a certificate of proficiency should be extended.

3. Consumers should be informed about the general and specific aspects of food hygiene.

Consumer educaton may be provided by adult education classes, the mass media and through consumer associations. Manufacturers should play a major role in consumer education through adequate labelling and by providing appropriate information on the storage and handling of their products.

Emphasis should be given to the hazards associated with home preservation of foods, especially non-acid foods, and attention drawn to the modes of transmission of hazardous organisms and their relevance to outbreaks of food poisoning.

4. Education in hygiene should be given by competent, specially trained personnel, such as domestic science teachers, biology teachers, dieti-

cians, home economists and other professional food advisers. The relevant authorities should be asked to consider the particular needs of food hygiene education when planning their school curricula. Teaching methods and materials should be planned in consultation with health authorities.

Visual display materials should be used whenever possible to illustrate and reinforce formal and informal instruction.

II. Invite the said governments to inform the Secretary General of the Council of Europe every five years of the action they have taken to implement this resolution.

Recommendation No. R (82) 9
on European Schools' Day

*(Adopted by the Committee of Ministers on 3 June 1982
at the 348th meeting of the Ministers' Deputies)*

The Committee of Ministers, under the terms of Article 15.*b* of the Statute of the Council of Europe,

Considering that the aim of the Council of Europe is to achieve a greater unity between its members;

Recalling that under the terms of the European Cultural Convention "the achievement of this aim would be furthered by a greater understanding of one another among the peoples of Europe";

Convinced that the European Schools' Day competition, which is open to schoolchildren in the member states, can develop that understanding of one another and promote awareness of Europe in schools;

Noting that participation in the competition is widespread in the majority of the member states and that other member states have announced their intention to be associated with it;

Acknowledging the efforts of the national committees which, often with meagre resources, are responsible for the smooth running and expansion of the competition in the participating countries;

Recalling its Resolution (69) 3 on wider support for European Schools Day at national level;

Recommends that the governments of all member states:

a. contribute actively to the development of European Schools Day;

b. grant or increase their financial and administrative support to the national committees for European Schools' Day.

Recommendation No. R (83) 4
concerning the promotion of an awareness of Europe in secondary schools

*(Adopted by the Committee of Ministers on 18 April 1983
at the 358th meeting of the Ministers' Deputies)*

The Committee of Ministers, under the terms of Article 15.*b* of the Statute of the Council of Europe,

Having regard to the European Cultural Convention (1954) which underlines the need for education for European understanding;

Recalling its Resolution (64) 11 on "Civics and European Education";

Having regard to the findings of the Council for Cultural Co-operation's Project No. 1 on secondary education, "Preparation for life" (1978-82);

Having regard to the Council of Europe's Second Medium-Term Plan (1981-86), and in particular to:

i. Objective 10.1 – the encouragement of an awareness of the cultural identity of Europe in its diversity and the recognition of possibilities of dialogue and mutual understanding with other parts of the world;

ii. Objective 11.3 – the enhancement of the contribution of national education systems to public awareness of Europe and the stimulation of active co-operation and communication among Europeans;

Noting the Recommendation concerning education for international understanding co-operation and peace and education relating to human rights and fundamental freedoms adopted by the General Conference of UNESCO at its 18th Session (Paris, 19 November 1974),

Recommends the governments of member states:

a. to take account, in the implementation of their policies for secondary education, of the principles set out in the Appendix to this recommendation, or to draw them to the attention of the competent bodies concerned, so that they can be considered and, where appropriate, taken into account;

b. to ensure that this recommendation is distributed as widely as possible among all persons and bodies concerned with the promotion of an awareness of Europe among pupils and teachers.

Appendix to Recommendation No. R (83) 4

Principles for the guidance of those drawing up educational programmes for the promotion of an awareness of Europe in secondary schools

1. Aims

1.1. Programme to promote an awareness of Europe in secondary schools may have a wide variety of content which will be determined by the needs and interests of individual countries, regions and schools.

1.2. In spite of any differences of content, these programmes should encourage all young Europeans to:

    i.   show respect for, and solidarity with, peoples of other nations and cultures;

    ii. see themselves not only as citizens of their own regions and countries, but also as citizens of Europe and of the wider world.

1.3. All young Europeans should be helped to acquire:

    i.   a willingness and ability to preserve and promote democracy, human rights and fundamental freedoms;

    ii. the knowledge and skills needed to cope with life in an interdependent world, characterised by diversity and by constant and rapid change;

    iii. an understanding of their common cultural heritage, its contribution to other civilisations, and the debt which it owes to those civilisations;

    iv. an awareness of the institutions and organisations set up to promote European co-operation and a willingness to support their ideals and activities.

2. Approaches

It is possible to teach about Europe in secondary schools through separate subjects, or through interdisciplinary courses. While schools must be allowed freedom to choose those approaches which best suit their particular situations, care should be taken to:

    i.   build on what will have been learned about Europe during the earlier years of schooling;

    ii. ensure that what is taught about Europe has an overall coherence. Fragmentation of knowledge and understanding can be avoided by careful planning and by cross-referencing (that is, co-ordination) between subjects.

3. Content

3.1. In teaching about Europe, secondary schools should seek to give pupils a full understanding of the following key concepts:

    i.   democracy, human rights and fundamental freedoms;

    ii. tolerance and pluralism;

    iii. interdependence and co-operation;

    iv. human and cultural unity and diversity;

    v. conflict and change.

3.2. These concepts can best be illustrated by themes and topics which demonstrate the need for international understanding and co-operation, such as:

    i.   the prevention of war and non-violent solution of conflict;

    ii. the conservation of the European cultural heritage;

iii. the impact of migration;

iv. the preservation of ecological balance;

v. the best use of energy and natural resources;

vi. changing needs with the developing countries.

vii relations with the developing countries.

3.3 It is obvious that modern languages, history, geography and social studies have a vital contribution to make to the promotion of an awareness of Europe in secondary schools. But due attention should be paid to the contribution which can be made by science and technology, artistic activities, music and indeed of almost all subjects in the secondary school curriculum.

4. Methods

4.1. The diversity of school systems in member states inevitably leads to differences in classroom practice. Nevertheless, in implementing programmes designed to increase an awareness of Europe, many teachers will wish to:

i. use methodologies which are active, investigational and discovery-based; use projects which involve personal research and interviewing; exploit local and national links with other countries;

ii. give young people opportunities for active participation, decision-making and responsibility within the school community in order to prepare them for life in a free democratic society;

iii. encourage pupils to participate in extra-curricular activities with an international dimension, for example participation in a European Schools Day competition, Unesco Clubs and the Unesco Associated Schools Project, the establishment of European clubs in schools, school correspondence and exchanges, visits to the European institutions and events linked to town twinnings;

iv. encourage pupils to take an informed and critical interest in coverage of international events by the mass media;

v. make use of primary sources and material from other countries and from international organisations both governmental and non-governmental.

4.2. As European society is becoming increasingly multicultural, schools should actively involve people from other cultural backgrounds in the learning process, wherever possible. This would help pupils to develop truly tolerant attitudes and a realisation that – despite differences of colour, creed and customs – all share a basic common dignity and basic common needs.

5. Teacher training

The success of programmes to develop an awareness of Europe in secondary schools depends, to a large extent, on the knowledge, skills and attitudes of those who teach them. It is, therefore, essential to provide appropriate courses of both pre-service and in-service education, not only for practising teachers, but also for senior administrators, inspectors, advisers and school principals. Furthermore, teachers and other educators should be encouraged to avail themselves of opportunities for studies in, and exchanges with, other European countries.

6. Monitoring and evaluation

In order to avoid duplication of effort and make the best possible use of resources, there should be careful monitoring and evaluation of programmes to promote an awareness of Europe in secondary schools in member states. This would ascertain the extent to which:

i.   the aims and objectives of the programmes are being achieved;

ii. the interests and needs of the learners are being satisfactorily met.

Such evaluation could also lead a sharing of experiences among member states and to the identification and dissemination of good practice.

Recommendation No. R (83) 13
on the role of the secondary school
in preparing young people for life

(Adopted by the Committee of Ministers on 23 September 1983
at the 362nd meeting of the Ministers' Deputies)

The Committee of Ministers, under the terms of Article 15.*b* of the Statute of the Council of Europe,

Having regard to the findings of Project No. 1 of the Council for Cultural Co-operation (CDCC) on secondary education, "Preparation for life" (1978-82);

Considering that Western Europe is undergoing a period of change and uncertainty, which varies in intensity from region to region;

Aware that many young people today are deeply concerned about the future, their roles in society and their chances of vocational training and work;

Believing that the future of European society depends on the ability and willingness of all its members:

i. to accept, preserve and promote human values, democracy and human rights;

ii. to further European co-operation, to display a sense of solidarity with the rest of the world and to work for peace;

iii. to understand and respect others, to be tolerant, to recognise the right to be different and to combat prejudice;

iv. to resolve conflict in an open and democratic manner;

v. to display positive attitudes towards learning and work;

vi. to respond with initiative to changing situations, including different patterns of employment;

vii. to understand the basic ideas of data processing and to take an informed and socially responsible stand on scientific and technological issues;

viii. to adopt discriminating attitudes towards the messages of the mass media and advertising;

ix. to display a sense of stewardship towards the environment;

Believing that these requirements can only be met by independent and responsible men and women;

Recognising that, although the school is not the only source of education, it has more than ever before, a crucial role to play in forming independent and responsible individuals,

Recommends the governments of member states:

a. to take account, in the implementation of their policies for secondary education, of the principles set out at the appendix hereto or to draw them to the attention of the competent bodies concerned so that they can be considered and, where appropriate, taken into account;

b. to ensure that this recommendation is distributed as widely as possible among all persons and bodies concerned with secondary education.

Appendix to Recommendation No. R (83) 13

Principles for the guidance of those responsible for programmes concerned with preparing young people for life

1. In preparing young people for life in society, special attention should be paid to their needs in the years just before and just after the end of compulsory education because:

    i.   these years are a period of intensive personal and social development;

    ii. during them, all young people have to take momentous decisions about their future;

    iii. in many member states, young people reach the age of majority a few years after the end of compulsory schooling.

2. Education systems should give all young people the opportunity to acquire essential knowledge, skills and attitudes in the following key areas, which are closely interdependent:

    i.   Preparation for life in a democratic society. This should cover human rights and fundamental freedoms, the duties and responsibilities of citizens, and politics and economics. It should help young people to participate in public life at local and national level and to understand international politics;

    ii. Preparation for personal life. This should include fundamental values and personal, family and community relations. Young people should be given experience in personal decision-making, problem-solving and planning;

    iii. Preparation for cultural life. This should enable young people to find sources of personal enrichment and to participate actively in cultural life. It should include an introduction to the cultural, spiritual, historical and scientific heritage, as well as preparation for life in a multicultural society. The concept of culture should be interpreted in a broad sense and culture should be given its rightful place in the teaching of all subjects;

    iv. Preparation for the world of work. In the compulsory secondary school, this should be concerned with providing a broad perspective on working life, and it should include both a theoretical introduction to the nature and forms of work and work experience. In technical and vocational studies, specialisation should be carried out gradually, wherever possible after a broad training in the elements which are common to a family of occupations. All young people should be aware of the important role that science and technology will play in their lives.

3. Schools should anticipate further studies and training by offering, in a perspective of lifelong learning, an appropriate counselling and guidance service on the possibilities offered by training schemes and by higher and adult education. In order to help young people to make the best use of these opportunities, schools should lay special emphasis on the acquisition of communication and study skills.

4. The preparation of young people for life will be facilitated by an active partnership between the school and other social institutions. In particular, the school could co-operate with advantage with:

    i.   the family, through close co-operation with parents;

    ii. the local community, through community involvement in the life of the school and voluntary involvement by young people in the life of the community;

    iii. social and political institutions, through discussions with leaders of public opinion, the study of and visits to local and national public institutions and appropriate out-of-school activities;

iv. other countries, through wide-ranging personal contacts, exchanges, and school twinning and correspondence. This will encourage the learning of foreign languages;

v. the world of work, through work experience and contacts with representatives of employers and of trade-unions;

vi. the world of culture in the widest sense, through active participation in social, artistic and scientific activities and sport.

5. The ethos, curricula and management of schools should be such as to allow young people opportunities for practical experience of the exercise of democratic values. Where appropriate, young people should be given opportunities:

i. to participate in informed decision-making with those responsible for their education;

ii. to assume responsibilities towards themselves, their classmates, their school, their family, their peer groups and their community;

iii. to practise forms of delegation and representation;

iv. to join school councils and informal students' groups.

6. School staff should be helped, through appropriate initial and in-service training, to acquire the knowledge, attitudes and skills required for counselling and guidance. In particular, they should be encouraged:

i. to understand the psychological and affective needs of their pupils;

ii. to develop sensitive democratic leadership;

iii. to use, as a resource, the different cultural and social backgrounds of their pupils;

iv. to have knowledge and even experience of the world of work outside the education system.

7. Educational authorities should allow schools both the flexibility and the time that they will require if they are to establish a partnership with other social institutions and create opportunities for pupil participation.

8. There should be a guarantee that, at the end of their compulsory education, all young people should be offered a job or further education or training. Special efforts should be made for vulnerable and disadvantaged groups. As policies for young people often concern several ministries and departments within ministries, member states may wish to review the existing links between them and, where necessary, take measures to ensure the coherence of such policies.

Recommendation No. R (84) 13
concerning the situation of foreign students[1]

*(Adopted by the Committee of Ministers on 21 June 1984
at the 374th meeting of the Ministers' Deputies)*

The Committee of Ministers, under the terms of Article 15.*b* of the Statute of the Council of Europe,

1.   Considering that the aim of the Council of Europe is to achieve a greater unity between its members, and that this aim can be pursued notably by common action in cultural matters;

2.   Having regard to the European Cultural Convention;

3.   Having regard to European Convention on the equivalence of diplomas leading to admission to universities;

4.   Having regard to the European Convention on the equivalence of periods of university study;

5.   Having regard to the European Convention on the academic recognition of university qualifications;

6.   Having regard to the European Agreement on continued payment of scholarships to students studying abroad;

7.   Considering that the Council of Europe has always encouraged academic mobility without any form of racial, religious, political or sexual discrimination;

8.   Considering that the political, economic, social, cultural, educational and scientific interdependence between the States Parties to the European Cultural Convention, and between those states and others, is getting closer and more intensive;

9.   Considering that the practice of study in a country other than a student's home country is likely to contribute to a student's cultural and academic enrichment;

10.   Considering that for the purpose of this recommendation the term "university" shall be understood in its broadest sense, that is to say implying:

---

1. When this recommendation was adopted, and in application of Article 10.2.c of the Rules of Procedure for the meetings of the Ministers' Deputies, the Representatives of Austria and Belgium reserved the right of their governments to comply or not with paragraph 12 of the appendix to the recommendation, and the Representative of the United Kingdom reserved the right of her government to comply or not with paragraphs 12 and 13 of the said appendix.

i. universities; and

ii. those other institutions of higher education and research not having the title of university but regarded as undertaking work of a generally equal nature by the competent authorities of the state in whose territory they are situated,

I.   Recommends the governments of member states:

a. to take account, in the establishment of their policies affecting universities, of the principles set out in the appendix hereto or to draw them to the attention of the competent bodies concerned, so that they can be considered and, where practicable and appropriate, taken into account;

b. to ensure that this recommendation is distributed as widely as possible among all persons and bodies concerned with the situation of foreign students;

II.   Instructs the Secretary General of the Council of Europe to transmit this recommendation to the governments of those contracting Parties to the European Cultural Convention which are not members of the Council of Europe.

Appendix to Recommendation No. R (84) 13

Principles for the formation of policies regarding the situation of foreign students

I. Study abroad: basic principles

A. *Preference for periods of study*

1.   In general, students should be encouraged to spend limited periods of study abroad, one or two years, depending upon the course of study.

2.   In the interest of the students themselves, studies should normally be begun and carried on in the country of origin for about two years, allowing the students to acquire the necessary grasp of their field of study, unless the very nature of the study requires that the courses be started abroad.

3.   Special encouragement should be given to any study abroad being planned and agreed by the institutions concerned as part of an integrated course or joint study programme.

B. *Students from developing countries*

4.   A special admission policy for students from developing countries favouring the needs of these countries should be encouraged.

5.   Students from developing countries should in general first complete university studies in their own country before embarking on professional specialisation by means of complementary intensification and research studies in foreign countries. Such further education should be recognised in their own countries.

6.   Where students from developing countries, because of the particular situation in their countries of origin, have reasons for pursuing full degree courses abroad, these courses should, if possible, take account of the problems and needs of the developing countries. The design of such courses necessitates a dialogue between the competent authorities in the countries of origin and in the states where such courses are held.

C. *Political refugees*

7.   Foreign nationals who have been granted the status of refugees under the Convention relating to the Status of Refugees (Geneva 1951) in a state, should be treated as a national of that state as far as access to universities is concerned, and, where necessary, special help should be given to acquire an adequate command of the language and to reach the required academic level.

II. Access of foreign students to universities

8.   In principle, the host state and/or its academic institutions should not accept a candidate who would not be entitled to go on to universities in his own country, but without taking possible admission limitations into consideration.

9.   If they so wish, a state and/or its academic institutions may institute more liberal measures; but their own requisite academic qualifications should in no case be altered.

10.   It is of paramount importance that the responsible body in the host country check that the candidates' command of the language is sufficient to enable them to understand the various courses they wish to follow before a place is offered in a university.

11. A special admission policy should be adopted for students coming from states with no universities, or without complete study courses.

12. As far as possible, where fees (registration, etc.) are payable, foreign students should not be required to pay higher fees than those applied to national students.

III. Return and reintegration

13. In admitting foreign students to university studies, the host countries proceed on the assumption that the foreign students, especially those who have been accepted for a full course of study, will return to their home country upon completing their courses of study and that they will on their own responsibility undertake every effort to secure their social and professional reintegration. Where necessary, measures to facilitate return and reintegration of foreign students should be introduced and/or improved.

IV. Information on studies abroad

14. Updated information on studies abroad should be furnished by the competent authorities of each state; it shall be distributed and where necessary supplemented by specialised departments in each university. The Council of Europe network of national mobility information centres should be put in a position to play an important role and exploited accordingly by all those concerned.

V. Financing and scholarships

15. Where appropriate, every effort should be made to establish or increase financial support for students wishing to study abroad in order to promote mobility.

16. Foreign students should be advised not to anticipate paid employment to meet their living costs, and before their arrival they should be requested to make provision for the financial means needed to complete their studies.

17. Each state, or university institution of such, should endeavour to set up, if such services are not provided for by other institutions, a University Solidarity Fund to assist students in temporary financial difficulties not due to their own fault (such as late payment of grants or scholarships).

VI. Reception services

18. To overcome the obstacles and the problems facing foreign students in their daily life, reception services (public or private, university or university-attached) should be set up, for effective reception, assistance, accommodation and guidance. Specialist staff should be trained for this type of work.

19. The administrative departments, both in the universities and in other responsible bodies, should simplify the various formalities that govern the personal situation of foreign students, notably the obtaining of residence permits and accommodation.

VII. Review, consultation and agreements between states

20. While respecting the responsibility of the individual states and institutions to determine their own policies on the admission of foreign students, states should be willing to undertake regular reviews of their own policies both by themselves and in consultation with other states, in order to monitor the effects of their own policies on student mobility.

VIII. Statistics and surveys

21.   Statistics regarding foreign students should be improved, harmonised and continually updated, in particular regarding the various main groups (students spending only a part of their period of study abroad, students completing a full course of study abroad).

Recommendation No. R (85) 7
on teaching and learning about human rights
in schools

*(Adopted by the Committee of Ministers on 14 May 1985
at the 385th meeting of the Ministers' Deputies)*

The Committee of Ministers, under the terms of Article 15.*b* of the Statute of the Council of Europe,

Considering that the aim of the Council of Europe is to achieve a greater unity between its members for the purpose of safeguarding and realising the ideals and principles which are their common heritage;

Reaffirming the human rights undertakings embodied in the United Nations' Universal Declaration of Human Rights, the Convention for the Protection of Human Rights and Fundamental Freedoms and the European Social Charter;

Having regard to the commitments to human rights education made by member states at international and European conferences in the last decade;

Recalling:

– its own Resolution (78) 41 on "The teaching of human rights";

– its Declaration on "Intolerance: a threat to democracy" of 14 May 1981;

– its Recommendation No. R (83) 13 on "The role of the secondary school in preparing young people for life";

Noting Recommendation 963 (1983) of the Consultative Assembly of the Council of Europe on "Cultural and educational means of reducing violence";

Conscious of the need to reaffirm democratic values in the face of:

– intolerance, acts of violence and terrorism;

– the re-emergence of the public expression of racist and xenophobic attitudes;

– the disillusionment of many young people in Europe, who are affected by the economic recession and aware of the continuing poverty and inequality in the world;

Believing, therefore, that throughout their school career, all young people should learn about human rights as part of their preparation for life in a pluralistic democracy;

Convinced that schools are communities which can, and should, be an example of respect for the dignity of the individual and for difference, for tolerance, and for equality of opportunity,

I.   Recommends that the governments of member states, having regard to their national education systems and to the legislative basis for them:

a. encourage teaching and learning about human rights in schools in line with the suggestions contained in the appendix hereto;

b. draw the attention of persons and bodies concerned with school education to the text of this recommendation;

II.   Instructs the Secretary General to transmit this recommendation to the governments of those states party to the European Cultural Convention which are not members of the Council of Europe.

Appendix to Recommendation No. R (85) 7

Suggestions for teaching and learning about human rights in schools

1. *Human rights in the school curriculum*

1.1. The understanding and experience of human rights is an important element of the preparation of all young people for life in a democratic and pluralistic society. It is part of social and political education, and it involves intercultural and international understanding.

1.2. Concepts associated with human rights can, and should, be acquired from an early stage. For example, the non-violent resolution of conflict and respect for other people can already be experienced within the life of a pre-school or primary class.

1.3. Opportunities to introduce young people to more abstract notions of human rights, such as those involving an understanding of philosophical, political and legal concepts, will occur in the secondary school, in particular in such subjects as history, geography social studies, moral and religious education, language and literature, current affairs and economics.

1.4. Human rights inevitably involve the domain of politics. Teaching about human rights should, therefore, always have international agreements and covenants as a point of reference, and teachers should take care to avoid imposing their personal convictions on their pupils and involving them in ideological struggles.

2. *Skills*

The skills associated with understanding and supporting human rights include:

    i.   *intellectual skills*, in particular:

– skills associated with written and oral expression, including the ability to listen and discuss, and to defend one's opinions;

    – skills involving judgement, such as:

      - the collection and examination of material from various sources, including the mass media, and the ability to analyse it and to arrive at fair and balanced conclusions;

      - the identification of bias, prejudice, stereotypes and discrimination;

    ii. *social skills*, in particular:

    – recognising and accepting differences;

    – establishing positive and non-oppressive personal relationships;

    – resolving conflict in a non-violent way;

    – taking responsibility;

    – participating in decisions;

    – understanding the use of the mechanisms for the protection of human rights at local, regional, European and world levels.

3. *Knowledge to be acquired in the study of human rights*

3.1. The study of human rights in schools will be approached in different ways according to the age and circumstances of the pupil and the particular situations of schools and education systems. Topics to be covered in learning about human rights could include:

    i.   the main categories of human rights, duties, obligations and responsibilities;

ii. the various forms of injustice, inequality and discrimination, including sexism and racism;

iii. people, movements and key events, both successes and failures, in the historical and continuing struggle for human rights;

iv. the main international declarations and conventions on human rights, such as Universal Declaration of Human Rights and the Convention for the Protection of Human Rights and Fundamental Freedoms.

3.2. The emphasis in teaching and learning about human rights should be positive. Pupils may be led to feelings of powerlessness and discouragement when confronted with many examples of violation and negations of human rights. Instances of progress and success should be used.

3.3. The study of human rights in schools should lead to an understanding of, and sympathy for, the concepts of justice, equality, freedom, peace, rights and democracy. Such understanding should be both cognitive and based on experience and feelings. Schools should, thus, provide opportunities for pupils to experience affective involvement in human rights and to express their feelings through drama, art, music, creative writing and audiovisual media.

4.   *The climate of the school*

4.1. Democracy is best learned in a democratic setting where participation is encouraged, where views can be expressed openly and discussed, where there is freedom of expression for pupils and teachers, and where there is fairness and justice. An appropriate climate is, therefore, an essential complement to effective learning about human rights.

4.2. Schools should encourage participation in their activities by parents and other members of the community. It may well be appropriate for schools to work with non-governmental organisations which can provide information, case-studies and first-hand experience of successful campaigns for human rights and dignity.

4.3. Schools and teachers attempt to be positive towards their pupils, and recognise that all of their achievements are important whether they be academic, artistic, musical, sporting or practical.

5.   *Teacher training*

5.1. The initial training of teachers should prepare them for their future contribution to teaching about human rights in their schools. For example, future teachers should:

i.   be encouraged to take an interest in national and world affairs;

ii.   have the chance of studying or working in a foreign country or a different environment;

iii. be taught to identify and combat all forms of discrimination in schools and society and be encouraged to confront and overcome their own prejudices.

5.2. Future and practising teachers should be encouraged to familiarise themselves with:

i.   the main international declarations and conventions on human rights;

ii.   the working and achievements of the international organisations which deal with the protection and promotion of human rights, for example through visits and study tours.

5.3. All teachers need, and should be given the opportunity, to update their knowledge and to learn new methods through in-service training. This could include the study of good practice in teaching about human rights, as well as the development of appropriate methods and materials.

6. *International Human Rights Day*

Schools and teacher training establishments should be encouraged to observe International Human Rights Day (10 December).

Recommendation No. R (88) 7 on school health education and the role and training of teachers

(Adopted by the Committee of Ministers on 18 April 1988 at the 416th meeting of the Ministers' Deputies)

The Committee of Ministers, under the terms of Article 15.*b* of the Statute of the Council of Europe,

Considering that the aim of the Council of Europe is to achieve a greater unity between its members and that this aim may be pursued, *inter alia*, by the adoption of a common approach in the health and social protection fields;

Recalling its Recommendation No. R (82) 4 on the prevention of alcohol-related problems especially among young people and its Recommendation No. R (82) 5 concerning the prevention of drug dependence and the special role of education for health, as well as the concerns which lay behind these two recommendations;

Considering that, in spite of the development of elaborate and specialised health systems combining general preventive measures and the availability of medical care services, numerous health problems continue to arise which do not respond to traditional preventive and curative measures;

Noting that the majority of these problems are linked to life-styles not conducive to health and that health education can contribute to avoiding them by promoting healthy attitudes and life-styles;

Noting that, alongside the central role of the family, the most appropriate structure for the introduction of health education is the school, as it regroups the young, the age-group which is most able to learn healthy behavioural patterns;

Conscious that the establishment of school health education programmes requires:

– guidelines for the planning and development of health education curricula;

– a clear definition of the role of the teacher in this field;

– basic, in-service and further training of all teachers to allow them to contribute within their field to the programmes in question,

Recommends that the governments of member states adopt a comprehensive policy for health education in schools, taking into account the matters contained in the appendix.

Appendix to Recommendation No. R (88) 7

1. *Basic concepts*

1.1. Health is more than the absence of infirmity or illness, it is a quality of life comprising social, mental, moral and emotional as well as physical dimensions. It is a dynamic asset to be acquired, defended and constantly rebuilt throughout life.

1.2. Health education essentially consists in:

– providing better information on factors which influence health,

– elucidating the relationships which exist between health and the physical and psycho-social environment,

– developing individual, family and collective awareness and a sense of responsibility in relation to health,

– promoting responsible attitudes and ways of life conducive to health.

1.3. Health education at school implies that children and adolescents are confronted with formal and informal experiences enabling them to acquire attitudes and behaviour patterns which have a positive effect on their health, and are given the information and capacities required in order to make free decisions. It is different from other "taught" school subjects in that it is an interdisciplinary activity which has to permeate the whole of school life and extend into the outside community, and requires a personal commitment on the part of all those involved.

2. *Objectives of school health education*

School health education should:

i. at pre-primary level, promote the mental, social and emotional development of children within the pre-school environment, stimulating them to become aware of their bodies in relation to others and the environment; and encourage experience of, and active participation in, the decision-making process;

ii. at primary level, allow pupils gradually to acquire knowledge of human growth and development, and awareness of the basic issues of the relationship between health and the environment;

iii. at secondary level, enable young people to develop their knowledge of human growth and of physical, psychological and social development, and of factors which have a positive or negative effect on health; to appreciate positively this period of physical and psychological change to attain a proper measure of self-esteem; to learn to analyse attitudes and behaviour which have an effect on health, in order to facilitate active training in decision-taking.

3. *Guidelines for the planning and development of a health education programme*

3.1. Health education programmes should take account of schoolchildren's social and cultural environment.

3.2. Programme planners should take account of:

i. state of health needs and health-related behaviour as identified by children and young people themselves and by their parents;

ii. state of health needs, as identified by doctors, practitioners and health inspectors;

iii. the state of health needs and types of health-related behaviour as they are seen by the community in which the children and young people live and by that in which they might later live.

3.3. Through a participative process, planners should develop a school health programme reflecting identified needs and priorities. School health education programmes should be articulated on three levels:

3.3.1. The health-promoting curriculum, including an overt "taught" component and different approaches incorporated in all aspects of the curriculum;

3.3.2. The ethos established at school or health in school. It is necessary to ensure that life within the school is consistent with the aims of the health educaton programme; it should ensure physical and mental health and good social relations;

3.3.3. The various provisions of the school health and social services. Good co-ordination between the school and health and social services is necessary just as much to ensure the involvement of these services in the development of school health education programmes as in their implementation.

3.4. The health-promoting curriculum should take account of changes and developments occurring within the school population and its environment.

3.5. Health education issues should be taken up repeatedly at different levels of increasing complexity, according to the level of understanding of children and young people, so that they relate to their interests and needs (spiral development of curriculum).

3.6. As the objectives range from imparting knowledge to modifying behaviour, all methods might be considered, from the most classical to the most modern: traditional classes, discussion, group work, socio-educational activities, communication techniques, etc. Whatever methods are adopted, their effectiveness is influenced by the involvement and degree of commitment of the teacher.

4.   *Research and evaluation*

4.1. Research could give a better understanding of the perceptions of pupils, teachers, parents, social services and health service staff and representatives of the community with regard to health, and could help in the development of teaching materials designed to improve working conditions in the classroom and taking account of the most recent scientific data.

4.2. All components of the curriculum should be evaluated and the achievement of objectives assessed in a formative and summative way; teachers, pupils, parents, social and health service staff, and community representatives should all be involved in this process.

5.   *Training of teachers*

5.1. In view of its differences from other "taught" subjects, all teachers need to be prepared for working in the field of health education, whether they are to play a major or a minor role.

5.2. Teacher training should be organised for primary school teachers preferably at both initial training and in-service levels. Secondary school teachers should be introduced to health education during their basic training, and should have the opportunity to extend their knowledge during the course of their work.

6.   *Professional preparation of teachers*

6.1. In general, teachers should be:

    i.   familiar with current theoretical bases of health education;

    ii.   aware of national developments in the field both within the educational system and in the community at large.

6.2. During training, the following issues should be stressed:

i.   the potential of the school as a forum for promoting the health of children individually and the "collective" health of the school community;

ii.   health education is not only concerned with giving information but involves the clarification of values, attitudes and beliefs with a possibility of multiple choice and is not free from ethical considerations;

iii.   health is multi-faceted and is influenced by decisions taken and policies adopted in a wide range of government sectors (for example health, social and economic fields);

iv.   health education needs to be seen as a democratic process where pupils are encouraged to seek out and use relevant information leading to appropriate decision-making in given situations.

6.3. Objectives to be pursued in the preparation of teachers for health education should include the following:

i.   increasing knowledge about health; this should include social, emotional, moral and mental as well as physical components;

ii.   increasing understanding of the relationships between health and other components of the curriculum;

iii.   helping teachers and students to see that health educaton is an essential element in the development of personal skills and the personality;

iv.   demonstrating that health issues can be integrated into other aspects of the curriculum;

v.   demonstrating the importance of a variety of informal approaches which should be congruent with the formal health education curriculum;

vi.   helping teachers and students learn the use of methods appropriate to health education;

vii.   helping teachers recognise the role of others in education for health and of pupil counselling; they should be encouraged to call upon the expertise of teaching colleagues, members of the school health service, community groups, parents, etc.

6.4. The contents of training should ensure that all teachers, in the course of their professional preparation:

i.   acquire a basic knowledge about and a sense of responsibility for creating a healthy school environment;

ii.   be made sensitive to the health needs of children;

iii.   obtain an insight into the basic growth and developmental processes of children;

iv.   acquire knowledge of the skills necessary to make independent decisions about one's own health;

v.   become familiar with the methodology to be used relevant to the cognitive and emotional elements of curriculum development;

vi.   become skilled in multidisciplinary work with colleagues in collaborative teaching strategies;

vii. become able to co-operate with other significant individuals, systems and services.

6.5. Teachers who are identified as having specific roles in the school health education programmes, for example, co-ordinators, those involved in teaching particular parts of the curriculum or particular groups of children, need to have appropriate skills in addition of those of other teachers. They should be familiar with all aspects of the curriculum related to health. They should, in particular:

446

i.   have special knowledge of how to develop comprehensive programmes and how to identify possible gaps;

ii.   play appropriate roles in implementing the programme;

iii.   be able to give advice to other teachers; and

iv.   assess the achievement of objectives, evaluate both the appropriateness of the methods employed and the effectiveness of the curriculum in contributing to pupils' health.

7.   Organisation of teacher training

7.1. Training colleges and other appropriate establishments, should gradually become organised in order to provide this type of training for teachers through multidisciplinary teams; in the absence of specialists, such colleges should appoint a co-ordinator to enlist specialists from a variety of disciplines from outside the college to ensure that the eclectic nature of health educaton is reflected in the teaching.

7.2. In-service training should be organised, preferably within the school, by co-ordinators belonging to the above institutions.

7.3. Training institutions responsible for the pre-service and in-service training of teachers should have at their disposal guidelines in the form of training documents which should be prepared at national level through co-operation between the health and education sectors. Such documents should contain:

i.   a guide to the training including both method and content;

ii.   all the necessary materials for teachers participating in the course.

7.4. In-service training should include examination of topical questions.

8.   Development of policies on health education

8.1. In order to ensure impact throughout the school system, policies need to be developed. Such policies should:

i.   ensure co-ordination at central, regional and local levels between the health and education sectors by means of co-ordinating committees supporting the intro-duction of health education in all school curricula;

ii.   provide for the appointment of persons responsible at regional level for developing strategies within schools in close co-operation with the head teacher and, if necessary, the school co-ordinating committee;

iii.   ensure that resources of time and materials are provided to support all those involved.

Recommendation No. R (91) 8
on the development of environmental education in school systems

(Adopted by the Committee of Ministers on 17 June 1991
at the 460th meeting of the Ministers' Deputies)

The Committee of Ministers, under the terms of Article 15.*b* of the Statute of the Council of Europe,

Having regard to the Stockholm Declaration on the Human Environment and the World Charter of Nature;

Having regard to the conclusions of the Unesco/UNEP Intergovernmental Conference in Tbilisi (1977), the Moscow International Congress (1987) and the various other international events and programmes on environmental education;

Having regard to the Convention on the Conservation of European Wildlife and Natural Habitats (Bern Convention);

Having regard to Resolution (71) 14 on the introduction of the principles of nature conservation into education, and considering its updating to be necessary in order to:

– take account of the aggravation of certain phenomena such as the population explosion and the appearance of new problems such as climatic changes and depletion of the ozone layer;

– ensure that educational curricula deal more fully with environmental problems and the risks facing the environment and society;

– reduce the discrepancy between advances in science and technology and their coverage by schools;

– include in curricula the increasingly numerous sources of information available to pupils;

Bearing in mind the revision of proposals made by the participants in the 38th Council of Europe Teachers' Seminar (Donaueschingen, November 1987);

Endorsing the conclusions of the report entitled "Our Common Future" by the World Commission on Environment and Development (Brundtland Report);

Aware that the state of the environment has reached a critical level;

Convinced that the present situation is the result of the juxtaposition of two phenomena, namely a dramatic increase in population and the globalisation of industrial society;

Underlining the planetary dimension of environmental problems and the need to promote a resources management model that takes more account of the interdependence of individuals and nations;

Noting that the tremendous development of science and the increase in technological power necessitates, on the part of individuals, an increased sense of responsibility for the environment, humanity's common heritage;

Recognising that people have the right to a healthy and ecologically balanced environment, on whose quality their dignity and well-being depend;

Convinced that environmental education is one of the best ways of restoring a balance between the individual and nature and guaranteeing a rational and reasonable management of planetary resources in a context of sustainable development;

Considering that the attention given to environmental protection in educational curricula should be increased and that appreciation of and respect for the environment should be basic principles of the teaching of all subjects;

Convinced that education should consist not only in developing a knowledge and understanding of ecology and biology but also in encouraging more positive individual attitudes towards nature and the environment;

Wishing that education be based on an ethical approach that it is essential for the judicious use of knowledge;

Being aware of emotional and affective relationship with nature and the environment;

Emphasising that environmental education in schools should not be separated from that provided in the home, in youth organisations and through out-of-school activities,

Recommends that the governments of member states:

– bear in mind, when drawing up or revising their environmental education policies, the guidelines set out in the appendix to this recommendation;

– ensure that teachers have an opportunity of revitalising and diversifying classroom activities and basic learning processes by providing them with resources enabling them:

- to use and develop active teaching methods aimed at the discovery and enhancement of the environment,

- to use out-of-school facilities for environmental education,

- to use the new technologies (for example audiovisual media, computer facilities and telematics) for the purpose of visualising the relevant concepts,

- to acquire teaching materials and educational modules meeting the aims of environmental education;

– promote working relations with research institutes in the field of natural science, social science and education;

– develop an active and stimulating policy for the initial and in-service training of teachers by:

- introducing appropriate elements into their training programmes,

- creating, within and around schools, educational areas conducive to the sensory awakening of pupils and to practical activities;

– create an infrastructure designed to help teachers and others involved in environmental education through the provision of consultants, a diversified range of curricula, training facilities and documentation;

– ensure wide distribution of this recommendation among all interest parties, especially curriculum developers, educational advisers, teacher trainers and teachers;

Instructs the Secretary General to transmit this recommendation to the governments of those states, Parties to the European Cultural Convention, which are not members of the Council of Europe.

Appendix to recommendation No. R (91) 8

Basic principles for the promotion of environmental education

I. *Contents*

Curricula should enable pupils:

– to gain a basic knowledge of ecology in its broadest sense and deal with themes relating to environment protection; teaching in this area should take into account the intellectual and psychological development of pupils;

– to learn to reason in terms of systems;

– to understand the economic, political and ecological interdependences.

It is advisable to:

– enhance, in curricula at all levels of education, the various subjects touching on questions of environmental and ecological protection: while biology and geography are the key subjects for this purpose, all other disciplines can help to promote the teaching of ecology and environment protection (civics, plastic arts, religion, etc.);

– encourage multidisciplinary schemes where every discipline helps to show how the various elements interact and contributes to a global perception of realities;

– mobilise the whole teaching profession around the subject of the environment.

II. *Methods*

Environmental issues cannot be taught solely in the form of knowledge. They should be related to the world in which pupils live and to real-life situations. Experience of nature is the best means of encouraging a favourable attitude towards the environment.

III. *Instruments*

The use of out-of-school teaching tools and facilities for environmental education enables teachers to diversify their teaching methods and stimulate school activities and basic learning processes.

These instruments also make an important contribution to a realisation of the requirements of the environment and should therefore be fully integrated into the educational process.

IV. *Teacher training*

Initial and in-service training of teachers is the key to the integration of environmental aspects into curricula.

The success of environmental education depends to a large extent on the knowledge, skills and attitudes of the teachers themselves.

Mass media

Table of contents

Parliamentary Assembly

Recommendation 952 (1982)[1]
on international means to protect freedom of expression by regulating commercial advertising

The Assembly,

1. Considering that freedom of expression is a fundamental right laid down in the constitutions of most Council of Europe member states and in the European Convention on Human Rights;

2. Considering that Article 10 of this convention reads as follows:

"1. Everyone has the right to freedom of expression. This right shall include freedom to hold opinions and to receive and impart information and ideas without interference by public authority and regardless of frontiers. This article shall not prevent states from requiring the licensing of broadcasting, television or cinema enterprises.

2. The exercise of these freedoms, since it carries with it duties and responsibilities, may be subject to such formalities, conditions, restrictions or penalties as are prescribed by law and are necessary in a democratic society in the interests of national security, territorial integrity or public safety, for the prevention of disorder or crime, for the protection of health or morals, for the protection of the reputation or rights of others, for preventing the disclosure of information received in confidence, or for maintaining the authority and impartiality of the judiciary.";

3. Considering that freedom of expression is a right which should enable individuals and groups to express themselves, but that due regard should be had to the rights of others;

4. Noting that, in accordance with the jurisprudence of the European Commission of Human Rights, the protection conferred by Article 10 is not normally withheld from statements of a commercial nature, but that the level of protection may be less than that accorded to the expression of political ideas with which the values underlying the concept of freedom of expression in the convention are chiefly concerned;

5. Desirous to counteract any abuses of human rights;

6. Considering that appropriate advertising is an essential element of the market economy;

---

1. *Assembly debate* on 1 and 2 October 1982 (12th, 13th and 14th Sittings) (see Doc. 4940, report of the Legal Affairs Committee).
   Text adopted by the Assembly on 2 October 1982 (14th Sitting).

7. Considering, however, that commercial advertising is often very intrusive, and that children especially may not possess adequate protection against its influence;

8. Considering that commercial advertising sometimes strives for the sale of goods and services which are dangerous to health or undesirable for other reasons;

9. Considering, in this respect, that there is, for instance, an alarming increase in the use of alcohol by youth in many of our member countries;

10. Referring to its Recommendation 716 (1973), on the control of tobacco and alcohol advertising, and on measures to curb consumption of these products;

11. Considering that mass media, especially in view of modern technical developments, such as cable television and direct television broadcasts by satellites, are not limited by national boundaries, but that they are frequently heard, watched or read in several of our member countries;

12. Considering that there is a danger of cultural messages, opinions and information being mixed with advertising, and that, as a consequence, the exercise of the right to freedom of expression may be undermined;

13. Considering, for that reason, that any action aimed at protecting freedom of expression by regulating commercial advertising is bound to fail unless it is taken up at international level;

14. Convinced that all action aimed at regulation or prohibition should be accompanied by a policy including measures such as better education of the young, strengthening of consumer associations and better use of leisure time;

15. Recalling its recent Recommendation 926 (1981) on questions raised by cable television and by direct satellite broadcasts;

16. Stressing the importance of:

i. the clear separation between programmes and advertising on the electronic media (see Recommendation 926, paragraph 18.iii);

ii. effective measures to guarantee that advertisers will comply with national and international provisions (see Recommendation 926, paragraph 15.ii);

iii. safeguards for the application of national legislation in the field of health, morals, public order, protection of children, etc.;

17. Considering that the overwhelming majority of newspapers and periodicals in our member states are dependent on a steady flow of advertisements without which they would not be able to exist;

18. Referring to the International Code of Advertising Practice of the International Chamber of Commerce;

19. Welcoming the work of the Council of Europe's Intergovernmental Steering Committee on the Mass Media;

20. Considering that this committee should, as a matter of urgency, study and propose adequate international measures, in particular:

i.   co-operation and co-ordination in respect of commercial advertising, especially on radio and television;

ii.   prohibition of misleading, hidden and subliminal advertising or messages;

iii.   promotion of the conditions under which a pluriform supply of information can exist;

iv.   introduction of a binding code of conduct for commercial advertising which should, in particular, take account of the effect of advertising on children, not be contrary to the process of emancipation, and promote as well as confirm the separation of advertising from information or opinions,

21. Recommends that the Committee of Ministers, in the light of Article 10 of the European Convention on Human Rights, instruct the Steering Committee on the Mass Media to examine international means to protect freedom of expression by regulating commercial advertising, especially on radio and television, and to make concrete proposals, possibly through the conclusion of a European convention.

Recommendation 963 (1983)[1]
on cultural and educational means of reducing violence

The Assembly,

A. *Introduction*

1. Having noted the report of its Committee on Culture and Education (Doc. 5013);

2. Taking note of the Hearing on Violence held by that Committee in Assisi from 1 to 3 September 1982 on the occasion of the 800th anniversary of the birth of St. Francis;

3. Gravely concerned at the occurrence of violence in modern society, in particular terrorism, but also delinquency, vandalism and rape;

4. Suspicious in principle of some of the justifications advanced for direct physical violence, but recognising that those in authority on certain occasions have to use varying acceptable degrees of force for the protection of society, of lives and of property;

5. Believing that violence in modern society is related to the stresses exercised on human nature by external factors of a social, economic and cultural character;

6. Recalling the report of its Committee on Culture and Education on war toys (Doc. 4742) and the resolution adopted on this subject by the European Parliament on 13 September 1982;

B. *Regarding terrorism*

7. Recalling its Recommendations 916 (1981) and 941 (1982) on the defence of democracy against terrorism in Europe;

8. Considering that terrorism is a permanent challenge to fundamental democratic values, and may well prompt states to take legislative, judicial or administrative measures (such as keeping records on individuals for the purposes of prevention, restrictions on personal freedoms, etc.) that may pervert the very character of democracy;

---

1. *Assembly debate* on 28 January 1983 (28th Sitting) (see Doc. 5013, report of the Committee on Culture and Education).
   Text adopted by the Assembly on 28 January 1983 (28th Sitting).

9. Aware of the fact that combating terrorism may, because of the growth of politically motivated crimes and offences, create imbalances in the arsenal of penalties, and disrupt prison systems;

10. Convinced that the symbolic, spectacular or revolting nature of terrorism and the exaggerated reflection sometimes given of it by the media helps it achieve a social impact out of all proportion to the resources it deploys and even to its ultimate goal, something which distinguishes it from ordinary violence;

11. Noting that terrorism imitates the methods, means and language of warfare without triggering off the usual collective defence mechanisms;

12. Conscious that terrorism is moreover a factor of major cultural destabilisation and can undermine the individual's confidence in the values, interests or institutions under attack;

13. Considering that measures to suppress terrorism must be based on an analysis of its causes,

14. Recommends that the Committee of Ministers invite member governments:

   a. to take the necessary steps to alert communities in which terrorism is breeding to the serious threat it presents to democracy and freedoms;

   b. to make available in all member countries a "White Paper on democracy and terrorism", a work which would be prepared by the Council of Europe and based on the European Convention on Human Rights, international agreements and member states' constitutions, and whose purpose would be to demonstrate the fact that terrorism is a major European problem imperilling democracy and to proclaim Europe's determination to combat political violence;

   c. to foster studies of the cultural and social causes of the growth of terrorism by giving thought to the setting up of an independent European Foundation for the study of terrorism;

C. *Regarding the media*

15. Concerned at the increasing tendency towards emphasis on violence in the media, and in particular on its portrayal in the visual media (television, video, film, advertising, comics, or still photography);

16. Conscious that prolonged exposure to such media violence can have a direct cumulative effect on young children and a minority of adults, and a growing effect on the accepted values of society;

17. Welcoming the recent Declaration by the Committee of Ministers on freedom of expression (1982), and recalling Article 10 of the European Convention on Human Rights (1950) and the United Nations Convention for the Repression of Obscene Publications (1947);

18. Concerned that artistic freedom should not be used as an alibi for purely commercial interests;

19. Believing that national legislative or voluntary restrictions are becoming increasingly impracticable in the light of direct broadcasting by satellite and other technological developments, and drawing attention to the fact that the production, distribution and sale of media software has already progressed beyond the control of individual states;

20. Stressing the urgency of co-ordinated action involving European states, broadcasting institutions and commercial audio-visual concerns,

21. Recommends that the Committee of Ministers:

a. request the broadcasting organisations to co-operate on the elaboration of codes of conduct or guidelines covering the portrayal of violence, including terrorism, that can apply to as broad an area in Europe as possible, and where necessary provide autonomous supplementary structures to enable the effective elaboration of such common codes;

b. encourage the elaboration of similar guidelines for other media such as films, written material, video and new forms of visual media that may be developed;

c. encourage the establishment in each member state of a. independent monitoring of broadcast and other visual media through viewer associations and other bodies, b. closer consultation between the public and the programme makers, and c. public accountability for media content whether to parliament, to the courts or to public opinion, and envisage at a subsequent stage closer co-ordination between member states on these aspects;

d. arrange for the regular publication of an up-to-date survey of existing guidelines, legislation and administrative structures regarding the media in all member states;

e. ask member governments:

i. to sponsor further independent research into the effects of the media;

ii. to consider introducing legislation to ensure that media violence involving individuals is condemned alongside incitement to racial hatred or obscenity;

iii. to take the appropriate measures to ensure that broadcasting companies give particular attention to means of protecting sensitive people, especially children, from prolonged exposure to media violence;

iv. to make clear to the press and to the audio-visual media their special responsibility as regards the dissemination of models of political violence, and therefore make proper understanding of the effects of the media a necessary part of the qualification of all personnel employed in the media field;

D. *Regarding sport*

22. Concerned with the continued presence of violence in sport and with the growth of violence associated with sport on local, national and international levels;

23. Welcoming the action already taken by the sports federations to reduce violence in sport by modifying the rules of individual and team games, with

special reference to violent sports such as boxing, and by increasing the authority of refereeing;

24. Questioning, however, the efficacy of existing sanctions, in particular in top-level professional sport, and believing that responsibility lies as much with trainers and management as with individual players;

25. Believing that concerted action by the public authorities and the sporting bodies is necessary to control violence associated with sport, and that the media could help in this action, and stressing the positive role to be played by responsible supporters' clubs;

26. Welcoming the activity of the International Alliance for Non-Violent Sport and for Fair Play, and noting the results of the symposium organised by the Alliance in Monte-Carlo on 16 and 17 November 1982;

27. Recalling the Council of Europe's European Sport for All Charter, and reaffirming its belief in the ideals and values of sport, especially Olympic sport as expressed in its Resolution 738 (1980), on the Olympic Games and the outlook for their future;

28. Believing that it is necessary to reaffirm and re-establish these positive values of sport and fair play as a direct contribution to solving the problem of violence in modern society;

29. Recalling the resolution on violence associated with sport, adopted by the Conference of European Ministers responsible for Sport in London 1978, and hoping that the ministers concerned will reconsider urgently the question of violence and sport,

30. Recommends that the Committee of Ministers:

   a. ask the Steering Committee for the Development of Sport to give consideration to effective European Intergovernmental co-operation on violence and sport, including the elaboration of a European convention, or other forms of European agreement on the introduction of specific legislation in member states;

   b. co-ordinate such activity with other sectors through the steering committees responsible for mass media, culture and education, and criminal matters;

   c. support the Campaign of the International Alliance for Non-Violent Sport and for Fair Play;

E. *Positive approaches, and in particular education*

31. Stressing the power of example of parent, teacher or state, and noting also the role played by the churches, youth organisations and other disinterested institutions in encouraging young people to participate in social goals;

32. Underlining the need for schools constantly to readjust to the changing patterns of modern society, and noting the conclusions reached by the Council for Cultural Co-operation project on "Preparation for life";

33. Insisting on the importance of the proper preparation of children to understand the messages put across by the media, and noting the positive contribution of the media in presenting society as condemning and rejecting violence;

34. Wishing to ensure that the systematic teaching of non-violent behaviour is an integral part of all compulsory education, and welcoming the proposal by the Quaker Council for European Affairs to conduct a study on existing models in Europe of such education;

35. Hoping that the Standing Conference of European Ministers of Education will pay close attention to the contribution education can make to encouraging constructive, non-violent behaviour,

36. Recommends that the Committee of Ministers:

   a. associate the Council for Cultural Co-operation with study of models of education for non-violent behaviour and co-operation;

   b. invite member governments or, through them, the local or regional authorities responsible for education:

   i. to review the content of existing school and university curricula in order to avoid thoughtless glorification of conflict and violence, and to introduce in schools the systematic teaching of non-violent behaviour;

   ii. to encourage the introduction in certain European universities of the study of terrorism;

   iii. to make available for use in schools, for example in the context of history lessons, material highlighting the odious and regressive nature of political violence and denouncing the ideologies that provoke and manipulate such violence;

   iv. to make it possible for young people to opt out of experiments involving violence to living animals should they object to these on grounds of conscience, without prejudice to their subsequent careers;

   v. to ensure that schools adhere to non-violent approaches with regard to their own internal problems and that they avoid any recourse to violent punishment;

   vi. to encourage real participation in school life by allowing the gradual development of pupil responsibility and the continued involvement of parents, and by permitting the school and its community to fulfil its indispensable educational role;

   vii. to introduce into the school curriculum the critical understanding of the media, and to provide the necessary in-service and preparatory training of teachers;

   viii. to ensure a proper place for sport (both individual and team sports) in schools, with particular stress on the principles of fair play.

Recommendation 996 (1984)[1]
on Council of Europe work
relating to the media

The Assembly,

1.   Having noted the resolutions on culture and communications technolo-gy, and on the distribution of video-cassettes portraying violence and brutal-ity, adopted by the European Ministers responsible for Cultural Affairs in Berlin in May 1984;

2.   Sharing the ministers' view that "technological innovation, with all the opportunities and dangers it entails, is producing fundamental changes in communication networks, making communications a major vehicle of further economic and cultural development and greater mutual understanding";

3.   Aware also of "the need to preserve and develop local, regional and national cultural identities at a time when frontiers are being opened up and production systems are being reorganised as a consequence of the introduc-tion of new technologies";

4.   Recalling its Recommendation 963 (1983), on cultural and educational means of reducing violence, and Recommendation 964 (1983), on a European award for non-violence, and welcoming the fact that the ministers in Berlin were equally concerned with media violence;

5.   Noting that the ministers for culture meeting within the Council of the European Communities in Luxembourg in June 1984 placed very similar emphasis on the need for concerted European action in the media field;

6.   Noting also the proposals made by the European Parliament in its reso-lution on the market of violent and horrific video-cassettes;

7.   In consequence, therefore, regretting all the more the over-cautious response of the Committee of Ministers to Recommendations 963 and 964, regarding the media,

8.   Recommends that the Committee of Ministers reconsider this response in the light of the positions adopted in Berlin and Luxembourg, and on the basis of closer co-ordination of the thinking of the Steering Committee for the Mass Media and of the Council for Cultural Co-operation;

---

1. *Assembly debate* on 2 and 3 October 1984 (18th, 19th and 20th Sittings) (see Doc. 5288, report of the Committee on Culture and Education).
   Text adopted by the Assembly on 3 October 1984 (20th Sitting).

9. Supports the request of the ministers in Berlin for an intensification of co-operation between Council of Europe member states, and stresses in particular the need for action relating to:

  a. the production and distribution of European programmes;

  b. copyright and other legal questions relating to the media;

  c. the quality of programme content and measures to regulate the distribution of video-cassettes portraying violence and brutality likely to have a pernicious influence on children and adolescents.

Recommendation 1067 (1987)[1]
on the cultural dimension
of broadcasting in Europe

The Assembly,

1.   Having considered the report by its Committee on Culture and Education (Doc. 5782) and the opinion of its Legal Affairs Committee (Doc. 5800);

2.   Recalling its Recommendation 926 (1981) on questions raised by cable television and by direct satellite broadcasts, and Recommendation 996 (1984) on Council of Europe work relating to the media;

3.   Recalling the Declaration on the Freedom of Expression and Information adopted by the Committee of Ministers in 1982;

4.   Drawing attention to the profound changes in the mass media field, and in particular in that of television, as a result of the introduction of new transmission techniques by satellite and cable, in conjunction with rapidly increasing commercialisation both in public broadcasting and through privatisation;

5.   Noting that such developments may have potentially positive effects, in particular through:

a.   increasing the opportunities and opening up new fields for cultural creation and expression;

b.   broadening the range of programmes;

c.   assisting awareness of other European languages and cultures;

6.   Believing however that such changes also carry serious cultural risks, notably:

a.   the encouragement of passive consumption of broadcast material;

b.   the reduction in programme diversity and the erosion of socially accepted standards of behaviour;

c.   the undermining of the cultural identity of smaller countries and minor language groups, and of the cultural diversity of Europe as a whole;

d.   lack of respect for copyright and neighbouring rights;

e.   economic and thereby cultural dependence on outside (largely commercial) factors;

1. *Assembly debate* on 8 October 1987 (18th Sitting) (see Doc. 5782, report of the Committee on Culture and Education, and Doc. 5800, opinion of the Legal Affairs Committee).
   Text adopted by the Assembly on 8 October 1987 (18th Sitting).

7.   Recognising that advertising provides an important occasion for artistic creation and is often of high quality, but at the same time wishing to prevent advertising destroying, for example by inappropriate juxtaposition or interruption, the cultural value of the programme it accompanies;

8.   Insisting on the need for an effective reassertion by governments of the public service nature of broadcasting (whether public or private), and of the political, educational and cultural roles of the mass media, and believing that greater emphasis should be placed on the mass media as a means of creative expression, cultural diversity and communication throughout Europe;

9.   Believing that, as a general principle, both public and private broadcasting should be subject to the same rules;

10. Stressing the importance for member states to concert policies and, when relevant, harmonise legal arrangements relating to the mass media, but in a manner that will respect national differences and also the independence of professional broadcasting bodies;

11. Repeating its concern, expressed in Recommendation 963 (1983) on cultural and educational means of reducing violence, that artistic freedom should not be used as an alibi for purely commercial interests;

12. Recalling its Recommendation 862 (1979) on cinema and the state, and stressing the need for closer co-ordination of mass media policies with those of other means of cultural expression;

13. Recalling also its Recommendation 928 (1981) on the educational and cultural problems of minority languages and dialects in Europe, and Recommendation 1043 (1986) on Europe's linguistic and literary heritage, and stressing the role that the cinema and mass media can play in promoting linguistic diversity and widening cultural appreciation;

14. Recalling its Recommendation 1018 (1985) on private sponsorship of the arts, and Recommendation 1059 (1987) on the economics of culture, and believing that considerably more resources should be channelled from the enormous profits made in the mass media business into direct encouragement of original production and the development of new and more varied talent;

15. Believing also that the governments of member states should review the fiscal incentives available to promote the re-investment of profits made in the mass media business in original domestic production and the development of new and more varied talent;

16. Recalling the long-standing concern of the Council for Cultural Co-operation and the Conference of European Ministers responsible for Cultural Affairs with the interaction between cultural policy and the communication media, and welcoming the proposal made by the ministers in Sintra (September 1987) for developing practical measures to promote European cultural diversity, taking into account the development of the communication technologies;

17. Having noted the texts adopted by the 1st European Ministerial Conference on Mass Media Policy (Vienna, December 1986), and welcoming in particular the direct request addressed by the Vienna conference to the Committee of Ministers for the rapid preparation, within the Council of Europe framework, of binding legal instruments on certain crucial aspects of transfrontier broadcasting;

18. Stressing the need for the participation of the European Community bodies in this initiative;

19. Underlining the need for speed in this area, in order to keep pace with technological advance and avoid cultural policies being dictated by such advances,

20. Recommends that the Committee of Ministers:

a. finalise and open for signature, early in 1988, a binding legal instrument on basic standards for transfrontier broadcasting by both public and private bodies, with a view to the possibility of its entering into force before the 2nd European Ministerial Conference on Mass Media Policy in Stockholm in November 1988, and set up an effective mechanism (including the representation of broadcasting bodies) to monitor the implementation of this instrument;

b. provide for the subsequent inclusion into such an instrument of binding agreements or additional protocols in other fields mentioned in the following paragraphs;

c. adopt a declaration on public responsibility for the mass media and the public service nature of broadcasting, with particular reference to the role of television in stimulating awareness of different cultures and developing the diversity of cultural and linguistic identities;

d. draw up proposals for maintaining and encouraging the linguistic diversity of the mass media, for example by:

i. joint production funds on which minor language nations may also draw;

ii. the inclusion of minor language interviews in news bulletins;

iii. the development of improved techniques for subtitling and the provision of dubbing on an optimal basis;

iv. ensuring the right for national languages, and where appropriate minor local and regional languages, to be carried on national, regional and local networks;

e. recognise advertising as a valid field of creative expression, but give consideration to means of ensuring that it does not shock or affect the cultural integrity of the programmes it may accompany;

f. accelerate and intensify its work on guidelines for reducing violence, brutality and pornography, with reference to national legislation, not only on videograms, but also with reference to broadcasting in general;

g. encourage increased participation by women in broadcasting (especially in the fields of production and programming);

h.   encourage media education, for example by:

   i. the introduction of school courses on critical appreciation of the media and audiovisual production;

   ii. the information of adults (and not only parents) as to developments in the mass media field;

i.   promote the use of the mass media in education and in particular in line with the objectives of the Council of Europe in such fields as human rights, tolerance and equality between the sexes;

j.   encourage the development of international concertation to promote the production and distribution of audiovisual works in Europe within the framework of overall cultural policies, including:

   i. training programmes, for example the setting up of training centres for those working in the broadcasting profession, and trainee exchange schemes;

   ii. protection of copyright and neighbouring rights;

   iii. the closer co-ordination of media policies, and in particular the relationship between cinema and television;

   iv. mechanisms of direct and indirect support for audiovisual creativity;

   v. special emphasis on co-production in the making of musical and other non-verbal programmes;

k.   maintain and encourage a continuing dialogue between all partners (government media, the public and interested non-governmental bodies) with a view to developing, by means of a series of suitable instruments, the basis for the free exchange of mass media material and professional experience between Council of Europe member countries, between Western and Eastern Europe, and between Europe and other parts of the world;

l.   conduct periodic reviews of international co-operation and research relating to broadcasting.

Recommendation 1136 (1990)[1]
on a European policy on alcohol

1.   Grave health and social problems are related to the excessive consumption of alcohol.

2.   The costs of excessive alcohol consumption pose a considerable burden on our societies both in human and economics terms.

3.   Excessive drinking can impose suffering on innocent people, as through motor vehicle accidents.

4.   Widely divergent alcohol traditions in different parts of Europe call for different national strategies in the effort to reduce the consumption of alcohol.

5.   Such national strategies may entail different levels of taxation in various countries; and fiscal harmonisation measures, however desirable in the pursuit of European integration, should allow for such variations to be retained.

6.   Cultural differences must also be taken into account in efforts to promote education and information about the physical and social effects of alcohol.

7.   Nevertheless, there is an important European dimension to the problem, and this warrants the elaboration of a common European policy on alcohol.

8.   The strength of producer, distributor and fiscal interests in the shaping of alcohol-related policy decisions is considerable and much greater weight should be given to public health considerations in the formulation of national alcohol policies.

9.   The Committee of Ministers has already made recommendations on questions pertaining to alcohol – in particular, on prevention of alcohol-related problems among young people; on prevention of drug dependence and the special role of education for health; and on strategies to combat smoking, alcohol and drug dependence in co-operation with opinion-makers and the media, including certain provisions of the European Convention on Transfrontier Television.

10. Moreover, member states of the World Health Organisation have undertaken to promote lifestyles conducive to health, with the target for 1995 of significant decreases in health-damaging behaviour – such as

---

1. *Assembly debate* on 4 October 1990 (18th Sitting) (see Doc. 6250, report of the Social, Health and Family Affairs Committee, Rapporteur : Mr Tarschys).
Text adopted by the Assembly on 4 October 1990 (18th Sitting).

over-use of alcohol and pharmaceutical products, use of illicit drugs and dangerous chemical substances, dangerous driving and violent social behaviour.

11. Accordingly, the Assembly recommends that the Committee of Ministers:

a.   urge governments of member states to adopt national targets for reducing alcohol consumption in line with the global strategy of "health for all by the year 2000" of the World Health Organisation;

b.   promote the introduction at both national and local levels of comprehensive programmes aimed at combating the abuse of alcohol by young people;

c.   instruct its European Health Committee:

    i.   to convene a group of experts for the purpose of sharing information and experience,

    ii. to reappraise and develop accordingly national strategies for combating immoderate consumption and preventing abuse;

d.   promote arrangements as soon as possible for discussion of alcohol policies in Europe at ministerial level.

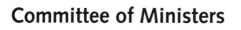

Committee of Ministers

Resolution (67) 13
The press and the protection of youth

(Adopted by the Ministers' Deputies on 29th June 1967)

The Committee of Ministers,

Considering the importance of the problem of juvenile delinquency in the modern world, and noting the serious manifestations of the phenomenon since the end of the second world war;

Drawing attention to the value attached by the authorities of all countries to research into the anti-social behaviour of juveniles and its causes;

Believing that encouragement and support must be given to all action, enlightened by research, which is calculated to render measures for the prevention of delinquency and for the resocialisation of young offenders more effective;

Approving to the full the initiative taken by the European Committee on Crime Problems in inaugurating a study of the influence of mass communication media – press, cinema, radio and television – on juveniles, and having taken note of the first report presented by the Committee concerning the press;

Considering the place of the press in modern society and stressing its impact on juveniles;

Wishing for a more detailed study of the influence of the press on the behaviour of children and adolescents and the adoption of suitable measures to enable the press to perform an educational function in relation to juveniles and, by eradicating the baneful influences that can be exerted by certain kinds of literature, to contribute to the prevention of juvenile delinquency,

Recommends to the member governments of the Council of Europe:

1. that the report "The press and the protection of youth" should be widely circulated among the authorities of member countries and brought to the attention of publishers, press associations and the general public;

2. that research should be encouraged into the mechanism by which the press influences children and adolescents and into the conditions of protection, distribution, sale and "consumption" of publications intended for juveniles;

3. that a series of enquiries should be made into specific ways and means of implementing measures for the protection of juveniles taken in the sphere

of the press and into their adequacy, including the effects of the restrictions on distribution which they seek to introduce;

4.   that those responsible for the publication of juvenile literature should be made clearly aware of the importance of observing certain educational standards.

Resolution (69) 6
Cinema and the protection of youth

(Adopted by the Ministers' Deputies on 7 March 1969)

The Committee of Ministers,

Considering the importance of the problem of juvenile delinquency in the modern world and noting the serious manifestations of the phenomenon since the end of the second world war;

Drawing attention to the value attached by the authorities of all countries to research into anti-social behaviour of juveniles and its causes;

Believing that encouragement and support must be given to all action, enlightened by research, which is calculated to render measures for the prevention of delinquency and for the resocialisation of young offenders more effective;

Approving to the full the initiative taken by the European Committee on Crime Problems in inaugurating a study of the influence of mass communication media – press, cinema, radio and television – on juveniles, and having taken note of the report presented by the committee concerning the cinema;

Considering the important role played in all countries by the cinema and its influence on the training and education of young people;

Welcoming the efforts already made in certain countries to assign to the cinema a positive role in the education of young people,

Recommends to the member governments of the Council of Europe:

1. That the report on "The cinema and the protection of youth" be widely circulated among government authorities and all interested organisations;

2. That the regulations governing the cinema should take biological, psychological and sociological factors into consideration in determining age groups;

3. That, whatever the form and methods of film censorship, use should be made of the views of those professionally concerned with films, of social scientists and of other suitable experts;

4. That censorship bodies should state the grounds for their decisions, at least when such decisions are of a restrictive character; that the persons concerned should have access to them and that they should be open to review;

5. That all action to promote the educational and cultural aims of the cinema should be encouraged and that the production and distribution of films

for young people and the teaching of film appreciation in schools should accordingly be intensified;

6. That experiments and research into the cinema should be undertaken with a view to better knowledge of its effects on young people and to allow its full exploitation for the prevention of delinquency and in youth education;

7. That censorship bodies should be encouraged to make their documentary material available to qualified research workers and facilitate their work;

8. That the exchange of information between states should be promoted, as well as relations between cinema organisations;

Invites member governments to send reports to the Secretary General of the Council of Europe in principle every five years, informing him of the action taken by them on these recommendations.

Recommendation No. R (84) 3
on principles on television advertising

(Adopted by the Committee of Ministers on 23 February 1984
at the 367th meeting of the Ministers' Deputies)

The Committee of Ministers, under the terms of Article 15.*b* of the Statute of the Council of Europe,

Considering that the aim of the Council of Europe is to achieve a greater unity between its members for the purpose of safeguarding and promoting the ideals and principles which are their common heritage;

Bearing in mind the Convention for the Protection of Human Rights and Fundamental Freedoms;

Recalling its commitment to the freedom of expression and the free flow of information and ideas as embodied, *inter alia*, in its Declaration of 29 April 1982;

Conscious that the electronic media enable a contribution of growing importance to be made towards communication and better understanding between individuals and peoples;

Aware that the development of new technologies, particularly involving the use of satellites, has made it more urgent to arrive at common European principles in the field of advertising on television;

Noting that member states adopt different attitudes towards advertising on television;

Conscious of the importance which advertising may have for the financing of the media;

Aware of the impact of television advertising on the attitudes and behaviour of the public;

Considering the importance of the portrayal of women and men by the media, particularly in television advertisements;

Mindful of the importance of securing the interests of the public in relation to advertising;

Welcoming the fact that codes of ethics and good advertising practice have been adopted on a voluntary basis by advertising organisations and professionals both on a national and an international basis;

Taking into account the independence of broadcasting organisations in matters of programming,

Recommends that the governments of member states:

a. satisfy themselves that the principles set out below concerning advertising on television are respected, and

b. to that end give these principles the widest possible circulation both to the competent bodies and to members of the public.

Principles

The following principles apply to television advertising, especially when transmitted by satellite:

I. *General principle*

1. Advertisements should be prepared with a sense of responsibility towards society, and give particular attention to the moral values which form the basis of every democratic society and are common to all member states, such as individual liberty, tolerance and respect for the dignity and equality of all human beings.

II. *Content*

2. All advertisements should be fair, honest, truthful and decent.

3. Advertisers should comply with the law applicable in the country of transmission and, depending on the proportion of the audience which is in another country, should take due account of the law of that country.

4. Utmost attention should be given to the possible harmful consequences that might result from advertisements concerning tobacco, alcohol, pharmaceutical products and medical treatments and to the possibility of limiting or even prohibiting advertisements in these fields.

5. Advertisements addressed to or using children should avoid anything likely to harm their interests and should respect their physical, mental and moral personality.

III. *Form and presentation*

6. Advertisements, whatever their form, should always be clearly identifiable as such.

7. Advertising should be clearly separated from programmes; neither advertisements nor the interests of advertisers should influence programme content in any way.

8. Advertisements should preferably be grouped and scheduled in such a way as to avoid prejudice to the integrity and value of programmes or their natural continuity.

9. The amount of time allowed for advertising should neither be excessive nor detract from the function of television as a medium of information, education, social and cultural development and entertainment.

10. No subliminal advertisements should be permitted.

Recommendation No. R (86) 14
on the drawing up of strategies to combat smoking, alcohol and drug dependence in co-operation with opinion-makers and the media

(Adopted by the Committee of Ministers on 16 October 1986
at the 400th meeting of the Ministers' Deputies)

The Committee of Ministers, under the terms of Article 15.*b* of the Statute of the Council of Europe,

Considering that the aim of the Council of Europe is to achieve a greater unity among its members and that this aim can be pursued, *inter alia*, by the adoption of common policies and regulations in the health field;

Considering that dependence on alcohol, tobacco and drugs is a major health problem, involving social, mental and pathological aspects;

Recalling the following recommendations: No. R (82) 4 on the prevention of alcohol-related problems, especially among young people; No. R (82) 5 concerning the prevention of drug dependence and the special role of education for health; and No. R (84) 3 on principles relating to television advertising;

Considering the need for a flexible policy of information and education, together with legislative, regulatory and economic measures, to encourage healthy lifestyles and reduce risk factors, and the key role which the media and other opinion-makers can have in reinforcing public awareness and acceptance of health education policies and other measures,

Recommends governments of member states to take account of the guidelines set out in the appendix to this recommendation, when promoting the development of strategies to combat smoking, excessive consumption of alcohol and drug dependence, in co-operation with opinion-makers and the media and when stressing the responsibility of those bodies in the shaping of public attitudes towards health.

Appendix to Recommendation No. R (86) 14

Guidelines for the development of strategies

Objectives

1.   The main objectives of health information and health education strategies should be to encourage healthy lifestyles, to promote a healthy environment and to reduce risk factors.

Policies

2.   A policy for health information and education should be carried out within a co-ordinated and integrated health-care system and, together with legislative, economic and other measures, should form part of a broader policy framework giving priority to underprivileged social groups.

3.   Such policies should be flexible and capable of implementation at local level in order to increase community and individual responsibility. They should also take into account the differences, between social groups and the need to give information which appeals to underprivileged sections of the population.

Co-ordination

4.   A co-ordination strategy should seek to involve various institutions, such as schools, public and private welfare and health institutions, the family, voluntary institutions, sport and recreation associations, as well as the media.

5.   Co-ordination should take place:

– horizontally, between institutions, services and individuals at the same level;
– vertically, between institutions, services and individuals operating at local, regional and national level;
– in time, to cover the individual's whole life-span.

Potential role of the media

6.   Efforts to collaborate with the media must respect the fundamental principles of independence and freedom of expression common to all member states and take into account the political, commercial and financial environment in which the media operate, which will vary from country to country. The aim should be to involve the media in stimulating the participation of the community and individuals in the promotion of their own health, and in strengthening the impact of educational campaigns aimed at the general public. Collaboration ought to extend to media participation in the definition and development of strategies.

7.   As far as possible, it is important to minimise contradictions between information disseminated by the media and the policies of health authorities. In particular, care should be taken to ensure that such information does not have the effect of suggesting that those who consume tobacco, or alcohol, or illicit drugs, are to be admired or copied, rather than those who do not.

8.   Public authorities and, in particular, health authorities, ought to provide the media with data needed to fulfil their function as a source of information. The information should be supplied in an appropriate form and reduced to its essentials so that the message is clear and comprehensible to the public.

9.   Ways should be considered of ensuring the expertise of individual journalists, for example through seminars or training courses or through the preparation of guide-

lines and reference materials (such as terminology). Encouragement should be given to the setting up of associations of journalists specialising in health.

Specific strategies

Tobacco

10. Strategies for discouraging the consumption of tobacco should essentially seek to :

– dissuade people, particularly young people, from beginning to smoke ;
– persuade smokers to stop smoking, or reduce their consumption.

Useful measures include :

– a ban on smoking in public places, school and hospitals, public transport, etc.;
– discouraging it in firms, offices, etc.;
– warnings on tobacco products.

Alcohol

11. Strategies aimed at reducing the consumption of alcohol should take into account the factors, such as economic and commercial interests, which are likely to constitute an obstacle to achieving the desired objectives. These objectives will include :

– promoting a moderate and responsible attitude, in particular in the working, school, military and sporting environments ;
– informing the public at large of the risks linked to alcohol abuse, particularly amongst pregnant women and young people :
– alerting the media to the implications of the way in which they portray the consumption of alcohol.

Drug addiction

12. Strategies for combating drug addiction should take account of the complexity of this phenomenon and the profound social isolation and maladjustment of many addicts who are victims in need of protection and not public curiosity. Information is needed at the local level for young people and their families, teachers and medical staff. Other measures may include restrictions on the distribution to young people of audiovisual or other material encouraging the use of drugs.

Evaluation

13. Health education campaigns and information programmes undertaken within the above framework should provide for a process of evaluation, with which the media should be associated, to make sure at least that the contents of the campaign have been accepted by the general public. Such evaluations should also take into account the risks relating to the different ways in which educational messages or information regarding health are perceived by different social groups. The results of the evaluation should be used for the planning of further campaigns.

Mediators

14. The health professions, teaching staff and socio-educational workers play a cardinal role in the dissemination of health information and should, as a matter of priority, be trained and kept informed regarding techniques and the most recent progress in child and adult health education.

15. Adequate means should be available to encourage and facilitate co-operation between those imparting information and consumer associations, trade unions, youth

movements and other non-governmental organisations interested in health and environmental problems, and to secure the active participation of all concerned. Co-operation might take the form of joint project teams to plan, execute and evaluate different campaigns. Opinion-leaders and representatives from these groups should be offered appropriate training where necessary.

16.   The introduction of a national prize should be considered in order to encourage and reward individuals or institutions which have made a major contribution to the development or implementation of strategies to combat dependence on tobacco, alcohol and drugs in line with the principles embodied in this recommendation.

Regulation of marketing and promotion

17.   A responsible policy should be implemented concerning the rules and regulations pertaining to the promotion and commercialisation of tobacco, alcohol and pharmaceutical products; where possible, voluntary co-operation with the producers should form part of this policy.

18.   Consideration should be given to policies which strictly limit all forms of promotion of tobacco and alcohol, not excluding the possibility of total prohibition in some cases, and to measures which prevent inappropriate promotion of drugs.

Recommendation No. R (89) 7
concerning principles on the distribution of videograms having a violent, brutal or pornographic content

(Adopted by the Committee of Ministers on 27 April 1989
at the 425th meeting of the Ministers' Deputies)

The Committee of Ministers, under the terms of Article 15.*b* of the Statute of the Council of Europe,

Considering that the aim of the Council of Europe is the achievement of greater unity between its members for the purpose of safeguarding and realising the ideals and principles which are their common heritage;

Bearing in mind the Convention for the Protection of Human Rights and Fundamental Freedoms, in particular Articles 8 and 10 thereof;

Recalling its commitment to freedom of expression and the free circulation of information and ideas, to which it gave expression, in particular, in its declaration of 29 April 1982;

Recalling Resolution No. 5 on the distribution of video-cassettes portraying violence and brutality adopted by the 4th Conference of European Ministers responsible for Cultural Affairs (Berlin, 23-25 May 1984);

Bearing in mind Recommendation 963 (1983) of the Parliamentary Assembly on cultural and educational means of reducing violence;

Recalling Recommendation 996 (1984) of the Parliamentary Assembly on Council of Europe work relating to the media, which stresses the need for action concerning in particular the quality of programme content and measures to regulate the distribution of video-cassettes portraying violence and brutality likely to have a pernicious influence on children and adolescents;

Having regard also to the final text of the 1st Conference of European Ministers responsible for Youth (Strasbourg, 17-19 December 1985), Recommendation 1067 (1987) of the Parliamentary Assembly on the cultural dimension of broadcasting in Europe and the conclusions and resolutions of the 16th Conference of European Ministers of Justice (Lisbon, 21-22 June 1988);

Being aware of the importance of strengthening action taken in respect of the distribution of videograms having a violent, brutal or pornographic content, as well as those which encourage drug abuse, in particular with a view to protecting minors,

1.   Recommends that the governments of the member states :

   a. take concrete measures to implement the principles set out below ;

   b. ensure, by all appropriate means, that these principles are known by the persons and bodies concerned ; and

   c. proceed to a periodical evaluation of the effective application of these principles in their internal legal orders ;

2.   Instructs the Secretary General of the Council of Europe to transmit this recommendation to the governments of those states party to the European Cultural Convention which are not members of the Council of Europe.

Principles

Scope

The following principles are designed to assist member states in strengthening their action against videograms having a violent, brutal or pornographic content – as well as those which encourage drug abuse – in particular for the purpose of protecting minors. They should be envisaged as a complement to other existing Council of Europe legal instruments.

These principles concern in particular the distribution of videograms.

1. *Systems for the distribution of videograms*

The member states should :

– encourage the creation of systems of self-regulation, or
– create classification and control systems for videograms through the professional sectors concerned or the public authorities, or
– institute systems which combine self-regulatory with classification and control systems, or any other systems compatible with national legislation.

In all cases, member states remain free to make use of criminal law and dissuasive financial and fiscal measures.

2. *Self-regulatory systems*

The member states should encourage, by appropriate means, the distributors of videograms to draw up codes of professional conduct and voluntary systems of regulation, which could comprise notably classification and control systems inspired by Principles 3 and 4 hereafter.

3. *Classification and control systems*

3.1. The member states should encourage the creation of systems of classification and control of videograms by the professional sectors concerned in the framework of self-regulatory systems, or through the public authorities. Such systems may be implemented either prior to, or following the distribution of videograms.

3.3. The classification and control systems shall involve either the issue of a free distribution certificate, a limited distribution permit specifying the videogram's distribution conditions, or possibly an outright prohibition.

3.4. Under the classification and control system, the age of the public to whom the videogram can be distributed shall be specified according to national criteria.

3.5. All classified videograms shall be registered and their material mediums (video-cassettes, videodiscs, etc.) shall display in a clear and permanent fashion the classification of the videograms and the public for whom they are intended. In the case of material mediums featuring several videograms, the member states shall take measures so that the most restrictive classification be applied.

3.6. When the video classification procedure is separate from that of cinematographic films, the member states shall look for consistency between the two, in so far as possible, but taking account of the differences between the two media.

3.7. Allowance should be made, within the classification and control system, for simplified procedures or exemption of procedures for certain types of programmes, such as material whose purpose is educational, religious or informative. These exemptions should not apply to programmes having an unduly pornographic or violent content.

3.8. The control of the distribution of videograms shall apply to the distribution of both nationally produced videograms and imported ones.

3.9. The establishment of a system designating which offers of a company should be liable for offences under the videogram classification and control system could be considered by the member states.

4. *Limitations on distribution*

4.1. Permits for limited distribution referred to in paragraph 3.3 above may include in particular:

    – a ban on commercial supplies or offers to supply to minors;
    – a ban on commercial supplies or offers to supply except at sales or rental outlets set aside for adults only;
    – a ban on advertising;
    – a ban on mail order sales.

4.2. The classification of each videogram should be specified on the packaging of the material medium and in video catalogues, advertisements, etc.

5. *Measures against offences to the classification and control systems*

5.1. The member states which have classification and control systems shall take appropriate measures to punish any infringement of these systems by dissuasive sanctions, for instance heavy fines, imprisonment, confiscation of the videograms and of the receipts gained from the unlawful distribution.

5.2. In member states where licensing exists, the authorities could envisage the suspension or withdrawal of the licence.

6. *Application of criminal law*

In conjunction with, parallel to, or independently from the application of classification and control systems, or as an alternative to such systems, the member states should consider the application of their criminal law concerning videograms is effective in dealing with the problem of videograms having a violent, brutal or pornographic content, as well as those which encourage drug abuse.

7. *Dissuasive financial and fiscal measures*

The member states should consider the possibility of taking measures of a financial and fiscal nature which discourage the production and distribution of videograms with a violent, brutal or pornographic content, as well as those which encourage drug abuse.

Recommendation No. R (90) 10
on cinema for children and adolescents

(Adopted by the Committee of Ministers on 19 April 1990
at the 438th meeting of the Ministers' Deputies)

1.   The Committee of Ministers, under the terms of Article 15.*b* of the Statute of the Council of Europe, having regard to the European Cultural Convention,

2.   Considering that the aim of the Council of Europe is to achieve a greater unity between its members, and that this aim may be achieved through common action in cultural matters;

3.   Considering that film, one of the dominant art forms of the twentieth century, has a significant and important role in articulating cultural issues and transmitting these to the world at large;

4.   Considering that the cinema has always been viewed as the best place to see films and that it serves an essential social purpose as a local pole of attraction;

5.   Considering that there is evidence that considerable cinema audiences can be found for films of cultural value;

6.   Considering that the specific developmental needs of children and adolescents gives them a distinct status as cinema audiences;

7.   Considering that the commercial sector only rarely responds to these needs in its present system of production, distribution and exhibition;

8.   Considering that whatever the provision of assistance by public authorities, it remains insufficient;

9.   Considering nevertheless that specific public measures are being taken by certain European countries including the provision of production finance for films for and/or by young people, and including the promotion of parallel distribution circuits and indirect measures designed to encourage film exhibition;

10. Considering also the development of policies designed to introduce young people to film in education systems;

11. Considering that cinema and television are substantially interdependent and that current indigenous production levels in Europe are inadequate at present to meet television's needs for films for young people;

12. Considering that generally there are benefits in providing a satisfactory cinema experience for young people, particularly because they comprise the potential adult audience of the future;

13. Considering that further studies could establish whether the creation of pooling arrangements or similar developments within the cinema trade might provide some financial risk cover for commercial producers and distributors;

14. Wishing to lay down appropriate measures, having regard in particular to the specific responsibilities of the Council of Europe for the welfare and development of children and adolescents,

15. Recommends that the governments of member states:

   a. encourage the adoption of appropriate arrangements of co-operation between film and television in the co-production of films for young people;

   b. promote close co-operation between the film industry and educational establishments;

   c. study and introduce all practical measures to promote the sub-titling and dubbing of films, with special regard to the needs of young people;

   d. ensure the adequate provision of auditoriums and programming for the exhibition of films for young people;

   e. encourage film shows for young people by providing financial support and/or tax benefits in order to minimise the financial disincentives of this form of exhibition;

   f. study and encourage the adoption of the best methods of ensuring the widest media coverage possible in this field;

   g. taking into account the established models already existing in certain countries, introduce systematic cinema and media education in schools and other institutions for young people;

   h. establish measures to encourage co-operation between film schools, centres for training in the language of image and sound and other educational institutions for young people;

   i. encourage research to determine the types of film which would both interest young people and meet their development needs;

   j. initiate studies covering all aspects of the cinema, in order to establish effective systems for the production, distribution and financing of films for young people;

   k. encourage educational work in specific areas of the cinema for young people, including cinema clubs, video libraries, festivals, colloquies and seminars, and special production projects which involve young people's participation and creative contributions;

   l. encourage the creation of a catalogue or data bank – with the help of bodies or organisations specialised in this field – of existing films for young people which would enable them to have a better idea of what is available to them;

16. Instructs the Secretary General of the Council of Europe to transmit this recommendation to the governments of those states party to the European Cultural Convention which are not members of the Council of Europe.

Recommendation No. R (92) 19
on video games with a racist content

(Adopted by the Committee of Ministers on 19 October 1992
at the 482nd meeting of the Ministers' Deputies)

The Committee of Ministers, under the terms of Article 15.*b* of the Statute of the Council of Europe,

Considering that the aim of the Council of Europe is to achieve a greater unity between its members, particularly for the purpose of safeguarding and realising the ideals and principles which are their common heritage;

Being aware that video games with a racist content, whose existence in member countries is unfortunately beyond doubt, convey a message of aggressive nationalism, ethnocentrism, xenophobia, anti-Semitism or intolerance in general, concealed behind or combined with violence or mockery;

Considering therefore that such games cannot be tolerated in democratic societies, which respect, *inter alia*, the right to be different, whether that difference be racial, religious or other;

Convinced that it is all the more necessary to take measures designed to put an end to the production and distribution of these games as they are used mainly by young people;

Recalling the terms of its Resolution (68) 30 relating to measures to be taken against incitement to racial, national and religious hatred and its Resolution (72) 22 on the suppression of and guaranteeing against unjustifiable discrimination;

Bearing in mind the Declaration regarding intolerance – a threat to democracy which it adopted on 14 May 1981;

Having regard to Recommendation No. R (89) 7 concerning principles on the distribution of videograms having a violent, brutal or pornographic content, and the European Convention on Transfrontier Television (European Treaty Series, No. 132),

Recommends that the governments of member states:

a. review the scope of their legislation in the fields of racial discrimination and hatred, violence and the protection of young people, in order to ensure that it applies without restriction to the production and distribution of video games with a racist content;

b. treat video games as mass media for the purposes of the application, *inter alia*, of Recommendation No. R (89) 7 concerning principles relating to the distribution of videograms having a violent, brutal or pornographic content, and of the European Convention on Transfrontier Television (European Treaty Series, No. 132).

Conventions and Charter
of the Council of Europe

European Convention
on the Adoption of Children

Preamble[1]

The member states of the Council of Europe, signatory hereto,

Considering that the aim of the Council of Europe is to achieve a greater unity between its members for the purpose, among others, of facilitating their social progress;

Considering that, although the institution of the adoption of children exists in all member countries of the Council of Europe, there are in those countries differing views as to the principles which should govern adoption and differences in the procedure for effecting, and the legal consequences of, adoption; and

Considering that the acceptance of common principles and practices with respect to the adoption of children would help to reduce the difficulties caused by those differences and at the same time promote the welfare of children who are adopted,

Have agreed as follows:

Part I – Undertakings and field of application

Article 1

Each Contracting Party undertakes to ensure the conformity of its law with the provisions of Part II of this Convention and to notify the Secretary General of the Council of Europe of the measures taken for that purpose.

Article 2

Each Contracting Party undertakes to give consideration to the provisions set out in Part III of this Convention, and if it gives effect, or if, having given effect, it ceases to give effect to any of these provisions, it shall notify the Secretary General of the Council of Europe.

Article 3

This Convention applies only to legal adoption of a child who, at the time when the adopter applies to adopt him, has not attained the age of 18, is not and has not been married, and is not deemed in law to have come of age.

---

1. European Treaty Series, No. 58. The Convention was opened for signature in Strasbourg, 24 April 1967.

Part II – Essential provisions

Article 4

An adoption shall be valid only if it is granted by a judicial or administrative authority (hereinafter referred to as the "competent authority").

Article 5

1   Subject to paragraphs 2 to 4 of this article, an adoption shall not be granted unless at least the following consents to the adoption have been given and not withdrawn:

  a   the consent of the mother and, where the child is legitimate, the father; or if there is neither father nor mother to consent, the consent of any person or body who may be entitled in their place to exercise their parental rights in that respect;

  b   the consent of the spouse of the adopter.

2   The competent authority shall not:

  a   dispense with the consent of any person mentioned in paragraph 1 of this article, or

  b   overrule the refusal to consent of any person or body mentioned in the said paragraph 1,

save on exceptional grounds determined by law.

3   If the father or mother is deprived of his or her parental rights in respect of the child, or at least of the right to consent to an adoption, the law may provide that it shall not be necessary to obtain his or her consent.

4   A mother's consent to the adoption of her child shall not be accepted unless it is given at such time after the birth of the child, not being less than six weeks, as may be prescribed by law, or, if no such time has been prescribed, at such time as, in the opinion of the competent authority, will have enabled her to recover sufficiently from the effects of giving birth to the child.

5   For the purposes of this article "father" and "mother" mean the persons who are according to law the parents of the child.

Article 6

1   The law shall not permit a child to be adopted except by either two persons married to each other, whether they adopt simultaneously or successively, or by one person.

2   The law shall not permit a child to be again adopted save in one or more of the following circumstances:

  a   where the child is adopted by the spouse of the adopter;

  b   where the former adopter has died;

c   where the former adoption has been annulled;

d   where the former adoption has come to an end.

Article 7

1   A child may be adopted only if the adopter has attained the minimum age prescribed for the purpose, this age being neither less than 21 nor more than 35 years.

2   The law may, however, permit the requirement as to the minimum age to be waived:

a   when the adopter is the child's father or mother, or

b   by reason of exceptional circumstances.

Article 8

1   The competent authority shall not grant an adoption unless it is satisfied that the adoption will be in the interest of the child.

2   In each case the competent authority shall pay particular attention to the importance of the adoption providing the child with a stable and harmonious home.

3   As a general rule, the competent authority shall not be satisfied as aforesaid if the difference in age between the adopter and the child is less than the normal difference in age between parents and their children.

Article 9

1   The competent authority shall not grant an adoption until appropriate enquiries have been made concerning the adopter, the child and his family.

2   The enquiries, to the extent appropriate in each case, shall concern, *inter alia*, the following matters:

a   the personality, health and means of the adopter, particulars of his home and household and his ability to bring up the child;

b   why the adopter wishes to adopt the child;

c   where only one of two spouses of the same marriage applies to adopt a child, why the other spouse does not join in the application;

d   the mutual suitability of the child and the adopter, and the length of time that the child has been in his care and possession;

e   the personality and health of the child, and subject to any limitations imposed by law, his antecedents;

f   the views of the child with respect to the proposed adoption;

g   the religious persuasion, if any, of the adopter and of the child.

3   These enquiries shall be entrusted to a person or body recognised for that purpose by law or by a judicial or administrative body. They shall, as far as practicable, be made by social workers who are qualified in this field as a result of either their training or their experience.

4   The provisions of this article shall not affect the power or duty of the competent authority to obtain any information or evidence, whether or not within the scope of these enquiries, which it considers likely to be of assistance.

Article 10

1   Adoption confers on the adopter in respect of the adopted person the rights and obligations of every kind that a father or mother has in respect of a child born in lawful wedlock.

Adoption confers on the adopted person in respect of the adopter the rights and obligations of every kind that a child born in lawful wedlock has in respect of his father or mother.

2   When the rights and obligations referred to in paragraph 1 of this article are created, any rights and obligations of the same kind existing between the adopted person and his father or mother or any other person or body shall cease to exist. Nevertheless, the law may provide that the spouse of the adopter retains his rights and obligations in respect of the adopted person if the latter is his legitimate, illegitimate or adopted child.

In addition the law may preserve the obligation of the parents to maintain (in the sense of l'obligation d'entretenir and l'obligation alimentaire) or set up in life or provide a dowry for the adopted person if the adopter does not discharge any such obligation.

3   As a general rule, means shall be provided to enable the adopted person to acquire the surname of the adopter either in substitution for, or in addition to, his own.

4   If the parent of a child born in lawful wedlock has a right to the enjoyment of that child's property, the adopter's right to the enjoyment of the adopted person's property may, notwithstanding paragraph 1 of this article, be restricted by law.

5   In matters of succession, in so far as the law of succession gives a child born in lawful wedlock a right to share in the estate of his father or mother, an adopted child shall, for the like purposes, be treated as if he were a child of the adopter born in lawful wedlock.

Article 11

1   Where the adopted child does not have, in the case of an adoption by one person, the same nationality as the adopter, or in the case of an adoption by a married couple, their common nationality, the

Contracting Party of which the adopter or adopters are nationals shall facilitate acquisition of its nationality by the child.

2 A loss of nationality which could result from an adoption shall be conditional upon possession or acquisition of another nationality.

Article 12

1 The number of children who may be adopted by an adopter shall not be restricted by law.

2 A person who has, or is able to have, a child born in lawful wedlock, shall not on that account be prohibited by law from adopting a child.

3 If adoption improves the legal position of a child, a person shall not be prohibited by law from adopting his own child not born in lawful wedlock.

Article 13

1 Before an adopted person comes of age the adoption may be revoked only by a decision of a judicial or administrative authority on serious grounds, and only if revocation on that ground is permitted by law.

2 The preceding paragraph shall not affect the case of:

a an adoption which is null and void;

b an adoption coming to an end where the adopted person becomes the legitimated child of the adopter.

Article 14

When the enquiries made pursuant to Articles 8 and 9 of this Convention relate to a person who lives or has lived in the territory of another Contracting Party, that Contracting Party shall, if a request for information is made, promptly endeavour to secure that the information requested is provided. The authorities may communicate directly with each other for this purpose.

Article 15

Provision shall be made to prohibit any improper financial advantage arising from a child being given up for adoption.

Article 16

Each Contracting Party shall retain the option of adopting provisions more favourable to the adopted child.

Part III – Supplementary provisions

Article 17

An adoption shall not be granted until the child has been in the care of the adopters for a period long enough to enable a reasonable estimate to be made by the competent authority as to their future relations if the adoption were granted.

Article 18

The public authorities shall ensure the promotion and proper functioning of public or private agencies to which those who wish to adopt a child or to cause a child to be adopted may go for help and advice.

Article 19

The social and legal aspects of adoption shall be included in the curriculum for the training of social workers.

Article 20

1 Provision shall be made to enable an adoption to be completed without disclosing to the child's family the identity of the adopter.

2 Provision shall be made to require or permit adoption proceedings to take place in camera.

3 The adopter and the adopted person shall be able to obtain a document which contains extracts from the public records attesting the fact, date and place of birth of the adopted person, but not expressly revealing the fact of adoption or the identity of his former parents.

4 Public records shall be kept and, in any event, their contents reproduced in such a way as to prevent persons who do not have a legitimate interest from learning the fact that a person has been adopted or, if that is disclosed, the identity of his former parents.

Part IV – Final clauses

Article 21

1 This Convention shall be open to signature by the member states of the Council of Europe. It shall be subject to ratification or acceptance. Instruments of ratification or acceptance shall be deposited with the Secretary General of the Council of Europe.

2 This Convention shall enter into force three months after the date of the deposit of the third instrument of ratification or acceptance.

3 In respect of a signatory state ratifying or accepting subsequently, the Convention shall come into force three months after the date of the deposit of its instrument of ratification or acceptance.

Article 22

1 After the entry into force of this Convention, the Committee of Ministers of the Council of Europe may invite any non-member state to accede thereto.

2 Such accession shall be effected by depositing with the Secretary General of the Council of Europe an instrument of accession which shall take effect three months after the date of its deposit.

Article 23

1 Any Contracting Party may, at the time of signature or when depositing its instrument of ratification, acceptance or accession, specify the territory or territories to which this Convention shall apply.

2 Any Contracting Party may, when depositing its instrument of ratification, acceptance or accession or at any later date, by declaration addressed to the Secretary General of the Council of Europe, extend this Convention to any other territory or territories specified in the declaration and for whose international relations it is responsible or on whose behalf it is authorised to give undertakings.

3 Any declaration made in pursuance of the preceding paragraph may, in respect of any territory mentioned in such declaration, be withdrawn according to the procedure laid down in Article 27 of this Convention.

Article 24

1 Any Contracting Party whose law provides more than one form of adoption shall have the right to apply the provisions of Article 10, paragraphs 1, 2, 3 and 4, and Article 12, paragraphs 2 and 3, of this Convention to one only of such forms.

2 The Contracting Party exercising this right, shall, at the time of signature or when depositing its instrument of ratification, acceptance or accession, or when making a declaration in accordance with paragraph 2 of Article 23 of this Convention, notify the Secretary General of the Council of Europe thereof and indicate the way in which it has been exercised.

3 Such Contracting Party may terminate the exercise of this right and shall give notice thereof to the Secretary General of the Council of Europe.

Article 25

1 Any Contracting Party may, at the time of signature or when depositing its instrument of ratification, acceptance or accession, or when making a declaration in accordance with paragraph 2 of

Article 23 of this Convention, make not more than two reservations in respect of the provisions of Part II of the Convention.

Reservations of a general nature shall not be permitted; each reservation may not affect more than one provision.

A reservation shall be valid for five years from the entry into force of this Convention for the Contracting Party concerned. It may be renewed for successive periods of five years by means of a declaration addressed to the Secretary General of the Council of Europe before the expiration of each period.

2 Any Contracting Party may wholly or partly withdraw a reservation it has made in accordance with the foregoing paragraph by means of a declaration addressed to the Secretary General of the Council of Europe, which shall become effective as from the date of its receipt.

Article 26

Each Contracting Party shall notify the Secretary General of the Council of Europe of the names and addresses of the authorities to which requests under Article 14 may be addressed.

Article 27

1 This Convention shall remain in force indefinitely.

2 Any Contracting Party may, in so far as it is concerned, denounce this Convention by means of a notification addressed to the Secretary General of the Council of Europe.

3 Such denunciation shall take effect six months after the date of receipt by the Secretary General of such notification.

Article 28

The Secretary General of the Council of Europe shall notify the member states of the Council and any state which has acceded to this Convention of:

a any signature;

b any deposit of an instrument of ratification, acceptance or accession;

c any date of entry into force of this Convention in accordance with Article 21 thereof;

d any notification received in pursuance of the provisions of Article 1;

e any notification received in pursuance of the provisions of Article 2;

f any declaration received in pursuance of the provisions of paragraphs 2 and 3 of Article 23;

g any information received in pursuance of the provisions of paragraphs 2 and 3 of Article 24;

h any reservation made in pursuance of the provisions of paragraph 1 of Article 25;

i the renewal of any reservation carried out in pursuance of the provisions of paragraph 1 of Article 25;

j the withdrawal of any reservation carried out in pursuance of the provisions of paragraph 2 of Article 25;

k any notification received in pursuance of the provisions of Article 26;

l any notification received in pursuance of the provisions of Article 27 and the date on which denunciation takes effect.

In witness whereof the undersigned, being duly authorised thereto, have signed this Convention.

Done at Strasbourg, this 24th day of April 1967, in English and in French, both texts being equally authoritative, in a single copy which shall remain deposited in the archives of the Council of Europe. The Secretary General of the Council of Europe shall transmit certified copies to each of the signatory and acceding states.

European Convention
on the Legal Status of Children
Born out of Wedlock

The member states of the Council of Europe, signatory hereto,[1]

Considering that the aim of the Council of Europe is to achieve a greater unity between its members, in particular by the adoption of common rules in the field of law;

Noting that in a great number of member states efforts have been, or are being, made to improve the legal status of children born out of wedlock by reducing the differences between their legal status and that of children born in wedlock which are to the legal or social disadvantage of the former;

Recognising that wide disparities in the laws of member states in this field still exist;

Believing that the situation of children born out of wedlock should be improved and that the formulation of certain common rules concerning their legal status would assist this objective and at the same time would contribute to a harmonisation of the laws of the member states in this field;

Considering however that it is necessary to allow progressive stages for those states which consider themselves unable to adopt immediately certain rules of this Convention,

Have agreed as follows :

Article 1

Each Contracting Party undertakes to ensure the conformity of its law with the provisions of this Convention and to notify the Secretary General of the Council of Europe of the measures taken for that purpose.

Article 2

Maternal affiliation of every child born out of wedlock shall be based solely on the fact of the birth of the child.

Article 3

Paternal affiliation of every child born out of wedlock may be evidenced or established by voluntary recognition or by judicial decision.

---

1. European Treaty Series, No. 85. The Convention was opened for signature in Strasbourg, 15 October 1975.

Article 4

The voluntary recognition of paternity may not be opposed or contested in so far as the internal law provides for these procedures unless the person seeking to recognise or having recognised the child is not the biological father.

Article 5

In actions relating to paternal affiliation scientific evidence which may help to establish or disprove paternity shall be admissible.

Article 6

1 The father and mother of a child born out of wedlock shall have the same obligation to maintain the child as if it were born in wedlock.

2 Where a legal obligation to maintain a child born in wedlock falls on certain members of the family of the father or mother, this obligation shall also apply for the benefit of a child born out of wedlock.

Article 7

1 Where the affiliation of a child born out of wedlock has been established as regards both parents, parental authority may not be attributed automatically to the father alone.

2 There shall be power to transfer parental authority; cases of transfer shall be governed by the internal law.

Article 8

Where the father or mother of a child born out of wedlock does not have parental authority over or the custody of the child, that parent may obtain a right of access to the child in appropriate cases.

Article 9

A child born out of wedlock shall have the same right of succession in the estate of its father and its mother and of a member of its father's or mother's family, as if it had been born in wedlock.

Article 10

The marriage between the father and mother of a child born out of wedlock shall confer on the child the legal status of a child born in wedlock.

Article 11

1 This Convention shall be open to signature by the member states of the Council of Europe. It shall be subject to ratification, acceptance or approval. Instruments of ratification, acceptance or approval shall be deposited with the Secretary General of the Council of Europe.

2 This Convention shall enter into force three months after the date of the deposit of the third instrument of ratification, acceptance or approval.

3 In respect of a signatory state ratifying, accepting or approving subsequently, the Convention shall come into force three months after the date of the deposit of its instrument of ratification, acceptance or approval.

Article 12

1 After the entry into force of this Convention, the Committee of Ministers of the Council of Europe may invite any non-member state to accede to this Convention.

2 Such accession shall be effected by depositing with the Secretary General of the Council of Europe an instrument of accession which shall take effect three months after the date of its deposit.

Article 13

1 Any state may, at the time of signature, or when depositing its instrument of ratification, acceptance, approval or accession, specify the territory or territories to which this Convention shall apply.

2 Any state may, when depositing its instrument of ratification, acceptance, approval or accession or at any later date, by declaration addressed to the Secretary General of the Council of Europe, extend this Convention to any other territory or territories specified in the declaration and for whose international relations it is responsible or on whose behalf it is authorised to give undertakings.

3 Any declaration made in pursuance of the preceding paragraph may, in respect of any territory mentioned in such declaration, be withdrawn according to the procedure laid down in Article 15 of this Convention.

Article 14

1 Any state may, at the time of signature, or when depositing its instrument of ratification, acceptance, approval or accession or when making a declaration in accordance with paragraph 2 of Article 13 of this Convention, make not more than three reservations in respect of the provisions of Articles 2 to 10 of the

Convention. Reservations of a general nature shall not be permitted; each reservation may not affect more than one provision.

2 A reservation shall be valid for five years from the entry into force of this Convention for the Contracting Party concerned. It may be renewed for successive periods of five years by means of a declaration addressed to the Secretary General of the Council of Europe before the expiration of each period.

3 Any Contracting Party may wholly or partly withdraw a reservation it has made in accordance with the foregoing paragraphs by means of a declaration addressed to the Secretary General of the Council of Europe, which shall become effective as from the date of its receipt.

Article 15

1 Any Contracting Party may, in so far as it is concerned, denounce this Convention by means of a notification addressed to the Secretary General of the Council of Europe.

2 Such denunciation shall take effect six months after the date of receipt by the Secretary General of such notification.

Article 16

The Secretary General of the Council of Europe shall notify the member States of the Council and any state which has acceded to this Convention of:

a any signature;

b any deposit of an instrument of ratification, acceptance, approval or accession;

c any date of entry into force of this Convention in accordance with Article 11 thereof;

d any notification received in pursuance of the provisions of Article 1;

e any declaration received in pursuance of the provisions of paragraphs 2 and 3 of Article 13;

f any reservation made in pursuance of the provisions of paragraph 1 of Article 14;

g the renewal of any reservation carried out in pursuance of the provisions of paragraph 2 of Article 14;

h the withdrawal of any reservation carried out in pursuance of the provisions of paragraph 3 of Article 14;

i any notification received in pursuance of the provisions of Article 15 and the date on which denunciation takes effect.

In witness whereof, the undersigned, being duly authorised thereto, have signed this Convention.

Done at Strasbourg, this 15th day of October 1975, in English and in French, both texts being equally authoritative, in a single copy which shall remain deposited in the archives of the Council of Europe. The Secretary General of the Council of Europe shall transmit certified copies to each of the signatory and acceding states.

European Convention
on Recognition and Enforcement
of Decisions concerning Custody
of Children and on Restoration
of Custody of Children

The member states of the Council of Europe, signatory hereto,[1]

Recognising that in the member states of the Council of Europe the welfare of the child is of overriding importance in reaching decisions concerning his custody;

Considering that the making of arrangements to ensure that decisions concerning the custody of a child can be more widely recognised and enforced will provide greater protection of the welfare of children;

Considering it desirable, with this end in view, to emphasise that the right of access of parents is a normal corollary to the right of custody;

Noting the increasing number of cases where children have been improperly removed across an international frontier and the difficulties of securing adequate solutions to the problems caused by such cases;

Desirous of making suitable provision to enable the custody of children which has been arbitrarily interrupted to be restored;

Convinced of the desirability of making arrangements for this purpose answering to different needs and different circumstances;

Desiring to establish legal co-operation between their authorities,

Have agreed as follows:

Article 1

For the purposes of this Convention:

a *child* means a person of any nationality, so long as he is under 16 years of age and has not the right to decide on his own place of residence under the law of his habitual residence, the law of his nationality or the internal law of the state addressed;

b *authority* means a judicial or administrative authority;

c *decision* relating to custody means a decision of an authority in so far as it relates to the care of the person of the child, including the right to decide on the place of his residence, or to the right of access to him;

---

1. European Treaty Series, No. 105. The Convention was opened for signature in Luxembourg, 20 May 1980.

d *improper removal* means the removal of a child across an international frontier in breach of a decision relating to his custody which has been given in a Contracting State and which is enforceable in such a state; improper removal also includes:

  i the failure to return a child across an international frontier at the end of a period of the exercise of the right of access to this child or at the end of any other temporary stay in a territory other than that where the custody is exercised;

  ii a removal which is subsequently declared unlawful within the meaning of Article 12.

Part 1 – Central authorities

Article 2

1 Each Contracting State shall appoint a central authority to carry out the functions provided for by this Convention.

2 Federal states and states with more than one legal system shall be free to appoint more than one central authority and shall determine the extent of their competence.

3 The Secretary General of the Council of Europe shall be notified of any appointment under this article.

Article 3

1 The central authorities of the Contracting States shall co-operate with each other and promote co-operation between the competent authorities in their respective countries. They shall act with all necessary despatch.

2 With a view to facilitating the operation of this Convention, the central authorities of the Contracting States:

  a shall secure the transmission of requests for information coming from competent authorities and relating to legal or factual matters concerning pending proceedings;

  b shall provide each other on request with information about their law relating to the custody of children and any changes in that law;

  c shall keep each other informed of any difficulties likely to arise in applying the Convention and, as far as possible, eliminate obstacles to its application.

Article 4

1 Any person who has obtained in a Contracting State a decision relating to the custody of a child and who wishes to have that decision recognised or enforced in another Contracting State may submit an application for this purpose to the central authority in any Contracting State.

2 The application shall be accompanied by the documents mentioned in Article 13.

3 The central authority receiving the application, if it is not the central authority in the state addressed, shall send the documents directly and without delay to that central authority.

4 The central authority receiving the application may refuse to intervene where it is manifestly clear that the conditions laid down by this Convention are not satisfied.

5 The central authority receiving the application shall keep the applicant informed without delay of the progress of his application.

Article 5

1 The central authority in the state addressed shall take or cause to be taken without delay all steps which it considers to be appropriate, if necessary by instituting proceedings before its competent authorities, in order:
   a to discover the whereabouts of the child;
   b to avoid, in particular by any necessary provisional measures, prejudice to the interests of the child or of the applicant;
   c to secure the recognition or enforcement of the decision;
   d to secure the delivery of the child to the applicant where enforcement is granted;
   e to inform the requesting authority of the measures taken and their results.

2 Where the central authority in the state addressed has reason to believe that the child is in the territory of another Contracting State it shall send the documents directly and without delay to the central authority of that state.

3 With the exception of the cost of repatriation, each Contracting State undertakes not to claim any payment from an applicant in respect of any measures taken under paragraph 1 of this article by the central authority of that state on the applicant's behalf, including the costs of proceedings and, where applicable, the costs incurred by the assistance of a lawyer.

4 If recognition or enforcement is refused, and if the central authority of the state addressed considers that it should comply with a request by the applicant to bring in that state proceedings concerning the substance of the case, that authority shall use its best endeavours to secure the representation of the applicant in the proceedings under conditions no less favourable than those available to a person who is resident in and a national of that state and for this purpose it may, in particular, institute proceedings before its competent authorities.

Article 6

1 Subject to any special agreements made between the central authorities concerned and to the provisions of paragraph 3 of this article:

   a communications to the central authority of the state addressed shall be made in the official language or in one of the official languages of that state or be accompanied by a translation into that language;

   b the central authority of the state addressed shall nevertheless accept communications made in English or in French or accompanied by a translation into one of these languages.

2 Communications coming from the central authority of the state addressed, including the results of enquiries carried out, may be made in the official language or one of the official languages of that state or in English or French.

3 A Contracting State may exclude wholly or partly the provisions of paragraph 1.b of this article. When a Contracting State has made this reservation any other Contracting State may also apply the reservation in respect of that state.

Part II – Recognition and enforcement of decisions and restoration of custody of children

Article 7

A decision relating to custody given in a Contracting State shall be recognised and, where it is enforceable in the state of origin, made enforceable in every other Contracting State.

Article 8

1 In the case of an improper removal, the central authority of the state addressed shall cause steps to be taken forthwith to restore the custody of the child where:

   a at the time of the institution of the proceedings in the state where the decision was given or at the time of the improper removal, if earlier, the child and his parents had as their sole nationality the nationality of that state and the child had his habitual residence in the territory of that state, and

   b a request for the restoration was made to a central authority within a period of six months from the date of the improper removal.

2 If, in accordance with the law of the state addressed, the requirements of paragraph 1 of this article cannot be complied with without recourse to a judicial authority, none of the grounds of refusal specified in this Convention shall apply to the judicial proceedings.

3 Where there is an agreement officially confirmed by a competent authority between the person having the custody of the child and another person to allow the other person a right of access, and the child, having been taken abroad, has not been restored at the end of the agreed period to the person having the custody, custody of the child shall be restored in accordance with paragraphs 1.b and 2 of this article. The same shall apply in the case of a decision of the competent authority granting such a right to a person who has not the custody of the child.

Article 9

1 In cases of improper removal, other than those dealt with in Article 8, in which an application has been made to a central authority within a period of six months from the date of the removal, recognition and enforcement may be refused only if:

a in the case of a decision given in the absence of the defendant or his legal representative, the defendant was not duly served with the document which instituted the proceedings or an equivalent document in sufficient time to enable him to arrange his defence; but such a failure to effect service cannot constitute a ground for refusing recognition or enforcement where service was not effected because the defendant had concealed his whereabouts from the person who instituted the proceedings in the state of origin;

b in the case of a decision given in the absence of the defendant or his legal representative, the competence of the authority giving the decision was not founded:

i on the habitual residence of the defendant, or

ii on the last common habitual residence of the child's parents, at least one parent being still habitually resident there, or

iii on the habitual residence of the child;

c the decision is incompatible with a decision relating to custody which became enforceable in the state addressed before the removal of the child, unless the child has had his habitual residence in the territory of the requesting state for one year before his removal.

2 Where no application has been made to a central authority, the provisions of paragraph 1 of this article shall apply equally, if recognition and enforcement are requested within six months from the date of the improper removal.

3 In no circumstances may the foreign decision be reviewed as to its substance.

Article 10

1 In cases other than those covered by Articles 8 and 9, recognition and enforcement may be refused not only on the grounds provided for in Article 9 but also on any of the following grounds:

   a if it is found that the effects of the decision are manifestly incompatible with the fundamental principles of the law relating to the family and children in the state addressed;

   b if it is found that by reason of a change in the circumstances including the passage of time but not including a mere change in the residence of the child after an improper removal, the effects of the original decision are manifestly no longer in accordance with the welfare of the child;

   c if at the time when the proceedings were instituted in the state of origin:

   i the child was a national of the state addressed or was habitually resident there and no such connection existed with the state of origin;

   ii the child was a national both of the state of origin and of the state addressed and was habitually resident in the state addressed;

   d if the decision is incompatible with a decision given in the state addressed or enforceable in that state after being given in a third state, pursuant to proceedings begun before the submission of the request for recognition or enforcement, and if the refusal is in accordance with the welfare of the child.

2 In the same cases, proceedings for recognition or enforcement may be adjourned on any of the following grounds:

   a if an ordinary form of review of the original decision has been commenced;

   b if proceedings relating to the custody of the child, commenced before the proceedings in the state of origin were instituted, are pending in the state addressed;

   c if another decision concerning the custody of the child is the subject of proceedings for enforcement or of any other proceedings concerning the recognition of the decision.

Article 11

1 Decisions on rights of access and provisions of decisions relating to custody which deal with the right of access shall be recognised and enforced subject to the same conditions as other decisions relating to custody.

2 However, the competent authority of the state addressed may fix the conditions for the implementation and exercise of the right of access taking into account, in particular, undertakings given by the parties on this matter.

3 Where no decision on the right of access has been taken or where recognition or enforcement of the decision relating to custody is refused, the central authority of the state addressed may apply to its competent authorities for a decision on the right of access, if the person claiming a right of access so requests.

Article 12

Where, at the time of the removal of a child across an international frontier, there is no enforceable decision given in a Contracting state relating to his custody, the provisions of this Convention shall apply to any subsequent decision, relating to the custody of that child and declaring the removal to be unlawful, given in a Contracting state at the request of any interested person.

Part III – Procedure

Article 13

1 A request for recognition or enforcement in another Contracting state of a decision relating to custody shall be accompanied by:

   a a document authorising the central authority of the state addressed to act on behalf of the applicant or to designate another representative for that purpose;

   b a copy of the decision which satisfies the necessary conditions of authenticity;

   c in the case of a decision given in the absence of the defendant or his legal representative, a document which establishes that the defendant was duly served with the document which instituted the proceedings or an equivalent document;

   d if applicable, any document which establishes that, in accordance with the law of the state of origin, the decision is enforceable;

   e if possible, a statement indicating the whereabouts or likely whereabouts of the child in the state addressed;

   f proposals as to how the custody of the child should be restored.

2 The documents mentioned above shall, where necessary, be accompanied by a translation according to the provisions laid down in Article 6.

Article 14

Each Contracting state shall apply a simple and expeditious procedure for recognition and enforcement of decisions relating to the custody of a child. To that end it shall ensure that a request for enforcement may be lodged by simple application.

Article 15

1 Before reaching a decision under paragraph 1.b of Article 10, the authority concerned in the state addressed:

   a shall ascertain the child's views unless this is impracticable having regard in particular to his age and understanding; and

   b may request that any appropriate enquiries be carried out.

2 The cost of enquiries in any Contracting state shall be met by the authorities of the state where they are carried out.

3 Request for enquiries and the results of enquiries may be sent to the authority concerned through the central authorities.

Article 16

For the purposes of this Convention, no legalisation or any like formality may be required.

Part IV – Reservations

Article 17

1 A Contracting state may make a reservation that, in cases covered by Articles 8 and 9 or either of these articles, recognition and enforcement of decisions relating to custody may be refused on such of the grounds provided under Article 10 as may be specified in the reservation.

2 Recognition and enforcement of decisions given in a Contracting state which has made the reservation provided for in paragraph 1 of this Article may be refused in any other Contracting state on any of the additional grounds referred to in that reservation.

Article 18

A Contracting state may make a reservation that it shall not be bound by the provisions of Article 12. The provisions of this Convention shall not apply to decisions referred to in Article 12 which have been given in a Contracting state which has made such a reservation.

Part V – Other instruments

Article 19

This Convention shall not exclude the possibility of relying on any other international instrument in force between the state of origin and the state addressed or on any other law of the state addressed not derived from an international agreement for the purpose of obtaining recognition or enforcement of a decision.

Article 20

1 This Convention shall not affect any obligations which a Contracting state may have towards a non-Contracting state under an international instrument dealing with matters governed by this Convention.

2 When two or more Contracting states have enacted uniform laws in relation to custody of children or created a special system of recognition or enforcement of decisions in this field, or if they should do so in the future, they shall be free to apply, between themselves, those laws or that system in place of this Convention or any part of it. In order to avail themselves of this provision the state shall notify their decision to the Secretary General of the Council of Europe. Any alteration or revocation of this decision must also be notified.

Part VI – Final clauses

Article 21

This Convention shall be open for signature by the member states of the Council of Europe. It is subject to ratification, acceptance or approval. Instruments of ratification, acceptance or approval shall be deposited with the Secretary General of the Council of Europe.

Article 22

1 This Convention shall enter into force on the first day of the month following the expiration of a period of three months after the date on which three member states of the Council of Europe have expressed their consent to be bound by the Convention in accordance with the provisions of Article 21.

2 In respect of any member state which subsequently expresses its consent to be bound by it, the Convention shall enter into force on the first day of the month following the expiration of a period of three months after the date of the deposit of the instrument of ratification, acceptance or approval.

Article 23

1 After the entry into force of this Convention, the Committee of Ministers of the Council of Europe may invite any state not a member of the Council to accede to this Convention, by a decision taken by the majority provided for by Article 20.d of the Statute and by the unanimous vote of the representatives of the Contracting states entitled to sit on the Committee.

2 In respect of any acceding state, the Convention shall enter into force on the first day of the month following the expiration of a period of three months after the date of deposit of the instrument of accession with the Secretary General of the Council of Europe.

Article 24

1 Any state may at the time of signature or when depositing its instrument of ratification, acceptance, approval or accession, specify the territory or territories to which this Convention shall apply.

2 Any state may at any later date, by a declaration addressed to the Secretary General of the Council of Europe, extend the application of this Convention to any other territory specified in the declaration. In respect of such territory, the Convention shall enter into force on the first day of the month following the expiration of a period of three months after the date of receipt by the Secretary General of such declaration.

3 Any declaration made under the two preceding paragraphs may, in respect of any territory specified in such declaration, be withdrawn by a notification addressed to the Secretary General. The withdrawal shall become effective on the first day of the month following the expiration of a period of six months after the date of receipt of such notification by the Secretary General.

Article 25

1 A state which has two or more territorial units in which different systems of law apply in matters of custody of children and of recognition and enforcement of decisions relating to custody may, at the time of signature or when depositing its instrument of ratification, acceptance, approval or accession, declare that this Convention shall apply to all its territorial units or to one or more of them.

2 Such a state may at any later date, by a declaration addressed to the Secretary General of the Council of Europe, extend the application of this Convention to any other territorial unit specified in the declaration. In respect of such territorial unit the Convention shall enter into force on the first day of the month following the expiration of a period of three months after the date of receipt by the Secretary General of such declaration.

3 Any declaration made under the two preceding paragraphs may, in respect of any territorial unit specified in such declaration, be withdrawn by notification addressed to the Secretary General. The withdrawal shall become effective on the first day of the month following the expiration of a period of six months after the date of receipt of such notification by the Secretary General.

Article 26

1 In relation to a state which has in matters of custody two or more systems of law of territorial application:

   a reference to the law of a person's habitual residence or to the law of a person's nationality shall be construed as referring to the system of law determined by the rules in force in that state or, if there are no such rules, to the system of law with which the person concerned is most closely connected;

b   reference to the state of origin or to the state addressed shall be construed as referring, as the case may, be to the territorial unit where recognition or enforcement of the decision or restoration of custody is requested.

2   Paragraph 1.a of this Article also applies *mutatis mutandis* to states which have in matters of custody two or more systems of law of personal application.

Article 27

1   Any state may, at the time of signature or when depositing its instrument of ratification, acceptance, approval or accession, declare that it avails itself of one or more of the reservations provided for in paragraph 3 of Article 6, Article 17 and Article 18 of this Convention. No other reservation may be made.

2   Any Contracting state which has made a reservation under the preceding paragraph may wholly or partly withdraw it by means of a notification addressed to the Secretary General of the Council of Europe. The withdrawal shall take effect on the date of receipt of such notification by the Secretary General.

Article 28

At the end of the third year following the date of the entry into force of this Convention and, on his own initiative, at any time after this date, the Secretary General of the Council of Europe shall invite the representatives of the central authorities appointed by the Contracting states to meet in order to study and to facilitate the functioning of the Convention. Any member state of the Council of Europe not being a party to the Convention may be represented by an observer. A report shall be prepared on the work of each of these meetings and forwarded to the Committee of Ministers of the Council of Europe for information.

Article 29

1   Any Party may at any time denounce this Convention by means of a notification addressed to the Secretary General of the Council of Europe.

2   Such denunciation shall become effective on the first day of the month following the expiration of a period of six months after the date of receipt of the notification by the Secretary General.

Article 30

The Secretary General of the Council of Europe shall notify the member states of the Council and any state which has acceded to this Convention, of:

a any signature;

b the deposit of any instrument of ratification, acceptance, approval or accession;

c any date of entry into force of this Convention in accordance with Articles 22, 23, 24 and 25;

d any other act, notification or communication relating to this Convention.

In witness whereof the undersigned, being duly authorised thereto, have signed this Convention.

Done at Luxembourg, the 20th day of May 1980, in English and French, both texts being equally authentic, in a single copy which shall be deposited in the archives of the Council of Europe. The Secretary General of the Council of Europe shall transmit certified copies to each member state of the Council of Europe and to any state invited to accede to this Convention.

European Convention
on the Exercise of Children's Rights

Preamble[1]

The member states of the Council of Europe and the other states signatory hereto,

Considering that the aim of the Council of Europe is to achieve greater unity between its members;

Having regard to the United Nations Convention on the rights of the child and in particular Article 4 which requires states Parties to undertake all appropriate legislative, administrative and other measures for the implementation of the rights recognised in the said Convention;

Noting the contents of Recommendation 1121 (1990) of the Parliamentary Assembly on the rights of the child;

Convinced that the rights and best interests of children should be promoted and to that end children should have the opportunity to exercise their rights, in particular in family proceedings affecting them;

Recognising that children should be provided with relevant information to enable such rights and best interests to be promoted and that due weight should be given to the views of children;

Recognising the importance of the parental role in protecting and promoting the rights and best interests of children and considering that, where necessary, states should also engage in such protection and promotion;

Considering, however, that in the event of conflict it is desirable for families to try to reach agreement before bringing the matter before a judicial authority,

Have agreed as follows:

Chapter I – Scope and object of the Convention and definitions

Article 1 – Scope and object of the Convention

1 This Convention shall apply to children who have not reached the age of 18 years.

2 The object of the present Convention is, in the best interests of children, to promote their rights, to grant them procedural rights and to facilitate the exercise of these rights by ensuring that chil-

---

1. European Treaty Series, No. 160. The Convention was opened for signature in Strasbourg, 25 January 1996.

dren are, themselves or through other persons or bodies, informed and allowed to participate in proceedings affecting them before a judicial authority.

3 For the purposes of this Convention proceedings before a judicial authority affecting children are family proceedings, in particular those involving the exercise of parental responsibilities such as residence and access to children.

4 Every state shall, at the time of signature or when depositing its instrument of ratification, acceptance, approval or accession, by a declaration addressed to the Secretary General of the Council of Europe, specify at least three categories of family cases before a judicial authority to which this Convention is to apply.

5 Any Party may, by further declaration, specify additional categories of family cases to which this Convention is to apply or provide information concerning the application of Article 5, paragraph 2 of Article 9, paragraph 2 of Article 10 and Article 11.

6 Nothing in this Convention shall prevent Parties from applying rules more favourable to the promotion and the exercise of children's rights.

Article 2 – Definitions

For the purposes of this Convention:

a the term "judicial authority" means a court or an administrative authority having equivalent powers;

b the term "holders of parental responsibilities" means parents and other persons or bodies entitled to exercise some or all parental responsibilities;

c the term "representative" means a person, such as a lawyer, or a body appointed to act before a judicial authority on behalf of a child;

d the term "relevant information" means information which is appropriate to the age and understanding of the child, and which will be given to enable the child to exercise his or her rights fully unless the provision of such information were contrary to the welfare of the child.

Chapter II – Procedural measures to promote the exercise of children's rights

A. Procedural rights of a child

Article 3 – Right to be informed and to express his or her views in proceedings

A child considered by internal law as having sufficient understanding, in the case of proceedings before a judicial authority affecting

him or her, shall be granted, and shall be entitled to request, the
following rights:

a   to receive all relevant information;

b   to be consulted and express his or her views;

c   to be informed of the possible consequences of compliance
    with these views and the possible consequences of any deci-
    sion.

Article 4 – Right to apply for the appointment of a special representative

1   Subject to Article 9, the child shall have the right to apply, in per-
    son or through other persons or bodies, for a special representative
    in proceedings before a judicial authority affecting the child where
    internal law precludes the holders of parental responsibilities from
    representing the child as a result of a conflict of interest with the
    latter.

2   States are free to limit the right in paragraph 1 to children who are
    considered by internal law to have sufficient understanding.

Article 5 – Other possible procedural rights

Parties shall consider granting children additional procedural rights
in relation to proceedings before a judicial authority affecting
them, in particular:

a   the right to apply to be assisted by an appropriate person of
    their choice in order to help them express their views;

b   the right to apply themselves, or through other persons or
    bodies, for the appointment of a separate representative, in
    appropriate cases a lawyer;

c   the right to appoint their own representative;

d   the right to exercise some or all of the rights of parties to such
    proceedings.

B. Role of judicial authorities

Article 6 – Decision-making process

In proceedings affecting a child, the judicial authority, before taking a decision, shall:

a   consider whether it has sufficient information at its disposal in
    order to take a decision in the best interests of the child and,
    where necessary, it shall obtain further information, in particu-
    lar from the holders of parental responsibilities;

b   in a case where the child is considered by internal law as having
    sufficient understanding:

    –   ensure that the child has received all relevant information;

- consult the child in person in appropriate cases, if necessary privately, itself or through other persons or bodies, in a manner appropriate to his or her understanding, unless this would be manifestly contrary to the best interests of the child;
- allow the child to express his or her views;

c give due weight to the views expressed by the child.

Article 7 – Duty to act speedily

In proceedings affecting a child the judicial authority shall act speedily to avoid any unnecessary delay and procedures shall be available to ensure that its decisions are rapidly enforced. In urgent cases the judicial authority shall have the power, where appropriate, to take decisions which are immediately enforceable.

Article 8 – Acting on own motion

In proceedings affecting a child the judicial authority shall have the power to act on its own motion in cases determined by internal law where the welfare of a child is in serious danger.

Article 9 – Appointment of a representative

1 In proceedings affecting a child where, by internal law, the holders of parental responsibilities are precluded from representing the child as a result of a conflict of interest between them and the child, the judicial authority shall have the power to appoint a special representative for the child in those proceedings.

2 Parties shall consider providing that, in proceedings affecting a child, the judicial authority shall have the power to appoint a separate representative, in appropriate cases a lawyer, to represent the child.

C. Role of representatives

Article 10

1 In the case of proceedings before a judicial authority affecting a child the representative shall, unless this would be manifestly contrary to the best interests of the child:

a provide all relevant information to the child, if the child is considered by internal law as having sufficient understanding;

b provide explanations to the child if the child is considered by internal law as having sufficient understanding, concerning the possible consequences of compliance with his or her views and the possible consequences of any action by the representative;

c determine the views of the child and present these views to the judicial authority.

2 Parties shall consider extending the provisions of paragraph 1 to the holders of parental responsibilities.

D. Extension of certain provisions

Article 11

Parties shall consider extending the provisions of Articles 3, 4 and 9 to proceedings affecting children before other bodies and to matters affecting children which are not the subject of proceedings.

E. National bodies

Article 12

1 Parties shall encourage, through bodies which perform, *inter alia*, the functions set out in paragraph 2, the promotion and the exercise of children's rights.

2 The functions are as follows:
   a   to make proposals to strengthen the law relating to the exercise of children's rights;
   b   to give opinions concerning draft legislation relating to the exercise of children's rights;
   c   to provide general information concerning the exercise of children's rights to the media, the public and persons and bodies dealing with questions relating to children;
   d   to seek the views of children and provide them with relevant information.

F. Other matters

Article 13 – Mediation or other processes to resolve disputes

In order to prevent or resolve disputes or to avoid proceedings before a judicial authority affecting children, Parties shall encourage the provision of mediation or other processes to resolve disputes and the use of such processes to reach agreement in appropriate cases to be determined by Parties.

Article 14 – Legal aid and advice

Where internal law provides for legal aid or advice for the representation of children in proceedings before a judicial authority affecting them, such provisions shall apply in relation to the matters covered by Articles 4 and 9.

Article 15 – Relations with other international instruments

This Convention shall not restrict the application of any other international instrument which deals with specific issues arising in the context of the protection of children and families, and to which a Party to this Convention is, or becomes, a Party.

Chapter III – Standing Committee

Article 16 – Establishment and functions of the Standing Committee

1 A Standing Committee is set up for the purposes of this Convention.

2 The Standing Committee shall keep under review problems relating to this Convention. It may, in particular:

a consider any relevant questions concerning the interpretation or implementation of the Convention. The Standing Committee's conclusions concerning the implementation of the Convention may take the form of a recommendation; recommendations shall be adopted by a three-quarters majority of the votes cast;

b propose amendments to the Convention and examine those proposed in accordance with Article 20;

c provide advice and assistance to the national bodies having the functions under paragraph 2 of Article 12 and promote international co-operation between them.

Article 17 – Composition

1 Each Party may be represented on the Standing Committee by one or more delegates. Each Party shall have one vote.

2 Any state referred to in Article 21, which is not a Party to this Convention, may be represented in the Standing Committee by an observer. The same applies to any other state or to the European Community after having been invited to accede to the Convention in accordance with the provisions of Article 22.

3 Unless a Party has informed the Secretary General of its objection at least one month before the meeting, the Standing Committee may invite the following to attend as observers at all its meetings or at one meeting or part of a meeting:

– any state not referred to in paragraph 2 above;

– the United Nations Committee on the Rights of the Child;

– the European Community;

– any international governmental body;

– any international non-governmental body with one or more functions mentioned under paragraph 2 of Article 12;

– any national governmental or non-governmental body with one or more functions mentioned under paragraph 2 of Article 12.

4   The Standing Committee may exchange information with relevant organisations dealing with the exercise of children's rights.

Article 18 – Meetings

1   At the end of the third year following the date of entry into force of this Convention and, on his or her own initiative, at any time after this date, the Secretary General of the Council of Europe shall invite the Standing Committee to meet.

2   Decisions may only be taken in the Standing Committee if at least one-half of the Parties are present.

3   Subject to Articles 16 and 20 the decisions of the Standing Committee shall be taken by a majority of the members present.

4   Subject to the provisions of this Convention the Standing Committee shall draw up its own rules of procedure and the rules of procedure of any working party it may set up to carry out all appropriate tasks under the Convention.

Article 19 – Reports of the Standing Committee

After each meeting, the Standing Committee shall forward to the Parties and the Committee of Ministers of the Council of Europe a report on its discussions and any decisions taken.

Chapter IV – Amendments to the Convention

Article 20

1   Any amendment to the articles of this Convention proposed by a Party or the Standing Committee shall be communicated to the Secretary General of the Council of Europe and forwarded by him or her, at least two months before the next meeting of the Standing Committee, to the member states of the Council of Europe, any signatory, any Party, any state invited to sign this Convention in accordance with the provisions of Article 21 and any state or the European Community invited to accede to it in accordance with the provisions of Article 22.

2   Any amendment proposed in accordance with the provisions of the preceding paragraph shall be examined by the Standing Committee which shall submit the text adopted by a three-quarters majority of the votes cast to the Committee of Ministers for approval. After its approval, this text shall be forwarded to the Parties for acceptance.

3   Any amendment shall enter into force on the first day of the month following the expiration of a period of one month after the date on which all Parties have informed the Secretary General that they have accepted it.

Chapter V – Final clauses

Article 21 – Signature, ratification and entry into force

1　This Convention shall be open for signature by the member states of the Council of Europe and the non-member states which have participated in its elaboration.

2　This Convention is subject to ratification, acceptance or approval. Instruments of ratification, acceptance or approval shall be deposited with the Secretary General of the Council of Europe.

3　This Convention shall enter into force on the first day of the month following the expiration of a period of three months after the date on which three states, including at least two member states of the Council of Europe, have expressed their consent to be bound by the Convention in accordance with the provisions of the preceding paragraph.

4　In respect of any signatory which subsequently expresses its consent to be bound by it, the Convention shall enter into force on the first day of the month following the expiration of a period of three months after the date of the deposit of its instrument of ratification, acceptance or approval.

Article 22 – Non-member states and the European Community

1　After the entry into force of this Convention, the Committee of Ministers of the Council of Europe may, on its own initiative or following a proposal from the Standing Committee and after consultation of the Parties, invite any non-member state of the Council of Europe, which has not participated in the elaboration of the Convention, as well as the European Community to accede to this Convention by a decision taken by the majority provided for in Article 20, sub-paragraph d of the Statute of the Council of Europe, and by the unanimous vote of the representatives of the contracting states entitled to sit on the Committee of Ministers.

2　In respect of any acceding state or the European Community, the Convention shall enter into force on the first day of the month following the expiration of a period of three months after the date of deposit of the instrument of accession with the Secretary General of the Council of Europe.

Article 23 – Territorial application

1　Any state may, at the time of signature or when depositing its instrument of ratification, acceptance, approval or accession, specify the territory or territories to which this Convention shall apply.

2　Any Party may, at any later date, by a declaration addressed to the Secretary General of the Council of Europe, extend the application of this Convention to any other territory specified in the declaration and for whose international relations it is responsible or on whose behalf it is authorised to give undertakings. In respect of such territory the Convention shall enter into force on the first day of the month following the expiration of a period of three months after the date of receipt of such declaration by the Secretary General.

3   Any declaration made under the two preceding paragraphs may, in respect of any territory specified in such declaration, be withdrawn by a notification addressed to the Secretary General. The withdrawal shall become effective on the first day of the month following the expiration of a period of three months after the date of receipt of such notification by the Secretary General.

Article 24 – Reservations

No reservation may be made to the Convention.

Article 25 – Denunciation

1   Any Party may at any time denounce this Convention by means of a notification addressed to the Secretary General of the Council of Europe.

2   Such denunciation shall become effective on the first day of the month following the expiration of a period of three months after the date of receipt of notification by the Secretary General.

Article 26 – Notifications

The Secretary General of the Council of Europe shall notify the member States of the Council, any signatory, any Party and any other State or the European Community which has been invited to accede to this Convention of:

a   any signature;

b   the deposit of any instrument of ratification, acceptance, approval or accession;

c   any date of entry into force of this Convention in accordance with Articles 21 or 22;

d   any amendment adopted in accordance with Article 20 and the date on which such an amendment enters into force;

e   any declaration made under the provisions of Articles 1 and 23;

f   any denunciation made in pursuance of the provisions of Article 25;

g   any other act, notification or communication relating to this Convention.

In witness whereof, the undersigned, being duly authorised thereto, have signed this Convention.

Done at Strasbourg, this 25th day of January 1996, in English and French, both texts being equally authentic, in a single copy which shall be deposited in the archives of the Council of Europe. The Secretary General of the Council of Europe shall transmit certified copies to each member state of the Council of Europe, to the non-member states which have participated in the elaboration of this Convention, to the European Community and to any state invited to accede to this Convention.

European Social Charter (extracts)

Extracts

Compliance with the commitments embodied in the Charter is sub-jet to international supervision on the basis of reports that the Contracting Parties, which currently number twenty,[1] submit at regular intervals.

Part I

The Contracting Parties accept as the aim of their policy, to be pursued by all appropriate means, both national and international in character, the attainment of conditions in which the following rights and principles may be effectively realised:

(...)

7 Children and young persons have the right to a special protection against the physical and moral hazards to which they are exposed.

(...)

16 The family as a fundamental unit of society has the right to appropriate social, legal and economic protection to ensure its full development.

17 Mothers and children, irrespective of marital status and family relations, have the right to appropriate social and economic protection.

(...)

19 Migrant workers who are nationals of a Contracting Party and their families have the right to protection and assistance in the territory of any other Contracting Party.

Part II

The Contracting Parties undertake, as provided for in Part III, to consider themselves bound by the obligations laid down in the following articles and paragraphs.

(...)

---

1. European Treaty Series, No. 35 The Convention was opened for signature in Strasbourg, 18 October 1961.

Austria, Belgium, Cyprus, Denmark, Finland, France, Germany, Greece, Iceland, Ireland, Italy, Luxembourg, Malta, Portugal, Netherlands, Norway, Spain, Sweden, Turkey and United Kingdom.

Article 7[1] – The right of children and young persons to protection

With a view to ensuring the effective exercise of the right of children and young persons to protection, the Contracting Parties undertake:

1   to provide that the minimum age of admission to employment shall be 15 years, subject to exceptions for children employed in prescribed light work without harm to their health, morals or education;

2   to provide that a higher minimum age of admission to employment shall be fixed with respect to prescribed occupations regarded as dangerous or unhealthy;

3   to provide that persons who are still subject to compulsory education shall not be employed in such work as would deprive them of the full benefit of their education;

4   to provide that the working hours of persons under 16 years of age shall be limited in accordance with the needs of their development, and particularly with their need for vocational training;

5   to recognise the right of young workers and apprentices to a fair wage or other appropriate allowances;

6   to provide that the time spent by young persons in vocational training during the normal working hours with the consent of the employer shall be treated as forming part of the working day;

7   to provide that employed persons of under 18 years of age shall be entitled to not less than three weeks' annual holiday with pay;

---

1. Article 7 para. 1 has been accepted by all the Contracting Parties except by Austria, Denmark, Germany, Iceland, Ireland, Norway, Turkey and United Kingdom.
Article 7 para. 2 has been accepted by all the Contracting Parties except by Cyprus, Denmark, Iceland and Turkey.
Article 7 para. 3 has been accepted by all the Contracting Parties except by Denmark and Iceland.
Article 7 para. 4 has been accepted by all the Contracting Parties except by Cyprus, Denmark, Iceland, Norway and United Kingdom.
Article 7 para. 5 has been accepted by all the Contracting Parties except by Cyprus, Denmark, Iceland and Sweden.
Article 7 para. 6 has been accepted by all the Contracting Parties except by Austria, Cyprus, Denmark, Finland, Iceland and Sweden.
Article 7 para. 7 has been accepted by all the Contracting Parties except by Denmark, Iceland, Ireland, Turkey and United Kingdom.
Article 7 para. 8 has been accepted by all the Contracting Parties except by Denmark, Iceland and United Kingdom.
Article 7 para. 9 has been accepted by all the Contracting Parties except by Cyprus, Denmark, Finland, Iceland, Ireland and Norway.
Article 7 para. 10 has been accepted by all the Contracting Parties except by Cyprus, Denmark, Iceland and Turkey.

8 to provide that persons under 18 years of age shall not be employed in night work with the exception of certain occupations provided for by national laws or regulations;

9 to provide that persons under 18 years of age employed in occupations prescribed by national laws or regulations shall be subject to regular medical control;

10 to ensure special protection against physical and moral dangers to which children and young persons are exposed, and particularly against those resulting directly or indirectly from their work.

(...)

Article 16[1] – The right of the family to social, legal and economic protection

With a view to ensuring the necessary conditions for the full development of the family, which is a fundamental unit of society, the Contracting Parties undertake to promote the economic, legal and social protection of family life by such means as social and family benefits, fiscal arrangements, provision of family housing, benefits for the newly married, and other appropriate means.

Article 17[2] – The right of mothers and children to social and economic protection

With a view to ensuring the effective exercise of the right of mothers and children to social and economic protection, the Contracting Parties will take all appropriate and necessary measures to that end, including the establishment or maintenance of appropriate institutions or services.

(...)

Article 19[3] – The right of migrant workers and their families to protection and assistance

With a view to ensuring the effective exercise of the right of migrant workers and their families to protection and assistance in the territory of any other Contracting Party, the Contracting Parties undertake:

---

1. Article 16 has been accepted by all the Contracting Parties except by Cyprus.
2. Article 17 has been accepted by all the Contracting Parties except by Cyprus.
3. Article 19 para. 1 has been accepted by all the Contracting Parties except by Denmark, Iceland and Malta.
Article 19 para. 2 has been accepted by all the Contracting Parties except by Denmark, Iceland and Malta.
Article 19 para. 3 has been accepted by all the Contracting Parties except by Denmark, Iceland and Malta (continued overleaf).

1   to maintain or to satisfy themselves that there are maintained adequate and free services to assist such workers, particularly in obtaining accurate information, and to take all appropriate steps, so far as national laws and regulations permit, against misleading propaganda relating to emigration and immigration;

2   to adopt appropriate measures within their own jurisdiction to facilitate the departure, journey and reception of such workers and their families, and to provide, within their own jurisdiction, appropriate services for health, medical attention and good hygienic conditions during the journey;

3   to promote co-operation, as appropriate, between social services, public and private, in emigration and immigration countries;

4   to secure for such workers lawfully within their territories, in so far as such matters are regulated by law or regulations or are subject to the control of administrative authorities, treatment not less favourable than that of their own nationals in respect of the following matters:

    a   remuneration and other employment and working conditions;

    b   membership of trade unions and enjoyment of the benefits of collective bargaining;

    c   accommodation;

5   to secure for such workers lawfully within their territories treatment not less favourable than that of their own nationals with regard to employment taxes, dues or contributions payable in respect of employed persons;

6   to facilitate as far as possible the reunion of the family of a foreign worker permitted to establish himself in the territory;

7   to secure for such workers lawfully within their territories treatment not less favourable than that of their own nationals in respect of legal proceedings relating to matters referred to in this article;

(continued) Article 19 para. 4 has been accepted by all the Contracting Parties except by Austria, Denmark, Iceland and Malta.

Article 19 para. 5 has been accepted by all the Contracting Parties except by Denmark, Iceland and Malta.

Article 19 para. 6 has been accepted by all the Contracting Parties except by Denmark, Iceland and Malta.

Article 19 para. 7 has been accepted by all the Contracting Parties except by Austria, Denmark, Iceland and Malta.

Article 19 para. 8 has been accepted by all the Contracting Parties except by Austria, Denmark, Iceland, Malta and Norway.

Article 19 para. 9 has been accepted by all the Contracting Parties except by Denmark, Iceland and Malta.

Article 19 para. 10 has been accepted by all the Contracting Parties except by Austria, Denmark, Finland, Iceland and Malta.

8   to secure that such workers lawfully residing within their territories are not expelled unless they endanger national security or offend against public interest or morality;

9   to permit, within legal limits, the transfer of such parts of the earnings and savings of such workers as they may desire;

10 to extend the protection and assistance provided for in this article to self-employed migrants in so far as such measures apply.

Part III

Article 20 – Undertakings

1   Each of the Contracting Parties undertakes:

a   to consider Part I of this Charter as a declaration of the aims which it will pursue by all appropriate means, as stated in the introductory paragraph of that part;

b   to consider itself bound by at least five of the following articles of Part II of this Charter: Articles 1, 5, 6, 12, 13, 16 and 19;

c   in addition to the articles selected by it in accordance with the preceding sub-paragraph, to consider itself bound by such a number of articles or numbered paragraphs of Part II of the Charter as it may select, provided that the total number of articles or numbered paragraphs by which it is bound is not less than 10 articles or 45 numbered paragraphs.

The Revised European Social Charter and Children's rights

The European Social Charter is the pendant of the European Convention on Human Rights with regard to the protection of economic and social rights. It is one of the main Council of Europe instruments in respect of children. The right of children and young people to protection is elaborated in detail in Article 7 of the charter. Other provisions of importance to children in the European Social Charter are Article 9 on the right to vocational guidance, Article 10, paragraph 2, on a system of apprenticeship for training young boys and girls; Article 16, on the right of the family to social, legal and economic protection; Article 17, on the right of mothers and children to social and economic protection; and Article 19, paragraph 6, on the reunification of the family of a migrant worker. These provisions assure the protection of children and adolescents in the workplace as well as the protection of those without any link to the working environment.

The revised Social Charter, drawn up by the Committee on the European Social Charter which, between 1990 and 1994 was entrusted with the relaunching of the charter, was adopted by the Committee of Ministers at the 562nd meeting of the Ministers' Deputies (1-4 April 1996) and opened for signature by Council of Europe member states. The revised charter increases the protection of young people at work and reinforces their protection outside the workplace. In addition, taking into account the importance of the right of children and adolescents to protection, the revised charter adds Article 7 to the main body of the charter.[1]

The protection of young people at work consists in prohibiting their employment under a certain age while authorising certain types of work, and in determining their working conditions as well as a number of other guarantees.

The charter sets at 15 years the minimum age for admission to employment (Article 7, paragraph 1) and sets a higher minimum age for admission to certain determined occupations considered as dangerous or unhealthy (Article 7, paragraph 2). The case law of the Committee of Independent Experts of the European Social Charter sets the age at 18 years for certain activities (for example work which involves contact with benzene). The revised charter generalises this solution. As to authorised work before the minimum age for admission to employment, only light work is permitted with no risk of adverse effects on children's health, morals or education (Article 7, paragraph 1) and, for children still subject to compulsory schooling, work which does not deprive them of the full benefit of this education (Article 7, paragraph 3).

The working conditions laid down by the Charter concern the limitation of working hours of workers aged under 16 (Article 7, paragraph 4 – in the

---

1. It is possible to enter only partially into the committments contained in Part II of the charter. However, certain provisions (referred to as the "compulsory nucleus") which are considered to be particularly important must be accepted upon ratification of the charter: Article 20, paragraph 1, of the charter and Article A, paragraph 1, of the revised charter.

revised charter this provision is intended for workers under 18 years of age), the remuneration of young workers and apprentices (Article 7, paragraph 5), the inclusion in the working day of the time spent in vocational training during the normal working hours with the consent of the employer (Article 7, paragraph 6), annual holiday with pay (Article 7, paragraph 7 – the revised charter increases the current allowance of three weeks to four) and the prohibition of night work for workers under 18 years of age (Article 7, paragraph 8).

This protection of young persons at work is completed by two other guarantees; the regular medical control of workers under 18 years of age employed in certain occupations prescribed by national laws or regulations (Article 7, paragraph 9) and special protection against the physical and moral dangers to which children and adolescents are exposed, and particularly against those resulting directly or indirectly from their work (Article 7, paragraph 10).

To this protection of young persons at work is added protection for those without any connection to the working environment: protection against physical and moral dangers, the protection of young offenders and special protection with regard to health. The revised charter reinforces certain of these guarantees and adds others.

The protection of young persons against physical and moral dangers outside the working environment is ensured by the adverb "particularly" used in Article 7, paragraph 10. The dangers which young people face have increased; traditionally they have been alcoholism, drug abuse and pornography, and, more recently, Aids. Now physical abuse must be added, including that of a sexual nature.

Very concerned about the protection needed by young persons, and conscious that this protection can be necessary even within the family, the committee of independent experts has decided to expand its control over three aspects of the protection of young persons that it considers at present to have priority: (i) the ill-treatment inflicted on young people, both within and outside the family with emphasis on the real importance of this problem and measures taken or envisaged to remedy the situation; (ii) the access of these young people to civil and criminal courts, *inter alia* when there are family conflicts; and (iii) the situation of young delinquents which requires particular attention.

As regards the protection of juvenile delinquents in the charter, this is mostly concerned with special institutions and courts. At present the charter also deals with the age at which criminal responsibility is set and the age at which sanctions may be pronounced, what sanctions may be applied and their forms of enforcement, as well as measures of protection, education and health care provided and effectively implemented.

With regard to health, Article 11 of the charter on the right to protection of health, deals with, *inter alia*, perinatal and infant healthcare. In addition, Article 8, paragraph 3, which guarantees work breaks – included in working time and paid as such – for mothers to nurse their infants, in practice allows mothers to continue nursing beyond the time allocated for maternity leave.

The revised charter establishes, in a new Article 17, the right of children and adolescents to social, legal and economic protection. This provision carries a package of measures, whose goal is to enable children and young persons to grow up in an environment conducive to the full development of their personality and of their physical and mental capacities. Besides the care, the assistance, the education and the training children and young people need, these measures expressly guarantee their protection against negligence, violence or exploitation, special protection for those who are deprived of their family's support, together with free primary and secondary education and regular school attendance.

These provisions apply to children and young persons as such,[1] though they do, in part, concern their protection within the family. Children and young persons are also protected as members of a family, on the one hand by the provisions concerning the status of the child and, on the other, by the protective measures specific to family life.[2]

---

1. See Children and adolescents, "Social Charter Monographs", No. 3.
2. See The Family, "Social Charter Monographs", No. 1.